GIANTS OF COUNTRY MUSIC

GIANTS OF COUNTRY MUSIC

CLASSIC SOUNDS AND STARS, FROM THE HEART OF NASHVILLE TO THE TOP OF THE CHARTS

NEIL HAISLOP
TAD LATHROP
HARRY SUMRALL

BILLBOARD BOOKS
An imprint of Watson-Guptill Publications/New York

Senior Editor: Paul Lukas
Book and Cover Design: Bob Fillie, Graphiti Graphics
Cover Illustration: Bill Nelson
Production Manager: Hector Campbell

First published 1995 by Billboard Books, an imprint of Watson-Guptill
Publications, a division of BPI Communications, Inc., 1515 Broadway,
New York, NY 10036.

Library of Congress Cataloging-in-Publication Data
Haislop, Neil
    Giants of Country Music: classic sounds and stars, from the heart
of Nashville to the top of the charts / Neil Haislop, Tad Lathrop,
Harry Sumrall.
        p.   cm.—(Billboard hitmakers series)
    Includes index.
    ISBN 0-8230-7635-0
    1. Country musicians–United States–Biography.   I. Lathrop, Tad.
II. Sumrall, Harry. III. Title. IV. Series.
ML385.H16 195
781.642'092'2--dc20
    [B]   95-36692

Manufactured in the United States of America

First Printing, 1995

1 2 3 4 5 6 7 8 9 / 99 98 97 96 95

CONTENTS

GIANTS OF COUNTRY MUSIC

Billboard is the home of the pop charts. For a century, those charts have chronicled the hit songs and albums that have come to represent the pinnacle of commercial achievement in the music industry.

But the charts are not the whole story. Of key importance both in and outside the industry are the artists — the rock and roll bands, soul singers, country musicians, and pop icons who produce the vast body of work from which chart successes emerge.

Billboard Hitmakers is about those artists.

The Hitmakers series presents a broad overview of popular music, with separate volumes devoted to such subject areas as Pioneers of Rock and Roll, Singer-Songwriters, Rhythm and Blues, and Country and Western. Each Hitmakers volume is designed to be enjoyed as a separate reference work dedicated to a distinct segment of the pop spectrum, but the books also complement and reinforce each other. Just as the music scene is constantly changing and growing, the Hitmakers series will expand as new volumes covering new subject areas are published. Taken together, the Billboard Hitmakers series adds up to a growing library of information on pop music's prime movers — with a unique Billboard slant.

Each book explores its topic in depth and detail via individual artist profiles arranged alphabetically, with the artists selected for inclusion on the basis of their commercial and/or aesthetic impact on the music scene — including, of course, their history of Billboard chart activity.

The artist profiles themselves provide more than just raw chart data, however. Along with biographical facts and career highlights, each profile gives a sense of the artist's impact, offers insights about the music, and places the subject in the grand musical scheme of things. Artists are viewed not as isolated entities but as contributors to an ever-changing soundscape, drawing music from the past, adding to it in the present, and passing it on to musicians of the future. The volumes in the Billboard Hitmakers series chronicle this ongoing evolution, providing a history of popular music as seen from the perspective of the artists who created it.

In addition, each Hitmakers profile lists the artist's significant songs and albums. Titles are chosen first from the top of the Billboard charts and are listed chronologically, along with the name of the record's label, its year of release, and its peak chart position. In cases where a profiled artist has no top 40 hits, the titles listed are those generally regarded as the artist's best or most significant recordings.

With rock and roll now moving toward the half-century mark and the originators of blues, gospel, country, and jazz slipping into history, popular music is steadily maturing. Its present-day boundaries encompass an intricate latticework of known genres, nascent movements, as-yet-unlabeled trends, and one-person sonic revolutions. Our intent with the Billboard Hitmakers series is to identify the major players within these diverse yet interrelated musical worlds and present their fascinating stories. And if the books also translate into print some of the musical pleasure these hitmakers have given us over the years, so much the better.

PREFACE

························

There are 180 stories told in this book, tracing the careers of country music's most significant and popular performers. These are the artists whose recordings attracted the greatest public interest and climbed the highest on the country charts. They are the ones who excelled in the making of that fundamental nugget of country music currency: the hit song.

This book chronicles the hits and examines other aspects of each hitmaker's rise to the top. But taken together, these profiles tell a single, much larger story: that of country music itself.

The country sound has been at the heart of American music from its very beginning. For three quarters of a century it has occupied an aesthetic niche of its own, along the way acquiring a set of labels—hillbilly music, familar tunes, mountain ballads, folk records, country and western, and its current name—evoking its rustic and homespun origins.

Yet nailing down a definition of just what country music is—especially in light of its later mergings with pop, rock, and other forms of mainstream entertainment—hasn't always been easy. Somebody once sidestepped the issue by stating simply, if music *sounds* country, it *is* country. That's a commendably brief assessment, but it doesn't entirely alleviate the need some feel to establish a few touchstones.

As revealed in the stories of country's artists, one of these touchstones is precisely the thing that makes country music difficult to define—its stylistic diversity. Country's variety began with its musical roots—from British folk ballads and 19th-century parlor melodies to African-American work songs and southern gospel music—and has increased ever since.

Before 1920, country music often took the form of story songs, dance accompaniments, and fiddle tunes played in various settings in the rural South. The primary performing unit was the string band, consisting of fiddle, banjo, and guitar. That format persevered into the 1920s, when record companies began promoting acts with names like the Hill Billies, the Possum Hunters, the Gully Jumpers, and the Fruit Jar Drinkers.

Divergent strains of country sound emerged in 1927 with Ralph Peer's historic Bristol, Tennessee, recordings of the Carter Family and Jimmie Rodgers. The Carters were purveyors of a traditional mountain folk blend emphasizing vocals. Rodgers, the legendary Singing Brakeman, mixed hillbilly music and the blues with tastes of jazz, Hawaiian guitar, and Mexican music. He established country as an evolving, flexible form, and his emulators were legion.

Among them was Gene Autry, who brought a western flavor to the music in the 1930s and '40s and became the original singing cowboy. Another, Ernest Tubb, employed electric instruments and drums to pioneer the rough-and-tumble honky-tonk sound in the 1940s.

Roy Acuff, on the other hand, reworked Carter Family material en route to mainstreaming country song, carrying his sincere vocals and traditional style to national popularity.

Country music branched out from these central points. In Texas in the 1930s and '40s, Bob Wills and His Texas Playboys (along with others) combined big-band dance music, hot jazz, and the country string-band sound to create western swing. Out of Kentucky, Bill Monroe and His Blue Grass Boys modernized the old-time string style to pioneer the intricate, high-energy sound of bluegrass.

One of the main conduits linking country artists to the country public was the "Grand Ole Opry," the radio program launched on Nashville station WSM in 1925 by announcer–station manager George D. Hay. Originally called the "Barn Dance," it became the Opry in 1927 and evolved into the most influential of the many radio programs that were crucial to the growth of country music from the 1930s on. (It established its long-term home at the Ryman Auditorium in 1943, remaining there until moving to its present-day Opryland location in 1974.)

Among stars of the Grand Ole Opry, smooth-toned singer Eddy Arnold was the most popular in the 1940s and perhaps the first country-to-pop crossover artist. But his musical influence was eclipsed by that of Hank Williams, whose mixture of the blues, gospel, and country of the Acuff–Carter Family variety drew disciples by the droves. Webb Pierce, Lefty Frizzell, and Ray Price championed it in the 1950s, and stars of the 1990s would continue to thrill audiences with classics from the Williams songbook.

With Kitty Wells, a female voice was added to the male-dominated honky-tonk chorus, and as the first woman to score a Number One country hit (1952), she opened the floodgates for every successful female artist to come.

The 1950s brought momentous change. Elvis Presley drew from country, gospel, and the blues to spearhead the new sound of rock and roll, while his Sun Records labelmates Carl Perkins, Jerry Lee Lewis, and Johnny Cash added rock-influencing sounds of their own. To remain current and commercially viable, the country establishment went back to the drawing board and developed—among other musical responses—the smoothed-out, sweetened, and urbanized Nashville Sound. As created primarily by producers Chet Atkins and Owen Bradley (and vocalized by Patsy Cline, Jim Reeves, and others), it took country into the pop mainstream and dominated the Nashville recording industry through the 1960s.

Others would compete with it. Buck Owens and Merle Haggard led a return to hard-driving, roughhouse honky-tonk—the Bakersfield Sound—in the 1960s. Flatt and Scruggs, former employees of Bill Monroe, drew acclaim from college-age folk audiences around the nation for their electrifying, state-of-the-art bluegrass music. Waylon Jennings rebelled against the Nashville Sound in the late 1960s, and he went on to gain fame as a country "outlaw" along with Willie Nelson and others.

Rock fed back into country starting with Bob Dylan and the Byrds in the late 1960s (notably with Dylan's *Nashville Skyline* album) and continuing in the 1970s by way of country rock. Emmylou Harris, a disciple of ex-Byrd Gram Parsons, forged a successful blend of electrified and traditional country sound. Linda Ronstadt, primarily a rock artist, also placed numerous songs on the country chart.

Country's impact on the pop mainstream grew in the 1980s, fueled at first by the contemporary-country "urban cowboy" movement of 1980 and driven by such singers as Dolly Parton and crossover artists Kenny Rogers and Eddie Rabbitt. In the middle of the decade it blew wide open, with newcomers George Strait and Ricky Skaggs spawning a movement of neotraditionalists that Randy Travis and Dwight Yoakam took further.

By the 1990s, country music was one of pop's dominant generes, its defining characteristics crumbling under an onslaught of power guitars and high-tech concert extravaganzas figureheaded by the likes of Garth Brooks, Clint Black, and Reba McEntire. Its boundaries had expanded to include such strains as southern rock, cowpunk, and punkabilly and such "progressive" artists as Lyle Lovett and k.d. lang.

Yet across this spectrum, characteristic sounds and inflections have always been discernible. The sliding, swelling cry of pedal-steel guitar; the emotional catch in a singer's voice; the "high and lonesome" vocal harmony blend; the bass-note twang of the Telecaster guitar—all are among the elements that singly or in combination signal that country music is being played, whether presented in unfettered form or dressed up with strings and synthesizers.

The picture of country music that this book's stories bring into focus involves more than multiple colors and forms. It's also a window on an aspect of America's social history. The makers of the songs—and, sometimes, the songs' protagonists—typically survive the hardships and struggles of everyday life, emerging from often impoverished origins in West Virginia, Kentucky, Tennessee, Alabama, Louisiana, Oklahoma, Texas, and elsewhere. They descend on Nashville or fan out to other music centers to try their luck at the country wheel of fortune. Ironically, how successful they are at transcending humble beginnings usually depends on how skilled they are at singing about them.

And here is another defining aspect of country music: song themes have remained consistent. Seven-ty-five years into its existence as a recording art, country still focuses on its favorite topics of human struggle, emotional conflict, and thwarted romance. At the same time, the mode of expression has acquired a standard form, with its own rules and conventions. Song titles often employ clever word-play, or use common expressions in new ways to characteristically country ends, as in "She Got the Goldmine (I Got the Shaft)," "What's Made Milwaukee Famous (Has Made a Loser Out of Me)," "Old Flames Can't Hold a Candle to You," "A Headache Tomorrow (Or a Heartache Tonight)," "I'm the Only Thing (I'll Hold Against You)," and "You're Out Doing What I'm Here Doing Without." At their best, titles can suggest an entire story in just a few words, as with Kitty Wells' "This White Circle on My Finger."

When country songs work, they naturally connect with an audience and, if popular enough, end up listed on the country charts. The *Billboard* charts have been used to measure the popularity of country music since 1944, when the magazine introduced its Juke Box Folk Records listing. Several other charts, covering retail sales and radio play, appeared during the 1940s and '50s (and used the label country and western). By 1958, one country singles chart was in place, and it remained unchanged until 1990, when it became known as Hot Country Singles and Tracks. A separate chart for country albums has been active since 1964.

Artists were chosen for this book primarily on the basis of their success on the charts—that is, they had significant numbers of high-ranking hits. In several cases, highly influential artists were included even though their commercial hits were relatively few; Merle Travis, Roy Acuff, and Flatt and Scruggs are among these. In all cases, performance on the chart determined the choice of songs in the discographies. Each list includes up to 10 songs and albums picked from the artist's highest-ranking hits and arranged chronologically. If the song crossed over to the top 40 of the pop chart, its pop ranking is shown. When an important song is not listed (because its rank was not high enough), it is ideally discussed in the text. Because country's emphasis has traditionally been on singles rather than albums, chart rankings are shown only for songs. Any albums listed are ones most representative of the artist's work.

A final word about a core aspect of country music: To its practitioners and fans, country music is expression of rare emotional directness and authenticity. Singer k.d. lang describes it as having "a real humanistic quality...[as] dealing with real human emotions." Emmylou Harris views it as "incredibly simple, yet poignant and moving." In essence, this book celebrates the people most responsible for making it so.

ACKNOWLEDGMENTS

NEIL HAISLOP: I wish to thank country music's artists, whose music entertains and touches fans around the world, and whose talent and incredible courage are driving forces in the industry. It has been a privilege to be able to sit down and talk to many of them about their lives, their careers, and country music.

I am also indebted to the talented publicists and public relations people who work hard to promote country performers and have allowed me access to their stars. Many of you have become close friends over the years, and I love you all.

Thanks to *American Country Countdown with Bob Kingsley* and *Country Fever* magazine for great jobs that put me inside the country music industry.

Thanks also to Billboard Books and Paul Lukas for taking a chance on an unproven author. Thanks especially to Tad Lathrop for his patient guidance and for joining in on this book, and to Harry Sumrall for coming aboard as well.

Special thanks to Patricia, for her loving support and patience and for keeping me sane and focused; to Keely, for being the light of my life; to Donald, for joining my life and enriching it—and Albert, that goes for you, too.

Also, thanks to Freddy for his faithful, warm, and purring presence atop my computer monitor.

TAD LATHROP: To Nancy, with my love and appreciation.

HARRY SUMRALL: Thanks to my wife, Leslie, and my son, Sam, for their love and patience (especially their patience). I wish to acknowledge Tad Lathrop and Paul Lukas, who brought me on board this project, as well as Neil Haislop, who seems to have every piece of information about country music that was ever printed. I would also like to dedicate my portion of this book to my dad, Harry G. Sumrall, who was a fan of country music long before his son.

In addition, the authors would like to thank the Country Music Foundation in Nashville, for its overall contribution to the research for this book.

ROY ACUFF

Roy Acuff

To use *Billboard* country chart activity as the sole indicator of Roy Acuff's importance as a performer would miss the point—not to mention a couple of his greatest records: "Great Speckled Bird" and the classic "Wabash Cannonball" were both recorded in 1936, eight years before *Billboard* officially began measuring country popularity. But Acuff had plenty of chart activity as well. The year the Juke Box Folk Records listing debuted (1944), Acuff scored three top 10 hits with "The Prodigal Son," "I'll Forgive You But I Can't Forget," and "Write Me Sweetheart."

Not regarded as the greatest vocalist ever to sing a country song, Acuff became popular largely because of his sincerity, showmanship, and natural ability as a master of ceremonies. He was active not only as a performer but also behind the scenes as a businessman, a key player in the evolution of Nashville as an important music center, and a life-long promoter of country music.

For Acuff (b. Roy Claxton Acuff, Sept. 15, 1903, Maynardsville, Tennessee), country music was neither his first love nor his first choice for a career. In the late 1920s, he pitched semi-pro baseball with enough skill to attract major league scouts. But two attacks of sunstroke while playing ball nearly killed him and squashed any hope of a future in athletics.

During his long recuperation he learned how to play the fiddle. A medicine show operator heard Roy playing the instrument one night in 1932 and hired him to help hawk Dr. Hauer's Mokiton Tonic. "On a medicine show you don't just play a fiddle or sing a song, you have to meet people and sell medicine," Acuff said in a *Billboard* interview. "So I played straight man, comic, and singer, and it gave me a wide experience."

Concluding that he didn't need to pitch anything but himself and his music, Acuff quit the medicine show, formed a band he called the Crazy Tennesseans, and quickly became a popular Knoxville-based radio performer. Recording sessions followed, yielding "Great Speckled Bird" and "Wabash Cannonball" on the American Record Corporation (ARC) label. Within two years—in February 1938—Acuff wrangled a guest shot on the Grand Ole Opry, the key to the big time in country music. It went so well it led to a permanent spot in the show. Subsequent exposure on national radio resulted in heavy record sales and a brief career in Hollywood, where he eventually made eight films.

During World War II, Roy became a kind of Bob Hope of country music as he toured the world entertaining the troops. His effectiveness in that role was reflected in the legendary Japanese broadcast that contained the cry, "To hell with Roosevelt, to hell with Babe Ruth, and to hell with Roy Acuff."

Roy's fame produced wealth that he invested well. Most significant for him—and for country music—was his founding of Acuff-Rose Publications with songwriter Fred Rose. It was the first major music publishing house in Nashville. With a catalogue that

TOP SONGS

GREAT SPECKLED BIRD (ARC, '36)

WABASH CANNONBALL (ARC, '36)

THE PRODIGAL SON (Okeh, '44, 4)

I'LL FORGIVE YOU BUT I CAN'T FORGET (Okeh, '44, 3, 21 Pop)

WRITE ME SWEETHEART (Okeh, '44, 6)

(OUR OWN) JOLE BLON (Columbia, '47, 4)

THE WALTZ OF THE WIND (Columbia, '48, 8)

ONCE MORE (Hickory, '58, 8)

Additional Top 40 Country Songs: 4

included the songs of Hank Williams, Pee Wee King, and Boudleaux Bryant, it boosted Nashville's efforts to become a major recording center.

In 1962, Acuff became the first living inductee to the Country Music Hall of Fame. "Even though you may not sing a song quite as well as somebody else," he told writer Gerry Wood, "you have to be able to sell yourself to an audience. I think they see within me what I want them to see: sincerity, honesty, and a man that's proud of who he is."

Until his death in 1992, Roy Acuff remained a popular and influential force in country music.

ALABAMA

In 1994, RCA Records announced that Alabama's worldwide album sales topped 60 million, placing them among the most popular bands of all time.

When Alabama appeared on the scene in the late 1970s, successful recording bands were practically nonexistent in country music. Alabama changed all that, opening the door to a succession of acts who followed their lead. In the process they became one of the most honored bands in the annals of country music, the dominant country act of the 1980s, and a major force on into the '90s.

Cousins Randy Owen (vocals, guitar; b. Dec. 13, 1949) and Teddy Gentry (bass, vocals; b. Jan. 22, 1952) grew up on adjoining farms in Adamsburg,

Alabama. Randy and Teddy were like brothers, spending much of their time together, swapping chords on guitar, and playing occasionally in local bands. While still teenagers they met a famous local musician from five miles away in Fort Payne named Jeff Cook (keyboards, fiddle; b. Aug. 27, 1949), who turned out to be another cousin. Jeff invited them to his home, where his room was full of expensive music equipment. One of them picked up a guitar and started singing. The others joined in with ear-pleasing results. Encouraged, they entered a talent contest in 1969, billing themselves as Young Country. They won, soon recruited drummer John Vartanian, and eventually changed their name to Wild Country.

Vartanian had contacts in Myrtle Beach, South Carolina. Starting in 1973, they played there six months out of the year until they began hitting the charts. During those years they combined the country, southern rock, and Beatles influences of Randy and Teddy with Jeff's love of rock and roll, developing their own brand of harmony-driven mainstream country rock and original songs.

Between 1973 and '77, they recorded three self-produced albums just to sell from the bandstand. They changed their name to the Alabama Band and then abbreviated it to Alabama when GRT Records picked up one of their songs and released the single "I Wanna Be with You Tonight" to mild chart success. After that small breakthrough, GRT folded, John Vartanian left the band, and drummer Rick Scott joined for a short time.

Discouraged, Alabama came close to calling it

Alabama

ing their own songs with a sound that was kind of southern rockabilly, mountain country with a little gospel and a few other elements thrown in for good measure."

Randy Owen drew praise for his lead vocals. He also earned recognition as a potential solo artist, although he put off suggestions that he move in that direction. "To go out on tour and be just Randy Owen is not something that really turns me on," he counters. "I spent my life and blood and my heart and my soul and my being, being part of Alabama and working toward the success of that group."

Alabama's timing was perfect. The sharply drawn line between country and pop had begun to blur with the advent of such '70s-born hybrids as country "outlaws," southern rockers, and country-tinged rock outfits like the Eagles. To country-inclined rock audiences, Alabama presented an attractive mix.

Country purists, however, were slow to embrace the band. "Most people don't realize it now," recalls Owen, "but when we were getting started we were these guys in T-shirts with long hair and their guitars all jumping around on stage, and we were really frowned on."

What ultimately secured them a permanent country home—carrying them through the wave of neo-traditionalist performers in the mid-1980s and early '90s—was the powerful country-roots strain that ran through their sound. Combining elements that seemed familiar yet new, innovative yet carved out of bedrock basics, Alabama helped redefine mainstream country music—and contributed significantly to the increase in popularity that country experienced toward century's end.

quits. Cook took pickup jobs in other bands; Gentry and Scott considered moving to Nashville to write songs. It looked like the group might split for good—until Randy and Teddy wrote "My Home's in Alabama." Randy had based the song on the notion that he had a home in the group. It provided an emotional rallying point for the members, who rededicated themselves to making Alabama work.

In 1979, Mark Herndon (b. May 11, 1955) took over on drums, and the act signed with an aggressive Dallas-based company, MDJ Records. That resulted in their first top 40 country hits, "I Wanna Come Over" (number 33, 1979) and "My Home's in Alabama" (number 17, 1980). "It gave us identity," said the group of the latter tune. "The title of the song and the name of the band tied in and helped people remember us."

In 1980, "Tennessee River," their initial release under the RCA Records banner, shot to Number One on the country chart. It was the first of a record-setting 20 consecutive Number One hits between 1980 and '86, shattering Sonny James' long-standing record of 16 consecutive top songs. Included in that incredible Alabama run were such '80s standouts as "Feels So Right," "Close Enough to Perfect," "Dixieland Delight," "Roll On," and "If You're Gonna Play in Texas (You Gotta Have a Fiddle in the Band)."

The reasons for success were numerous. Harold Shedd, who produced their records through 1988, cited eclecticism, pointing to the fact that they were "four guys who were playing their own music, writ-

BILL ANDERSON

A South Carolina–born, Georgia-raised gentleman with a middle-class upbringing, Bill Anderson (b. Nov. 1, 1937, Columbia, S. C.) first aimed at playing the hits as a disc jockey rather than a musician. Yet he spent the better part of 30 years as one of the most important writer-performers in the business.

Anderson was just nine years old when his family moved from the Carolinas to the Atlanta suburb of Decatur, where his interest in music blossomed. He entered Avondale High School and became the leader of a hillbilly band he called the Avondale Playboys.

At age 17 Anderson landed his first country disc jockey job at a radio station in Commerce, Georgia. He worked as a broadcaster to pay his way through the University of Georgia, eventually earning a degree in broadcast journalism. At first he viewed music as a hobby and success in the field as an impossible dream. That attitude began to change when, as a college freshman, he got his first song published. "No Love Have I" was recorded by an artist named Arkansas Jimmy on TNT Records out of San Antonio, Texas. "My first royalty check was for $2.52 cents," says Anderson. "I've got it framed."

While he was still in school, Bill wrote and recorded "City Lights" for TNT. Ray Price covered it and scored a Number One hit in 1958. Doors in Nashville began to open. "People would ask what I'd done," Anderson recalls. "I'd say I wrote 'City Lights,' and they would say, 'Come on in.'"

One of the opening doors was that of Decca Records. For the next 16 years (1958 to '74) Anderson cut discs for the label under the production guidance of the legendary Owen Bradley. His breakthrough came in 1960–61 when he scored three consecutive top 10 country hits: "The Tip of My Fingers," "Walk Out Backwards," and "Po' Folks." He followed them in 1962 with his first two Number Ones, "Mama Sang a Song" and "Still."

In 1964, at the height of his popularity, Bill had enough influence to become a star *maker*. He was the judge of a talent contest near Columbus, Ohio, where a housewife named Connie Smith impressed him. He got her to Nashville and RCA records and not only produced her records but also wrote most of her hits—including her debut Number One, "Once a Day."

From 1966 to 1971 the other major female country artist in Anderson's career was Jan Howard. Bill and Jan recorded a series of successful duets together-

er, scoring a run of four top five hits that included the Number One "For Loving You."

Anderson did not waste his degree in broadcasting. He bought radio stations and hosted TV music and quiz shows as well as "Back Stage at the Opry" telecasts and various Nashville Network programs; he also had a recurring role on the soap opera "One Life to Live."

His greatest legacy may be the sophisticated, classic country songs he wrote. According to Anderson, his father put his career in proper perspective when he said, "I knew Bill had a good imagination and began to suspect he had some talent when he wrote "City Lights" in Commerce, Georgia—because there ain't no lights in Commerce, Georgia."

JOHN ANDERSON

One of the most recognizable voices in country music belongs to John Anderson (b. John David Anderson, Dec. 13, 1954, Orlando, Florida). He debuted on the *Billboard* country chart in 1977 and broke through to prominence in the early 1980s. But his ride was far from smooth: Anderson faced possible career oblivion in the late '80s before pulling out one of the great comebacks in country music history.

Raised in the Orlando suburb of Apopka, Florida, Anderson was inspired early by his guitar-playing sister, Donna. Although she forbid him to touch it, seven-year-old John secretly borrowed her guitar to teach himself how to play. He became so proficient on his own, she simply gave it to him. By eighth grade he'd formed his first serious band, a heavy metal group called the Weed Seeds (later, the Living End). John continued playing rock until he was 15.

A neighbor named Roy Tillman was a lover of old-time country music, and he taught John the songs of Jimmie Rodgers and the Delmore Brothers. "I was just picking right along with him, and I loved it," Anderson recalls. "It grew on me, and before long I traded in all my electric stuff, got me a Martin flattop guitar, and was learning how to fingerpick." After high school graduation in 1972, Anderson followed in the footsteps of his sister Donna and moved to Nashville to try for a music career.

Too young to be taken seriously by Music City bigwigs, Anderson survived by working construction

John Anderson

charters of the decade, the quirky "Swingin'," a Number One hit (and million-selling single) that earned the Country Music Association's Single of the Year award. "It took us over a year to write that song," Anderson commented. "We kept picking it apart trying to make sure it didn't sound stupid. I'm not sure we ever fixed it, but I guess it doesn't matter now."

The year 1983—with "Swingin'" and yet another Number One song, "Black Sheep"—marked the high point of Anderson's success in the '80s. After that, his chart activity was spotty at best, resulting in a slow, steady decline that found him completely off the charts and, by 1990, without a record company. "We weren't having much luck," he says. "I always knew that I would never stop playing music. I just wondered how far it would go. Would I end up back in the bars, just me and my guitar, like I started?"

That question was answered in 1991 with the arrival of BNA Entertainment, a new label that needed a male artist and believed that John was still a viable act. They were proved right when his second BNA single, "Straight Tequila Night," hit Number One and *Seminole Wind* became his first platinum (million-selling) album. It was a remarkable comeback, especially given its timing: a new wave of young country artists had wiped away the careers of several veteran acts of previous decades.

"I tried to play some country music that was acceptable to a younger crowd, back when a younger crowd was real hard to find in country music," notes Anderson. "We used to search and

jobs (he built concrete forms for the roof of the new Grand Ole Opry house) and performing occasionally in a duo with his sister. In 1974 he signed with Ace of Hearts, an independent label that didn't have the resources to break him as an act. Frustrated, he left Nashville briefly to work in Colorado and Texas. He returned to begin networking with other hopeful young writers and performers and met Lionel Delmore (son of Alton Delmore of the Delmore Brothers). As writing partners they came up with material that helped John get signed to Warner Brothers Records in 1977, resulting in his first two top 40 country hits, "The Girl at the End of the Bar" and "Low Dog Blues."

"1959" hit number seven in late 1981, becoming the first of 10 top 10 songs through 1984—a noteworthy run for a traditional artist at a time when country music was still pop influenced. More hits—including "I'm Just an Old Chunk of Coal," "Chicken Truck," and "Wild and Blue" (Number One in 1982)—nailed down Anderson's offbeat sound and distinctive singing style. Then he and Delmore wrote what became one of the most memorable country

TOP ALBUMS

JOHN ANDERSON (Warner, '77)
JOHN ANDERSON—2 (Warner, '81)
WILD AND BLUE (Warner, '82)
SEMINOLE WIND (BNA, '91)
COUNTRY 'TIL I DIE (BNA, '94)

TOP SINGLES

WILD AND BLUE (Warner, '82, *1*)
SWINGIN' (Warner, '83, *1*)
BLACK SHEEP (Warner, '83, *1*)
STRAIGHT TEQUILA NIGHT (BNA, '91, *1*)
MONEY IN THE BANK (BNA, '93, *1*)

Additional Top 40 Country Songs: 27

search to find people our own age to play to. It's wonderful to see that things have turned around and that now country music is as acceptable to young folks as it is. But I hope that I can just be remembered as one of the artists who was real and pretty much stayed true to the music."

LYNN ANDERSON

Lynn Anderson

Lynn Anderson (b. Sept. 26, 1947, Grand Forks, North Dakota) emerged in the late 1960s to become one of the most important women in country music. Raised in Sacramento, California, she didn't have a thick "country" accent, and she fought against any preconceived, "born in a barn" notions of country performers, all the while helping to introduce the music to millions of new listeners.

Lynn's mother, Liz Anderson, was the composer of Merle Haggard's first top 10 hit, "(My Friends Are Gonna Be) Strangers" (number 10 country, 1965), and his first Number One, "The Fugitive" (1966). Liz herself placed 19 songs on the charts between 1966 and '72, including the top five "Mama Spank" in 1967.

Lynn's mother had landed her own record deal based on songwriting demo tapes she had been sending to Nashville. Fortunately, those tapes included Lynn singing background and some lead vocals, and they ended up launching her career as well. According to Lynn, "I went to Nashville with Mom when Chet Atkins called her there to make a record. I went there just to see the sights, but a small label called Chart Records heard my voice on the demo tapes and asked me to record something with them while I was in town. The result was that a few months after mother hit the charts, I had a top 40 chart record with a song she wrote called 'Ride, Ride, Ride'" (number 36, 1966).

In 1967 Lynn scored a top five with "Promises, Promises." Her music and good looks were noticed by Lawrence Welk, Jr. He talked his father into giving her an audition that earned her a guest spot on "The Lawrence Welk Show." The next year she became a regular on the program, thrusting Lynn—and country music—into the national spotlight and making her one of the few country artists to appear regularly on network television. Lynn welcomed the exposure but staged a revolt when they dressed her in high-button shoes and a bustle, handed her a

TOP ALBUMS

ALL THE KING'S HORSES (Columbia, '76)
LYNN ANDERSON (Columbia, '77)
OUTLAW IS JUST A STATE OF MIND (CBS, '79)

TOP SONGS

IF I KISS YOU (WILL YOU GO AWAY) (Chart, '67, 5)
PROMISES, PROMISES (Chart, '67, 4)
ROSE GARDEN (Columbia, '70, 1, 3 Pop)
YOU'RE MY MAN (Columbia, '71, 1)
HOW CAN I UNLOVE YOU (Columbia, '71, 1)
KEEP ME IN MIND (Columbia, '73, 1)
WHAT A MAN MY MAN IS (Columbia, '74, 1)

Additional Top 40 Country Songs: 40

parasol, and told her to sing "Buttons and Bows." "I was very young," she says. "I don't know how I had the courage to do it, but I went to Mr. Welk himself and said, 'I'll have to quit the show. You can't refer to me as the little country singer, dress me like this, and have me sing 20-year-old tunes. That's not what country music is all about. . . . Lawrence understood, but it was still a battle after that to keep them from putting me in stereotypical settings surrounded by wagon wheels and hay bales."

Anderson had her greatest impact in 1970 when "Rose Garden" became a huge country-to-pop crossover hit and made her a household name. "Between 1970 and 1980 there were only two records bigger than 'Rose Garden': 'Hey Jude' and 'Bridge over Troubled Water,'" claims Anderson. "It hit on the country, pop, and R&B charts and in 15 foreign countries. For a Nashville-created, country-produced record to do that back then was phenomonal."

Lynn never found another "Rose Garden," but she remained a dominant force through the 1970s with additional chart-topping hits like "You're My Man," "How Can I Unlove You," and "What a Man My Man Is." She also remained a stalwart defender of the true nature of country music and its fans. "To misrepresent country music would be to misrepresent myself," she says. "I think because the country music audience identifies so much with the music, they want to feel they can trust the person singing it to them."

EDDY ARNOLD

It would be an understatement to call Eddy Arnold a giant of American music. He scored 58 consecutive top 10 country hits between his debut in 1945 and 1954, never scored lower than a top 40 hit during the first 21 years of his career, charted over 140 records, and sold a staggering total of over 85 million records. Not bad for a fellow dubbed the Tennessee Plowboy because he *was* a former Tennessee plowboy.

Arnold (b. Richard Edward Arnold, May 15, 1918, Henderson, Tennessee) was born the son of a sharecropper and raised in rural Tennessee. His father was a country fiddler who encouraged his son's musical talents and scraped together enough money to get his boy a guitar at age 10. His earliest

---

TOP ALBUMS

ANYTIME (RCA, '58)
EDDY ARNOLD (RCA, '59)
CATTLE CALL (RCA, '63)

TOP SONGS

I'LL HOLD YOU IN MY HEART (TILL I CAN HOLD
    YOU IN MY ARMS) (RCA VICTOR, '47, 1)
ANYTIME (RCA VICTOR, '47, 1, 17 Pop)
BOUQUET OF ROSES (RCA VICTOR, '48, 1, 13 Pop)
THERE'S BEEN A CHANGE IN ME (RCA, '51, 1)
THE CATTLE CALL (RCA, '55, 1)
WHAT'S HE DOING IN MY WORLD (RCA, '65, 1)
MAKE THE WORLD GO AWAY (RCA, '65, 1, 6 Pop)

Additional Top 40 Country Songs: 121

---

public performances were in grade school. By the time he entered high school he had become a local star. With the Great Depression in full swing, Eddy was forced to leave school to help out on the farm and work as a mortuary assistant. His performing was relegated to occasional local functions, to which he'd travel riding a mule with his guitar slung on his back.

Like other country artists of the time, Arnold earned his ticket to stardom performing live on radio. He debuted on a Jackson, Tennessee, station in 1936, becoming a regional star there, and later worked in St. Louis, Missouri. From 1940 to '43 he appeared on the Grand Ole Opry with Pee Wee King. He signed with RCA Victor Records in 1944, and since he'd been billing himself as the Tennessee Plowboy and His Guitar, that was the name that appeared on his records until 1954.

Arnold's first chart record, "Each Minute Seems a Million Years," hit number five to begin that string of 58 consecutive top 10 hits. In 1947 Arnold scored his first three Number One country hits, "What Is Life Without Love," "It's a Sin," and "I'll Hold You in My Heart (Till I Can Hold You in My Arms)," with the latter staying at the top for 21 weeks. The following year, Arnold hit the peak with two of his signature songs, "Anytime" and "Bouquet of Roses." At this point, with songs also appearing on the *Billboard* pop chart, he had become the first true country-to-pop crossover artist.

Reaching a wider audience was Arnold's goal

when he moved beyond simple country instrumentation. "I had recorded with a little group of musicians for so long that there wasn't anything else for me to do from an instrumental standpoint," he said. "I had to be reborn. My songs were good lyrically and melodically; I just needed to change the background a little. I went in and did some things with violins, and *boom.*"

Eddy Arnold became universally popular and a perennial star, charting records over a span of five decades, with Number One hits into the late 1960s and top 10s into the '80s, including such classics as "Cattle Call," "Make the World Go Away," and "What's He Doing in My World." After a seven-year hiatus he was back in the studio in 1990.

In addition to setting a standard for musical achievement and longevity, Arnold was an exemplary manager of his show business fortune. "I saved the first dollar I ever made, and I've been saving and investing my money ever since," he recalled. "I never forgot how it felt to be poor." He ultimately became one of the wealthiest men in show business.

Arnold was inducted into the Country Music Hall of Fame in 1966.

ASLEEP AT THE WHEEL

The award-winning Asleep at the Wheel came together in 1970 on a back-holler farm near the town of Paw Paw in the eastern panhandle of West Virginia. Guitarist-singer Ray Benson (b. Mar. 16, 1951, Philadelphia)—along with Rueben "Lucky Oceans" Gosfield (pedal steel guitar), Danny Levin (fiddle, mandolin), and Chris O'Connell (vocals, guitar)—launched the group to play their favorite kinds of American roots music. A quarter-century later, Benson was the only remaining founder, the band's membership having at one time expanded to 11 musicians, and the total number of players who'd passed through the band having neared 80. During that time Asleep at the Wheel attained cult status as promulgators of western swing, a style pioneered in the 1930s and '40s by Bob Wills and the Texas Playboys.

Benson and crew were starving musicians in 1971 when the manager of Commander Cody and the Lost Planet Airmen suggested they check out the active music scene in San Francisco. They took the

Asleep at the Wheel

advice and, amid 1,500 other bands in the Bay Area vying for work, began to perform regularly at the Long Branch Saloon in Berkeley. Counterculture audiences soon discovered them and coalesced into a tight following.

In 1973 the band released their first album, *Comin' Right at Ya,* establishing their reputation as western swing specialists. "Asleep at the Wheel was formed to do what I now term 'forgotten music,'" Ray Benson points out. "Back then we were doing hillbilly music, when hillbillies refused to do hillbilly music. We did Buck Owens, Merle Haggard, the old kind of stuff, and Hank Williams and Bob Wills and Cajun music and boogie-woogie. That was the whole idea—to do music other people had passed over in the popular music arena."

They issued about an album a year. Though critically acclaimed (earning three Grammies for instrumental performance), the discs tended to steer clear of the charts' upper reaches, with the exception of 1975's top 10 single "The Letter That Johnny Walker Read" and the *Texas Gold* LP. "A lot of stuff was way out of the mainstream, and totally noncommercial," Benson told Jack Hurst, *Chicago Tribune.* "It's satisfying to have gotten it all on vinyl, but it was not marketable." Albums sold in the area of 100,000 copies each.

From 1974 on they based themselves in Austin, Texas, increasing their identification with western swing. "Standards, blues, western music, pop, jazz—anything can be done in a western swing mode, because it's so improvisational," claims Benson.

TOP ALBUMS

COMIN' RIGHT AT YA (United Artists, '73)
ASLEEP AT THE WHEEL 10 (Epic, '87)
WESTERN STANDARD TIME (Epic, '88)
KEEPIN' ME UP NIGHTS (Arista, '91)
ASLEEP AT THE WHEEL: TRIBUTE TO THE MUSIC OF
    BOB WILLS AND THE TEXAS PLAYBOYS (Liberty, '93)

TOP SINGLES

THE LETTER THAT JOHNNY WALKER READ
    (Capitol, '75, 10)
BUMP BOUNCE BOOGIE (Capitol, '75, 31)
HOUSE OF BLUE LIGHTS (Epic, '75, 17)

Additional Top 40 Country Songs: 3

In 1993 the band finally got around to recording their tribute to Bob Wills. The Liberty Records project *Asleep at the Wheel: Tribute to the Music of Bob Wills and the Texas Playboys* included guest performances by George Strait, Vince Gill, Merle Haggard, Garth Brooks, Willie Nelson, Lyle Lovett, and others and became the biggest-selling Asleep at the Wheel album.

CHET ATKINS

He was a teenager when people started hiring him for his guitar playing and then firing him because he lacked any personality as a performer. Chet Atkins (b. Chester Burton Atkins, June 20, 1924, Luttrell, Tennessee) claims he was so shy that he was afraid to speak when he performed, much less reveal any personality. He overcame that shyness to become one of the top instrumentalists in country music, a legendary record producer, and a powerful record industry executive who played a role in the careers of some of the most popular artists in America. These accomplishments earned him a spot as the youngest inductee into the Country Music Hall of Fame (at age 49) and a Lifetime Achievement Grammy Award.

Atkins' father was an itinerant voice and piano teacher who left his family when his son was just six years old. Chet inherited his father's talent and love of making music, and at age six he fashioned his own first instrument, a crude ukulele with screen wire strings. "I didn't have that long," he recalls. "I was plunking on it one day when my mother asked me to go to the spring to get some water. I didn't go quick enough, so she took it out of my hands and hit me over the head with it and broke the neck off. After that, I traded an old, broken, Owl's-head revolver for a cheap Stella guitar and started to teach myself how to play."

Chet's home was in a poor, rural area just below the Kentucky border, replete with backwoods virtuosos playing what they referred to as "string" music, by which they meant guitar, mandolin, banjo, and fiddle.

"I started playing for square dances when I was still real little," he says. "I played guitar, some mandolin, and I even learned to play the fiddle some. I knew all the music, all the chords the other people knew in the countryside where I lived."

Before long, Chet was learning from music he heard on the radio (Les Paul, George Barnes, and Merle Travis, among others) and every record he could get his hands on. "It wasn't long before I could play just like Django Reinhardt or Andres Segovia," he claims. "People would say, 'You sound just like them.' Right then I realized I had to learn my own style." That's when he developed his distinctive fingerpicking technique—an intricate five-fingered approach to playing simultaneous melodies and harmonies.

At 17 he got his first job on the radio for Knoxville's WNOX. He was hired as a fiddle player for Archie Campbell, but when the station discovered his guitar playing he soon had his own spot on the show. In 1946 he landed a key stint with Red Foley's radio program out of Chicago, recorded with Wally Fowler's Georgia Clodhoppers on Capitol, and made his first solo recording with Bullet Records. A year later he signed with RCA, his professional home until 1982.

Chet moved to Nashville in 1950, joining Mother Maybelle Carter and the Carter Sisters as a regular on the Grand Ole Opry. He became a top session player, contributing to records by artists as diverse as Hank Williams, Hank Snow, Johnny and Jack, Andy Williams, the Everly Brothers, and Elvis Presley.

He began arranging music on the early RCA sessions for Elvis—"Hound Dog" and "Heartbreak Hotel" among them. He graduated to hit producer when sessions with Don Gibson produced such successes as "Oh Lonesome Me" and "I Can't Stop Loving You." At one point he was producing as many as 40 artists a year, including Jim Reeves, Dottie West, Waylon Jennings, Bobby Bare, Perry Como, Eddie Arnold, and Al Hirt. As RCA A&R chief and later vice president, Chet signed Steve Wariner, Jennings, Dolly Parton, and Charley Pride. During his years as a kingpin he helped modernize recording studios and recording techniques and was a key factor in solidifying Nashville's place as a major recording center.

He left RCA in 1982. The reason, he said, was that "they didn't want to promote my albums, since they were signing so many younger artists." Moving across town, Atkins continued his recording career with Epic Records.

"I'm not the greatest talent," Atkins once said on the Nashville Network, "but I have originality. I'm a famous guitar player, I'll admit to that. . . . There are many better players than me; I just got there first."

Chet Atkins

TOP ALBUMS

GALLOPIN' GUITAR (RCA, '53)
DOWN HOME (RCA, '62)
ME AND JERRY (RCA, '70)
GUITAR MONSTERS (RCA. '78)
STANDARD BRANDS (RCA, '81)
CHET ATKINS, C.G.P. (Columbia, '89)
READ MY LICKS (Columbia, '94)

TOP SONGS

MISTER SANDMAN (RCA, '55, *13*)
SILVER BELL (RCA, '55, *15*)
YAKETY AXE (RCA, '65, *4*)

Additional Top 40 Country Songs: 3

GENE AUTRY

To anyone born in the latter part of the twentieth century, Gene Autry (b. Orvon Gene Autry, Sept. 29, 1907) was best known as a millionaire businessman owner of a broadcasting empire and the California Angels baseball team. To those born between 1930 and 1960, Gene was a superstar of radio, records, motion pictures, and television. He was the original "singing cowboy," and most of his fans can still sing his theme song, "Back in the Saddle Again," word for word.

Gene was born in Tioga Springs, Texas, lived for a while in Oklahoma, and then returned to Texas. Although he had naturally picked up cowboy and country songs, he had no real plans to become a musician. After graduating from high school he worked some as a cowboy and then took a night-shift job as a railroad telegraph operator. To keep from getting bored, Gene picked up a guitar and entertained himself by singing and writing songs to while away the hours. His life changed when the legendary humorist Will Rogers stopped by to send a telegram. He heard Gene playing and told him he was in the wrong business and ought to go sing on the radio.

Gene told writer Bob Thomas that he took Rogers' advice but his show business career had actually started earlier. "My first show was when I was very young, 16," he said. "I worked in a medi-cine show playing guitar and singing while the 'doctor' sold elixirs."

He claimed that his first real professional job was in 1929 at Tulsa radio station KVOO, where he was billed as Oklahoma's Singing Cowboy. That job led Autry to the American Record Company and their subsidiary, Okeh Records, for whom he made some of the earliest recordings of cowboy songs. In 1930 he landed his own show at WLS radio in Chicago and performed on the "Barn Dance" until 1934. At the same time, his recording and writing career began to take off (the 1931 release of his original composition "Silver Haired Daddy of Mine" eventually sold over 5 million copies). Autry ultimately wrote over 250 songs, including "You're the Only Star in My Blue Heaven" and the Christmas classic "Here Comes Santa Claus."

In 1934 the Singing Cowboy went to Hollywood. Starting with a well-received bit part in the western *In Old Santa Fe,* Gene established a screen presence that gave a boost to western film as a genre.

From radio, recording, and the movies Gene was making an estimated $600,000 a year when he put

Gene Autry

TOP ALBUMS

GREATEST HITS (Columbia, '61)
GOLDEN HITS (RCA, '62)
GREAT AMERICAN SINGING COWBOYS (Republic, '76)

TOP SONGS

I HANG MY HEAD AND CRY (Okeh, '44, 4)
DON'T FENCE ME IN (Okeh, '45, 4)
BUTTONS AND BOWS (Columbia, '48, 6, 17 Pop)
PETER COTTONTAIL (Columbia, '50, 3, 5 Pop)
HERE COMES SANTA CLAUS (Columbia, '48, 4, 8 Pop)
RUDOLPH THE RED-NOSED REINDEER
    (Columbia, '49, 1, 1 Pop)
FROSTY THE SNOWMAN (Columbia, '50, 4, 7 Pop)

Additional Top 40 Country Songs: 18

his career on hold to enlist in the service in 1942. During World War II, Gene's only income was from his royalties and endorsements, and he realized that fame and fortune could both be fleeting. "I was okay [financially] while I was performing," he said. "But what if my voice failed, or I became ill and couldn't work? I learned a lesson every performer should learn, and that's when I decided to invest in some kind of business."

Although he would become a millionaire from those other businesses (radio and TV stations, hotels, and sports), he never really needed the extra income. After the war he began his long-running radio series "Melody Ranch," renewed his film career, and branched into television. He also revived his recording career, moving from Okeh to Columbia Records in 1945 and releasing such timeless songs as "Buttons and Bows," "Peter Cottontail," and one of the biggest hits of the century, "Rudolph the Red-Nosed Reindeer." The latter went on to sell over 10 million copies.

HOYT AXTON

Hoyt Axton (b. May 25, 1938, Duncan, Oklahoma) may never have done an interview without fielding a question about his mother, Mae Axton, who co-wrote Elvis Presley's first million seller, "Heartbreak Hotel." Said Axton, "When I saw how much fun she had and how much money she made, I said, 'That's what I'm going to do.'" What followed was a writing and performing career that has seen him explore folk, blues, and rock as well as country music. As a songwriter Axton scored with hits for the Kingston Trio, Three Dog Night, and Ringo Starr. He made his own mark as the deep-voiced interpreter of some his best material and, later, as an actor.

Hoyt was 15 when "Heartbreak Hotel" hit and he wrote his first songs—"mostly cowboy ballads and gunfighter things," he recalls. Aside from the influence of his mother, Axton drew inspiration for his eclectic output from Woodie Guthrie, Hank Williams, Chuck Berry, Jackson Browne, Joni Mitchell, and Bach.

He started out in the late 1950s, singing folk music on the West Coast coffee-house circuit. In 1962 the mainstream folk act the Kingston Trio gave Axton his first big show business break when they scored a pop hit with his "Greenback Dollar." That

same year Axton released his own first record, "Follow the Drinking Gourd."

In the early 1970s he wrote Steppenwolf's "The Pusher" and two hits for Three Dog Night. The first was "Never Been to Spain," a composition Axton describes as "a silly little song written in 20 minutes that didn't mean a thing." It hit the pop top 10. The other was based on a demo of a tune called "Joy to the World," for which he'd only written temporary words. He never had a chance to write permanent ones, because Three Dog Night recorded it as it was and made it the number one pop hit of 1971. During this same period Axton co-wrote what may be the highest-charting anti–substance abuse song in history: "The No-No Song." Inspired by a friend who died of a drug overdose, it was a number three hit for former Beatle Ringo Starr.

Axton first entered the country chart in 1974 with the number 10 "When the Morning Comes." He followed it with "Boney Fingers," another top 10 and one of his more memorable tunes. Later in the 1970s came "Della and the Dealer" and "A Rusty Old Halo" along with extensive touring, which continued into the 1980s.

Axton launched an acting career that yielded appearances in commercials, television, and motion pictures, with starring roles in *The Black Stallion* (1979) and *Gremlins* (1984).

Axton was once asked which of his talents he'd keep if he had to give the rest up. "I'd have to be the songwriter," he said. "I like to write songs. I like the process, the way it feels to write a song. Writing is when I have the most freedom."

TOP ALBUMS

FEARLESS (A&M, '76)
SNOWBLIND FRIEND (MCA, '77)
ROAD SONGS (A&M, '77)
A RUSTY OLD HALO (Jeremiah, '79)

TOP SONGS

WHEN THE MORNING COMES (A&M, '74, *10*)
BONEY FINGERS (A&M, '74, *8*)
DELLA AND THE DEALER (Jeremiah, '79, *17*)
A RUSTY OLD HALO (Jeremiah, '79, *14*)
WILD BULL RIDER (Jeremiah, '80, *21*)

Additional Top 40 Country Songs: 2

RAZZY BAILEY

Razzy Bailey

His laid-back, sophisticated singing style was perfect for the pop-influenced country music of the late 1970s and early '80s, and Razzy Bailey (b. Rasie Michael Bailey, Feb. 14, 1939, Five Points, Alabama) was one of the hottest acts of the period. From his first release for RCA Records in 1978 through the middle of 1982 he scored 13 top 10 songs, including five Number One hits.

Razzy (he changed the spelling from Rasie because nobody pronounced it properly) was raised on a farm in an area where neighbors relied on each other for help and where making music was the chief form of social entertainment. "On weekends several families from miles around would get together at our house to have weenie roasts, make homemade ice cream, and make music," he says. "My father was my greatest influence, because he would write poems for us kids, and he'd write songs for the songfests. We would also listen to the Grand Ole Opry radio broadcasts, and I thought, 'Wouldn't this be a great way to make a living?' Trouble was, it took a long time before I could make a living with music."

Bailey began performing at age 15, but his musical career was delayed when he got married right out of high school and started a family. For the next 15 years music was mostly part-time as he worked the honky-tonk circuit in Alabama, Georgia, and Florida and held a series of day jobs. He wrote songs and send them to Atlanta producer/entrepreneur Bill Lowery, who gave him feedback. "At first, if he rejected my songs, I'd throw them away thinking they were no good," Bailey says. "He finally told me, 'Razzy, just because I can't use your song it doesn't mean it isn't a good song. Don't ever throw your songs away. Hang on to them.'"

Bailey would occasionally try to get things going on a large scale, beginning with a pop band he formed in 1958 called Daily Bread. He recorded with the Aquarians in 1972 and in '74 was signed briefly by MGM Records as "Razzy." Nothing panned out for him, and by the mid-1970s his singing and songwriting career was at a standstill. He became so frustrated that he went to a Florida psychic. According to Bailey, she correctly predicted he would soon break through: "I never knew what to think about such things until right after that, Dickey Lee recorded a song I'd written 10 years earlier called '9,999,999 Tears,' and sure enough it almost went to the top [number three] in 1976."

A contract with RCA Records soon followed. Beginning with "What Time Do You Have to Be Back to Heaven," Bailey was out of the country top 10 only once during the next four years.

TOP ALBUMS

RAZZY (RCA, '80)
MAKIN' FRIENDS (RCA, '81)
FEELIN' RIGHT (RCA, '82)
A LITTLE MORE RAZZY (RCA, '82)

TOP SONGS

LOVING UP A STORM (RCA, '80, 1)
I KEEP COMING BACK (RCA, '80, 1)
FRIENDS (RCA, '81, 1)
MIDNIGHT HAULER (RCA, '81, 1)
SHE LEFT LOVE ALL OVER ME (RCA, '81, 1)

Additional Top 40 Country Songs: 13

His urban country sound drew criticism from country purists, prompting Bailey to claim, "I'm as country as they come. I was born on a farm with no indoor plumbing or electricity, and I plowed behind a mule. I sing the best songs I can find, and I don't put limits on myself because of where I came from."

But country music took a swing toward more traditional artists. Bailey's run of hits stopped, and years later he would look back on the early '80s as the zenith of his recording career.

MOE BANDY

Born in Mississippi but raised in San Antonio, Texas, he did what many tough, young Texans do: he headed for a career in the rodeo as a wild-bull rider. Several broken bones later he turned in his chaps and picked up a guitar to see if someday he could ride some songs to the top of the charts. Moe Bandy succeeded, becoming one of the hottest singers of the 1970s and '80s. A traditional, honky-tonk–style artist a decade before the resurgence of interest in traditional acts, he was curiously passed over when the neotraditional movement achieved full force.

Bandy (b. Marion Franklin Bandy, Jr., Feb. 12, 1944, Meridian, Mississippi) drew his love of music from his parents—a guitar-playing father and piano-playing mother—and from simply being raised in Texas. Following his rodeo stint, he took a day job as a sheet-metal worker to support his family while he tried to establish his singing career at night and on weekends. In 1964 he formed a band called Moe Bandy and the Mavericks that became popular on the San Antonio club circuit. Bandy and his band became local TV stars when they joined a program called *Country Corner*.

After recording for a series of regional, independent record labels, Bandy made a stab at Nashville without actually going to Music City. When Nashville producer Ray Baker visited San Antonio, Bandy says, "I found out what hotel he was staying in and just went and knocked on his door. I said, 'I'd like to cut a record in Nashville; I thought you could help me.'" Baker took a tape of Moe's songs and gave him the perfunctory, "I'll be glad to listen, but no promises." But he heard poten-

tial and ended up helping Bandy get a start on the national scene.

Beginning with "I Just Started Hatin' Cheatin' Songs Today" in 1974, Bandy scored five top 40 songs, including two top 10 hits, with GRC Records. Columbia picked him up and in 1975 rode with him to number two on the track "Hank Williams, You Wrote My Life." Over the next 10 years Bandy was a constant presence in the country top 40, scoring his first Number One in 1979 with "I Cheated Me Right Out of You."

With a series of duet partners, Moe found success that both helped and ultimately hurt his career. He and Janie Fricke hit number two in 1979 with "It's a Cheating Situation"; he scored in the top 10 with Judy Bailey in 1981 ("Following the Feeling") and Becky Hobbs in 1983 ("Let's Get Over Them Together"). His favorite duet partner, however, was Joe Stampley. Moe and Joe released five duet albums between 1979 and '85 that yielded the Number One *Just Good Ol' Boys* and three more top 10s, including one called *Where's the Dress*. The latter was a parody of cross-dressing pop star Boy George of Culture Club; Moe and Joe actually dressed in drag for the video of the song.

Although Bandy and Stampley had great fun and success with the duets, "we went too far with it," Bandy says. "Radio began ignoring the singles we released as solo artists and wanted more duets." They recognized their mistake too late, and each of their solo careers lost crucial momentum at a time

---

TOP ALBUMS

HANK WILLIAMS, YOU WROTE MY LIFE (Columbia, '76)
IT'S A CHEATIN' SITUATION (Columbia, '79)
THE CHAMP (Columbia, 80)
JUST GOOD OL' BOYS (with Joe Stampley, Columbia, '79)
HEY JOE—HEY MOE (with Joe Stampley, Columbia, '81)

TOP SONGS

HANK WILLIAMS, YOU WROTE MY LIFE (Columbia, '76, 2)
IT'S A CHEATING SITUATION (with Janie Fricke, Columbia, '79, 2)
JUST GOOD OL' BOYS (with Joe Stampley, Columbia, '79, 1)
I CHEATED ME RIGHT OUT OF YOU (Columbia, '79, 1)
SHE'S NOT REALLY CHEATIN' (SHE'S JUST GETTIN' EVEN) (Columbia, '82, 4)

Additional Top 40 Country Songs: 39

when new traditionalists like Dwight Yoakam, Randy Travis, and Ricky Van Shelton were arriving on the scene.

Moe briefly regained his momentum in 1987 and '88 when he moved over from Columbia to MCA/Curb Records and collected two more top 10 songs. By the beginning of the 1990s, Moe had quit the field in Nashville and opened a highly successful theater in Branson, Missouri.

BOBBY BARE

His career began like an episode of "The Twilight Zone." In 1958, one day before Bobby Bare entered the military, he recorded a song in California called "The All American Boy." He sold it for 50 dollars and headed off to basic training. A few months later the song came on the radio, and he told his barracks buddies, "Hey, that's me singing that song." Nobody believed him, especially when the deejay identified the singer as Bill Parsons. Mislabeled by accident or design, "The All American Boy" hit number two on the pop charts and sold a million, with Bare cut out of the glory and money. He didn't let the injustice bother him for long. Bare returned to make his own indelible mark beginning in 1962 with a series of crossover hits that included the classic "Detroit City" and "500 Miles Away from Home."

Bare (b. Robert Joseph Bare, Apr. 7, 1935, Ironton, Ohio) grew up poor in rural Ohio near the Kentucky border. His mother died when he was five. His father had a rough time after that, even putting one of his daughters up for adoption because there were too many mouths to feed. His extended family included several music-playing uncles, and by the time Bobby was 11, he knew he wanted to become a performer. "I was 15 or 16 years old and organized my first band," he says. "I think it was called the Drifting Pioneers. I started out playing bass, but I found out that you get more girls if you play guitar and sing."

When he turned 19 he moved to the West Coast. He had just started to make inroads as a writer and singer when he was drafted into the Army. After the debacle involving "The All American Boy," he left the service and returned to the music business. "I was in search of another hit song and just working all over the country when I got word that Chet

Atkins was interested in talking to me," he says. "We never connected until I went to Nashville, looked him up, and he said, 'I think I can cut some hit records with you.'" Beginning in 1962 with "Shame on Me," Bare's first four singles hit both the country and pop charts. Two of them were significant pop hits: "Detroit City" hit number six country and 16 pop (it was a Grammy Award winner in 1963), and "500 Miles Away from Home" peaked in the country top five and went to number 10 pop.

"Detroit City" was originally recorded and released by Billy Grammer with the title "I Want to Go Home." Grammer's version failed to chart, but Bare says he thought it was a hit: "I was living in Hollywood the first time I heard that being played on the radio. I said, 'Damn, that's the greatest song I ever heard in my life. That's me. I can really relate to that.'" With "500 Miles Away from Home," Bobby heard Peter, Paul and Mary sing a version of the song and fell in love with the melody. He wanted to record it but could only find an instrumental version of the song, so he wrote his own lyrics.

Bobby Bare

TOP ALBUMS

THIS IS BOBBY BARE (RCA, '73)
HARD TIME HUNGRIES (RCA, '75)
THE WINNER AND OTHER LOSERS (RCA, '75)

TOP SONGS

500 MILES AWAY FROM HOME (RCA, '63, *5, 10 Pop*)
MILLER'S CAVE (RCA, '64, *4, 33 Pop*)
FOUR STRONG WINDS (RCA, '64, *3*)
(MARGIE'S AT) THE LINCOLN PARK INN (RCA '69, *4*)
HOW I GOT TO MEMPHIS (Mercury, '70, *3*)
DADDY WHAT IF (RCA, '73, *2*)
MARIE LAVEAU (RCA, '74, *1*)

Additional Top 40 Country Songs: 51

As with Waylon Jennings and Johnny Cash, Bare's appeal came not from his raw vocal talent but from the emotion and heart he put into his songs. "He doesn't just sing the lyrics, he knows what they're all about," said Chet Atkins, who called Bare "one of the most intelligent artists I've worked with."

Bare's charisma made him an appealing touring act. He also had a sense of humor about himself and his music that came out in songs like "Drop Kick Me, Jesus" and the Number One smash "Marie Laveau," about the legendary Cajun witch. A singer's singer, Bare garnered the respect of his peers for both his talent and his generosity toward other artists. In 1979, he and a fledgling named Rosanne Cash recorded a duet called "No Memories Hangin' Round" that hit number 17 and launched her recording career.

Bare is "basically honest," he says, "probably to a fault. My mother died when I was a kid. I didn't have a lot of guidance. But, along about 10 or 11 years old, I figured it out myself. I decided that if it's right, do it. If it's wrong, don't. I've kept it just that simple my whole life."

BELLAMY BROTHERS

In 1976 the Bellamy Brothers hit Number One on the *Billboard* pop chart with "Let Your Love Flow." Their record company and managers geared up to make them the newest pop icons when the brothers abruptly turned their backs on a pop music career. "We are basically country musicians," they explained. "We just realized that we were headed in the wrong direction." More than a few people thought they had lost their minds until 1979, when "If I Said You Have a Beautiful Body Would You Hold It Against Me" became their first of many top country hits. By the mid-1980s, Howard and David were one of the most successful brother duos in country music history, regularly climbing the charts with inventive, original songs that often showed their sense of humor and sometimes incorporated unlikely influences, from reggae and calypso to R&B and rap music.

Raised on a central Florida farm that had been in their family for more than a century, Howard (b. Feb. 2, 1946, Darby, Florida) and David (b. Sept. 16, 1950, Darby) became best of friends in spite of a four-and-a-half-year age difference. "We liked each other and never fought," says Howard. "Good thing, too, since we lived out in the country and other playmates were miles away." The brothers shared a common passion for making music, and the isolation of rural life gave them plenty of time to pick and sing together (Howard played guitar, mandolin, and banjo; David played accordion, organ, piano, banjo, mandolin, and fiddle). The music they produced was essentially country (influenced by their father, Homer, who sang and played guitar, dobro, and fiddle), yet it layered pop influences they absorbed from the radio. They discovered their greatest asset early on. "We knew when we were younger we had a vocal blend that you don't find everyday," Howard recalls, "and we always thought that was our strong point. So we developed the writing and just tried to stay with our original sound."

Songwriting provided their big break when they moved to Los Angeles in the early 1970s. Jim Stafford recorded one of David's compositions called "Spiders and Snakes" and scored a number three pop hit. Their own recording contract with Warner Brothers/Curb Records followed, yielding their pop chart-topper.

The brothers' subsequent shift from pop to country was just one example of their independence. For most of their career they were self-managed and placed their mother in charge of their finances. They shunned Nashville, choosing instead to live on the land they were born to and even building a recording studio on the family ranch, where they recorded several pre-digital albums.

"If I Said You Have a Beautiful Body Would You Hold It Against Me" signaled that they would be musical mavericks as well. The playful sexual innuendo and the rhythm, arrangement, melody, and harmonies defined much of their musical personality, which continued to shine through on such hits as "Do You Love As Good As You Look," "Redneck Girl," "Old Hippie," and "Rebels Without a Clue." Incidentally, the only time this brother duo recorded with another act was with a quartet of sisters: the Bellamy Brothers and the Forester Sisters hit Number One in 1986 with "Too Much Is Not Enough."

Each brother approached writing in his own way. Howard was only inspired when a recording date approached. David was more compulsive and prolific. To make sure their songs were commercial, they conducted research to see what fans and radio stations wanted. "But most of the time we wrote what inspired us," says David, "and that worked, too."

For most of their career the Bellamys were a Curb Records act that recorded at various times in con-

TOP ALBUMS

THE BELLAMY BROTHERS (Warner/Curb, '76)
THE TWO AND ONLY (Warner/Curb, '79)
YOU CAN GET CRAZY (Warner/Curb, '80)
HOWARD AND DAVE (MCA/Curb, '85)

TOP SONGS

IF I SAID YOU HAVE A BEAUTIFUL BODY
    WOULD YOU HOLD IT AGAINST ME
    (Warner/Curb, '79, 1, 39 Pop)
SUGAR DADDY (Warner/Curb, '80, 1)
DANCIN' COWBOYS (Warner/Curb, '80, 1)
DO YOU LOVE AS GOOD AS YOU LOOK
    (Warner/Curb, '81, 1)
FOR ALL THE WRONG REASONS (Elektra/Curb, '82, 1)
REDNECK GIRL (Warner/Curb, '82, 1)

Additional Top 40 Country Songs: 29

Bellamy Brothers

junction with Warner Brothers, Elektra, and MCA. In 1991 they were signed briefly to Atlantic. In '92 they formed their own label, Bellamy Brothers Records. Their explanation: "It was a combination of major labels being reluctant to sign acts our age, our dissatisfaction with our last couple of record deals, and the desire to develop other artists as well as to continue our career."

CLINT BLACK

One could say that the surge in country music popularity that marked the early 1990s actually began in February of 1989 with the release of Clint Black's debut single, "Better Man." That song became the first of four consecutive Number One hits from his initial album, *Killin' Time*, proving what research surveys for the Country Music Association postulated in 1986: country fans wanted more young, traditional country performers along the lines of mid-'80s sensations Randy Travis and Dwight Yoakam.

Black's spectacular start made him, briefly, the most important new act in country music. By early 1991, Black was overshadowed—but not diminished—by the phenomenal success of Garth Brooks. Black's importance and continued popularity were assured by his unique voice and the freshness of his original material.

Black (b. Clint Patrick Black, Feb. 4, 1962, Long Branch, New Jersey) grew up in the Houston suburb of Katy, Texas. His early musical influences came from his father's country music collection and his brother's hard rock albums. He was strictly a listener until age 13, when at one point he was housebound with a broken arm. "I was moping on the porch, because I couldn't ride my bike or skateboard, when this harmonica player named Leslie Stoffard came down the sidewalk," says Black. "He took pity on me and gave me a harmonica to pass the time. By the time I got that cast off I was playing songs like 'Old Joe Clark' and 'Mama's Little Baby Loves Shortnin' Bread.' Sometimes family friends would toss me a quarter to play for them, and I was hooked."

Black's first real music job was playing bass guitar in his older brother Kevin's band (he sat in with him periodically from age 14 to 18). During this time his musical influences broadened. He recalls

Clint Black

that "Haggard, James Taylor, Jimmy Buffett, Don Henley, and Glenn Frey were influences. I'd also be listening to Loggins and Messina and Black Sabbath while Johnny Winter and James Cotton put the blues in me."

For the first eight years of his music career, Black preferred to perform solo. He became a teenage troubadour who would cruise the streets and parks of Katy and would play for anybody who'd stop to listen to him. Later he began working the local coffee house, restaurant, and bar circuit. He would sit on a stool with his guitar and harmonica to perform the requisite cover tunes along with the original songs he was beginning to write.

In 1987 he met a top guitar player and serious songwriter named Hayden Nicholas. "What was great is that Hayden had a little recording studio in his house where we could make demos," says Black. It was a providential meeting. They clicked immediately, each possessing strong music and lyric writing skills that, when combined, began to produce material stronger than much of what they'd written individually. (Nicholas would play a key role in Black's career as his bandleader, lead guitarist, and co-writer of most of his hits.) The new collaboration with Nicholas gave Black the caliber of songs he needed to find a strong manager who he hoped could pitch him as a recording act. Armed with tunes like "Better Man," "Killin' Time," and "Nobody's Home," he approached Bill Ham (the high-powered manager of the rock act ZZ Top). Ham took Black on as a client and helped him land a contract with RCA Records Nashville.

Black's debut album yielded five hit singles. "Better Man," "Killin' Time," "Nobody's Home," and "Walkin' Away" went to Number One, with "Nothing's News" peaking at number three. That beginning established him well enough to hold his own against competition from Garth Brooks and other young stars who debuted in 1989, such as Travis Tritt and Alan Jackson, and from new challengers who followed, like Doug Stone, Joe Diffie, and a host of others. Black maintained his momentum with the release of his second album, *Put Yourself in My Shoes*. Even though he felt this album suffered in quality because recording sessions had to be squeezed into the busy schedule of his first year of stardom, it yielded four more top 10 hits, including the Number One songs "Loving Blind" and "Where Are You Now."

In 1992 Black and his manager Bill Ham quarreled over their original agreement (that Black contended gave Ham excessive percentages and publishing rights). Black severed the relationship, and a legal battle followed that all but brought his career to a standstill. He was not able to release new material from his third album, *The Hard Way*, until June 1992. Black had been anxious for this disc to appear, since he'd stepped up as co-producer. "The album was more me than the first two albums," he claims. "I produced every recording session and mixing session." Black's song selection for *The Hard Way* created a bit of controversy with his record company, which was nervous about some of the more esoteric material, like "Wake Up Yesterday," a tune about a poltergeist. Black held his ground and has since enjoyed a high degree of creative control of his albums. "To me an album is like a movie. If people are going to listen to it, it has to be dynamic, it has to change tone and flavor, and they [the listeners] have to go through a range of emotions. Also, I don't use the same instrumentation for every song just because something worked on radio before. I try to sound different but familiar at the same time."

He applied that theory to his fourth album, *No Time to Kill*, which included a hit duet with Wynonna Judd called "A Bad Goodbye." The duet inspired the "Black and Wy" co-tour that bolstered both their careers and made them one of the biggest concert draws of 1993.

In the fall of '94 Black released *One Emotion*. The album included a hit song, "Untanglin' My Mind," that his idol Merle Haggard had begun and Black had finished writing.

Taking control of both the business and creative aspects of his career is something Black says he felt bound to do. "When my time here is through, I want to have worked a lot. I want to have exercised all my creativity. I want to feel like a farmer feels: that nobody else plowed his field, nobody else harvested his crop. It's not as much fun if you're not digging your own dirt from under your fingernails."

TOP ALBUMS

KILLIN' TIME (RCA, '89)
PUT YOURSELF IN MY SHOES (RCA, '90)
THE HARD WAY (RCA, '92)
NO TIME TO KILL (RCA, '93)
ONE EMOTION (RCA, '94)

TOP SONGS

BETTER MAN (RCA, '89, 1)
NOBODY'S HOME (RCA, '89, 1)
LOVING BLIND (RCA, '91, 1)
WHERE ARE YOU NOW (RCA, '91, 1)
WHEN MY SHIP COMES IN (RCA, '93, 1)

Additional Top 40 Country Songs: 10

SUZY BOGGUSS

Suzy Bogguss epitomizes the singer who performs simply because she loves it: at one point she toured the Northwest alone in a small pickup truck with a camper shell, playing any dinner club, honky-tonk, or dance hall that would hire her. She finally broke through in 1992 with a series of top 10 hits and moved on to establish herself as a skilled songwriter and record producer.

The youngest of four children, Bogguss (b. Suzy Kay Bogguss, Dec. 30, 1956, Aledo, Illinois) was encouraged in music and taught to read it by her piano-playing mother. Her father introduced her to country music, allowing only the tapes of his favorite country singers to be played in the family car while he was driving. An outgoing youth, Suzy was a cheerleader and acted and sang in various musicals, choirs, and choruses through high school and college.

The day she graduated with a degree in art (her concentration was metallurgy and jewelry design) from Illinois State University, she decided she wanted to live a little before settling down. Music was her ticket to freedom. "I wasn't ready to take a job as a metalsmith and work towards becoming a designer," she says. "I decided to take my music and travel with it. It wasn't long after I started singing for my living that music became a fever and I couldn't quit, even when I didn't make more than 20 dollars a night for almost two years."

From 1978 to '84, she toured widely, from the Great Lakes to the Pacific Ocean. Bogguss favored Wyoming and Montana, where she could sing cowboy songs—especially old tunes like Patsy Montana's "I Want to Be a Cowboy's Sweetheart," complete with yodel. (Bogguss is one of the few contemporary female country artists who has mastered yodeling.)

In 1983, Bogguss took on a duet partner, Lisa Smith. They performed for the better part of a year as Bogguss and Smith, until Smith went back to school and Bogguss headed for Nashville on Thanksgiving Day, 1984.

Bogguss immediately found work singing in a restaurant and recording demos for music publishers. Her big break came in 1986 when she headlined a daily show at Dolly Parton's Dollywood amusement park in East Tennessee. Executives from Capitol Records caught her show there and offered her a singles deal. Her first release, "I Don't Want to Set

Suzy Bogguss

the World on Fire" (number 68, 1987), didn't set the world on fire, nor did her next few releases. Yet Capitol had enough faith in her to match her with producer Wendy Waldman for her first album, *Somewhere Between*. The great-sounding result was curiously more memorable for its instrumental tracks than for the vocals, although it did yield Bogguss' first top 40 hit, "Cross My Broken Heart" (number 14, 1989).

In 1990, Capitol Nashville's CEO, Jimmy Bowen, stepped in to co-produce her sophomore album, *Moment of Truth*. It did little more than establish their working relationship. Then, in 1991, Suzy got a needed boost from Lee Greenwood when their duet version of "Hopelessly Yours" from Lee's *Perfect 10* CD hit number 12.

Her follow-up collection, *Aces*, was a watershed—and perhaps a career saver. Her version of Ian

Tyson's "Someday Soon" went to number 12, followed by two top 10 hits: "Outbound Plane" and "Aces." Bogguss felt validated by *Aces.* "I worked very hard to find songs that portrayed what I wanted to be as an artist; there was no compromising," she says. "I was very fortunate to have people behind me that believed in me, who saw that I was coming around and gave me the opportunity to learn about myself as I went along."

Her *Voices in the Wind* album contained the number two hit "Drive South," written by John Hiatt, and the number six "Letting Go," written by her husband, Doug Crider, and Matt Rollings.

Bogguss included her own material on her albums, including at least one song on each written with her husband. Her biggest hit as a writer was "Hey Cinderella," a collaboration with Matraca Berg and Gary Harrison that hit number five in 1994.

Bogguss' first solo effort as a record producer was the critically acclaimed CD *Simpatico,* a project undertaken with her close friend Chet Atkins. "George Massenberg was supposed to produce the album," explains Bogguss. "He had to bow out and said to me, 'Why don't you produce it?' The thought of producing a great artist who is also a great producer made me stop and think. Luckily, Chet approved, and he made it easy."

"I'm not finished," says Bogguss of her country music involvement. "There are many sides to me. I just kind of keep experimenting, and country music is letting me do that. I guess I'm a work in progress."

TOP ALBUMS

ACES (Capitol, '91)
VOICES IN THE WIND (Capitol, '92)
SOMETHING UP MY SLEEVE (Liberty, '93)
SIMPATICO (with Chet Atkins, Liberty, '94)

TOP SONGS

OUTBOUND PLANE (Capitol, '92, 9)
ACES (Liberty, '92, 9)
LETTING GO (Liberty, '92, 6)
DRIVE SOUTH (Liberty, '92, 2)
JUST LIKE THE WEATHER (Liberty, '93, 5)
HEY CINDERELLA (Liberty, '93, 5)

Additional Top 40 Country Songs: 5

BROOKS & DUNN

In October 1990, Kix Brooks and Ronnie Dunn were singer-songwriters in search of individual solo careers. Tim DuBois, head of Arista Records Nashville, listened to a demo tape of songs they had written and sung together and told them, "You've got a record deal." Surprised, they asked, "Which one of us?" "Both of you," he answered, and the pair, who'd just joined forces as writers three weeks earlier, were suddenly a recording act called Brooks & Dunn. Within a short time they were issuing top 10 hits and multimillion-selling albums and were on their way to becoming one of the dominant country acts of the 1990s.

Brooks (b. Leon Eric Brooks, May 12, 1955, Shreveport, Louisiana) and Dunn (b. Ronnie Gene Dunn, June 1, 1955, Coleman, Texas) have similar cultural backgrounds. "We were raised the same, in the same part of the country," says Dunn. "Our fathers were laborers in the oil field business. So we felt a certain kinship from the start." Brooks was six when his grandmother sparked his interest in music with a mail-order ukulele. By age 12 he had formed his first band. Dunn's main musical influence was his father, the leader of a band that backed up Sonny James when he went to west Texas to perform. The band met at the Dunn home to practice. "There were always jam sessions at our home while I was growing up," Dunn says. "I remember lying awake as a little kid until two or three in the morning in the summertime listening to them picking on the front porch, just going for it." Dunn eventually joined his father's band to begin his career in music.

In 1976, Brooks headed north to work on the Alaskan pipeline. "I got first-hand experience being drunk and tired for eight months," he notes. "What a great foundation for writing country songs." By 1981 he was in Nashville writing for Charlie Daniels' publishing company. Over the next several years his songs were cut by the Oak Ridge Boys, Crystal Gayle, and Sawyer Brown. He then wrote two Number One hits: John Conlee's "I'm Only in It for the Love" and the Nitty Gritty Dirt Band's "Modern Day Romance." In 1988, Brooks signed with Capitol Records. After two failed single releases he pulled the plug himself. "Rather than beat a dead horse, I asked them if I could walk, and they let me," he says. "I thought I'd be better off to write and regroup until I found another project."

Brooks & Dunn

Dunn took a brief break from music to study for the Baptist ministry. But by his senior year he was violating school rules by sneaking out to play honky-tonks on weekends. The dean of the school found out and told him to quit making music or quit school.

Dunn decided his true calling was music, and he headed to Tulsa. There he fell into a fertile music scene surrounding Leon Russell's Shelter Records. He found himself hanging out with icons of the rock world like Leon, Joe Cocker, and members of Eric Clapton's road band.

After a short-lived deal on Church Hill Records, Dunn got his big break through onetime Clapton sideman Jamie Oldaker. In 1989, on a lark, Oldaker entered Dunn in the Marlboro Country Talent Contest. Dunn was the winner. "One of the prizes was a 40-hour recording session with Barry Beckett and

TOP ALBUMS

BRAND NEW MAN (Arista, '91)
HARD WORKIN' MAN (Arista, '93)
WAITIN' ON SUNDOWN (Arista, '94)

TOP SONGS

BRAND NEW MAN (Arista, '91, *1*)
MY NEXT BROKEN HEART (Arista, '91, *1*)
NEON MOON (Arista, '92, *1*)
BOOT SCOOTIN' BOOGIE (Arista, '92, *1*)
SHE USED TO BE MINE (Arista, '93, *1*)
THAT AIN'T NO WAY TO GO (Arista, '94, *1*)
SHE'S NOT THE CHEATIN' KIND (Arista, '94, *1*)

Additional Top 40 Country Songs: 4

Scott Hendricks," he says. "That is where the Arista connection came in. Scott was producing Alan Jackson when the label started up, and he took my tape to their head guy, Tim DuBois." DuBois encouraged Dunn to move to Nashville. In 1990, DuBois saw an opportunity for a new duo in the void created by the departure of the Judds and thought of both Brooks and Dunn, whom he liked but couldn't fit into his roster as solo artists. He put them together, hoping they would gel as writers and sound good together as singers. After hearing the fruits of their first sessions, he offered them the deal.

Their first single, the title tune of their first album, *Brand New Man,* appeared on the chart in June 1991, becoming the first of four consecutive Number One songs. Barely six months after their debut they were in the top ranks of country acts, attracting a large core audience with songs that reflected both youthful exuberance ("Boot Scootin' Boogie") and experience that comes with age ("Hard Workin' Man," "She Used to Be Mine"). By the early 1990s Brooks and Dunn were positioned for a long run on record and on stage.

GARTH BROOKS

Garth Brooks moved to Nashville in 1987 and in just two years went from boot store manager to songwriter and demo singer to one of the hottest young acts in the music business. The top 10 performance of his first chart record—an impressive feat for a newcomer at the time—was just the slightest hint of what was to come. He soon became the driving wind behind the firestorm of country music popularity that swept the nation in the early 1990s. With hit songs and charismatic appeal, Brooks became an entertainment phenomenon, transcending country without alienating his strong country base of fans.

Raised in Yukon, Oklahoma, the son of an ex-Marine and former country recording artist Colleen Carroll (who recorded for Capitol Records in the mid-1950s), Brooks (b. Feb. 7, 1962, Luba, Oklahoma) was often the star of weekend family performance gatherings. He veered more toward an athletic career until he went to college at Oklahoma State University, failing as a javelin tosser but succeeding in hooking up with musicians like Ty England (lead guitarist and future solo artist) to begin his career in country music. In 1985 he made a trip to Nashville, hoping to be discovered. He became so discouraged by the industry and his own naiveté that he turned back around and went home after only 23 hours.

He returned in 1987 and began networking with writers and producers. "I was turned down by every label in town until Capitol Records gave me a live audition," Brooks recalls. "They passed on me, too, at first." Just six weeks after Capitol passed, one of their executives saw him sing "If Tomorrow Never Comes" at the Bluebird Cafe. That convinced the company to reconsider and sign him to a contract in 1988.

Brooks debuted in 1989 at the same time as three other future stars: Clint Black, Alan Jackson, and Travis Tritt. Brooks hit number eight with his debut single, "Much Too Young (To Feel This Damn Old)." But Clint Black grabbed the most attention by scoring four consecutive Number One hits. Brooks' second release, "If Tomorrow Never Comes," hit Number One but was still not enough to overcome the Black onslaught. "We're just going to keep our heads, keep pace, and just keep laying a foundation as thick as we can," Brooks said at the time.

Brooks eventually pulled ahead with two high-impact Number One records: "The Dance" (supported with an inspired video that presented scenes of heroic figures) and "Friends in Low Places" (from the second album, *No Fences*). Together, they established the qualities of youthful exuberance and sensitivity that became Brooks' key attractions for country fans.

The *No Fences* CD and the third album, *Ropin' the Wind,* each sold over 10 million copies, with the latter becoming the first album in history to debut at Number One on both the *Billboard* country and pop album charts. Brooks' high-tech, rock-style stage show boosted album sales and regularly sold out 60,000-seat stadiums within minutes.

"Garth Brooks has been the single most important thing that's happened to country music," says Jimmy Bowen, former president of Brooks' second label, Liberty Records. "Because of the tremendous impact of his music at retail, the retailers, the rack jobbers in this country, have a whole other attitude toward country music than they had a few years ago, and that helped all the other new stars."

Lacking the raw sex appeal of an Elvis Presley, Brooks (who battles a weight problem and is balding and prematurely gray) built a broad constituency by

Garth Brooks

successfully emphasizing sincerity and the appearance of accessibility. In spite of his extravagant show, he comes across as honest, humble, and unpretentious. He reached out to young audiences and at the same time endeared himself to the country establishment by paying homage to its institutions and the stars who influenced him. He joined the Grand Ole Opry and appeared there regularly while opting not to perform his more pop-oriented material "in that sacred place." He once said, "I won't feel that I've really accomplished something in country music until I've sustained a career as long as those of Reba McEntire and George Strait."

"I'm hoping my contribution was good," says Brooks, "and they don't look back and say that was the decline, the time when big sales was all that mattered. A lot of new companies have rushed in [to Nashville] because of the dollars, and I think that the two main ingredients of country, honesty and sincerity, are being forfeited. It scares me not only for Nashville's sake but more importantly for the sake of country music."

TRACY BYRD

It took about 40 years after George Jones emerged from Beaumont, Texas, for Mark Chesnutt to appear. It was only a matter of months before Beaumont yielded its next star, Tracy Byrd. In 1990, Byrd (b. Dec. 17, 1966), raised in nearby Vidor, took over from Chesnutt as the headliner of a local club called Cutters when Mark signed a record contract. Byrd quickly established his own reputation there, and when his managers pitched him to MCA less than a year later, he filled the label's need for another young, traditional singer. He broke through in 1993 when he hit Number One with his third single, "Holdin' Heaven."

The son of a chemical plant worker, Byrd is one of the rare country singers who didn't grow up performing music with family or friends. His ambition to perform was driven by random discoveries of his singing talent. He was a teenager when he attracted his first fans. "I would drive up to the teller window at the bank," he says, "and while I waited, I'd sing along with Merle Haggard or George Strait, whoever I was listening to. I didn't know for six months that the ladies would turn up the intercom so they could all listen to me sing." Later, he'd sing while

TOP ALBUMS

GARTH BROOKS (Capitol, '89)
NO FENCES (Capitol, '90)
ROPIN' THE WIND (Capitol, '91)
THE CHASE (Liberty, '92)
IN PIECES (Liberty, '93)

TOP SONGS

IF TOMORROW NEVER COMES (Capitol, '89, 1)
THE DANCE (Capitol, '90, 1)
FRIENDS IN LOW PLACES (Capitol, '90, 1)
WHAT SHE'S DOING NOW (Liberty, '92, 1)
AIN'T GOING DOWN (TIL THE SUN COMES UP)
    (Liberty, '93, 1)

Additional Top 40 Country Songs: 15

Tracy Byrd

cruising around town in a pickup truck with his best friend. "He would say, 'You really sing good, you ought to do something with it.' I'd say, 'That's just something I do, I'd never get anywhere with that.'"

Curious about how he might sound on record, he made a $7.95 recording at a local emporium. "The lady working at the studio there worked with this 'Opry' show in Beaumont at a theater," says Byrd. "They have this amateur hour. I got up, sang two songs, and got a standing ovation. I thought, 'This is great, I have to feel this again." By the time he entered college he'd obtained a guitar and begun picking and singing wherever he could. When his junior year at Beaumont's Lamar University rolled around, Byrd quit school to become a full-time performer.

He began as a solo act but was soon sitting in with various local bands on the regional club circuit, which included Cutters. In 1990, when he was chosen to replace Chesnutt, they co-headlined for six months before Mark hit the road to support his first album. Byrd attracted a couple of local backers who financed a Nashville showcase performance for him in March 1991 that attracted interest from both Warner Brothers and MCA. Byrd opted for MCA, where his friend Chesnutt had gone and where his idol George Strait resided.

Byrd's debut album, *Tracy Byrd,* was recorded in 1992. It was not released immediately, because the label had him scheduled for 1993, and they wanted to record several additional songs. The delay was frustrating for Byrd, but one of the late songs was "Holdin' Heaven," which became the first album's only hit and his first Number One song. The second album, *No Ordinary Man,* was released in the summer of 1994.

Between the two discs, claims Byrd, he learned an important lesson: "To go with my gut instinct on songs. First time, I was talked out of ones I believed in. On the second album I went more with my raw instincts. I felt better, and it worked out with songs I fought for, like 'Lifestyles of the Not So Rich and Famous,' 'Watermelon Crawl,' and 'The First Step.'"

TOP ALBUMS

TRACY BYRD (MCA, '93)
NO ORDINARY MAN (MCA, '94)

TOP SONGS

HOLDIN' HEAVEN (MCA, '93, *1*)
LIFESTYLES OF THE NOT SO RICH AND FAMOUS
    (MCA, '94, *4*)
WATERMELON CRAWL (MCA, '94, *4*)

Additional Top 40 Country Songs: 1

GLEN CAMPBELL
• •

Glen Campbell

Glen Campbell once described his music as "a crock," his tongue-in-cheek answer to people who would categorize him as either a country or a pop artist. From his country beginnings in Arkansas and Texas, to his years as a top pop session guitarist in Los Angeles, through stints with the Champs and the Beach Boys, Campbell laid a foundation in both musical worlds. When he became a recording artist in the early 1960s, it was not surprising that his biggest country hits, like "Wichita Lineman," "Galveston," and "Rhinestone Cowboy," were also huge pop hits. Campbell portrays himself as "not country per se, but I am a country boy who sings"—an accurate enough description of a man who became an icon of American music and whose universal appeal spans four decades.

Campbell (b. Apr. 22, 1936, Billstown, Arkansas) was raised in Delight, Arkansas, among 10 other children in a family where everybody picked and sang. Handed his first guitar when he was just four, he learned from siblings and relatives at first. Later he listened to such masters as Django Reinhardt and Barney Kessel while developing his vocal ability by singing in a local church.

By age 14, he was ready to move on and plunge further into music. "I spent the early part of my life looking at the north end of a southbound mule," he says, "and it didn't take long to figure out that a guitar was a lot lighter than a plow handle." He headed for New Mexico and Houston, Texas, but he didn't stray too far from the family circle. He spent several years in the band of his uncle, Dick Bills, touring what Campbell calls the "dancin' and fightin' clubs." "I joined his band when I was 15, and we had a half-hour show, five days a week, on station KOBE in Albuquerque. That experience gave me an appreciation for a variety of music. We played everything . . . old country standards . . . we did old pop standards and current hits from Hank Cochran to Elvis. I went to college working for Dick."

At 22, Campbell moved to California. By 1960 he was in Los Angeles and having little trouble adjusting to big city life. "I used growing up in the country as an advantage," he told reporter Scott Cohen. "People are curious when you have an accent. Then I started doing studio work. Musicians don't care where you're from or what color you are. They judge you by your talent." His talent was world class, landing him work on records by Frank Sinatra, Bobby Darin, Rick Nelson, the Monkees, the Mamas and the Papas, the Association, Merle Haggard, Ray Charles, and Elvis Presley.

He made his first chart appearance in 1962, scoring a top 20 country hit as the featured singer and picker with the Green Mountain Boys. At one point he toured with the Champs, and in 1965 he became a temporary member of the Beach Boys. After filling in for Brian Wilson for six months he was asked to become a permanent member. "But they withdrew the offer when I asked for an equal split," Campbell recalls. Just a few months later, he had his own recording contract with Capitol Records.

His first single, "Burning Bridges," demonstrated his potential as a country act when it hit number 18 in early 1967. In the summer of that year he released "Gentle on My Mind." It only reached number 30 on the country chart, but it put his name on the pop listings and laid the groundwork for his next release, "By the Time I Get to Phoenix," a number two country smash that crossed over to 26 pop. More big hits followed in rapid succession, including "I Wanna Live," "Dreams of the Everyday Housewife," and "Wichita Lineman." The success of the latter (Number One country, number three pop) helped Campbell land his own national television show, "The Glen Campbell Good Time Hour," which ran from 1968 to 1972.

Campbell became a perennial presence on the country chart through to the 1990s, contributing

TOP ALBUMS

RHINESTONE COWBOY (Capitol, '75)
BLOODLINE (Capitol, '76)
SOUTHERN LIGHTS (Capitol, '77)
LETTER TO HOME (Atlantic America, '84)

TOP SONGS

BY THE TIME I GET TO PHOENIX
   (Capitol, '67, 2, 26 Pop)
I WANNA LIVE (Capitol, '68, 1, 36 Pop)
WICHITA LINEMAN (Capitol, '68, 1, 3 Pop)
GALVESTON (Capitol, '69, 1, 4 Pop)
RHINESTONE COWBOY (Capitol, '75, 1, 1 Pop)
SOUTHERN NIGHTS (Capitol, '77, 1, 1 Pop)

Additional Top 40 Country Songs: 48

classic crossover hits like "Galveston" and the country and pop Number Ones "Rhinestone Cowboy" and "Southern Nights."

A truly exceptional guitarist, able to hold his own with such virtuosos as jazzman George Benson, Campbell has long considered himself primarily a guitar player who sings. He almost always plays lead guitar on his recordings. "If there is a guitar solo, I might as well play the guitar, because I have to do it on stage," he says. "Besides that, I don't know anybody who can do it better."

MARY CHAPIN CARPENTER

In 1988 few country music pundits gave Mary Chapin Carpenter more than a slim chance of making it. She was an outsider with few Nashville connections and fewer expectations that her music would be embraced by the country establishment. Her country recording career was born in the midst of a powerful return to traditional influences. Yet Carpenter's decidedly nontraditional sound not only survived but served to broaden the boundaries of the music, putting her in the ranks of country's most important artists.

Carpenter (b. Feb. 21, 1958, Princeton, New Jersey) was raised in New Jersey and Japan. Her father was a business manager for *Life* magazine who spent a few years in Tokyo as the publisher of the Asian edition. She had grown up listening to the music of Woody Guthrie and Judy Collins, but she didn't start performing until the family had moved to Japan. There, in an international school, she joined an informal gathering of students to play music each day after school. It was a life-altering experience. Playing guitar and singing led to writing songs, which eventually became her reason for staying in the music business. "I didn't begin to play music because I had a huge ego that needed to be in front of people," she says. "Music became a cathartic outlet for expressing myself, to deal with my feelings and emotions."

The family returned to the United States, settling in Washington, D.C. Through high school and her college years at Brown University, Carpenter remained a closet performer—until around the age of 19 or 20. "My father got tired of me playing my

*Mary Chapin
Carpenter*

music in my room. One night he just came in and said, 'Why don't you go down to that bar down the street that has an open mike and get up there and sing?' I thought, 'Oh God,' but I did it. I went there to Gallagher's Pub, got up on a stool, did three songs, didn't die of fright, and a year later I was a regular at the club." Carpenter went on to become one of the most popular D.C. area performers.

She had amassed a catalog of original songs by the time she met guitarist and record producer John Jennings. Impressed with the freshness of her sound and the highly personal and intelligent lyrics of her songs, he helped convince Carpenter to record her material. Together they produced an album, *Hometown Girl,* hoping to perhaps attract the interest of a small label. A copy made its way to Rounder Records, who made an offer. Some visionary at Columbia Records responded as well, and just two days away from signing with Rounder, Columbia intervened and signed her up.

Following the release of *Hometown Girl,* Columbia executive Roy Wunsch called her music "a high risk for the format." It proved true at first, as nothing from the album worked commercially. "The

album wasn't written for radio," she claims. "It was just to show off my songs, most of which were over five minutes long. We had a better idea of what radio needed when we went in to record the second album."

Impressed with the quality of her debut disc, Columbia allowed Jennings and Carpenter to return to Washington to record *State of the Heart.* The label's trust was validated when the record yielded her first four hits—songs that would define her music. The first, "How Do," showcased her way with words and sense of humor and at the same time showed she could connect with the mainstream country audience. "I got letters from places in the Deep South from guys telling how much their gals liked that song," she recalls. She followed "How Do" with her first two top 10s, "Never Had It So Good" and "Quittin' Time," each the kind of auto-biographical, cathartic message from her heart that became a mainstay of her work.

In 1990 Carpenter released *Shooting Straight in the Dark,* her first gold album largely due to the strength of its number two single, "Down at the Twist and Shout," a Cajun-tinged tune that featured members of the group Beausoleil. Then, in June 1992, she issued what became her breakthrough disc, *Come On Come On,* which yielded seven hit singles, three Grammy Awards, and sales of over 2.5 million. That success led to her being named the Country Music Association's Female Vocalist of the Year in 1993.

Carpenter's fifth album, *Stones in the Road,* produced "Shut Up and Kiss Me," her first Number

---

TOP ALBUMS

STATE OF THE HEART (Columbia, '89)
SHOOTING STRAIGHT IN THE DARK (Columbia, '90)
COME ON COME ON (Columbia, '92)
STONES IN THE ROAD (Columbia, '94)

TOP SONGS

NEVER HAD IT SO GOOD (Columbia, '89, *8*)
QUITTIN' TIME (Columbia, '90, *7*)
DOWN AT THE TWIST AND SHOUT (Columbia, '91, *2*)
I FEEL LUCKY (Columbia, '92, *4*)
PASSIONATE KISSES (Columbia, '93, *4*)
SHUT UP AND KISS ME (Columbia, '94, *1*)

Additional Top 40 Country Songs: 7

One song. She notes that *Stones* bears similarities to the album that led to the "former folk singer" reputation she has always rejected. "Look at this album and look at all the albums in between, then look at the first album, *Hometown Girl*. From a production value and instruments used and everything, there's no difference."

Carpenter, "former folk singer" and onetime "high risk to the format," remains a flourishing artist and a unique voice in country music.

CARLENE CARTER

Carlene Carter was born of country royalty, but she's been as troubling at times to her elders as the younger generation of British royalty has been to the House of Windsor. Carlene (b. Rebecca Carlene Smith, Sept. 26, 1955, Madison, Tennessee) is the daughter of country singer Carl Smith (a popular star of the 1950s and '60s) and June Carter (daughter of Mother Maybelle Carter and member of the legendary Carter Family). In spite of growing up in Nashville immersed in country music traditions, Carter rebelled and first sought a career in rock and roll. Drawn back into the country fold in the mid-1980s by the Carter sisters (June, Anita, and Helen), Carlene committed to a country recording career in 1990 that led to her biggest hits.

Carlene was just two years old when June divorced Carl Smith. Smith became less of an influence in her life, particularly after June married Johnny Cash. Carlene's grandmother, Maybelle, taught her to play guitar; her mother and aunts taught her to sing harmony; she took classical piano lessons; and Johnny and his peers Kris Kristofferson, Willie Nelson, and Waylon Jennings introduced her to the progressive, "outlaw" element of country music. Although she performed occasionally with the Carter Family and the Johnny Cash show in the late 1960s and early '70s, it was no surprise to her stepfather when Carlene gravitated to the rock world. "She started playing rock and roll at the house when she was 12 years old," Cash observed.

Strong-willed and wildly independent, Carlene left home at age 15 and was married with child at 16. By the time she recorded her first album at age 22 she had two children and was married to her third husband, producer and performer Nick Lowe.

Her early recordings (*Carlene Carter* and *Two* Sides to Every Woman*) were heavy on the rockabilly, and even though she charted country twice (in 1979 and 1980), she was ultimately rejected by both the country and pop worlds. "There's a certain tone in my voice from the Carters that assured that I could never stop being country," she says, "but I was always infuriated when they had to label you as something. I wanted to rock a little harder than what was happening in country at the time, so I was labeled too rock for country. I was thought of as such a country person that I couldn't fit into the rock thing either."

Carter moved to England, where she recorded five albums that mixed R&B, rock, and rockabilly. She cited that period as one of absolute freedom to create any music she wanted to. As she matured, however, her deep country roots came out. Her transition back to country was helped along in 1986 when the Carter Sisters came through England on tour. When aunt Anita fell ill one night, Carlene filled in for her; she ended up working with them for two years. Her marriage to Nick Lowe ended, and she returned to the U.S., where, with her friend and collaborator Howie Epstein, she began writing songs aimed at getting her back into country.

The result of that move was a contract with Reprise Records and a solid, fresh-sounding disc in 1990 called *I Fell in Love*. That album and the follow-up, 1993's *Little Love Letters* on Giant Records, brought her five consecutive top 40 hits, including three top 10s. "I feel I came full circle," Carter said. "I feel that my songs have come from the same place the old Carter tunes came from, but they are new Carter Family songs." Perhaps her return to the fold was predictable given her decision, when starting out as a performer, to use the last name of Carter instead of Smith. "I picked up Carter

---

TOP ALBUMS

I FELL IN LOVE (Reprise, '90)
LITTLE LOVE LETTERS (Giant, '93)

TOP SONGS

I FELL IN LOVE (Reprise, '90, 3)
COME ON BACK (Reprise, '90, 3)
EVERY LITTLE THING (Giant, '93, 3)

Additional Top 40 Country Songs: 3

because my grandmother was getting pretty old and there weren't any male Carters left doing music," she explains. "I felt in a way that I needed to carry on the Carter name."

JOHNNY CASH

The word *legend* is so carelessly applied that it has all but lost its meaning. Yet it is appropriate for Johnny Cash. In a career that spans five decades he has become nearly as much a pop icon as a country megastar. Since his debut on Sun Records in 1955 he has recorded over 500 albums. From them came over 140 country hit singles and nearly 50 that made the *Billboard* Hot 100 pop chart. He was there at Sun Records with other legends-to-be Roy Orbison, Carl Perkins, Jerry Lee Lewis, and Elvis Presley—all of whom contributed to the birth of rock and roll while Cash simultaneously helped to redefine country music. He is the only artist enshrined in both the Country Music Hall of Fame and the Roll and Rock Hall of Fame.

Cash (b. J. R. Cash, Feb. 28, 1932, Kingsland, Arkansas) grew up in Dysess Colony in northeast Arkansas surrounded by the images and influences that would shape his autobiographical songs. For 15 years he lived on the Mississippi River, next to sharecroppers and cotton pickers, near the trains that passed by their farm, and within earshot of the fire-and-brimstone messages and soul-grabbing music of the Pentecostal church his mother attended. He absorbed the music that came from the Grand Ole Opry and he idolized Ernest Tubb, Hank Williams, Roy Acuff, and Hank Snow. He also watched his brother Roy put a band together in the 1940s called the Dixie Rhythm Ramblers.

Sun Records' Sam Phillips recognized talent when John Cash (he was born with only the initials J. R.; John evolved as a name; Phillips changed it to Johnny) auditioned for him in 1955. Cash had moved to Memphis to attend a disc jockey school on the G.I. Bill. He thought he was auditioning to be a gospel singer, but Phillips had other plans. During the audition Johnny sang an original song called "Hey Porter." Phillips ordered his engineer to start recording and told Cash, "Sing it again." That was his first recording. Phillips then said to him, "Now go home and write me a hit to go with it." The result was Sun's first country chart hit, "Cry! Cry! Cry!"

Although Phillips considered Johnny to be the most "country" of his stable of future legends, the lines between musical genres were blurred back then, and radio played anything that was a hit. Between 1955 and 1958, Johnny released a string of Sun recordings that would become American classics, like "Folsom Prison Blues," "I Walk the Line," "Ballad of a Teenage Queen," and "Guess Things Happen That Way." The broad appeal of the records stemmed from their simple arrangements stripped of the usual steel guitar, background vocals, and fiddle licks that characterized "country and western" at the time. "Sam Phillips had a vision," said Cash to writer Bill Flanagan. "He saw another direction for the music, and I did, too. I never liked fiddle and steel guitar on my music, and Nashville was grinding out songs that sounded the same, calculated and predictable. My music wasn't done to sound like somebody else in Nashville or in rock."

Cash was lured away from Phillips in 1958 by Columbia Records, his musical home for the next 32 years (1958 to 1990). From the late 1950s through the early '70s Johnny issued a slew of country releases that nearly all crossed over to the pop chart, with "A Boy Named Sue" (Number One country) peaking at number two pop in 1969. Cash became particularly visible in pop in the late 1960s, pairing with Bob Dylan on the song "Girl from the North Country," included on Dylan's *Nashville Skyline* album (for which Cash wrote the liner notes).

TOP ALBUMS

AT FOLSOM PRISON/AT SAN QUENTIN (Columbia, '75)
GREATEST HITS VOL. 1 (Columbia, '67)
AMERICAN RECORDINGS (American Records, '94)

TOP SONGS

FOLSOM PRISON BLUES (Sun, '56, 4; Columbia, '68, 1)
I WALK THE LINE (Sun, '56, 1, 17 Pop)
BALLAD OF A TEENAGE QUEEN (Sun, '58, 1, 14 Pop)
DON'T TAKE YOUR GUNS TO TOWN
    (Columbia, '59, 1, 32 Pop)
RING OF FIRE (Columbia, '63, 1, 17 Pop)
A BOY NAMED SUE (Columbia, '69, 1, 2 Pop)
HIGHWAYMAN (with Waylon Jennings, Willie Nelson,
    and Kris Kristofferson, Columbia, '85, 1)

Additional Top 40 Country Songs: 95

The Man in Black, as he became known, tended to transcend categorization while remaining as fond of country tradition as he was of new musical directions. He sang roots country and gospel with his wife June Carter and her sisters; he recorded "Highwayman" with country "outlaws" Willie Nelson, Waylon Jennings, and Kris Kristofferson. He supported the progressive music of his daughter Rosanne Cash and stepdaughter Carlene Carter. He drew material for his recordings from such non-country artists as Bruce Springsteen.

As happened with many of his peers, Cash's presence on the country chart diminished in the late 1980s and early '90s. That did not signal the end of his career. In 1994, Rick Rubens (producer of Red Hot Chili Peppers and other rock acts) approached

Johnny Cash

Cash about recording an acoustic record for his American Records label. The CD *Johnny Cash: American Recordings* became his best-selling album in a decade, its stark, guitar-backed vocals and songs like "Deliah's Gone," "Drive On," "The Man Who Couldn't Cry," and "Redemption" drawing critical acclaim and sparking the interest of young listeners discovering him for the first time. "There are more young people coming to my shows than ever before," he told writer Linda Cauthen. "I don't know if they are going to respond by buying millions of my records, but this album is an expression of my art that I've always wanted to do, just to sit down with my guitar and sing a song, just me and you, personal and close up to let people hear what I really am."

That up-close-and-personal projection of his big, earthy, and instantly recognizable voice remained the anchor of Cash's appeal. As June Carter Cash told *The Nashville Banner,* "He has such dynamic charisma on stage that he can make a person half a mile away from the stage think he is seeing the pupil of John's eye."

ROSANNE CASH

In 1973, Rosanne Cash was a petrified teenager when she made her first stage appearance as part of father Johnny Cash's show. In 1979, she was a shy 24-year-old when Bobby Bare joined her for a duet that became her first country chart hit, "No Memories Hangin' Round." A year later she stepped onto the country stage as a solo artist. Almost before people could question whether she would climb out of the shadow of her father, Rosanne confidently established her own identity with sharply written, emotional hits like "Seven Year Ache" and "Blue Moon with Heartache." She eventually evolved into one of the most eloquent female voices for the affairs of the heart and one of the key country stars of the 1980s.

Cash (b. May 24, 1955, Memphis, Tennessee) began life in the same year and the same place her father's recording career began. When she was three the family moved to California, and eight years later Johnny and her mother, Vivian, divorced. "My whole childhood was pretty traumatic," she recalls. "My dad was gone a lot, and my mother was trying to handle four kids by herself." Cash managed to

maintain a long-distance relationship with her father. After high school, she and her sister Rosie went on the road with his show, working in the wardrobe department. Eventually he had them both up on stage singing. "It was a real protective atmosphere," she says. "I never had to fall on my face. It was a stage where people automatically liked me, and I learned a lot about stage presence by watching dad."

In 1978 Cash went to Germany and recorded her first album, on Ariola Records. She was mismatched with a producer who tried to get her to record disco songs along with pop and country tunes. The album was never released in the United States, but the head man at Columbia Records Nashville heard it and liked one song well enough to recruit Rosanne for the label. The song was "No Memories Hangin' Round," written by her soon-to-be husband, singer-songwriter Rodney Crowell. Rodney ended up producing the song in a duet arrangement (with Bobby Bare). It turned out so well he produced her first album, *Right or Wrong.* (He would also produce *Seven Year Ache, Somewhere in the Stars,* and *King's Record Shop.*) "I was intimidated by [Crowell's] talent at first," says Cash. "He's such a good writer that for a long time I didn't want to write anything. I was embarrassed, but I got over that and just decided to start writing."

Cash's writing ability proved to be prodigious. Her sophomore album, *Seven Year Ache,* spawned three Number One songs, of which two, the title song and "Blue Moon with Heartache," were her

---

TOP ALBUMS

SEVEN YEAR ACHE (Columbia, '81)
SOMEWHERE IN THE STARS (Columbia, '82)
RHYTHM & ROMANCE (Columbia, '85)
KING'S RECORD SHOP (Columbia, '87)

TOP SONGS

SEVEN YEAR ACHE (Columbia, '81, *1, 22 Pop*)
BLUE MOON WITH HEARTACHE (Columbia, '81, *1*)
NEVER BE YOU (Columbia, '85, *1*)
TENNESSEE FLAT TOP BOX (Columbia, '87, *1*)
RUNAWAY TRAIN (Columbia, '88)
ON THE SURFACE (Columbia, '91)

Additional Top 40 Country Songs: 15

Rosanne Cash

World" (from his album *Diamonds and Dirt*) in 1988.

In the 1990s, Rosanne experienced sweeping changes in both her personal and professional life. She and Rodney Crowell divorced, she moved from Tennessee to New York City, and while country music moved more towards the traditional, Rosanne's musical self-expression became more poetic and esoteric. Her album *Interiors* yielded a country Number One, "On the Surface," but the balance of that album and a subsequent release, *The Wheel*, effectively moved her out of the country camp.

MARK CHESNUTT

In the late 1980s Mark Chesnutt made occasional trips from Texas to Nashville to make contacts and to search for material to record. On one of those trips he got his hands on a really good song. He recorded and released it on a small Texas label. It became a big enough regional hit to come to the attention of a Houston-based promotion man for MCA Records in Nashville. The label went looking for the man who recorded it and signed him up. In 1990, that song, "Too Cold at Home," became Mark's debut single, hitting number three in the nation and thrusting him into the ranks of viable new artists. He proved his viability by becoming a solid, platinum-selling 1990s star.

Chesnutt (b. Sept. 6, 1963, Beaumont, Texas) lists the usual musical influences—Haggard, Jones, Presley, and Hank Williams (Sr. and Jr.)—but claims he owes his career to his father, Bob Chesnutt. Mark's earliest memories are of his father writing and performing country music in preparation for the serious run at Nashville he made when Mark was eight years old. Bob went to Music City and was gaining publishing and recording interest in his talent when he abruptly pulled the plug on his recording career, opting instead to be a family man. Says Chesnutt, "He just quit it cold turkey and never performed seriously again."

Though disillusioned, Chesnutt's father encouraged his son's interest in music. Around 1980, Chesnutt was out of high school and beginning to make his living in the local honky-tonks. His father advised and supported him when he needed new equipment, and when Chesnutt decided he wanted to make a record, his father financed his son's first

own compositions. "Within a year's time, from this kind of shy woman that recorded *Right or Wrong*," noted Crowell, "she became this powerful, evocative *Seven Year Ache* artist, a modern woman with a feminist image."

Country purists were hesitant to embrace her. "I don't think my music fit into the boxes or definitions people apply to country music today," she admits. "I feel that I'm a country artist breaking new ground."

Rosanne continued to release albums full of insightful original songs and her distinctive versions of songs written by others, like John Hiatt's "The Way We Make a Broken Heart" and the John Lennon–Paul McCartney tune "I Don't Want to Spoil the Party." She also managed to pay tribute to her father by writing and recording "My Old Man." After scoring a Number One hit with his "Tennessee Flat Top Box," she received a letter in which he wrote, "Your own 'My Old Man' is one of my life's greatest joys, but your success with 'Tennessee Flat Top Box' is one of my life's greatest fulfillments."

The one time Cash and Crowell recorded together they scored a Number One hit: "It's Such a Small

TOP ALBUMS

Too Cold at Home (MCA, '90)
Longnecks and Short Stories (MCA, '92)
Almost Goodbye (MCA, '93)
What a Way to Live (Decca, '94)

TOP SONGS

Too Cold at Home (MCA, '90, 3)
Brother Jukebox (MCA, '90, 1)
I'll Think of Something (MCA, '92, 1)
It Sure Is Monday (MCA, '93, 1)
I Just Wanted You to Know (MCA, '93, 1)
She Dreams (Decca, '94, 1)

Additional Top 40 Country Songs: 6

ROY CLARK

Guitarist-singer Roy Clark (b. Apr. 15, 1933, Meherrin, Virginia) became well known via some 50 country-charting songs—including the Number One "Come Live with Me" and the crossover hit "Yesterday, When I Was Young." But most Americans know him through his appearances on national television. For over 30 years, Clark's infectious grin, effervescent personality, and incredible picking ability lit up numerous late-night talk shows and musical variety programs. He also had a recurring role in the TV series "The Beverly Hillbillies" and a long run as a co-host of "Hee Haw."

Clark grew up near Washington, D.C. He was the son of a mid-level government worker and didn't experience the poverty-stricken, rural upbringing typical of his musical peers. That didn't stop him from falling in love with country music and the instruments used to make it, all of which he would eventually learn how to play. Just how good he was at doing that was revealed in the late 1940s when he won the first of two national banjo playing championships at age 14. He added to his repertoire of instruments and developed his talent as a musician and humorist on a circuit of clubs in the D.C. and Baltimore area. That led to a spot on a local TV show called "The Hayloft Conservatory of Musical Interpretation." Other TV appearances followed, along with opportunities to tour with such country stars as Wanda Jackson and Hank Thompson.

Clark recorded a few times on small record labels before Capitol signed him to his first recording contract in 1963. Clark responded by scoring a top 10 hit with his debut single, "Tips of My Fingers."

recording session. Between 1981 and '89 they recorded one local single a year. They sent them to local radio stations and got them into a few jukeboxes. Each time they did that, the feedback and inspiration of hearing himself on the radio fueled Chesnutt's determination to stay in the business. Meanwhile, he developed his stage act in the local clubs and during a short stint as a regular performer at Jones Country, an east Texas music theme park owned by George Jones. Later, Chesnutt settled in to a headlining spot at a popular Beaumont club called Cutters.

He was doing well as a local hero, but he wanted more. "There were times that I could have given up," he says. "Daddy seemed to sense that, and he'd ask me if still wanted to try to make it in the music business. I'd mumble, 'Yes,' and he would say, 'Well, if you want to keep going, I think it's time to put out another record.'" Somehow his father would scrape up the money to make the record. In 1989 it was the recording of "Too Cold at Home," and it paid off with the MCA contract. Bob Chesnutt was able to witness the first year or so of Mark's success before he died.

Chesnutt came right back after the top three performance of his first national release and scored a Number One with "Brother Jukebox." Others followed, including "I'll Think of Something," "It Sure Is Monday," and "She Dreams." In 1994, MCA reactivated Decca Records and moved Chesnutt over to become the new company's flagship act. *What a Way to Live* was his first Decca album.

TOP SONGS

Tips of My Fingers (Capitol, '63, 10)
Yesterday, When I Was Young (Dot, '69, 9, 19 Pop)
I Never Picked Cotton (Dot, '70, 5)
The Lawrence Welk–Hee Haw–Counter
    Revolution Polka (Dot, '70, 9)
Come Live with Me (Dot, '73, 1)
Somewhere Between Love and Tomorrow
    (Dot, '73, 2)
If I Had It to Do All Over Again (ABC/Dot, '76, 2)

Additional Top 40 Country Songs: 17

He never became a star vocalist, but given the right song for his distinctive voice, Roy could deliver a hit—and he did so with nine top 10 songs. One of them was 1969's "Yesterday, When I Was Young," which peaked at number nine on the country chart and rose to number 19 pop. "I don't consider myself a fantastic musician. I just have fun with picking," he says. "I know I'm not the greatest player, comedian, or a great singer. When people ask me what I do, I just tell them I'm an entertainer."

In the late 1980s Roy established a lucrative theater in Branson, Missouri, capping a career that included two extensive tours of Russia (1976 and 1988) and induction into the Grand Ole Opry.

PATSY CLINE

It has been said that "the light that shines twice as bright burns half as long." The truth of that assertion seemed evident on March 5, 1963, when Patsy Cline, who had become the first major female country-to-pop crossover star, died in a Tennessee plane crash barely six years after her first chart appearance. But Cline's story has since proven that a bright light cut short can sometimes return to shine brighter than ever: Her sophisticated "country-politan" sound is more popular in the 1990s than it was during her lifetime. She sells over 100,000 albums a

Patsy Cline

year and continues to inspire legions of new female country artists.

Cline (b. Virginia Patterson Hensley, Sept. 8, 1932, Winchester, Virginia) once credited a near-death experience for her million-dollar voice. As a young girl she experienced a throat infection so severe that it briefly stopped her heart. "I was placed in an oxygen tent and brought back to life," she told a Washington, D.C., newspaper. "I recovered from the illness with a voice that boomed forth like Kate Smith." She grew up in a rural setting with parents wise enough to recognize her talent and provide her with music and dance lessons. She had to leave school as a teenager to help support the family after her father deserted them; she supplemented her drugstore wages by singing in area clubs and on a local radio show for station WINC.

Cline was confident of her talent and aggressive enough to take advantage of opportunities when they came along. At a performance by Grand Ole Opry star Wally Fowler in her hometown, she talked him into giving her an audition, and he hired her to become part of his road show. It eventually got her to Nashville, where she wrangled an appearance on radio station WSM. But she couldn't crack the Opry or a record company and soon returned to Virginia.

Cline persisted, and thanks in part to the door-opening success of Kitty Wells (the first female to score a Number One country hit), she landed a contract with 4 Star Records in 1954.

The first three years of her recording career were not happy ones, marred by battles over the kind of music she wanted to record. Trying to sound like

Kitty Wells wasn't working, and she didn't want to sing pop. In 1957 she was about to lose her contract when she reluctantly recorded a song called "Walkin' After Midnight." She was soon glad she did. Before the song was released she used it to audition for the nationally broadcast "Arthur Godfrey's Talent Scouts" show. She ended up singing that song on the show and winning the "talent scouts" contest. It sparked a nationwide demand for Cline and the song. Her label, which had formed a partnership with Decca Records, had to rush to get the record out to radio stations and the public. "Walkin' After Midnight" became a huge country and pop hit.

Cline's career took off in 1961, when she was signed exclusively to Decca. She released "I Fall to Pieces" that year, and it became her first Number One country hit. She followed it with another country and pop chart success—a song called "Crazy" written by a struggling writer named Willie Nelson.

As one of the most successful female acts of the early 1960s, Cline helped and encouraged other aspiring artists, including Barbara Mandrell and Loretta Lynn. "She helped me so much," Lynn said on the "American Country Countdown with Bob Kingsley" radio show. "She taught me how to go on and come off stage and advised me about what clothes to wear."

Cline became one of the chief purveyors (along with Brenda Lee) of the Nashville Sound, a pop-oriented style that was also dubbed "country-politan." Her record producer, Owen Bradley, was one of the architects of the sound. "She sounded like a pop singer in a lot of ways," says Bradley. "That was a minus for a long time, and now, 30 some years after her death, it has become a plus. My bosses used to tell me to make albums that would last 10 years. But I don't think anybody in their wildest dreams thought they'd last this long."

JESSI COLTER

Jessi Colter has been involved with music nearly all her life and literally married to it all her adult life (her first husband was Duane Eddy, and she later married Waylon Jennings). A writer of note, she reserved her own place in music history when she recorded her tender, across-the-board smash, "I'm Not Lisa." In a career that has been on and off, she is guilty by association of being a country "outlaw."

Colter (b. May 25, 1947, Phoenix, Arizona) is the great-great-great-grandniece of an actual outlaw. Her real name is Miriam Johnson; she took her performing name from her ancestor, Jesse Colter, who once ran with the Jesse James gang. Jessi was one of seven children born to a multifaceted father (an inventor, race car builder, and mining engineer) and a mother who became a preacher. She began her music career at age 11 playing piano and accordion in her mother's church.

Her marriage to Duane Eddy (originator of the "twangy" guitar sound) lasted roughly from 1961 to '68. Somewhere along the line she became a convert to country music. "The first time I heard the music of Hank Williams, Jr., and George Jones, I said to myself, 'What's that?'" recalls Colter. "But after I got into it I considered discovering country music as the greatest thing that ever happened in my creative life." She began writing country songs and had some luck when Don Gibson and Dottie West cut her material. Her life changed dramatically after she first saw Waylon Jennings sing in a Phoenix nightspot called JD's. They met and were married in 1969. "I always knew that my man and my music would have to be together," she says, "but I didn't count on marrying one of the greatest singers in the world and the most brilliant producer I know."

Colter's first chart appearances were duets with Waylon, in 1970 on "Suspicious Minds" (a cover of Elvis Presley's smash from the year before) and in 1971 with "Under Your Spell Again." Meanwhile,

---

TOP ALBUMS

I'M JESSI COLTER (Capitol, '75)
JESSI (Capitol, '76)
DIAMOND IN THE ROUGH (Capitol, '76)

TOP SONGS

I'M NOT LISA (Capitol, '75, *1, 4 Pop*)
WHAT'S HAPPENED TO BLUE EYES (Capitol, '75, *5*)
IT'S MORNING (AND I STILL LOVE YOU)
    (Capitol, '76, *11*)
SUSPICIOUS MINDS (with Waylon Jennings, RCA, '76, *2*)
WILD SIDE OF LIFE / IT WASN'T GOD WHO MADE
    HONKY TONK ANGELS (with Waylon Jennings,
    RCA, '81, *10*)

Additional Top 40 Country Songs: 4

Waylon encouraged Jessi's writing. Of her own work, Colter once said, "All my songs are an expression of where I live at that particular moment." It took all of five minutes for her to write a tender tale of a woman trying to assure her lover that she won't let him down like another had done. In 1975, with Waylon and Ken Mansfield producing, that song, "I'm Not Lisa," became her debut single, rising to Number One country and number four pop. She followed it with a number five called "What's Happened to Blue Eyes," and in 1976, capitalizing on that success, the duet "Suspicious Minds" was rereleased and sped to number two.

That two-year period was the pinnacle of Colter's recording career. In 1979 she pulled away from the business to write and raise her children. Aside from a brief return in the early 1980s, she has limited herself mainly to occasional spiritual albums and duets and stage appearances with her husband. But Colter will always be remembered for "I'm Not Lisa," a song thought by most to be an American classic.

CONFEDERATE RAILROAD

Confederate Railroad chugged onto the national scene in 1992, fueled by a supply of light-hearted, southern rock–based tunes that set them apart not only from most other country bands (save the Charlie Daniels Band) but also from most other country artists (save Travis Tritt, who also tries to infuse his music with southern rock sounds). Known for eight years as Danny Shirley and the Crossroads Band, they were one of the most successful acts on the southeastern club circuit, often working as the road band for David Allen Coe. Their first hit, "Jesus and Mama," brought them wide recognition.

The band consists of drummer Mark Dufresne, keyboardist Chris McDaniel, guitarist Michael Lamb, bassist Wayne Secrest, Gates Nichols on steel, and leader and founder Danny Shirley on guitar and lead vocals. In 1976 Danny Shirley made his professional debut in the shadow of Lookout Mountain at a club called the Ranch House. It was a simple, sit-down-on-a-stool solo gig, but the applause and the 30 bucks a night he was earning were enough to hook him on show business. It was part-time until

Confederate Railroad

April 1982, when Shirley quit working for his father's construction company, formed his band (including Dufresne and McDaniel), and began playing Chattanooga area clubs. He named the band after a restaurant his grandparents had owned called Crossroads.

The band was heavily influenced by the '70s country "outlaw" movement led by Waylon Jennings and Willie Nelson and by southern rockers like the Allmans and Lynyrd Skynyrd. But that style of music didn't cut it in Nashville, as Shirley discovered when he made his first run there in the early 1980s. "The going thing then was George Strait, and Randy Travis was the rising star of the future," Shirley remembers. "It was the music of Waylon and Willie that got me into the business, and Nashville was going real traditional. I had to decide to either play that game or just keep doing what we were doing,

enjoy it, and wait till it came back in style."

He decided to wait. They continued to work occasionally for David Allen Coe but eventually became regulars at a well-known club called Miss Kitty's in Marietta, Georgia, a suburb of Atlanta. The Crossroads Band and Travis Tritt were the top drawing acts at the club (and were sometimes not-so-friendly rivals). Travis was soon off to his Nashville career, and that spurred Danny and company to want to make records.

They had recorded three independent albums before their music came to the attention of the head man at Atlantic Records. "He liked our southern rock influences and put us with producer Barry Beckett, who had worked with guys like Bob Dylan, Bob Seger, and Hank, Jr.," says Shirley. "[He] figured he could help come up with a sound that was us and would work today." They got that sound plus a

TOP ALBUMS

CONFEDERATE RAILROAD (Atlantic, '92)
NOTORIOUS (Atlantic, '94)

TOP SONGS

JESUS AND MAMA (Atlantic, '92, 4)
QUEEN OF MEMPHIS (Atlantic, '92, 2)
TRASHY WOMEN (Atlantic, '93, *10*)
DADDY NEVER WAS THE CADILLAC KIND
(Atlantic, '94, 9)

Additional Top 40 Country Songs: 2

new moniker inspired by a stretch of railroad track between Kinnesaw, Georgia, and Chattanooga, where the famous Civil War train called the General once ran. Shirley, figuring a southern band should have a southern name, chose Confederate Railroad.

Six singles were released from their *Confederate Railroad* debut CD, including three top 10s—"Jesus and Mama," "Queen of Memphis," and "Trashy Women"—that put them on the map and drove the album to million-seller status.

They held their platinum celebration party in a Nashville Harley-Davidson shop, the appropriate venue for a bunch of road warriors whose image is of guitar-toting, partying biker outlaws—complete with a pro-wrestling stage manager named Dawg— and whose sense of good-ol'-boy fun is largely what attracted their core audience.

"I met [Nashville songwriter-producer Mark Wright] not long after the first album came out," says Shirley. "He came up and introduced himself and said, 'The thing that strikes me about your album the most is that I believe every word you're saying.' He couldn't have paid us a better compliment, because that's what we're going for: honesty."

JOHN CONLEE

When John Conlee signed a record contract in the late 1970s, it made him a quadruple threat: recording artist, broadcaster, farmer, and mortician. The only job he gave up after scoring a top five hit with "Rose Colored Glasses" was his job as a disc jockey and music director at a Nashville radio station. He continued to live on a working farm and renewed his old mortician's license every year, "just in case my show business career doesn't pan out," he explained. Conlee didn't have to think about that from the late 1970s through the early '90s as he racked up over two dozen chart hits, including seven Number One songs.

Conlee (b. Aug. 11, 1946, Versailles, Kentucky) made his public debut at age eight singing "Love Me Tender" in a grade school assembly. When he didn't die of fright, he liked the feeling well enough to keep music as a serious hobby. He sang in school choruses and choirs and a barbershop quartet. After high school he turned down a college grant to go to mortician's school and later became a practicing undertaker. He worked at that job for six years before becoming a broadcaster at a Versailles all-news station. Eventually Conlee wanted to move to a bigger market and chose Nashville mainly because his sister lived there and he would have a place to stay while he went job hunting at Music City radio stations. He landed a job at sister stations WKQB-FM and WLAC-AM, working as a disc jockey on FM and music director and assistant program director on the AM side.

Conlee quickly caught the fever of being in the country music capital. He and a couple of friends at the radio station began writing together and trying to figure out how to get their songs recorded. John looked at songwriting as a means to an end. "Having a song to pitch was a way of getting heard as a singer, and being heard as a singer was more important to me," he says. Singing provided his big break. "In 1976 I got a job to sing in the barbecue tent after a celebrity golf tournament. Producer Bud Logan was sitting in the audience and loved what I did. We started working together, and I ended up with a deal at ABC Records."

Conlee's early releases—including the debut single, "Backside of Thirty," which he'd co-written— went unnoticed. That changed in May 1978, when he issued "Rose Colored Glasses," a Conlee original. People began tuning in to his voice, a sonic mixture of Lefty Frizzell and Merle Haggard, and "Rose Colored Glasses" broke through to the top five. He followed it with "Lady Lay Down," his first Number One. Then, in the spring of 1979, his label did something unusual. "They rereleased 'Backside of Thirty,'" says Conlee. "Same voice track, same record, and it went to Number One."

After that, Conlee recorded under the MCA ban-

TOP ALBUMS

Rose Colored Glasses (ABC, '78)
Busted (MCA, '82)
In My Eyes (MCA, '83)

TOP SONGS

Rose Colored Glasses (ABC, '78, 5)
Lady Lay Down (ABC, '78, 1)
Backside of Thirty (ABC, '79, 1)
Common Man (MCA, '83, 1)
I'm Only in It for the Love (MCA, '83, 1)
In My Eyes (MCA, '83, 1)
Domestic Life (Columbia, '87, 4)

Additional Top 40 Country Songs: 20

ner until 1986, hitting his stride and scoring most of his biggest '80s hits. Songs like "Miss Emily's Picture" and "I'm Only in It for the Love" solidified his place as a purveyor of heartfelt balladry. He gravitated to songs with working-class values, like "Common Man," "Working Man," and a remake of Ray Charles' 1963 top four pop hit "Busted."

In addition to his tobacco-farm heritage, Conlee has credited his experience as a broadcaster with giving him the ability to recognize and write hit material, all elements that combined with his vocal talent to make him one of the outstanding country acts of the 1980s.

EARL THOMAS CONLEY

One of country music's more soulful singers and poetic writers, Earl Thomas Conley first song-wrote his way onto the national music scene in 1975 when Mel Street hit with his "Smokey Mountain Memories" and Conway Twitty scored a Number One with "This Time I've Hurt Her More Than She Loves Me." That same year, Earl debuted as a charting vocalist with "I Have Loved You Girl (But Not Like This Before)." What followed was a remarkable run of success through the 1980s and into the '90s, during which Conley scored an extraordinary total of 18 Number One country hits.

Conley (b. Oct. 17, 1941, Portsmouth, Ohio) grew up in poverty, one of eight children of a railroad worker and a staunchly religious mother. He had an artistic, sensitive nature that struggled to survive in his tough Portsmouth, Ohio, neighborhood and lifestyle. "As a kid I discovered I could draw and paint, but I couldn't let the gang I hung out with know that I liked to do that," he recounts. "I'd be out in the streets acting like a tough guy, then I'd go back home and literally hide in a closet and paint so nobody would know what I was doing." (Conley eventually worked as a portrait painter and commercial artist.) Admits Conley, "I grew up feeling guilty and insecure all the time because of my mother's strict, moralistic discipline and the fact we were poor." Things got even tougher when Earl was 10 and his father was laid off by the railroad. By the time Conley turned 14, his older sister Joyce Ann had married a banker and moved to Xenia, Ohio. She feared that his creativity would be stifled at home and invited him to live with her. According to Earl, that saved his life. "She took me out of all that poverty and put me in dress pants," he says. "She gave me a car to drive to school, and I felt like a rich kid. More than that, she encouraged my art and convinced me I could do anything I wanted to with my life."

When Earl was 21, his sister was killed in a car crash. He enlisted in the Army to sort out her loss and to give his aimless life some direction. Up to that point music had been in the background. It didn't surface until one of his barracks mates in Germany taught him how to play the guitar. They would sit around drinking strong German beer and singing Everly Brothers songs, and by the time Earl left the service he'd decided to pursue music as a career. His first real music experience came when he returned to Ohio and joined his aunt and uncle in a gospel group.

Conley became conflicted again about the meaning of his life and began to study various philosophies and religions. He claims he didn't begin to find answers until he looked inward and began writing and then singing what he wrote. "I began writing to dig into my own mind and find out what goes on there," he claimed. "I first found some dark things and wrote about them. Then I had to go in and find the positive side, and I wrote about that, too."

Conley made a few tentative journeys to Nashville to try to peddle his songs, but nothing happened. Later, he moved to Huntsville, Alabama,

Earl Thomas Conley

where he worked in a steel mill by day and wrote and sang country music by night. His writing improved, and his first songs were cut by Billy Larkin and Bobby G. Rice, followed by the breakthrough hits by Mel Street and Conway Twitty in 1975.

In Nashville, Conley began his own recording career on the independent GRT label. After four low-charting releases he moved over to Warner Brothers in 1979 and promptly scored his first top 40 hits with "Dreamin's All I Do" and "Stranded on a Dead End Street" (a song he released under the name the ETC Band). In 1980 he was enticed to join an ambitious new label called Sunbird Records. The result was an astonishingly good, and now collectible, LP titled *Blue Pearl*. The first single, "Silent Treatment," went to number seven, and the followup, "Fire and Smoke," went all the way to Number One—an amazing achievement for an independent company. That was not lost on RCA Records, who struck a deal with Sunbird to immediately take over Earl's contract and then included four cuts from *Blue Pearl* on his debut RCA album, *Fire and Smoke*. They saw gold in his writing and instantly recognizable, soulfully resonant voice, and they were right. Between 1982 and '89 alone, beginning with "Heavenly Bodies," Conley scored 21 consecutive top 10 songs, including 17 Number Ones—making him one of the dominant stars of the 1980s.

Conley had additional success recording duets, including pairings with Gus Hardin, Anita Pointer, and Emmylou Harris. In 1987 he recorded "Broth-

---

TOP ALBUMS

BLUE PEARL (Sunbird, '80)
FIRE AND SMOKE (RCA, '81)
SOMEWHERE BETWEEN RIGHT AND WRONG (RCA, '82)
TOO MANY TIMES (RCA, '86)

TOP SONGS

FIRE AND SMOKE (Sunbird, '81, *1*)
SOMEWHERE BETWEEN RIGHT AND WRONG (RCA, '82, *1*)
HOLDING HER BUT LOVING YOU (RCA, '83, *1*)
ONCE IN A BLUE MOON (RCA, '86, *1*)
RIGHT FROM THE START (RCA, '87, *1*)
LOVE OUT LOUD (RCA, '89, *1*)

Additional Top 40 Country Songs: 26

erly Love," a duet with labelmate Keith Whitley. Shelved after Whitley's death in 1989, it was released as a single two years later and became a top two hit.

BILLY "CRASH" CRADDOCK

Rock and roll is a child of country music, so it's not surprising that many country performers gravitated to it. Billy "Crash" Craddock (b. June 16, 1939, Greensboro, North Carolina) is one of those who did. In his teens, Craddock and his brother, Ronald, formed a rock and roll band, and he's had one foot in rock and the other in country ever since.

He was born the thirteenth child in his family, and he learned how to be a survivor just by growing up in a house full of so many siblings. He was a hard-hitting, star halfback in high school and thus picked up the nickname "Crash"—a moniker that would later apply just as well to his energetic, hip-swiveling stage demeanor. He was encouraged as a performer when he and his brother's band, the Four Rebels, became locally famous as perennial winners of a radio talent contest.

Eventually, Craddock moved on alone and began recording in 1957 with Colonial and then Date Records, cutting a tune called "Ah, Poor Little

---

TOP ALBUMS

TWO SIDES OF CRASH (ABC/Dot, '73)
EASY AS PIE (ABC/Dot, '76)
THE FIRST TIME (ABC/Dot, '77)

TOP SONGS

KNOCK THREE TIMES (Cartwheel, '71, 3)
DREAM LOVER (Cartwheel, '71, 5)
RUB IT IN (ABC, '74, 1, 16 Pop)
RUBY, BABY (ABC, '74, 1, 33 Pop)
EASY AS PIE (ABC/Dot, '75, 2)
BROKEN DOWN IN TINY PIECES (ABC/Dot, '76, 1)
IF I COULD WRITE A SONG AS BEAUTIFUL AS YOU
    (Capitol, '79, 4)

Additional Top 40 Country Songs: 27

Baby" that didn't hit but led to a major label contract with Columbia Records. When nothing happened for him at Columbia during the mid-'60s, he left the business.

He didn't stay away long. After signing with Cartwheel Records, he launched the most successful phase of his career starting in 1971, when his country version of "Knock Three Times" (a Number One pop hit for Dawn that same year) knocked the doors open for him. It was his first chart record and hit number three. He then scored a total of five top 10s on Cartwheel by covering pop material, including "Dream Lover" (a number two pop hit for Bobby Darin in 1959) and "I'm Gonna Knock on Your Door" (a number 12 pop hit in 1961 for Eddie Hodges). By then Craddock knew that he would always be a country act with a pop edge, so he cultivated an image borrowed from Elvis Presley, down to the sideburns and a white jumpsuit (bearing in mind the importance of sex appeal, he asked the press to downplay the fact that he was married).

Craddock reached his peak in 1974 when he released back-to-back Number One country hits— "Rub It In" and "Ruby, Baby"—that both crossed over to the pop chart. Another country Number One, "Broken Down in Tiny Pieces," registered in 1977.

Years later, even after his chart activity ceased at the end of the 1980s, "Crash" would be remembered as a man who made country music with a pop flair, and did it long before performers like Garth Brooks and Travis Tritt hit mass popularity using a similar approach.

RODNEY CROWELL

Rodney Crowell (b. Aug. 7, 1950, Houston, Texas) distinguished himself in each of his many musical roles: recording artist (once setting the record for the most consecutive Number One hits from a single album), record producer (most notably of his ex-wife, Rosanne Cash), and songwriter (writing hits for the Oak Ridge Boys, Alan Jackson, and many others).

Crowell's professional career began when he played drums in the country band led by his father, J. W. Crowell, at age 11. "He was a local in Houston and was very good," Rodney says. "He played a lot of good, moving dance music and all the hits of the day. I worked a lot with him." He bought

Rodney Crowell

Starting in 1975, Crowell toured as a member of Emmylou Harris' Hot Band, leaving to begin his own recording career with Warner Brothers Records in 1978. Critics hailed his three Warner albums for their sophisticated writing and fresh-sounding music. Country radio, on the other hand, stopped short of embracing his singles, tagging his music as too esoteric or not country enough—characterizations that would dog him throughout his career. Crowell's highest-charting solo record in the early 1980s was "Stars on the Water," which peaked at number 30.

From 1983 to '86 he concentrated on writing and producing the albums of his wife, Rosanne Cash. He had resisted signing with his wife's label but finally joined her on Columbia Records and renewed his recording career with the release of *Street Language*. Again, charges of "good, but not country" surfaced. Frustrated, he went back into the studio and recorded a spectacular straight-country album, *Diamonds & Dirt*. Beginning with the January 1988 release of a lovely duet with Rosanne called "It's Such a Small World," the album yielded five consecutive Number One hits.

In subsequent albums he went back to a mixture of straight country and innovative songs and lost the momentum he'd achieved with *Diamonds & Dirt*.

Crowell left Columbia and recorded for MCA Records in the 1990s, remaining a favorite of critics and an artist's singer-songwriter. "I came in the back door in terms of being different," he says, "and it took people a while to take me seriously. If you're

records from a local grocery store called Weingarten's. "I could go in there and from the same rack I could buy the latest from Buck Owens, the Beatles, Barbra Streisand, or the Beach Boys. There were no categories. That's why my music is a synthesis of all the music I've enjoyed and held close to my heart. It ranges from Hank Williams to Prince."

In 1965 he started his own band, the Arbitrators, and experimented musically until he decided to head to Nashville in 1972 with the aim of learning to write like his idols, Townes Van Zandt, Mickey Newbury, and Guy Clark. He landed a job at Jerry Reed's music publishing company. "They sure must have hired me on my potential," he says, "because it took a while before I turned out anything anybody thought was good enough to pitch." Eventually he scored a number of successes, including "Shame on the Moon" for Bob Seger (number two pop, 1982), "I Ain't Living Long Like This" for Waylon Jennings (Number One country, 1980), "Leaving Louisiana in the Broad Daylight" for the Oak Ridge Boys (Number One country, 1980), and "An American Dream" for the Nitty Gritty Dirt Band (number 13 pop, 1980).

TOP ALBUMS

RODNEY CROWELL (Warner, '81)
DIAMONDS & DIRT (Columbia, '88)
KEYS TO THE HIGHWAY (Columbia, '89)

TOP SONGS

IT'S SUCH A SMALL WORLD (Columbia, '88, *1*)
I COULDN'T LEAVE HER IF I TRIED (Columbia, '88, *1*)
HE'S CRAZY FOR LEAVIN' (Columbia, '88, *1*)
AFTER ALL THIS TIME (Columbia, '89, *1*)
ABOVE AND BEYOND (Columbia, '89, *1*)
MANY A LONG AND LONESOME HIGHWAY
    (Columbia, '89, *3*)
IF LOOKS COULD KILL (Columbia, '90, *6*)

Additional Top 40 Country Songs: 7

different they don't take you seriously, and to me, the different people are exactly who you *should* take seriously. I figure as an artist the best thing you can do is just follow your heart, and if your heart is marketable, then you win."

BILLY RAY CYRUS

Billy Ray Cyrus' arrival in the 1990s demonstrated what can happen when the right artist, the right song, and the right marketing converge at exactly the right time. It took just such a fusion of elements to bring about the monumental success of "Achy Breaky Heart" and the album that contained it, *Some Gave All.*

Billy Ray Cyrus

Cyrus (b. Aug. 25, 1961, Flatwoods, Kentucky) grew up near the point in the Ohio River where Kentucky, West Virginia, and Ohio meet. He was a quiet, introspective kid who responded to the music his father made as part of a gospel quartet. As a teenager, he listened to everything from Lynyrd Skynyrd and Led Zeppelin to Bill Monroe and Hank Williams, but he didn't start a music career until he bought a guitar at age 20. The very next day he formed his band, Sly Dog.

He began to make a name for himself on the tri-state club circuit, working mostly in the biggest town in the region, Huntington, West Virginia. In 1984, instead of heading to Tennessee, Cyrus traveled to Los Angeles, where he tried, but failed, to begin a recording career.

In '86, he returned to Kentucky, reactivated his band, and began to set his sights on Music City. "In 1989, I made 42 trips to Nashville," he recalls. "I'd work all week at a club in Huntington and drive to Tennessee and spend three days there trying to meet people."

Those trips paid off when he connected with Grand Ole Opry star Del Reeves. Reeves arranged demo sessions for him and introduced him to artist manager Jack McFadden. That led to meetings with Mercury Records, who sent emissaries to watch him perform live. They liked his rugged looks, his rocking style of country music, and the effect that combination had on his local audiences, who treated him like a major star. They guessed that if they could find the right song to appeal to the female country audience, he could be big.

That's when they found a silly-sounding ditty that had been kicking around Nashville for a while. Billy Ray and Sly Dog took it into a recording studio and revved it up. The result was a danceable, driving number that seemed like a hit. "Then we saw that wherever we tried 'Achy Breaky Heart' out on audiences, no matter what age people were, it got them up on their feet dancing," Cyrus says. "That's when the idea to do the dance and video came up."

Instead of taking a traditional, country

radio approach to promotion, Mercury Records decided to break Cyrus using video and country dance clubs. They commissioned choreographer Melanie Greenwood to devise an Achy Breaky dance. They went to a theater on Cyrus' home turf and taped a performance video that made him look like a superstar. The video was an instant hit, and dance clubs embraced Billy Ray immediately. By the time the single and album were released to radio and the general public, there was already a huge demand for them.

In 1992 the song shot to Number One country and remained there five weeks. It powered his debut album to sales of over 11 million worldwide, creating one of the all-time great country music success stories.

The downside for Cyrus was that the song received a bashing from critics. However, outside of a few detractors among performers, the recording industry welcomed the Cyrus phenomenon. "I'm very happy about it," said Jimmy Bowen, former president of Liberty Records (who'd seen Cyrus outsell Garth Brooks at one point). "It's good for all of us. Like Garth, Billy Ray gets new buyers into record stores, and while they're there, they might pick up the latest by Clint [Black] or Alan [Jackson] or Reba [McEntire]."

Though not able to duplicate the success of "Achy Breaky Heart" and the incredible sales of his debut album, Cyrus avoided one-hit wonder status. His second album, *It Won't Be the Last* sold two million copies, and his third, *Storm in the Heartland* sold over a million. He established a huge base of fans who continue to make him a top draw on the

---

TOP ALBUMS

SOME GAVE ALL (Mercury, '92)
IT WON'T BE THE LAST (Mercury, '93)
STORM IN THE HEARTLAND (Mercury, '94)

TOP SONGS

ACHY BREAKY HEART (Mercury, '92, 1, 4 Pop)
COULD'VE BEEN ME (Mercury, '92, 2)
SHE'S NOT CRYING ANYMORE (Mercury, '92, 6)
IN THE HEART OF A WOMAN (Mercury, '93, 3)
SOMEBODY NEW (Mercury, '93, 9)

Additional Top 40 Country Songs: 1

---

concert circuit. "I got into this business to get up on stage and perform for the people," he says. "That's all that really matters to me, that time with them."

LACY J. DALTON

Lacy J. Dalton became an instant sensation in 1979 with a husky voice and bluesy, country style that were new and full of promise. But she differed in appearance and style from the Nashville norm. Aggressive on stage, wearing jeans instead of a dress, eschewing makeup, she seemed more a country Janis Joplin than, say, a glamorous Crystal Gayle.

Dalton (b. Jill Byrem, Apr. 24, 1946, Bloomsburg, Pennsylvania) was born to a country-singing game warden, who filled their home with the sounds of guitar, mandolin, and banjo. "When I was young, I didn't like the sound of the music," she admits, "but I liked the lyrics, the storytelling aspect of country music." Before she left home, her father gave her a guitar, hoping it might inspire her to play. By the time she got to California—by way of Utah—she was performing folk and blues in coffeehouses. She moved to a commune near Santa Cruz, California, and made a name for herself on the local club scene. Later, in Los Angeles, she was offered a pop recording contract only to turn it down because they wanted her but not her band. "After that mistake, I moved back to Santa Cruz and worked as a crepe chef," she recalls.

By 1979 she was both singing and writing country music. A fellow named David Woods heard an independent album she had recorded under her married name, Jill Croston. Woods encouraged her to make a demo tape, which earned her a contract with Columbia Records in Nashville. They manufactured the more country persona of Lacy J. Dalton and released her self-penned first single, "Crazy Blue Eyes" (1979). It hit number 17, a major accomplishment at that time for a new artist.

Over the next few years she scored such top 10s as "Hard Times," "Takin' It Easy," and "16th Avenue." She had the respect of her peers and seemed headed for major stardom. In the mid-1980s, however, she became embroiled in contract disputes with management and came down on the losing side of a political battle at her record label. Her career was never the same. By 1989, when she was able to

Lacy J. Dalton

TOP ALBUMS

LACY J. DALTON (Columbia, '79)
HARD TIMES (Columbia, '80)
TAKIN' IT EASY (Columbia, '80)

TOP SONGS

CRAZY BLUE EYES (Columbia, '79, 17)
HARD TIMES (Columbia, '80, 7)
HILLBILLY GIRL WITH THE BLUES (Columbia, '80, 8)
WHISPER (Columbia, '81, 10)
TAKIN' IT EASY (Columbia, '81, 2)
EVERYBODY MAKES MISTAKES (Columbia, '81, 5)
16TH AVENUE (Columbia, '82, 7)
DREAM BABY (Columbia, '83, 9)

Additional Top 40 Country Songs: 12

move on to other record companies, it was too late to recapture her place in the increasingly youth-oriented country industry of the time.

Dalton remains a popular touring artist and one of the finest vocalists to appear in country music. Her most recent chart success was the top 15 hit "Black Coffee" in 1990.

THE CHARLIE DANIELS BAND

A timeless standard-bearer of southern rock, Charlie Daniels caught that wave in the early 1970s and has been riding it ever since. Although country to the core, Daniels kept his music and recording contracts in the pop divisions of his record labels until he shifted, in the mid-1980s, to the country side of the spectrum and later to gospel music.

In spite of his rock orientation, Charlie never sought to distance himself from his country roots. He once took on drummer Buddy Rich and bandleader Stan Kenton after they said disparaging things about country music. "I said, 'If you guys are such geniuses, why don't you come show us how to do it? I'll give either one of you $10,000 if you can come to Nashville and record a decent country single,'" Daniels recalls. "Of course, they couldn't do it."

Daniels (b. Oct. 28, 1936, Wilmington, North Carolina) grew up in Gulf, North Carolina, the son of a timber salesman. Unlike many country musicians, he was from a nonmusical family. "I traced both sides of my family all the way back to the Civil War," he says, "and not a one of them was musical. I just loved music and wanted to do it ever since I was eight or nine years old and started going to see people play country music." At 15, he joined a bluegrass group called the Misty Mountain Boys—"a ripoff of Flatt and Scruggs' Foggy Mountain Boys," he confesses.

During the mid-1950s Charlie worked a factory job making TV and radio capacitors during the day and on weekends played in every country, rock, and R&B band he could join. In 1958 the factory announced worker layoffs that included a friend of Charlie's who had a family. Charlie gave his own job to the friend and quit to do music full-time. In 1959 he joined the Jaguars (through '67), an eclectic band that played a variety of styles including "jazzy, Louis Prima–style shuffles and songs like 'Mack the Knife,'" according to Daniels. In 1964 he turned toward country and rock and began to write. He co-wrote "It Hurts Me," which ended up on the flip side of Elvis Presley's "Kissin' Cousins."

In 1967 he moved to Nashville and began a successful stint as a session guitarist and fiddle player, lending his talent to records by Marty Robbins and to such visiting musical potentates as Ringo Starr and Bob Dylan. "Ironically, working on Dylan's *Nashville Skyline* was the first time I felt at home in Nashville," Daniels claims. "I'd been told by some producers I played too loud. Dylan just liked what I did, and I felt a sense of freedom I hadn't felt before." In 1970 he recorded his first solo album for Capitol Records, *Charlie Daniels*. He became part of the first wave of southern rockers and formed the Charlie Daniels Band.

He moved over to Kama Sutra Records, and his second album for the label, *Honey in the Rock* (1972), yielded "Uneasy Rider," a number nine pop hit spoof about a hippie who enters a biker lounge. He followed it with "The South's Gonna Do It Again" and "Long Haired Country Boy." In 1976 his last single for Kama Sutra, "Texas," became his first top 40 country song (number 36). That year the Charlie Daniels Band switched to Epic Records, his home for the next decade and a half.

He began to appear more regularly on the country chart and in 1979 scored the biggest hit of his

Charlie Daniels

career, "The Devil Went Down to Georgia," a country-pop smash. "We were recording *Million Mile Reflections* and hadn't found a good fiddle tune," Daniels says, "so the boys and I just sat down and came up with one. Turned out to be a good one." (He released two versions of the song, a country version referring to the devil as a "son of a gun" and a pop version with the words "son of a bitch.") "The Devil" earned Daniels the Country Music Association Single of the Year award and a Grammy for Best Country Vocal. That was the high point of his chart career, but he continued to be a gold- and platinum-selling act as well as a top concert draw through the 1980s.

In the 1990s Daniels signed with Liberty Records and proceeded to record both country and gospel music. "It doesn't bother me at all not to be able to be categorized," he says. "It don't ruffle my feathers a bit. Defying description is a role I don't mind playing, because I don't put any titles on our music. I call it CDB music."

TOP ALBUMS

HONEY IN THE ROCK (Kama Sutra, '72)
NIGHT RIDER (Kama Sutra, '75)
MILLION MILE REFLECTIONS (Epic, '79)
WINDOWS (Epic, '82)
HOMESICK HEROES (Epic, '88)
SIMPLE MAN (Epic, '90)

TOP SONGS

THE DEVIL WENT DOWN TO GEORGIA
   (Epic, '79, *1, 3 Pop*)
IN AMERICA (Epic, '80, *13, 11 Pop*)
DRINKIN' MY BABY GOODBYE (Epic, '86, *8*)
BOOGIE WOOGIE FIDDLE COUNTRY BLUES (Epic, '88, *10*)

Additional Top 40 Country Songs: 8

BILLY DEAN

Billy Dean (b. William Harold Dean, Apr. 1, 1962, Quincy, Florida) carved out a niche as the opposite of the neotraditionalist, hat-wearing, cowboy-style stars with whom he was competing in the early 1990s. In the process he became one of country music's finest smooth-singing balladeers.

Dean grew up using the name Harold, but his nickname was Little Billy because he idolized his father, Billy Dean. His father's band, the Country Rocks, was locally famous, and not surprisingly, dad was Little Billy's biggest musical influence. He started his son out with acoustic guitar, and when his boy was 10 years old he gave him his first electric guitar for Christmas.

"Right after that I formed a little band, and I played that guitar," Dean says. "I think we called ourselves the Country Rocks, just like my dad's band, and we had little fringe outfits, the whole thing." His father would continue to set a musical example up until he died of a heart attack. "It was after that, as a tribute to him, that I adopted Billy as my stage name," Dean explains.

His other influences were Merle Haggard, Jim Reeves, Marty Robbins, and Dean Martin. "I used to sing it a lot more country back home and when I first got to Nashville," he says. "That's when people told me I sounded too much like Merle, so I changed my style." He developed a mellow croon that drew especially from Reeves and Robbins.

The name of the younger Billy Dean became popular in clubs and restaurant lounges from Tallahassee to Tampa. What got him to Nashville was becoming a finalist in the national Wrangler Talent Search contest held at the Grand Ole Opry in 1982. He didn't win the contest, but he got encouragement to move to town to write. He managed to get songs cut by Ronnie Milsap and Randy Travis and came to the attention of Capitol Nashville in 1989.

At the time, his debut was delayed while Capitol struggled to keep up with the explosive success of Garth Brooks. But then Dean's second single, "Only Here for a Little While," charted in late 1990 and put him on the map when it hit number three. He went on to distinguish himself from his contemporaries with a run of seven consecutive top 10 singles, including his own compositions "Somewhere in My Broken Heart" and "Billy the Kid."

Billy Dean

TOP ALBUMS

YOUNG MAN (Capitol, '90)
BILLY DEAN (Capitol, '91)
FIRE IN THE DARK (Liberty/SBK, '92)

TOP SONGS

ONLY HERE FOR A LITTLE WHILE (Capitol, '90, 3)
SOMEWHERE IN MY BROKEN HEART
 (Capitol/SBK, '91, 3)
YOU DON'T COUNT THE COST (Capitol/SBK, '91, 4)
ONLY THE WIND (Capitol/SBK, '91, 4)
BILLY THE KID (Liberty/SBK, '92, 4)
IF THERE HADN'T BEEN YOU (Liberty/SBK, '92, 3)
TRYIN' TO HIDE A FIRE IN THE DARK
 (Liberty/SBK, '92, 6)

Additional Top 40 Country Songs: 3

JOHN DENVER

To some, he was essentially a pop star with country leanings. Others tagged him as a country ambassador to the pop mainstream. Still others viewed him as folk music's gift to both pop and country. But few disputed John Denver's status, for a time, as one of music's superstars, a top performer of multiple Number One hits on both the country and pop charts, and the skilled writer of such standards as "Country Roads" and "Leaving on a Jet Plane." Named the poet laureate of Colorado, he was also the symbol of Rocky Mountain clean living, wholesomeness, and ecological awareness before environmentalism became a national trend.

Denver was born Henry John Deutschendorf, Jr. (Dec. 31, 1943, Roswell, New Mexico) to an Air Force pilot, and he grew up in various parts of the Southwest. When he was eight his grandmother gave him a 1910 Gibson guitar, and Denver became an accomplished player. After attending college at Texas Tech, where he studied architecture, Denver moved to Los Angeles to pursue a music career.

Learning of the Chad Mitchell Trio's plan to replace the departing Chad, Denver auditioned and was chosen from among 250 applicants. He stayed with the group for nearly four years.

In 1969 he signed as a soloist with RCA Records, releasing the album *Rhymes and Reasons*. One of its songs, "Jet Plane," found its way into the repertoire of folk singers Peter, Paul and Mary, who rode it to the top of the *Billboard* singles chart in late 1969.

Two more albums—*Take Me to Tomorrow* and *Whose Garden Was This*—came and went before Denver first cracked the top 40 of the album chart with 1971's *Poems, Prayers, and Promises* (number 15). One of its tracks was the stirring anthem "Take Me Home, Country Roads," which Denver co-wrote with Bill Danoff and Taffy Nivert (later of the Starland Vocal Band on Denver's own Windsong label). It was a million seller and Denver's first entry as a singer into both the country and pop charts (at numbers 50 and two, respectively). He bettered that album's performance with the follow-up, *Rocky Mountain High* (number four, 1972), the title track of which gained status as a classic in the pop realm (at number nine) while making nary a ripple in the country-oriented airwaves.

The mid-'70s were the years of Denver's breakthrough. It started with the Number One pop hit "Sunshine on My Shoulder," a song imbued with the optimism and euphoria that were fast becoming his signature. His mid-1974 album *Back Home Again* hit Number One, its track "Annie's Song" topping the pop Hot 100 and the title tune doing the same on the country chart.

The hit streak continued into 1975. The live LP *An Evening with John Denver* yielded one of the singer's two country-rock crossover Number Ones, the foot-stomping "Thank God I'm a Country Boy." The follow-up album, *Windsong* (another Number One disc), spun off the second, "I'm Sorry" (the flip side of which, "Calypso," hit number two pop).

The flurry of activity carried over to television: he hosted a "John Denver Special" in 1974 and did so again in '75, the second one earning an Emmy Award for Best Musical Variety Special. Another— "Thank God I'm a Country Boy"—ran on ABC in 1977. In that same year, Denver successfully invaded the movies, starring opposite George Burns in *Oh God!*

John Denver

Denver's live shows at the time were often described as "dazzling," "exhilarating," "masterful," hailed as much for the star's personality and enthusiasm as for musicianship (during 1977–78 he toured with a "dream band" that included ex–Elvis Presley guitarist Jim Burton and veteran studio drummer Hal Blaine).

Social and environmental causes drew much of Denver's attention. He became actively involved in such organizations as Friends of the Earth, the World Wildlife Fund, and the Hunger Project. He backed the documentary *John Denver's Alaska: The American Child* and on one occasion sang a song about the environment, "To the Wild Country," before the U.S. Congress.

Reaction to Denver was not unanimously positive. Some decried him as "the Norman Rockwell of pop," too sunny, bland, and conventional. Country purists were less than enthusiastic when Denver—whom they considered "pop"—received the Country Music Association's Entertainer of the Year Award in 1975. On the nonmusical front, one report had protesters charging him with hypocrisy for attempting to build giant gas storage tanks near his home—an apparent no-no for an environmental activist.

After 1975, Denver's rankings on the singles charts lowered, but his albums continued to score impressively: he amassed a total of 15 in the top 40 between 1971 and 1982.

In the 1980s, Denver was more successful on the country chart than in pop, though he was active in both arenas. Several of his key releases were collaborative efforts, including "Perhaps Love," with opera star Placido Domingo (59 pop, 1982); "Wild Montana Skies," with Emmylou Harris (14 country, 1983); and "And So It Goes," with the Nitty Gritty Dirt Band (14 country, 1989).

THE DESERT ROSE BAND

It would be difficult to assemble a more talented group of musicians than the original Desert Rose Band, which included Chris Hillman, Herb Pedersen, and John Jorgenson. Though putting together quality players doesn't guarantee success, it did in this case. In the late 1980s and early 1990s the Desert Rose Band had a run of top 10 singles, including two Number One hits, that helped establish them as one of the leading country groups of their day.

Leader Chris Hillman and Herb Pedersen had common beginnings: they crossed paths on the California bluegrass circuit in the early 1960s, when Hillman was a member of the Golden State Boys and Pedersen was with the Pine Valley Boys. In 1963 Hillman formed the Hillmen with Vern and Rex Gosdin. A year later he co-founded the first of two seminal folk-country-rock acts, the Byrds, with Roger McGuinn, David Crosby, Gene Clark, and Michael Clarke, yielding the hits "Mr. Tambourine Man" and "Turn! Turn! Turn!" and numerous other late-'60s classics. The second was the Flying Burrito Brothers, which he formed with Gram Parsons soon after they both left the Byrds. From 1972 to 1985, Chris played a part in a number of other bands that included Manassas; Souther, Hillman, Furay; and McGuinn, Clark and Hillman. He also recorded four solo albums.

In 1985, for a one-time appearance at a Los Angeles street festival, Chris hooked up with the superbly talented multi-instrumentalist John Jorgenson (lead guitar and vocals), Pedersen (banjo and guitar), Bill Bryson (bass), Jay Dee Maness (steel), and Steve Duncan (drums). Bryson, Maness, and Duncan, all top session players and sidemen, had worked with everyone from Buck Owens to Freddy Fender to Ricky Nelson. When the six veterans started jamming, it was a serendipitous experience that kept the group together long enough to be heard by

TOP ALBUMS

BACK HOME AGAIN (RCA, '74)
WINDSONG (RCA, '75)

TOP SONGS

ANNIE'S SONG (RCA, '74, 9, 1 Pop)
BACK HOME AGAIN (RCA, '74, 1, 5 Pop)
SWEET SURRENDER (RCA, '75, 7, 13 Pop)
THANK GOD I'M A COUNTRY BOY (RCA, '75, 1, 1 Pop)
I'M SORRY (RCA, '75, 1, 1 Pop)
FLY AWAY (RCA, '75, 12, 13 Pop)
SOME DAYS ARE DIAMONDS (SOME DAYS ARE STONE) (RCA, '81, 10, 36 Pop)
DREAMLAND EXPRESS (RCA, '85, 9)

Additional Top 40 Country Songs: 6

Desert Rose Band

Curb Records executive Dick Whitehouse a year later at the legendary Palomino Club in North Hollywood, leading to a recording contract.

The name Desert Rose Band came from a song Chris wrote in the early 1980s ("Desert Rose") inspired by his daughter's middle name, Rose. To go with the name, they came up with a sound infused

with all the bluegrass, folk, country, and rock influences of a collective century and a quarter of musical experience. According to Hillman, who had a hand in writing much of the material on the band's 1987 debut album, it was "a highly evolved version of what Gram Parsons and I were trying to do in the late '60s with the Flying Burrito Brothers." Superb musicianship supporting distinctive three-part harmonies (Jorgenson, Pedersen, and Hillman) was the essence of the Desert Band approach.

After scoring their first country chart hit with the number 26 "Ashes of Love," the band racked up a total of eight top 10 singles, including the Number One songs "He's Back and I'm Blue" and "I Still Believe in You," between 1987 and 1990. During this time their live performances were superb, earning them Top Touring Band honors from the Academy of Country Music.

After 1990, the band lost momentum at country radio and never again hit the top 10. By '92, Jorgenson, Duncan, and Maness had exited the band. Hillman and Pedersen tried to regroup with new members to no avail, and the Desert Rose Band made its last chart appearance in late 1993.

Hillman, the veteran of nearly a dozen bands, had always been philosophical about the Desert Rose Band and its chances. "We just do what we do and hope it flies," he said in 1990. "The Desert Rose

TOP ALBUMS

CHRIS HILLMAN AND THE DESERT ROSE BAND
 (Curb/MCA, '87)
RUNNING (Curb/MCA, '88)
PAGES OF LIFE (Curb/MCA, '90)

TOP SONGS

LOVE REUNITED (Curb/MCA, '87, 6)
ONE STEP FORWARD (Curb/MCA, '87, 2)
HE'S BACK AND I'M BLUE (Curb/MCA, '88, 1)
SUMMER WIND (Curb/MCA, '88, 2)
I STILL BELIEVE IN YOU (Curb/MCA, '88, 1)
SHE DON'T LOVE NOBODY (Curb/MCA, '89, 3)
START ALL OVER AGAIN (Curb/MCA, '89, 6)
STORY OF LOVE (Curb/MCA, '90, 10)

Additional Top 40 Country Songs: 4

Band will never sit back and go, 'Oh, we have to emulate, we have to do a song like *this* if we're going to get on radio.' I never want to be in that position, because we'll never catch up to what's current."

DIAMOND RIO

Diamond Rio began its career by making history, releasing "Meet in the Middle" in 1991 and becoming the first country group to hit Number One with a debut single. From that spectacular entrance the sextet remained an important country act, a self-contained recording-performing entity noted for instrumental skill.

They came together, member by member, in the early 1980s performing for Nashville's Opryland Amusement Park as the Grizzly River Boys, named after a popular ride at the park. They broke free of the park in the mid-'80s, changed their name to the Tennessee River Boys, and began making their mark with a bluegrass-tinged country sound that wasn't surprising given the musical backgrounds of some of the members. Dana Williams (bass, vocals) is the nephew of bluegrass artists Bobby and Sonny Osborne and grew up picking and singing his uncles' brand of music. Gene Johnson (mandolin, fiddle),

whose high harmonies are a key Diamond Rio ingredient, worked with the likes of Keith Whitley and the progressive bluegrass band J. D. Souther and New South. Jimmy Olander (lead guitar) taught banjo to others from the time he was 12. Marty Roe (lead vocals) began singing at a very early age, belting out a version of Merle Haggard's "The Fugitive" as a three-year-old. Rounding out the lineup are drummer Brian Prout and classically trained pianist Dan Truman (piano), who the others claim "adds the class to the band."

Diamond Rio's breakthrough came in 1989 when they landed a spot opening for George Jones at a concert in Alabama attended by Tim DuBois of Arista Records. DuBois began developing them as an act and co-producing their albums with Monty Powell. Around that time the band came up with a new name using a source—Diamond Reo trucks—that had also inspired REO Speedwagon.

The recording of their debut album, *Diamond Rio,* was interrupted twice by freak accidents. Johnson, although a master cabinetmaker, nearly severed his thumb with a saw. Then, six weeks later, Williams' leg was nearly severed while he was waterskiing. "When we showed up for a recording session, two of us truly the walking wounded, Tim DuBois turned pale and sent us back home to recover," they claim.

Diamond Rio

TOP ALBUMS

DIAMOND RIO (Arista, '91)
CLOSE TO THE EDGE (Arista, '92)
LOVE A LITTLE STRONGER (Arista, '94)

TOP SONGS

MEET IN THE MIDDLE (Arista, '91, 1)
MIRROR MIRROR (Arista, '91, 3)
MAMA DON'T FORGET TO PRAY FOR ME (Arista, '91, 9)
NORMA JEAN RILEY (Arista, '92, 2)
IN A WEEK OR TWO (Arista, '92, 2)
OH ME, OH MY SWEET BABY (Arista, '93, 5)
LOVE A LITTLE STRONGER (Arista, '94, 2)

Additional Top 40 Country Songs: 2

When the first album finally saw the light of day, the song "Meet in the Middle" rose to the chart peak and launched a run of seven more top 10 country singles. Recognition from the country music community came quickly: both the Academy of Country Music and Country Music Association voted Diamond Rio Best Vocal Group.

JOE DIFFIE

Joe Logan Diffie (b. Dec. 28, 1958, Tulsa, Oklahoma) turned a layoff notice into a ticket to Nashville. Then, riding a swelling wave of country music popularity in 1990, Diffie hit Number One with his first chart record. He's since remained one of country's leading '90s-born acts.

Diffie was raised in Duncan, Oklahoma, in a musical family. "My mother just sang," Diffie says. "[Dad] sang and played guitar, banjo, and piano. My grandpa played guitar and fiddle, and I have a bunch of aunts, uncles, and cousins who were good pickers and singers."

After high school, Joe went to work in a foundry and performed music at nights and on weekends. He sang country and spent four years as part of a local bluegrass group called the Special Edition. As the owner of a small, eight-track recording facility, he taped himself and some local bands and produced a few commercials.

In 1987 Diffie divorced his first wife and was laid off from the foundry. "Suddenly I didn't have anything keeping me in Oklahoma," he says, "so I borrowed three hundred bucks from a friend and headed to Tennessee." In Nashville Joe landed a job as a quality control inspector at the Gibson guitar factory and began to write songs and get work as a session singer. With the vocal range he developed singing bluegrass he was soon in demand. In 1989, Epic Records signed him to a contract, and the next year his debut album, *A Thousand Winding Roads*, was released. Beginning with his debut Number One, "Home," Joe established himself with six consecutive top five hits, including his second Number One, "If the Devil Danced (In Empty Pockets)."

Mary Chapin Carpenter, who invited Diffie to record with her on the song "Not Too Much to Ask," describes him as "a 'modern' country singer. He's of this generation but has an understanding of what made classic, stylist-oriented singers of years ago great and seminal. . . . They invest in their singing an emotional quality; they're giving everything to it, without it being acrobatic or gratuitous. Joe Diffie does the same thing."

"I'm not trying to make any particular mark or statement with my music," Diffie says. "I'm just trying to sing, enjoy what I do, and hopefully make a difference in somebody's life." Having gained respect as both a singer and a writer—penning such hits as "There Goes My Heart Again," "New Way to Light Up an Old Flame," and "Honky Tonk Attitude"—Diffie was made a member of the Grand Ole Opry in 1993.

TOP ALBUMS

A THOUSAND WINDING ROADS (Epic, '90)
A REGULAR JOE (Epic, '92)
HONKY TONK ATTITUDE (Epic, '93)
THIRD ROCK FROM THE SUN (Epic, '94)

TOP SONGS

HOME (Epic, '90, 1)
IF THE DEVIL DANCED (IN EMPTY POCKETS) (Epic, '91, 1)
NEW WAY (TO LIGHT UP AN OLD FLAME) (Epic, '91, 2)
PROP ME UP BESIDE THE JUKEBOX (IF I DIE) (Epic, '93, 3)
THIRD ROCK FROM THE SUN (Epic, '94, 1)
PICKUP MAN (Epic, '94, 1)

Additional Top 40 Country Songs: 5

HOLLY DUNN

She hit Nashville in the early 1980s and worked as a writer and demo singer before hooking up with a brand new Nashville record company, MTM Records. With her good looks, unique voice, and considerable writing talents, Holly Dunn broke through to the top 10 in 1987 and went on to become one of the top female country artists of the late '80s.

Dunn (b. Holly Suzette Dunn, Aug. 22, 1957, San Antonio, Texas) was born to a preacher father and a mother who is an accomplished landscape artist. Holly showed musical ability at age six, when she was given her first musical instrument, a drum set. By age eight she was putting pen to paper. She was 16 when she wrote her first song, a ditty called "Moonwind."

Her brother, Chris Waters (he changed his last name because there was another Chris Dunn in the Nashville writing community), was the first in the family to head to Nashville, eventually making a name for himself as the writer of such titles as Dr. Hook's "Sexy Eyes" and Ronnie McDowell's "In a New York Minute." Holly, in the meantime, went off to college to major in advertising and public relations. One summer she visited Chris in Nashville, and they ended up writing a song called "Out of Sight, Not Out of Mind" that found its way onto a disc recorded by country-gospel artist Cristy Lane.

Encouraged, Dunn moved to Tennessee permanently in 1979, put her degree away, and took whatever jobs she could get until she landed a writing deal. She found one with CBS Music and had her songs cut by Louise Mandrell, Sylvia, Marie Osmond, and the Whites. Newly formed MTM Records signed her as an artist, and she made her first mark on the chart in 1985.

Following two low-charting songs and one that barely made the top 40, Dunn hit number seven in 1986 with "Daddy's Hands," a song written as a Father's Day gift. "Dad and I were always close, but it was unspoken; he was not good at expressing his feelings," says Dunn. "What I expressed in the song provided a breakthrough moment for us emotionally."

Dunn followed "Hands" with a run of top 10 hits. Among them was "A Face in the Crowd," a 1987 top four duet with Michael Martin Murphy released on Warner Brothers Records. In 1988 MTM Records folded and Holly moved over to Warner, where she scored a pair of Number One hits with "Are You Ever Gonna Love Me" and "You Really Had Me Going."

Dunn's success proved something of a model for aspiring female performers, demonstrating that being able to write songs is an important asset for women in a field where male performers generally have an easier time getting started.

After beginning the 1990s with the chart-topping song "You Really Had Me Going," Dunn experienced only spotty success between 1991 and '93 and ultimately left Warner Brothers. "I took two years off basically to decide what to do next," she explained. "I always have the option to write, but I decided I still have something to say as an artist." In 1994 she signed on as the flagship star of a new label called River North Records.

TOP ALBUMS

HOLLY DUNN (MTM, '86)
CORNERSTONE (MTM, '87)
ACROSS THE RIO GRANDE (MTM, '88)
BLUE ROSE OF TEXAS (Warner, '89)
HEART FULL OF LOVE (Warner, '90)

TOP SONGS

DADDY'S HANDS (MTM, '86, 7)
LOVE SOMEONE LIKE ME (MTM, '87, 2)
ARE YOU EVER GONNA LOVE ME (Warner, '89, 1)
THERE GOES MY HEART AGAIN (Warner, '89, 4)
YOU REALLY HAD ME GOING (Warner, '90, 1)

Additional Top 40 Country Songs: 8

THE EVERLY BROTHERS

The relationship between country and rock and roll was never closer than in the 1950s, and few acts bridged the two worlds as easily as the Everly Brothers. Their country roots were deep, but from the time they began recording in Nashville in 1955, the universal appeal of their incredible born-and-bred harmonies made them equally important as pop and country performers. They influenced gener-

TOP SONGS

Bye Bye Love (Cadence, '57, 1, 2 Pop)
Wake Up Little Susie (Cadence, '57, 1, 1 Pop)
This Little Girl of Mine (Cadence, '58, 4)
Should We Tell Him (Cadence, '58, 10)
All I Have to Do Is Dream (Cadence, '58, 1, 1 Pop)
Claudette (Cadence, '58, 15)
Bird Dog (Cadence, '58, 1, 1 Pop)
Devoted to You (Cadence, '58, 7, 10 Pop)
Problems (Cadence, '58, 17, 2 Pop)
('Til) I Kissed You (Cadence, '59, 8, 4 Pop)

Additional Top 40 Country Songs: 2

ations of artists—most notably the Beatles—and along the way sold many millions of records.

Don (b. Isaac Donald Everly, Feb. 1, 1937) and Phil (b. Jan. 19, 1939) were born in Brownie, Kentucky, to Ike and Margaret Everly, popular country performers on the southern and midwestern circuit. Don and Phil joined their parents on tour while very young (Don was just eight and Phil only six) and remained with them until out of high school.

In 1955 the brothers launched their recording career in Nashville with a single on Columbia Records. It flopped, Columbia cut them loose, and the Everlys shopped around for another label. Through guitarist Chet Atkins they landed a songwriting deal with the publisher Acuff-Rose, and in 1957 they signed with Cadence Records. That same year, the Everlys met writers Felice and Boudleaux Bryant, who provided them with the song "Bye Bye Love." It was a smash, spending seven weeks at Number One on the country chart and four weeks at number two pop. Thus began a run of what would become Everly Brothers classics, including "Wake Up Little Susie" (Number One country, 1957) and the country-pop crossover Number Ones "All I Have to Do Is Dream" and "Bird Dog," both in 1958. Their debut on the Grand Ole Opry came in 1957. "It was my proudest moment," Don recalled to the *Nashville Tennessean*'s Walter Carter. "It was my life's ambition. It was Hank Williams' home, and that's who I wanted to be, Hank Williams."

A label change to Warner Brothers resulted in more pop hits, including the chart–topping "Cathy's Clown" and the number seven "Walk Right Back," but, like many other American rock acts of the era, the Everly Brothers found their fame fading with the British Invasion of the mid-'60s, something they curiously didn't resent. "Thank God for the British," Don said. "They took American rock and roll, made it literate, and gave it back to us. The Beatles gave it back to us in a better state than it was in."

The Everlys tried returning to their country roots with a few albums, including *Roots* in 1968, before breaking up acrimoniously during a performance at California's Knotts Berry Farm in 1973. "The Everly Brothers got to be so Siamese-like," Don commented. "It was debilitating emotionally. People have a tendency to talk about you as one person. We're not alike that much. We're not twins." They reunited a decade later and scored one of their last hits with the Paul McCartney tune "On the Wings of a Nightingale" in 1984.

Although best remembered for their vocal blend, the Everlys were also adept songwriters who wrote some of their own biggest hits, including "Cathy's Clown," "Till I Kissed You," "Devoted to You," and "When Will I Be Loved." In 1986, Don and Phil were inducted into the Rock and Roll Hall of Fame.

EXILE

E xile was the first band to benefit from the ground-breaking early '80s success of Alabama, who paved the way for Exile to shift from pop to a sound that fit well with the pop-dominated country music of the time. Impetus was added to the band's desire to explore country music when member J. P. Pennington co-wrote (with then-member Mark Gray) two chart-topping songs for Alabama: "Take Me Down" (1982) and "The Closer You Get" (1983). It was in late 1983 that they released the first of 10 Number One country hits of their own.

The group was founded as the Fascinations in Richmond, Kentucky, in 1963. Membership included J. P. (James Preston) Pennington on guitar, Jimmy Stokely on vocals, and Buzz Cornelison on keyboard. They changed the name to the Exiles in 1965 and to Exile in 1973, the same year keyboardist Marlon Hargis joined up. "It originally started as a rhythm and blues group," Hargis says. "When I joined, it had developed into a rock and roll band, I suppose because it was the thing to do at the time, even though we all grew up with country music." (Pennington's mother, Lily Mae Ledford, had performed with a popular country act called the Coon

Creek Girls.) After they scored a Number One pop hit in 1978 with "Kiss You All Over" it became less likely that they would ever explore their country roots. Yet that song proved to be the zenith of their pop career. When their popularity wavered, lead singer Jimmy Stokely left the group and was replaced by singer-songwriter Les Taylor.

Taylor worked out, but the music wasn't working. As the 1980s began they knew it was time for a change. "At that point, we decided we were beating our heads against the wall pursuing our material in a sort of Europop vein," says Hargis. They moved to Lexington, Kentucky, to reinvent themselves as a country act, a shift that took place about the time Pennington's songs were hitting for Alabama. Those hits added to the group's country credibility and led to a record contract with Epic. Exile, which then consisted of Pennington, Hargis, Taylor, bassist Sonny Lemaire, and drummer Steve Goetzman, quickly scored the Number One country hits "Woke Up in Love," "I Don't Have to Be a Memory," "Give Me One More Chance," "Crazy for Your Love," and "She's a Miracle." It was one of the key success stories of the 1980s, since country music has historically resisted pop-to-country crossover acts.

Beginning in the late 1980s, in spite of the group's consistent presence at the top of the country charts, Exile began to lose members. Hargis departed and was replaced by Lee Carroll, formerly with the Judds. Taylor then left for a solo career, as did founder Pennington. So essential had Pennington and Taylor been to the overall vocal sound that Exile lost momentum, and Epic dropped the band. Lemaire attempted to resurrect the act with Paul Martin as lead vocalist, signing with Arista Records and managing two more top 10 hits, "Nobody's Talking" and "Yet," in 1990. Unable to sustain the momentum, Exile charted a final time in 1991 and then disbanded.

TOP ALBUMS

EXILE (Epic, '83)
KENTUCKY HEARTS (Epic, '84)
HANG ON TO YOUR HEART (Epic, '85)

TOP SONGS

WOKE UP IN LOVE (Epic, '83, 1)
I DON'T WANT TO BE A MEMORY (Epic, '84, 1)
GIVE ME ONE MORE CHANCE (Epic, '84, 1)
CRAZY FOR YOUR LOVE (Epic, '84, 1)
SHE'S A MIRACLE (Epic, '85, 1)
HANG ON TO YOUR HEART (Epic, '85, 1)
I COULD GET USED TO YOU (Epic, '86, 1)

Additional Top 40 Country Songs: 12

Exile

DONNA FARGO

Donna Fargo lived the prototypical small-town-girl-makes-good story: After getting discovered, she became one of the most famous performers in the pop and country worlds, joining Loretta Lynn and Dolly Parton in the ranks of country's premier female singer-songwriters.

The Happiest Girl in the Whole U.S.A. was born Yvonne Vaughn on November 10, 1949, in Mount Airey, North Carolina. She sang in church and was a high school cheerleader and homecoming queen. "I grew up in North Carolina listening to all kinds of music," she recalled to *Billboard*'s Bob Kirsch in 1974. "I didn't really distinguish between categories of music during my childhood. I always had the desire to sing."

After attending High Point, North Carolina, Teachers' College, she migrated to southern California and soon was teaching school by day and singing in nightclubs in the evenings under her stage name, Donna Fargo. She met record producer Stan Silver, who taught her to play guitar and encouraged her songwriting. "The only thing I'd ever done was a little poetry in high school and college—not even much of that," she told writer Patsi Cox in 1986. "But Stan understood what makes songs work, and he critiqued my work a great deal at first. Little by little, it started coming together." After marrying Silver in 1969, Donna recorded for the Ramco and Challenge labels and achieved mild chart success in California.

During Donna's Easter vacation in 1972, the Silvers traveled to Nashville to record a demo session that they paid for themselves. Donna returned to her teaching job while Stan shopped the tape to record labels. Jim Fogelsong of ABC/Dot heard one song and jumped to sign Donna. Her first charting single was also her biggest: "The Happiest Girl in the Whole U.S.A." held down the Number One slot for three weeks in 1972 and won the award for Single of the Year from the Country Music Association. As the song was climbing the charts, Donna finally gave up teaching and moved to Nashville. "I was still teaching when 'Happiest Girl' hit," she told Kirsch, "and I had to make the decision as to whether to go out as a singer or keep teaching. In June of 1972 the record was Number One, but it was still quite a decision."

The next three years brought a string of Number One hits, including "Funny Face," "Superman," "You Were Always There, "Little Girl Gone," and "You Can't Be a Beacon (If Your Light Don't Shine)." She became the first female in country music history to have back-to-back million-selling singles with "Happiest Girl" and "Funny Face."

Unlike many female country stars of the era, Donna wrote most of her own material. "It's much easier to cut something you've written yourself," she told Kirsch, "because you almost arrange the song when you've written it. The song almost develops a soul of its own."

After changing labels to Warner Brothers in 1976, she charted regularly but scored only one more Number One—"That Was Yesterday"—in 1977. In 1978 she was diagnosed with multiple sclerosis, but she continued to record and tour. "I knew I had to get back on schedule, so I did and that helped," she told Laura Eipper in 1980. "I decided to read and study and really discipline myself. I decided that I just couldn't give up." She overcame the effects of MS and subsequently worked diligently to aid others afflicted with the disease.

Fargo's last top 10 single was "Somebody Special" in 1979.

TOP SONGS

THE HAPPIEST GIRL IN THE WHOLE U.S.A.
   (Dot, '72, *1, 11 Pop*)
FUNNY FACE (Dot, '72, *1, 5 Pop*)
SUPERMAN (Dot, '73, *1*)
YOU WERE ALWAYS THERE (Dot, '73, *1*)
YOU CAN'T BE A BEACON (IF YOUR LIGHT DON'T
   SHINE) (Dot, '74, *1*)
THAT WAS YESTERDAY (Warner, '77, *1*)
DO I LOVE YOU (YES IN EVERY WAY) (Warner, '78, *2*)

Additional Top 40 Country Songs: 18

FREDDY FENDER

Freddy Fender was one of the first great Latino country artists. He overcame poverty and the school of hard knocks to become a major star, hitting the charts a number of times in the 1970s with a sound he referred to as "Chicano country."

Fender (real name, Baldermar Huerta) was born June 4, 1937, in San Benito, Texas, on the Mexican border. His parents were migratory workers, and his childhood was spent following the crops as they came to harvest. While his parents weren't musical, they listened to traditional Mexican music, and it seeped into the young Fender's consciousness at an early age. His mother bought him his first guitar.

To escape from his family's modest circumstances, Fender quit school and joined the Marines when he was 16. When he was released from the military in the late 1950s he returned to San Benito and began to pursue a musical career, performing Mexican music at local dances.

But it soon became clear to him that he would have to broaden his musical outlook in order to succeed. "I just couldn't feel it [Mexican music]," he said. "I never liked Chicano music. I liked to listen to it, but not deliver it. I've just always been into gringo music." When he began playing songs that were more country and rock and roll, he came to the attention of local promoter Wayne Duncan, who signed Fender to his Duncan label. At that time, he also changed his name to Fender, basing it on the name of the famous electric guitar.

With Duncan's assistance as producer and co-composer, Fender recorded a demo that subsequently came to the attention of Imperial Records in 1960. That same year, Imperial released the single "Wasted Days and Wasted Nights," which catapulted Fender into the charts.

But his fledgling career was interrupted in May 1960 when Fender was arrested for possession of drugs in Louisiana. Convicted, he was sentenced to

Freddy Fender

five years in the state penitentiary. "My records were doing great for awhile," Fender said. "Then on May 13, 1960, I found myself in jail for three years. . . . While in prison, I studied my music and got a lot of practice while performing for the convicts on weekends." In 1963, he was paroled with the encouragement of the state's governor, Jimmie Davis.

He worked at various odd jobs over the next decade and more. While he did not release any records during this period he did continue to perform at various clubs and dances on the local level. It was at one of these, in 1974, that he came into contact with producer Huey Meaux, who began to record Fender performing in a pop-oriented country vein.

The result of their efforts was the single "Before the Next Teardrop Falls," a gigantic hit in 1975 on the ABC/Dot label. With his plaintive vocal sound and homespun sincerity, Fender was as much in the mainstream of country music as anyone. But his Latino background was a public relations bonus that set him apart and drew in a new range of fans.

Fender rapidly became a star of major proportions. In 1975 his hit record was honored as Single of the Year by the Country Music Association, which also named him Male Vocalist of the Year. His success continued through the end of the decade, with such releases as "Secret Love," "You'll Lose a

TOP SONGS

BEFORE THE NEXT TEARDROP FALLS
  (ABC/Dot, '75, *1, 1 Pop*)
WASTED DAYS AND WASTED NIGHTS
  (ABC/Dot, '75, *1, 8 Pop*)
SINCE I MET YOU BABY (GRT, '75, *10*)
SECRET LOVE (ABC/Dot, '75, *1, 20 Pop*)
WILD SIDE OF LIFE (GRT, '76, *13*)
YOU'LL LOSE A GOOD THING (ABC/Dot, '76, *1, 32 Pop*)
VAYA CON DIOS (ABC/Dot, '76, *7*)
LIVING IT DOWN (ABC/Dot, '76, *2*)
THE RAINS CAME (ABC/Dot, '77, *4*)
IF YOU DON'T LOVE ME (WHY DON'T YOU JUST
  LEAVE ME ALONE) (ABC/Dot, '77, *11*)

Additional Top 40 Country Songs: 6

Good Thing," "The Rains Came," and "Talk to Me" all making the charts. Fender also charted with a rendition of the Mexican traditional song "Vaya Con Dios."

Fender's version of country music was hardly revolutionary. Like most of his country counterparts, he adhered to a simple style that was low on glitz and high on basic emotion. There were love songs such as "Teardrop" and paeans to home like "If You're Ever in Texas." But Fender also added the energy and punch of rock and roll, particularly on the album *Rock 'n' Country.*

Following his 1970s heyday, Fender was unable to maintain his success. But he didn't fade from the scene entirely. In 1991, he appeared in the film *The Milagro Beanfield War.* And in 1990 he joined rocker Doug Sahm and others in the Texas Tornados, a group that specialized in the tangy blend of Tex-Mex rock, pop, and country that Fender had performed in his younger days in San Benito.

LESTER FLATT

One of the kings of bluegrass, Lester Raymond Flatt rode to fame as half of the influential duo Flatt and Scruggs. For some 20 years with that act, and over a career that spanned five decades, Flatt's high-pitched voice, straightforward rhythm guitar, and simple but memorable songs helped define the traditional acoustic string-band style. His so-called Flatt G-run became a signature country guitar lick. His 16-year presence—with Scruggs—on the *Billboard* country singles chart spread bluegrass far beyond the southeastern U.S. enclaves where it originated.

He was born on June 28, 1914, in Overton County, Tennessee, the son of a sharecropper who had a musical bent. Lester married young—at age 17—and went to work in a local mill. But over the next 10 years he became increasingly involved in music making, joining a group called the Harmonizers and then, in the early 1940s, singing and playing mandolin with Charlie Monroe and His Kentucky Pardners.

He quit Monroe in 1944 but was quickly recruited to sing lead and handle guitar for Charlie's brother, Bill Monroe, whose Blue Grass Boys were a rising attraction on the "Grand Ole Opry" at the time. A 20-ish banjo wiz named Earl Scruggs joined the group in 1945, and for the next several years Mon-

roe and the Boys virtually invented the bluegrass style, laying smooth and high vocal harmonies over fast and intricate instrumentals—in their case anchored by Flatt's alternating bass-chord rhythm picking. Flatt's songwriting matured with the Blue Grass Boys: the Monroe-Flatt collaboration "Will You Be Loving Another Man" is now considered one of the key early bluegrass records. (Two other Blue Grass Boys songs from this period—"Kentucky Waltz" and "Footprints in the Snow," both from 1946—scored in the top 10 of the *Billboard* Juke Box Folk Records chart, the precursor to the country singles listing.)

Flatt took leave of the Monroe enterprise in 1948, and he was followed shortly by Scruggs. The two promptly assembled an outfit they called Lester Flatt, Earl Scruggs, and the Foggy Mountain Boys, enlisting the aid, over time, of ex-Monroe bassist Cedric Rainwater, guitarist-vocalist Mac Wiseman, and fiddler Jim Shumate. The act toured energetically, broadcast over a number of radio stations in the Southeast, signed with Mercury Records, and steadily built a base of popularity, by 1950 issuing the song "Foggy Mountain Breakdown," an eventual bluegrass standard.

In 1951 Flatt and Scruggs moved over to Columbia Records, launching a run of what would be 20 country chart singles in *Billboard* through 1968. They got a boost in 1953 when the Martha White Flour company sponsored them for a daily live radio

---

TOP ALBUMS

Flatt and Scruggs:
AT CARNEGIE HALL (Columbia, '62)
GOLDEN ERA 1950–55 (Rounder, '78)

TOP SONGS

Flatt and Scruggs:
'TIS SWEET TO BE REMEMBERED (Columbia, '52, *9*)
CABIN ON THE HILL (Columbia, '59, *9*)
POLKA ON A BANJO (Columbia, '60, *12*)
GO HOME (Columbia, '61, *10*)
THE BALLAD OF JED CLAMPETT (Columbia, '62, *1*)
PEARL, PEARL, PEARL (Columbia, '63, *8*)
YOU ARE MY FLOWER (Columbia, '64, *12*)
PETTICOAT JUNCTION (Columbia, '64, *4*)

Additional Top 40 Country Songs: 7

show, "Martha White Biscuit Time," on station WSM in Nashville. With an invitation to join the Grand Ole Opry in 1955, the foundation of the Flatt and Scruggs career was solidly in place.

During the late 1950s and early 1960s, the group broke out of the confines of Nashville and broadened its appeal, reaching a growing college-age audience of folk music listeners. Then, in 1962, they were asked to perform the theme—titled "The Ballad of Jed Clampett"—for the popular television series "The Beverly Hillbillies." With the Number One hit success of that song, the duo's cameo appearances on the show, and the inclusion, in 1968, of "Foggy Mountain Breakdown" on the soundtrack of the movie *Bonnie and Clyde,* Flatt and Scruggs almost single-handedly brought bluegrass into the mainstream.

Came the late 1960s and the newly mind-expanding sounds of rock, and the bonds of the Flatt-Scruggs union began to weaken. Scruggs was inclined to evolve and modernize with the time, leading to Flatt and Scruggs' cover of Bob Dylan's "Like a Rolling Stone" in 1968 and their appearance in such counterculture spawning grounds as San Francisco's Avalon Ballroom. Flatt, however, preferred the more traditional sounds of his bluegrass heyday. The two parted ways in 1969.

Flatt followed his inclination and formed the Nashville Grass, recalling the Foggy Mountain Boys format. With it, he spent 10 years playing to his longtime southern audience, touring, recording, and remaining active even after undergoing open-heart surgery in 1975.

Flatt died of heart failure on May 11, 1979, several months after discussing the possibility of a reunion with Scruggs. He left behind a series of albums—on RCA and other labels—and the group Lester Flatt's Nashville Grass, which continued performing under the experienced leadership of mandolinist and onetime Flatt and Scruggs sideman Curtis Seckler.

Flatt and Scruggs were inducted into the Country Music Hall of Fame in 1985.

RED FOLEY
· · · · · · · · · · · · · · · ·

One of country music's key figures in the late 1940s and early '50s, singer Red Foley was also one of its great popularizers. Onstage, on radio, and later on television, Foley brought

TOP SONGS
· · · · · · · · · · · · ·

SMOKE ON THE WATER (Decca, '44, *1, 7 Pop*)

SHAME ON YOU (Decca, '45, *1*)

NEW JOLIE BLONDE (NEW PRETTY BLONDE) (Decca, '47, *1*)

TENNESSEE SATURDAY NIGHT (Decca, '48, *1*)

CHATTANOOGIE SHOE SHINE BOY (Decca, '50, *1, 1 Pop*)

BIRMINGHAM BOUNCE (Decca, '50, *1, 14 Pop*)

MISSISSIPPI (Decca, '50, *1, 22 Pop*)

MIDNIGHT (Decca, '52, *1*)

GOODNIGHT IRENE (Decca, '50, *1, 10 Pop*)

ONE BY ONE (Decca, '54, *1*)

Additional Top 40 Country Songs: 50

country music out of the commercial woods and into the musical mainstream.

Born Clyde Julian Foley on June 17, 1910, in Bluelick, Kentucky, Foley was the right age for membership in country's founding generation, which emerged in the 1930s. He began his career at the start of that decade when he won a talent contest in Louisville in 1930. Encouraged to move to Chicago to seek his fortune in the larger musical world (like a generation of southern bluesmen of the same period), he did so in the same year, joining the Cumberland Ridge Runners on the WLS "National Barn Dance" show, which he starred in until 1937. The leader of that group, John Lair, subsequently teamed with Foley later in the decade, and the two created "The Renfro Valley Show." These radio programs gave Foley the perfect background for his subsequent teaming with the comedian Red Skelton, in 1939, on "Avalon Time," which made Foley the first country star to have his own radio show on a network. His radio performances brought him national recognition and put country on the musical map.

In the 1940s Foley became a star at the Grand Ole Opry and began to pursue a recording career that eventually eclipsed his success on the airwaves. Initially he recorded versions of traditional songs like "Tennessee Saturday Night" and "Tennessee Polka," which hit the top 10 in 1949. He followed them with "Birmingham Bounce," a country Number One in 1950. Other hits, such as "Alabama Jubilee," "Shake a Hand," "Jilted," and "Hearts of Stone," made the top 10 through the mid-1950s.

While these songs and others were mainstream country, Foley also recorded a number of religious and gospel-based songs during the same period, to tremendous acclaim and success. "Just a Closer Walk with Thee" and "Steal Away" sold a million copies apiece in 1950, and "(There'll Be) Peace in the Valley (For Me)" made the country top five in 1951.

Foley was one of the artists (others included Hank Williams, Hank Snow, and Tennessee Ernie Ford) who made the period from 1949 to 1955 a musical and commercial golden age for country music. As he had done on radio in the 1930s, Foley brought country music to television—and to a wide audience—in the 1950s. He hosted one of the first country TV series, ABC's "Ozark Jubilee," from his home base of Springfield, Missouri, in 1954. He also co-starred with Fess Parker on the series "Mr. Smith Goes to Washington" in the 1960s.

For his simple and direct style, his pioneering music, and his unerring use of media—from records to radio and television—to promulgate country music as a commercial and artistic force, Foley was elected into the Country Music Association's Hall of Fame in 1967, a year before his death in Fort Wayne, Indiana on September 19, 1968.

TENNESSEE ERNIE FORD

H e dubbed himself the Pea Picker, coddling fans with phrases like "Bless your li'l pea-pickin' hearts" in a voice as low, warm, and cozy as an old dog curled near a fireplace. The result was impressive: in his peak period of fame, Tennessee Ernie Ford ranked high on the roster of America's favored entertainers. A combination hitmaker, TV star, radio personality, and gospel crooner, Ford brought country music—and his own brand of homeyness and small-town charm—deep into the pop mainstream.

Ernest Jennings Ford (b. Feb. 13, 1919, Bristol, Tennessee) exhibited musical inclinations even as a youngster. He sang in the local Methodist church and learned to play the trombone, and after high school—and a stint as an announcer at a Bristol radio station—he studied voice at the Cincinnati Conservatory of Music.

Radio announcing jobs were to be his indirect entrée into the world of music making. He left Cincinnati to deejay first at an Atlanta station and then at another in Knoxville. Following active duty as a bombardier in the Army Air Corps during World War II, Ford relocated to California and settled for a spell in front of the microphone at station KFXM in San Bernardino. That led to further deejay duties at KXLA in Pasadena—and a career breakthrough. When not handling his own morning program, "Bar Nothing Ranch Time," Ford would sidle in to another studio where musician Cliffie Stone was emceeing the "Dinner Bell Round Up," and he would tell jokes and sing along with the band. Stone, consequently, invited Ford to be a regular on his Saturday night show, "Hometown Jamboree." He also connected Ford with Lee Gillette, an A&R man at Stone's label, Capitol Records, which led to the signing of a contract in early 1949.

Ford began issuing records on which he was the singer—"Tennessee Border," "Mule Train," and "Anticipation Blues" among the first. They rapidly began registering on the *Billboard* country chart and, just as quickly, crossing over to the magazine's pop listings. A rollicking, boogie-flavored sound characterized a number of these early discs, including "Smokey Mountain Boogie," "The Shot Gun Boogie" (penned by Ford), and "Blackberry Boogie," which scored country chart rankings of eight, one, and six, respectively. And these were only the beginning. Ford would ultimately place 20 songs in the country top 40 and 15 in the top 100 of the pop chart, making him one of the key movers in the mass-popularization of country.

A career peak was reached in 1955. First, Ford scored a top 10 hit with "Ballad of Davy Crockett"

TOP SONGS

MULE TRAIN (Capitol, '49, *1, 9 Pop*)

ANTICIPATION BLUES (Capitol, '49, *3*)

THE CRY OF THE WILD GOOSE (Capitol, '50, *2, 15 Pop*)

AIN'T NOBODY'S BUSINESS BUT MY OWN (with Kay Starr, Capitol, '50, *5*)

I'LL NEVER BE FREE (with Kay Starr, Capitol, '50, *2, 3 Pop*)

THE SHOT GUN BOOGIE (Capitol, '50, *1, 14 Pop*)

MISTER AND MISSISSIPPI (Capitol, '51, *2, 18 Pop*)

BLACKBERRY BOOGIE (Capitol, '52, *6*)

BALLAD OF DAVY CROCKETT (Capitol, '55, *4, 5 Pop*)

SIXTEEN TONS (Capitol, '55, *1, 1 Pop*)

Additional Top 40 Country Songs: 10

(a tune rapidly recollected today by anyone of the baby-boom generation or older). Then he recorded a coal miner's song written by his friend Merle Travis. Titled "Sixteen Tons," it topped both the country and pop listings, selling in massive quantities both initially and over its lifetime.

At the time, Ford was already hosting his own television show for NBC five days a week. Previously, while issuing records, he had deejayed on the ABC radio network and begun making guest appearances on such series as "I Love Lucy." The success of "Sixteen Tons" smoothed the way for continued television activity and extramusical celebrity. From 1956 to '61, Ford hosted "The Ford Hour," a weekly variety show. He starred in another series through 1965, and over the years he guested on such programs as "Make Room for Daddy," "The Jack Benny Show," and "Hee Haw."

Later in his career, Ford concentrated on gospel music, starting in 1956 with the album *Hymns*—which spent nearly three years in the top 40 albums chart—and including the 1964 collection *Great Gospel Songs,* a Grammy winner in the religious music category.

Though Ford's heyday was over by the mid-'60s, career highlights were yet to come. In 1974 he led a troupe of performers on a State Department–sponsored tour of the Soviet Union—the first visit of a country music group to that country. Ten years later, Ford was awarded the Medal of Freedom. And in 1990 he was elected to the Country Music Hall of Fame.

Shortly after Ford's death on October 17, 1991, Cliffie Stone described Ford to *People* magazine as "just an ordinary person, not an actor. So many people try to be somebody else, and they're not really good at it. He was totally unique."

THE FORESTER SISTERS

The Forester Sisters are members of the generation of country artists who grew up in the rock and roll era. While their music is part traditional country (in its melodic makeup and lyrical approach), it is also a product of the country-rock age, with a feel and energy that come as much from the work of artists like Linda Ronstadt, Bonnie

TOP SONGS

I FELL IN LOVE AGAIN LAST NIGHT (Warner, '85, *1*)
JUST IN CASE (Warner, '85, *1*)
MAMA'S NEVER SEEN THOSE EYES (Warner, '86, *1*)
LONELY ALONE (Warner, '86, *2*)
TOO MUCH IS NOT ENOUGH (with the Bellamy Brothers, Warner, '86, *1*)
TOO MANY RIVERS (Warner, '87, *5*)
YOU AGAIN (Warner, '87, *1*)
LYIN' IN HIS ARMS AGAIN (Warner, '87, *5*)
LOVE WILL (Warner, '89, *7*)
LEAVE IT ALONE (Warner, '89, *7*)

Additional Top 40 Country Songs: 5

Raitt, and the country-era Byrds as from the country masters.

The group is made up of four sisters: Kathy (b. Jan. 4, 1955), June (Sept. 22, 1956), Kim (Nov. 4, 1960), and Christy (Dec. 21, 1962). Kathy, June, and Kim began performing in the 1970s at various shows and events in and around their hometown of Lookout Mountain, Georgia. They were joined in 1982 by Christy and soon became an opening act for the Gatlin Brothers. At about the same time, they recorded a demo at Muscle Shoals studios that came to the attention of producer Jim Ed Norman of Warner Brothers Records. Norman signed them to a contract in 1984, and the sisters began to record their first album.

With Kim and Kathy providing most of the lead vocals (along with guitar and keyboard work, respectively) and June and Christy adding their crystalline harmonies, the Foresters created a sound that proved accessible to a wide range of listeners. It was the country equivalent of the pop "girl group" style of the 1960s, "a fresh, uncomplicated sound," as Christy described it. "We're not as progressive as the Judds, and we're not as traditional as the Whites." Its trademark was the sisters' sibling harmony, an oddly alike sort of vocal approach that had set apart such other groups as the Bee Gees and the Beach Boys. "You can have close, tight harmonies," Kim said, "but there's nothing like family harmonies. I think a lot of it has to do with facial structure—families get the same resonances in their voices. The speech inflections are the same and the way you think—it's like ESP. Everybody knows how far everyone else can go vocally."

Forester Sisters

The sound had immediate commercial impact. The Foresters' debut single, "(That's What You Do) When You're in Love," reached number 10 on the country chart in 1985, the first in a series of top 10 hits during the latter part of the decade. The group's next three singles, 1985's "I Fell in Love Again Last Night" and "Just in Case" and 1986's "Mama's Never Seen Those Eyes," were all chart-toppers.

The sisters teamed with the Bellamy Brothers in 1986 and recorded "Too Much Is Not Enough," another country Number One (they would team with the Bellamys again on John Hiatt's "Drive South" in 1990). "You Again" became the Foresters' fifth Number One, reaching that peak in 1987.

The late-'80s songs "Lyin' in His Arms Again," "Letter Home," "Sincerely," "Love Will," "Don't You," and "Leave It Alone" all made the top 10. But in the 1990s, the sisters' career began to slide. With the exception of 1991's "Men," the group's singles increasingly languished in the lower levels of the charts.

But the music of the Forester Sisters was important in the way it bridged the musical gap between rock and pop and country at a time when the commercial status of country was on the rise. The success of the Forester Sisters was emblematic of the crossover sound and across-the-board popularity that were to become new facets of the country scene.

RADNEY FOSTER

Radney Foster has the distinction of having been both a part of an important country duo—Foster and Lloyd—and an important solo artist.

Foster was born (July 20, 1959, Del Rio, Texas) into a family of lawyers and was expected to follow his grandfather and father into the practice of law. That might have happened if his father hadn't taught him how to play the guitar at age 12 and if as a teenager Foster hadn't become fascinated by music. "I think what influenced me most were the acts that were singer-songwriter–based," he says, "whether groups like the Beatles or Crosby, Stills and Nash or

Radney Foster

guys like Merle Haggard." Foster wrote his first song at age 15.

While attending the University of the South in Sewanee, Tennessee, just a hundred miles from Nashville, Foster took to performing his original songs at local clubs on weekends. One night, a patron with Nashville connections was impressed by his writing and singing and encouraged Foster to visit Music City. He took the next year off from school and moved to Nashville to see what he could accomplish.

In 1985 he landed a writing job with MTM Music Publishing. Two months later Bill Lloyd joined the company. "Somebody suggested I hang out with the new guy," Foster remembers, "but it was the hot summer that drove us together as a team. Neither of our air conditioners worked in our apartments, so we spent a lot of time together at MTM Music just to keep cool."

Their first break as a writing team came when they wrote "Since I Found You"—a top 10 single for Sweethearts of the Rodeo in 1986. Foster then teamed up with Holly Dunn to write her 1987 number two hit, "Love Someone Like Me." That year RCA Records heard some demo tapes of Foster and Lloyd's songs and signed them as a duo. They scored four top 10s over the next two years, starting with "Crazy over You" and including "Sure Thing,"

TOP ALBUMS

Foster and Lloyd:
FOSTER & LLOYD (RCA, '87)

Radney Foster:
DEL RIO, TEXAS, 1959 (Arista, '92)

TOP SONGS

Foster and Lloyd:
CRAZY OVER YOU (RCA, '87, *4*)
SURE THING (RCA, '87, *8*)
WHAT DO YOU WANT FROM ME THIS TIME
   (RCA, '88, *6*)
FAIR SHAKE (RCA, '89, *5*)

Radney Foster:
JUST CALL ME LONESOME (Arista, '92, *10*)
NOBODY WINS (Arista, '93, *2*)

Additional Top 40 Country Songs: 4

"What Do You Want from Me This Time," and "Fair Shake." Then, as suddenly as they'd sprung to prominence, they cooled off at radio, hitting the top 40 one more time before parting company in 1991. "I had been writing some things that were very different from what Foster and Lloyd were doing," explains Foster, "and I felt [the duo] wasn't the vehicle for those songs. After a lot of soul-searching and some heartfelt conversations with Bill, we parted ways."

In 1992, Arista Nashville executive Tim DuBois heard Foster perform at the Bluebird Cafe and offered him a contract on the spot. The result was Foster's first solo album, *Del Rio, Texas, 1959*. It yielded four consecutive top 40 hits, of which two, "Just Call Me Lonesome" and "Nobody Wins," rose to the top 10. Radney's second disc, *Labor of Love,* was released to critical acclaim in early 1995. Both albums indicated that Foster was evolving into one of country music's best writers, bringing a distinctively new-age tone to an intrinsically country style.

JANIE FRICKE

Going against the professional grain, Fricke emerged from the ranks of the Nashville session scene to become one of the biggest singing stars of the country world in the 1980s.

Fricke (who sometimes spelled her last name Frickie) was born December 19, 1947, in South Whitney, Indiana. She came from a musical family, her father being a guitarist and her mother an organist at their local church. She began her career—or, rather, the first phase of her career—as a session vocalist for television and radio jingles while she was a student at Indiana State University. After college, she continued her commercial efforts in Dallas, Memphis, and Los Angeles at the start of the 1970s.

Fricke moved to Nashville in the mid-'70s and began to get work as a vocalist on the thriving session scene. At a session with Johnny Duncan in 1975, Fricke was asked to sing several lines of the song "Jo and the Cowboy." Released as a single—credited to Duncan—the record hit the top 10. With this success, Fricke rose to membership in Nashville's session elite. Over the next two years, she contributed vocals to top 10 hits by numerous leading country performers. At various points, she worked with such stars as Elvis Presley, Crystal Gayle, Dolly Parton, Ronnie Milsap, and Billy Swan.

These records and others led to the offer of a contract with Columbia Records in 1977. Fricke's debut single, "What're You Doing Tonight," was released in September 1977 and became a modest hit at number 21. Several more minor hits, including "Baby It's You" and "Please Help Me, I'm Falling (In Love with You)," followed.

Fricke continued to have success with other artists. She hit the top five with Duncan on a remake of Jay and the Americans' 1964 hit "Come a Little Bit Closer" in October of 1977 and then topped the charts in 1978 with Charlie Rich with "On My Knees."

Her recording career ignited when she began collaborating with producer Jim Ed Norman, first issuing "Down to My Last Broken Heart," a number two hit in 1980. Phenomenal success followed. In 1981 the singles "I'll Need Someone to Hold Me (When I Cry)" and "Do Me with Love" hit number four. And in May 1982, Fricke had her first chart-topping record with "Don't Worry 'Bout Me Baby." From there, the hits seemed to keep coming every few months. "It Ain't Easy Bein' Easy" topped the charts in September of that year. In 1983–84, Fricke scorched the charts with seven top 10 hits, five of which reached Number One. The last of those, "A Place to Fall Apart," was another duet, this time with Merle Haggard.

Along the way, Fricke was voted Female Vocalist of the Year in 1982 and 1983 by the Country Music Association. She also emerged from the studio sessions (her own and others) to form her own group, the Heart City Band, and began touring on a steady basis.

TOP SONGS

ON MY KNEES (Epic, '78, 1)
DOWN TO MY LAST BROKEN HEART (Columbia, '80, 2)
DON'T WORRY 'BOUT ME BABY (Columbia, '82, 1)
IT AIN'T EASY BEIN' EASY (Columbia, '82, 1)
HE'S A HEARTACHE (LOOKING FOR A PLACE TO
     HAPPEN) (Columbia, '83, 1)
TELL ME A LIE (Columbia, '83, 1)
LET'S STOP TALKIN' ABOUT IT (Columbia, '84, 1)
YOUR HEART'S NOT IN IT (Columbia, '84, 1)
A PLACE TO FALL APART (Epic, '84, 1)
ALWAYS HAVE ALWAYS WILL (Columbia, '86, 1)

Additional Top 40 Country Songs: 22

The mid-1980s saw five more of Fricke's singles hit the top 10. Of these, "She's Single Again" peaked at number two in 1985 and "Always Have Always Will" made it to Number One in 1986. But the fire then subsided. By the end of the 1980s, Fricke's impressive chart run was over. Her final entry was "Give 'Em My Number" in late 1989.

DAVID FRIZZELL

From the time he went pro in the mid-1950s, it took David Frizzell about a quarter-century's worth of trying before he reached that country music pot of gold: a pair of Number One hits and a string of tunes in the top 40. The glow of stardom was especially bright in light of the route he'd taken to find it—a career path ever shadowed by the fame of his older sibling, music veteran Lefty Frizzell. "I didn't want to come back [to Nashville] and be 'Lefty's brother,'" he told writer Dolly Carlisle in 1982.

The son of an oil driller and itinerant farmer, and one of eight children, David (b. Sept. 26, 1941, El Dorado, Arkansas) moved frequently as a youth, reportedly attending 15 schools in one year. By 1956, brother Lefty—13 years older—had made deep professional inroads as a singer in the honky-tonk style. The 15-year-old David, also musically inclined, dropped out of school to work with Lefty on the road. Four years later he joined the Air Force, finished high school, and then embarked on what would be his long trek to establish a solo career.

Recordings were made and issued, but hits were few, although the track "I Just Can't Help Believing" charted top 40 (country) in 1970. A stint with Buck Owens added a valuable credential to his resumé, while a couple more low-charting singles kept him afloat into late 1976.

It was in California in 1977 that Frizzell met Shelly West, aspiring singer, fiancée of his brother Allen, and daughter of country star Dottie West. While recording a demo, David invited Shelly to join him on a duet. The resulting sound found the ears of producer Snuff Garrett, who saw the glimmer of gold in the notion of Lefty's brother and Dottie's daughter forming a team. The two didn't disagree with him. After a period of working in clubs (backed by guitarist Allen), they put together an album for release by Casablanca West, a label run by bubblegum/Kiss/disco entrepreneur Neil Bogart. But the

label folded, and the duo, deal-less, had to go shopping for another company to put out the record. Takers were not instantly forthcoming.

Enter Clint Eastwood, a partner with Snuff Garrett in Warner/Viva Records. At the time, moviedom's Man with No Name was working on the film *Any Which Way You Can,* and he felt the Frizzell-West track "You're the Reason God Made Oklahoma" would spice up the audio.

The tune was included on the soundtrack album amid songs by other, "bigger-name" acts. "Oklahoma" was the fifth cut to be released as a single, but it became the biggest hit of all, rising with haste to the pinnacle of the *Billboard* country chart. Popular attention rapidly turned to the pair, the Country Music Association named them Duo of the Year in 1981, and the stages of Lake Tahoe and Sparks, Nevada, beckoned, welcoming an act that included crowd-pleasing nods to family lineage (David covering Lefty, and Shelly singing a medley of Dottie tunes).

Solo, Frizzell repeated the chart-topping achievement in 1982 with "I'm Gonna Hire a Wino to Decorate Our Home" (he'd revisit the booze theme with the next year's "A Million Light Beers Ago") and then output numerous discs of decreasing popularity. He did this while concurrently issuing Frizzell and West singles (also of decreasing popularity, with the

---

TOP SONGS

David Frizzell and Shelly West:
YOU'RE THE REASON GOD MADE OKLAHOMA (Warner, '81, *1*)
A TEXAS STATE OF MIND (Warner, '81, *9*)
HUSBANDS AND WIVES (Warner, '81, *16*)
ANOTHER HONKY-TONK NIGHT ON BROADWAY (Warner, '82, *8*)
I JUST CAME HERE TO DANCE (Warner, '82, *4*)
SILENT PARTNERS (Viva, '84, *20*)
IT'S A BE TOGETHER NIGHT (Viva, '84, *13*)

David Frizzell:
I'M GONNA HIRE A WINO TO DECORATE OUR HOME (Warner, '82, *1*)
LOST MY BABY BLUES (Warner, '82, *5*)
WHERE ARE YOU SPENDING YOUR NIGHTS THESE DAYS (Viva, '83, *10*)

Additional Top 40 Country Songs: 2

exception of 1984's number 13 "It's a Be Together Night").

By the late 1980s David was back out of the limelight, but his reputation as one of country's finer singers was secure—as was his own place right next to Lefty in the country music history books.

LEFTY FRIZZELL

Lefty Frizzell was one of the most important country artists of the 1950s and '60s. He contributed some timeless hits to country music, and the influence of his distinctive vocal delivery can still be heard today in the songs of artists who freely admit they copied him, including Merle Haggard, Keith Whitley, and John Anderson.

Frizzell was born William Orville Frizzell in Corsicana, Texas, on March 31, 1928. He acquired his nickname after dispatching several contenders during a short-lived stint as a boxer. He began playing music as a child and won a talent contest at the age of 12. By his teen years, he was playing in bars in his native Texas, covering the hits of his idol, Jimmie Rodgers.

Frizzell scored his first charting record for Columbia in 1950 with the two-sided country Number One smash "If You've Got the Money, I've Got the Time" b/w "I Love You a Thousand Ways." The next year, three of his seven singles went to Number One and, in combination, held the top spot for half the year: "I Want to Be with You Always" for 11 weeks, "Always Late (With Your Kisses)" for 12, and "Give Me More, More, More (Of Your Kisses)" for three. Riding high on the charts, Frizzell toured with another honky-tonk legend, Hank Williams. "Hank and I did shows together," Lefty recalled to John Lomax. "We'd flip a coin to see who'd go on first." Between 1950 and 1954, Lefty charted with 15 consecutive top 10 country hits. In 1952, he became the first and only country artist to have four songs in the top 10 at the same time.

Soon after his initial success, Lefty moved to California, where he appeared on the TV shows "Town Hall Party" and "Country America."

"Run 'Em Off" (1954) marked the end of his winning streak. He came back with only one more top 10 single ("The Long Black Veil" in 1959) and one more Number One ("Saginaw, Michigan" in 1964).

TOP ALBUMS

LEFTY'S 20 GOLDEN HITS (Columbia, '82)
HIS LIFE, HIS MUSIC (Bear Family, '84)

TOP SONGS

IF YOU'VE GOT THE MONEY, I'VE GOT THE TIME (Columbia, '50, 1)
I LOVE YOU A THOUSAND WAYS (Columbia, '50, 1)
I WANT TO BE WITH YOU ALWAYS (Columbia, '51, 1)
ALWAYS LATE (WITH YOUR KISSES) (Columbia, '51, 1)
GIVE ME MORE, MORE, MORE (OF YOUR KISSES) (Columbia, '51, 1)
SAGINAW, MICHIGAN (Columbia, '64, 1)

Additional Top 40 Country Songs: 20

Frizzell continued to record for Columbia until 1972 and issued several singles for ABC in the mid-'70s, but he was never able to come near his chart success of the early 1950s. His last single, "Falling," was charting when he died on July 19, 1975, following a stroke. He was elected to the Country Music Hall of Fame in 1982.

Frizzell's younger brother David went on to his own success in country music, both as a solo performer and in partnership with Shelly West. David, who toured with his Lefty as a teenager, told Robert K. Oermann, "Lefty was the greatest country singer that ever was. He didn't need all that extra stuff to make him sound good. He was a genius all alone."

LARRY GATLIN AND THE GATLIN BROTHERS

For Larry Gatlin and his brothers Steve and Rudy, music was a family affair. Larry was the first to become a star; he brought his brothers along, and by the time their career peaked, they were one of the top acts in country.

It started in the early 1950s when Larry (b. May 2, 1948, Seminole, Texas), Steve (Apr. 4, 1951, Olney, Texas), Rudy (Aug. 20, 1952), and one of their sisters, LaDonna, formed a gospel group. They toured in the South for a number of years and had their own television show in Abilene.

Larry went on his own during the 1960s and eventually became a vocalist with the Imperials, who were part of the Jimmy Dean show in Las Vegas. It was there that he first met Dottie West, who encouraged him to begin a songwriting career. He did just that, moving to Nashville in 1972 to become the first staff writer at West's First Generation Music Company. He composed material for West—including "You're the Other Half of Me," "Once You Were Mine," and "My Mind's Gone Away"—and during the same period also wrote songs for Elvis Presley, Glen Campbell, Tom Jones, and others. Gatlin songs were also used in the Johnny Cash film *The Glory Road*.

Gatlin secured gigs as a session vocalist in Nashville. He sang harmonies on Kris Kristofferson's breakout hit, "Why Me," in 1973 and became friends with Kristofferson, who encouraged Monument Records to sign Gatlin to a contract. That same year, Gatlin released his debut record, "Sweet Becky Walker," which made it to number 40 on the country chart.

Meanwhile, Steve, Rudy, LaDonna, and Tim Johnson (LaDonna's husband) formed a group of

TOP SONGS

Larry Gatlin with Family and Friends:
I DON'T WANNA CRY (Monument, '77, 3)
LOVE IS JUST A GAME (Monument, '77, 3)
I JUST WISH YOU WERE SOMEONE I LOVE
    (Monument, '77, 1)

Larry Gatlin:
NIGHT TIME MAGIC (Monument, '78, 2)

Larry Gatlin and the Gatlin Brother Band:
ALL THE GOLD IN CALIFORNIA (Columbia, '79, 1)
WHAT ARE WE DOIN' LONESOME (Columbia, '81, 4)
HOUSTON (MEANS I'M ONE DAY CLOSER TO YOU)
    (Columbia, '83, 1)

Larry Gatlin and the Gatlin Brothers:
THE LADY TAKES THE COWBOY EVERYTIME
    (Columbia, '84, 3)

Larry, Steve, Rudy: The Gatlin Brothers:
SHE USED TO BE SOMEBODY'S BABY (Columbia, '86, 2)
TALKIN' TO THE MOON (Columbia, '86, 4)

Additional Top 40 Country Songs: 24

Larry Gatlin and the Gatlin Brothers

their own, Young Country, and toured with Tammy Wynette.

During the mid-1970s, Gatlin flirted with success, releasing several records that stalled at lower chart levels (1974's "Delta Dirt" the best received, at number 14). But his fortune improved at the end of 1975 when he teamed with Steve and Rudy and others as Larry Gatlin with Family and Friends. "We are basically of one mind, one spirit, and one heart," Gatlin said at the time. "And now we're doing what we were born to do, which is stand up there and sing. ...We can do everything from what we call good ole time traditional-type country to a little harder country and even some rock 'n' roll. But we sing Gatlin music. It's country-oriented music done our way."

With the single "Broken Lady," they scored a number five hit and won a Grammy Award for Best Country Song in 1976. Momentum continued with 1976's "Statues Without Hearts" and 1977's "I Don't Wanna Cry" and "Love Is Just a Game," the former hitting number five and the latter two hitting number three (credited to Larry Gatlin with Brothers and Friends). They scored their first Number One record in 1977 with "I Just Wish You Were Someone I Love."

Gatlin recorded as a solo artist in 1978, releasing three singles that made the top 20. When he and his brothers re-formed the next year as Larry Gatlin and the Gatlin Brothers Band, they began an astonishing five-year run on the charts that included 15 top 40 hits, starting with 1979's Number One "All the Gold in California" and continuing with "Take Me to Your Lovin' Place" (1980), "What Are We Doin' Lonesome" (1981), and "Houston (Means I'm One Day Closer to You)" (1983).

Using various different names—including Larry Gatlin and the Gatlin Brothers; Larry, Steve, Rudy: the Gatlin Brothers; and the Gatlin Bros.—they charted in the mid-1980s with "The Lady Takes the Cowboy Everytime" (number three, 1984), "Talkin' to the Moon" (number four, 1986), and others. They also hit with 1987's "From Time to Time (It Feels Like Love Again)," credited to Larry Gatlin and Janie Frickie (with the Gatlin Brothers).

There were problems along the way. In 1984, Larry Gatlin was admitted to a drug and alcohol rehabilitation center in California. And the group's popularity—at least as measured in chart rankings—began to decline in 1988.

In 1991, the group concluded what it called its "Adios" tour and went into semi-retirement. Larry Gatlin reappeared the following year in the Broadway musical *The Will Rogers Follies*.

CRYSTAL GAYLE

Although Crystal Gayle and Loretta Lynn are sisters, they don't look, talk, or sing alike, which explains how Gayle managed to avoid the comparisons that siblings of stars often endure. She did fine on her own: during the 1970s, '80s, and into the '90s she amassed 45 top 40 hits and 18 Number Ones—including the classic country-pop smash "Don't It Make My Brown Eyes Blue"—enroute to becoming an American music icon.

Gayle (b. Brenda Gail Webb, Jan. 9, 1951, Paintsville, Kentucky), the last of the eight Webb children, spent her first three years in the family's now famous Butcher Hollow home. Unlike her famous sister, nearly 17 years her senior, Gayle was raised in Wabash, Indiana, where the family moved because of her father's failing health from black lung, the coal miner's disease.

Gayle's singing career began when she was around five years old, when her mother and visiting aunts and uncles would entice her to sing by paying her a nickel a song. "They had to start bribing me because my mother used to make me get up and sing, so I started hiding when company came," she says. "Now I'm glad she kept after me about it."

In Indiana, Gayle sang informally in local choirs,

TOP SONGS

DON'T IT MAKE MY BROWN EYES BLUE
 (United Artists, '77, *1, 2 Pop*)
READY FOR THE TIMES TO GET BETTER
 (United Artists, '78, *1*)
TALKING IN YOUR SLEEP (United Artists, '78, *1, 18 Pop*)
WHY HAVE YOU LEFT THE ONE YOU LEFT ME FOR
 (United Artists, '78, *1*)
TOO MANY LOVERS (Columbia, '81, *1*)
YOU AND I (with Eddie Rabbitt, Elektra, '82, *1, 7 Pop*)
'TIL I GAIN CONTROL AGAIN (Elektra, '82, *1*)
MAKIN' UP FOR LOST TIME (Warner, '85, *1*)
CRY (Warner, '86, *1*)
STRAIGHT TO THE HEART (Warner, '86, *1*)

Additional Top 40 Country Songs: 35

Crystal Gayle

and she gained exposure to an array of country, folk, pop, and gospel styles. She also went on the road with her older sister for a few weeks each summer. Loretta Lynn encouraged Gayle's singing ambitions, but once advised her not to limit herself to country music. "She didn't want me to be compared to her, because she knew I wouldn't make it if that happened," recalls Gayle. "She helped me realize that I could record anything I wanted to in Nashville."

When Gayle turned 18, Lynn played a major role in getting her started. She helped open the door to Decca Records, who signed Gayle to a contract in 1970. She suggested the stage name Crystal ("Gayle" was an altered spelling of her middle name, Gail). Lynn also wrote Gayle's debut top 20 hit, "I've Cried (The Blues Right Out of My Eyes)," and arranged to use her as the opening act on tour.

The association had its drawbacks. People accused Gayle of riding her sister's coattails, and Lynn and her husband began to argue over what Gayle should sing and how she should act on stage. "I was out with them about three days and knew this wasn't going to work," says Gayle. "I didn't want to

cause problems between them. And I realized that if I just tagged along with my sister and kept asking, 'What should I do and how should I do it?' I knew I'd never find my own creative self."

In 1973, she left Lynn and Decca. Soon settled at United Artists, she began working with Allen Reynolds (producer of Don Williams, Kathy Mattea, and Garth Brooks, among others). He gained her confidence, she says, "by respecting me and giving me the freedom to be myself as an artist." "Some of the early stuff I cut on her included a song her husband had written called 'Beyond You,'" says Reynolds. "I just loved her performance on it. So I told her that I thought she ought to just go ahead and be as good as she wants to be, because I just had the feeling after hearing that song that this person had the makings of a major artist."

Beginning with "Wrong Road Again" in 1974, Gayle scored a total of 11 top 10 hits on the UA label. In 1977, "Don't It Make My Brown Eyes Blue" climbed to Number One country and number two pop, blowing her career wide open. International fame followed. Francis Ford Coppola hired her to sing on the soundtrack of his film *One from the Heart* (some of her finest vocal work), and she became an in-demand guest on variety and late-night talk shows. Signed to Columbia, and later Warner Brothers, she accrued such additional hits as "If You Ever Change Your Mind," "Too Many Lovers," "Cry," and "Straight to the Heart."

Amid more traditional country artists like Loretta Lynn and Tammy Wynette, Crystal Gayle proved, as Patsy Cline had done a decade before her, that it's possible to appeal to pop audiences by forging a mainstream sound and still succeed in the country arena.

DON GIBSON

He wrote "Sweet Dreams," the classic Patsy Cline hit that became the title of her 1985 film biography. He also penned "Oh Lonesome Me," which Neil Young introduced to rock audiences in 1970, and "I Can't Stop Loving You," a 1962 Number One hit for Ray Charles. As a performer, he racked up 65 top 40 hits—and a number of pop ones—over a 40-year span starting in 1956. Self-dubbed the King of Country Soul, Don Gibson was a major, if not universally recognized, player on the country music stage.

Born in Shelby, North Carolina, on April 3, 1928, Gibson learned guitar "the same way thousands of other 'down-home' pickers learned," he told *Guitar Player,* "sitting on the back porches where the local musicians gathered. The older fellows would teach licks and runs to us younger guys."

At 19 he swung in to Knoxville, Tennessee, where he auditioned for the "American Barn Dance" program on KNOX radio and got hired as a rhythm guitar player. An occasional singer and regular presence on the show, he built popularity over time. RCA Records took notice and signed him in 1950, but success on vinyl was, at first, elusive. Two years later he shifted to Columbia; luck was no better.

Wesley Rose, of the music publishing giant Acuff-Rose, heard Gibson perform in a Knoxville club. Impressed with the singer, and especially with his tune "Sweet Dreams," Rose signed him on as a writer in what would be the beginning of a long and fruitful association.

"Sweet Dreams," issued on MGM in 1956, became Gibson's first hit (number nine). Over at RCA, guitarist Chet Atkins, in his capacity as producer, brought Gibson on board as Atkins' first signing to the label. Under Atkins' guidance, Gibson modernized his sound and struck gold in 1958 with the two-sided smash, "Oh Lonesome Me" (Number One) and "I Can't Stop Loving You" (number seven). For the next decade, Gibson rode the crest of his wave of fame, scoring the chart-topping "Blue Blue Day" and a collection of other hits and joining the Grand Ole Opry, where he handled multiple duties as a singer, guitarist, songwriter, and bandleader.

Despite personal problems in the late '60s, Gibson stayed on the charts, although his run of singles in the pop listings—which had lasted four years—never repeated. A switch over to the Hickory label in 1969 brought some revitalization, peaking with the Number One country "Woman (Sensuous Woman)" in 1972.

Noted for writing durable songs "as well known by the patrons of a fancy nightclub as they are by customers at a rural roadside tavern," as Robert Hilburn wrote in *BMI* magazine, Gibson heard his best material covered by a varied roster of interpreters. Emmylou Harris took "Sweet Dreams" to Number One in 1976, topping the success of other versions by Faron Young, Troy Seals, Reba McEntire, and Cline. Similarly, a Conway Twitty recording of "I Can't Stop Loving You" hit the chart peak, surpassing attempts by Kitty Wells, Sammi Smith, Mary K. Miller, and dozens of others. The haunting "Oh Lonesome Me" has enhanced the repertoires of Loggins and Messina, Johnny Cash, Stonewall Jackson, and the Kentucky Headhunters. Such has been the impact of the latter song that Gibson's reputation as a songwriter of lasting significance might have rested comfortably on it alone.

VINCE GILL

A gifted triple-threat talent—singer, instrumentalist, and songwriter—Vince Gill scored his first national chart success as lead singer for the rock band Pure Prairie League. In the mid-1980s he dedicated himself to country music and succeeded both as a highly respected session musician and as a solo recording artist noted especially for his smooth, compelling tenor voice and his handling of simple but powerful ballads.

Born the grandson of farmers and the son of a federal judge, Gill (b. Vince Grant Gill, Apr. 12, 1957, Norman, Oklahoma) was introduced to music early on by his banjo-playing father, Stan, who formed a country band when Vince was eight years old. "We'd play on flatbed trucks in parades in little towns," says Gill. "I still have a picture of the first time I played in front of anybody. I had this little four-string tenor guitar." At age 10 he was given a Gibson ES 335 electric guitar by his parents. Vince thrashed on that instrument over the next few years, and while still in high school he joined a local country-rock band called Mountain Smoke. They ended up recording a version of John Stewart's "July

TOP SONGS

OH LONESOME ME (RCA, '58, *1*)

BLUE BLUE DAY (RCA, '58, *1, 20 Pop*)

GIVE MYSELF A PARTY (RCA, '58, *5*)

WHO CARES (RCA, '59, *3*)

DON'T TELL ME YOUR TROUBLES (RCA, '59, *5*)

JUST ONE TIME (RCA, '60, *2, 29 Pop*)

SEA OF HEARTBREAK (RCA, '61, *2, 21 Pop*)

LONESOME NUMBER ONE (RCA, '61, *2*)

RINGS OF GOLD (RCA, '69, *2*)

WOMAN (SENSUOUS WOMAN) (Hickory, '72, *1*)

Additional Top 40 Country Songs: 45

Vince Gill

While in Kentucky, Gill met Ricky Skaggs and worked a short stint in Ricky's band, Boon Creek. Then, in 1979, he heard that Pure Prairie League was holding auditions for a lead singer. He went to the audition just to see if they remembered him from the time he'd opened for them in Oklahoma. They did and hired him on the spot as lead vocalist and lead guitarist. Gill wrote several songs that appeared on the three albums he recorded with the band, and he sang lead on their only top 10 hit, "Let Me Love You Tonight." After three years with the band, Vince quit and headed to Nashville. "I told them going in that my intention was to return to country music, so it wasn't a surprise to them," he explains.

Gill quickly established himself as a top session instrumentalist and background singer and spent a short time playing in Rodney Crowell's band the Cherry Bombs (as well as in Emmylou Harris' Hot Band) before signing with RCA Records. In 1984, he scored his first country chart record, a top 40 hit called "Victim of Life's Circumstances." He broke into the top 10 for the first time with "If It Weren't for Him" (featuring guest vocals by Rosanne Cash) in 1985.

Gill scored two more top 10 hits with RCA, but he never seemed to gain full acceptance at country radio or with the public. When he tried to take his music in a more traditional vein, RCA seemed less than enthusiastic. Gill requested that he be let out of his contract, and RCA agreed.

You're a Woman" that became a regional hit. "That was the first time I ever heard myself on the radio," Gill claims. "It was a blast, and being in a band was great—I was making four, five hundred dollars a week, which was pretty good for a kid." The band was good enough to open for acts like the Nitty Gritty Dirt Band and Pure Prairie League when they came through Oklahoma City.

Vince's musical focus shifted when he was 16. One day, after breaking a string on his father's banjo, he sought out a local fellow who played and fixed stringed instruments. "He asked me if I knew any bluegrass music," Gill recalls. "I said, 'Not much,' and he got out his acoustic guitar and played me some Flatt and Scruggs, Stanley Brothers, and Bill Monroe. He invited me to a couple of bluegrass gatherings, and I was hooked." Gill eventually added dobro, mandolin, fiddle, and banjo to the list of instruments he could play, and after graduating from high school, he passed up a golf scholarship to college and headed to Louisville, Kentucky, to briefly join a band called the Bluegrass Alliance.

TOP ALBUMS

WHEN I CALL YOUR NAME (MCA, '89)
POCKET FULL OF GOLD (MCA, '91)
I STILL BELIEVE IN YOU (MCA, '92)

TOP SONGS

WHEN I CALL YOUR NAME (MCA, '89, 2)
I STILL BELIEVE IN YOU (MCA, '92, 1)
DON'T LET YOUR LOVE START SLIPPIN' AWAY
(MCA, '92, 1)
THE HEART WON'T LIE (with Reba McEntire,
MCA, '93, 1)
ONE MORE LAST CHANCE (MCA, '93, 1)
WHENEVER YOU COME AROUND (MCA, '94, 1)

Additional Top 40 Country Songs: 27

He moved over to MCA Records and scored a number two smash in 1989 with the title tune of his first album for the label, "When I Call Your Name." The song included some memorable harmonies from Patty Loveless and became the Country Music Association's Single of the Year. That slow, heartfelt country ballad was a prototype for some of his biggest hits to follow, such as "Look at Us" and "I Still Believe in You."

Gill entered the 1990s with an impressive track record as a recording artist. He added to it by becoming one of the top 10 draws on the concert trail as well as a two-time winner of the Country Music Association's Entertainer of the Year award. "I just want to be remembered as someone that cared about country music in its entirety," he says. "About the players, about the writers, about the business, and about the history—where it started and where it's headed."

MICKEY GILLEY

Ferriday, Louisiana, is not a big town, but it produced three very famous Americans: Reverend Jimmy Swaggart, Jerry Lee Lewis, and their cousin, Mickey Gilley. For a long time Gilley lived in the shadow of his more famous kin, accused of copping Jerry Lee's piano style during early years on the tough southwestern honky-tonk circuit and in failed attempts to start a recording career. That all changed in 1971, when he became part owner of a sprawling nightclub in the Houston suburb of Pasadena, Texas. Gilley and his club drew national attention when it became the setting for the 1979 John Travolta film *Urban Cowboy*. The resulting burst of country music popularity added to what would be Gilley's final tally of 17 Number One country hits.

Gilley (b. Mar. 9, 1936) says that when he was growing up in Ferriday, Swaggart and Lewis were as close to him as brothers. He recalls sitting beside Jerry Lee at the piano as they played with the wild, home-grown style that characterizes their keyboard artistry. "At one point I decided to take piano lessons, thinking I should know how to read music, but the teacher refused to give me lessons because it might mess me up more than help me," Gilley says. At first, Gilley didn't take music as seriously as Lewis, and he headed off to Houston when he was

17 to take a job as a mechanic. Not long after that, Lewis scored his first hit, "Crazy Arms," and Gilley went to see him in concert. "I took him to the airport afterwards," Gilley recalls, "and he pulled out a big wad of hundred dollar bills. It made me decide right then that I was in the wrong business."

He spent the late 1950s and '60s working Houston area clubs and then moved to New Orleans, Biloxi, Mobile, and Lake Charles, Louisiana. Along the way he recorded for Dot Records and a succession of small labels, even charting in 1969 for Paula Records. He just couldn't find the handle, and for a short time gave up on the music business. He moved back to Houston and worked construction for six months. Then he got a gig at a Pasadena nightclub called the Nasadel. Without the pressure to "make it" in the business, Gilley slowly built a local following and started making good money. He met a local businessman named Sherwood Cryer who believed in Gilley's talent enough to go into business with him, and together they opened Gilley's Club.

The more the club prospered, the less Gilley was motivated to put himself through the agony of searching for a record contract. However, in 1973 a local jukebox distributor talked him into recording a couple of songs for her string of jukeboxes. Getting him back in the studio resulted in his recording "Room Full of Roses." Released on Astro Records, it became a big regional hit before being picked up by Playboy Records and taken to the top of the country chart and to number 50 on the pop chart.

Between 1974 and '78, Gilley scored a total of seven Number One songs with Playboy, including "City Lights," "Don't the Girls All Get Prettier at

---

TOP SONGS

ROOM FULL OF ROSES (Playboy, '74, *1*)
DON'T THE GIRLS ALL GET PRETTIER AT CLOSING
    TIME (Playboy, '77, *1*)
TRUE LOVE WAYS (Epic, '80, *1*)
STAND BY ME (Full Moon, '80, *1, 22 Pop*)
THAT'S ALL THAT MATTERS (Epic, '80, *1*)
A HEADACHE TOMORROW (OR A HEARTACHE
    TONIGHT) (Epic, '81, *1*)
PUT YOUR DREAMS AWAY (Epic, '82, *1*)
TALK TO ME (Epic, '82, *1*)
FOOL FOR YOUR LOVE (Epic, '83, *1*)

Additional Top 40 Country Songs: 32

Closing Time," and "She's Pulling Me Back Again." When he moved over to Epic in 1978 he continued as a top 10 act, but after the release of the *Urban Cowboy* movie he was seldom out of the top spot for the next three years. Included among the new string of country chart-toppers was "Stand by Me" (also number 22 pop), from the movie soundtrack album.

In 1986 Gilley and Sherwood Cryer dissolved their partnership, and Gilley's Club eventually closed down. Gilley's chart presence diminished as well. His most recent chart appearance occurred in 1989, the year of a new surge in country music popularity and exactly 10 years after the so-called urban cowboy movement in which Gilley had played such a key role.

VERN GOSDIN

As a member of the Gosdin Brothers and as a solo artist over three decades, Vern Gosdin developed a classic country vocal style that made him a favorite among his peers and inspired

Vern Gosdin

TOP ALBUMS

CHISELED IN STONE (Columbia, '88)
ALONE (Columbia, '89)

TOP SONGS

HANGIN' ON (the Gosdin Brothers, Bakersfield International, '67, *37*)
IF YOU'RE GONNA DO ME WRONG (DO IT RIGHT) (Compleat, '83, *5*)
WAY DOWN DEEP (Compleat, '83, *5*)
I CAN TELL BY THE WAY YOU DANCE (YOU'RE GONNA LOVE ME TONIGHT) (Compleat, '84, *1*)
DO YOU BELIEVE ME NOW (Columbia, '87, *4*)
SET 'EM UP JOE (Columbia, '88, *1*)
WHO YOU GONNA BLAME IT ON THIS TIME (Columbia, '89, *2*)
I'M STILL CRAZY (Columbia, '89, *1*)

Additional Top 40 Country Songs: 23

critics to rank him up with Merle Haggard and George Jones as one of the best to ever sing a country song.

He was born in Woodland, Alabama, on August 5, 1934, to a farm family. "I've been singing as long as I can remember," he says. "I sang in church and always loved it. If you loved singing as much as I did, I don't think there was any way to get away from it." With his brothers Rex and Ray, he organized the Gosdin Family Gospel Show that appeared on radio in Birmingham. In 1953 he drifted to Atlanta and later to Chicago, where he opened a country nightclub called the D&G Tap.

In 1960, Vern joined his brother Rex in California. They hooked up with a bluegrass band called the Golden State Boys that eventually included Chris Hillman and evolved into the Hillmen. The brothers decided to move on to country music, and in 1967 they scored a top 40 hit on Bakersfield International with "Hangin' On"—the one and only hit for the brothers and the label. While they were trying to hang on in California, Vern wrote a song called "Someone to Turn To" that ended up in the popular film *Easy Rider*. Unable to get something else going on the West Coast, the frustrated brothers retired from show business and each opened a window glass business in Atlanta.

Gosdin stayed out of the music industry for the

next several years. Then, in 1976, producer Gary Paxton talked him into recording again. This time it was as a solo artist on Elektra Asylum Records. His first solo release—a top 20 country hit—was a remake of "Hangin' On."

Gosdin remained a frequent visitor to the top 40 through the late 1970s, hitting the top 10 with "Yesterday's Gone," "Till the End," and "Never My Love."

He stayed in the top 10 in the early '80s in spite of a series of label changes, collecting his first Number One in 1984 on Compleat Records with "I Can Tell by the Way You Dance (You're Gonna Love Me Tonight)." In 1987, Gosdin's career seemed to slip again, and he left Compleat. "I was about to give up on Nashville and go out to California," he says. "Merle [Haggard] had offered to record some stuff at his studios that I might pitch on TV, but when Bob Montgomery [head of Columbia Nashville] heard about that, he offered to sign me at Columbia Records." That turned out to be a great move for both label and Gosdin. His album *Chiseled in Stone* was recorded for a measly $30,000, yet it became Gosdin's first gold record, was nominated for a Grammy, and yielded four top 10 hits, including Gosdin's second Number One, "Set 'Em Up Joe," a marvelous tribute to country legend Ernest Tubb.

Gosdin's run of success on Columbia continued into the 1990s, when, in his fifties, he was at the peak of his career amid a youth movement sweeping country music.

JACK GREENE

Early in the 1960s, before he embarked on his solo career, Greene earned the nickname the Jolly Green Giant. For a time in the later part of that decade, he was a giant of country music.

Greene (b. Jan. 7, 1930, Maryville, Tennessee) began his career in the late 1940s when he played guitar for the Atlanta-based group the Cherokee Trio. A multi-instrumentalist, Greene became the drummer of the Rhythm Ranch Boys in 1950 and the Peachtree Cowboys later in the decade. But he began earning a reputation more as a vocalist than a guitarist or drummer.

While a member of Ernest Tubb's Texas Troubadours in the 1960s, Greene pursued a solo career. In

---

TOP SONGS

THERE GOES MY EVERYTHING (Decca, '66, *1*)
ALL THE TIME (Decca, '67, *1*)
WHAT LOCKS THE DOOR (Decca, '67, *2*)
YOU ARE MY TREASURE (Decca, '68, *1*)
LOVE TAKES CARE OF ME (Decca, '68, *4*)
UNTIL MY DREAMS COME TRUE (Decca, '68, *1*)
STATUE OF A FOOL (Decca, '69, *1*)
BACK IN THE ARMS OF LOVE (Decca, '69, *4*)
WISH I DIDN'T HAVE TO MISS YOU (Decca, '69, *2*)
I NEED SOMEBODY BAD (Decca, '73, *11*)

Additional Top 40 Country Songs: 13

1965, he recorded the single "Ever Since My Baby Went Away," the middling success of which was enough to encourage him to continue full-time. He formed his own group, the Jolly Green Giants (later named the Renegades), and recorded the single "There Goes My Everything" in 1966. It hit Number One on the country chart and brought Greene rapid recognition. In 1967, he dominated the Country Music Association awards, winning in the categories of Best Male Vocalist, Best Album, Best Single, and Best Song.

Greene remained on the country charts through the end of the decade, scoring four more Number One hits. At that point he changed course and teamed with Jeannie Seely, his co-star on the Ernest Tubb television show. The two fashioned a glitzy touring show with a Las Vegas feel that was far different from the traditional approach Green had taken up to that point.

But if the new act was different from his old, it was just as successful, onstage and on record, starting out with the number two hit "Wish I Didn't Have to Miss You" in 1969. Over the next 12 years, the duo performed at various major venues all over the world, including New York's Madison Square Garden and London's Wembley arena.

When they dissolved the act, Greene returned to music that was much closer to his original country sound. He signed with the Frontline label and recorded the singles "Yours for the Taking," "The Rock I'm Leaning On," and "Devil's Den." In 1983 he switched to the EMH label. Although subsequent chart entries remained at lower levels, Greene continued to record and perform on a steady basis.

LEE GREENWOOD

T he 1980s were the years of Reagan, MTV, Madonna, and Michael Jackson's *Thriller*. They also encompassed Lee Greenwood's years of peak activity on the country music airwaves and popularity charts. His distinctly middle-of-the-road style of country pop, yielding seven Number One hits from 1983 to '86 and the Country Music Association's 1984 Song of the Year, "God Bless the USA," proved him ideally suited to the tastes of a mainstream, slightly older listenership. Though he came late to the recording industry—debuting when he was about 39—Greenwood's prior years were spent productively, in an appropriate training ground for the kind of music he opted to perform.

His mother had been a professional pianist, his father had played saxophone, and Lee (b. Melvin Lee Greenwood, Oct. 27, 1942, Southgate, California) was destined to play both. Raised in Sacramento, he was blowing saxophone by age 12 and doing it professionally in the band of Del Reeves (who hit Number One in 1965 with "Girl on the Billboard") by his mid-teens. Later, he formed the Moonbeams and then the Apollos, who landed a contract to play in Las Vegas. When the band left for Hawaii, Greenwood stayed behind, beginning what would be two decades of activity on the Nevada casino-and-lounge circuit.

A big break just missed him in the mid-'60s: Greenwood's road gig with a group called the Scotties came to an end. Two of the members invited Lee to work with them in a band; Greenwood opted instead for the security of Vegas. Had he decided otherwise, he might have rocketed to fame with the two musicians, Felix Cavaliere and Dino Danelli, and their band, the Young Rascals. Greenwood missed out again in 1971 when he signed with Paramount Records only to have his first single, "My First Day Alone with You," shelved and his recording career put on hold.

In Nevada, Greenwood honed his skills in the ultimate boot camp of the entertainment business, writing and arranging show tunes, singing, playing keyboards and saxes (occasionally two at a time), leading bands, and covering pop, rock, and country styles—and dealing cards when not on stage. It was at a piano bar in Reno that Mel Tillis' bassist heard Greenwood performing and suggested he cut records in Nashville. A contract with MCA soon followed,

along with a debut single, "It Turns Me Inside Out," produced by MCA exec Jerry Crutchfield.

Greenwood's distinctively husky voice was the chief sales tool for his outpouring of product, and it worked through a run of top 10 country hits that was broken only once between 1982 and late 1987. The country music establishment took near-immediate notice. For two years in a row—1983 and '84—Greenwood was voted Male Vocalist of the Year by the Country Music Association. (It was a month after receiving the first of these honors that he scored his first Number One hit, "Somebody's Gonna Love You.") In 1984 he won a Grammy Award for Top Country Vocal Performance by a Male (for his work on the number six hit "I.O.U."). And in that same year—just three years into his recording career—he paired with country icon Barbara Mandrell for an album, *Made for Each Other*, and single, "It Should Have Been Love by Now."

Following four Number One hits in a row in 1985–86, plus a top 10 and another Number One, Greenwood's popularity began to dim slightly. When he switched from MCA to Capitol Records in 1990 a boost resulted ("Holdin' a Good Hand," number two, 1990), preceding a return to middling chart rankings.

As eclectic in fields of involvement as in types of instruments played and music performed, Greenwood has had parallel success as a songwriter, plac-

TOP ALBUMS

INSIDE OUT (MCA, '82)
SOMEBODY'S GONNA LOVE YOU (MCA, '83)

TOP SONGS

SOMEBODY'S GONNA LOVE YOU (MCA, '83, *1*)
GOING, GOING, GONE (MCA, '83, *1*)
DIXIE ROAD (MCA, '85, *1*)
I DON'T MIND THE THORNS (IF YOU'RE THE ROSE) (MCA, '85, *1*)
DON'T UNDERESTIMATE MY LOVE FOR YOU (MCA, '85, *1*)
HEARTS AREN'T MADE TO BREAK (THEY'RE MADE TO LOVE) (MCA, '86, *1*)
MORNIN' RIDE (MCA, '86, *1*)
HOLDIN' A GOOD HAND (Capitol, '90, *2*)

Additional Top 40 Country Songs: 45

ing his material with Kenny Rogers ("A Love Song," number three, 1982) and with such notable others as Brenda Lee, Mel Tillis, and T. G. Sheppard. And ever the musical journeyman, he's sidelined as a jingle singer—even during country fame.

MERLE HAGGARD

Merle Haggard

Few country artists have had a life as full of experience, from the disastrous to the triumphant, as Merle Haggard. Childhood poverty, the early death of his father, a troubled youth, prison, a tumultuous personal life, substance abuse—he's lived it all. Even fewer country artists can translate their experiences into musical expression with the eloquence that Haggard has on the way to becoming a country legend in his own time—a singer and songwriter whose influence will assuredly be timeless thanks to classic songs like "Mama Tried," "Okie from Muskogee," and "Big City."

Haggard (b. Merle Ronald Haggard, Apr. 6, 1937, Bakersfield, California) was born into a family of Oklahomans who had migrated to California during the Great Depression to find a better life. For a while, life did get mildly better. His father got a job with the railroad, and they moved into an old railroad car that his father turned into a home. "This lady had an old Santa Fe refrigerator car on her property," Haggard recalls. "My dad made a deal with her that he'd convert it into a house. He cut the back and front sides out, built rooms out from that, and made it a fairly livable situation."

Haggard's grandfather and father were fiddle players, and his dad filled their home with the music of Jimmie Rodgers and Bob Wills. (Haggard learned to play fiddle and would play the music of Bob Wills in his shows throughout his career.) His brother provided his first guitar; a patron at a service station where his brother worked hocked the guitar for a couple of dollars worth of gas and never reclaimed it. It was Haggard's mother who taught him his first chords.

Haggard's life took a sharp turn when he was nine years old. His father died of a brain tumor, and the son reacted with anger at the loss. He began running away by jumping freight trains. "I grew up fast," he recalls. "At 12 or 13 I was full grown. I just wanted to go to work so I wouldn't be a burden to my mother. My truancy problem began then, and

they threw me into juvenile hall. Finally I got to thinking I was an outlaw and started acting like one."

He once broke into a fire prevention store to steal a chest protector and then, with some drunken buddies, broke through the back door of a bar that happened to be open for business. He got six months to 15 years in San Quentin prison. After spending some of his time near death row, he vowed to turn his life around. Already a country performer, he was inspired by a Johnny Cash show at the prison in the late 1950s. Haggard went from troublemaker to model prisoner, joined the warden's band, and was paroled at age 21.

He went back to Bakersfield, where he dug ditches by day and began singing in the rough honky-tonks at night. By the early 1960s, Bakersfield had become a thriving music center boasting the likes of Buck Owens, Ferlin Husky, and Bonnie Owens. In 1962, Haggard became part of it when he was signed by Louis Tally to Tally Records.

Haggard's first chart record, "Sing a Sad Song," appeared in late 1963 and peaked at number 19. He collected two more top 40 hits with Tally, including his first top 10 "(My Friends Are Gonna Be) Strangers," before switching to Capitol Records.

In 1966, his second Capitol release, "Swinging Doors," hit top five, and Haggard's career rocketed. From 1966 to '77, he released 38 records, only two of which scored lower than the top 10; the remainder charted in the top five and included 24 Number One songs. "The Fugitive" was the first to top the chart, followed soon by such classics as "Branded Man," "Sing Me Back Home," "Mama Tried," "Hungry Eyes," "Workin' Man Blues," and "Okie from Muskogee."

"Okie from Muskogee" hit in 1969 at the height of the antiwar and counterculture movements in America. It became an anthem for a segment of the populace—later dubbed "the silent majority"—who reacted against hippies and the general social upheaval. According to Haggard, the song polarized the two groups. It also triggered some surprising reactions. "I was on a plane one time," says Haggard, "and a well-dressed guy tapped me on the shoulder and said, 'I was one of those hippies you were singing about on Hollywood Boulevard, and your song "Muskogee" turned my life around. Now I'm an attorney.'"

Throughout his career, Haggard continued to stand for patriotism and concerns of the common man with songs like "The Fightin' Side of Me," "Big City," "I Think I'll Just Stay Here and Drink," and "It's Been a Great Afternoon."

Married several times (Bonnie Owens and Leona Williams were country-singing wives), Haggard remains a complex man who describes himself as "very unpredictable." The future impact of his music, however—given his legacy of beautiful country songs and his astounding lifetime total of 36 Number One hits—is anything but unpredictable.

TOP SONGS

THE FUGITIVE (Capitol, '66, 1)

SING ME BACK HOME (Capitol, '67, 1)

MAMA TRIED (Capitol, '68, 1)

WORKIN' MAN BLUES (Capitol, '69, 1)

OKIE FROM MUSKOGEE (Capitol, '69, 1)

BIG CITY (Epic, '82, 1)

GOING WHERE THE LONELY GO (Epic, '82,)

THAT'S THE WAY LOVE GOES (Epic, '83, 1)

NATURAL HIGH (Epic, '85, 1)

TWINKLE TWINKLE LUCKY STAR (Epic, '87,)

Additional Top 40 Country Songs: 72

TOM T. HALL

The writer of Jeannie C. Riley's massive 1968 Number One country and pop hit, "Harper Valley P.T.A.," Tom T. Hall is known as the Storyteller, and his style of writing has been described as "musical journalism." Dipping into his own life experiences for subject matter, he has produced a catalog of songs unique in their vivid imagery and characterizations, slice-of-life authenticity, and humorous turns of phrase. That has made Hall outstanding among songwriters in any style, as indicated by his 54 top 100 country hits registered between 1967 and 1986.

He has also been a deejay, copywriter, touring performer, writer of an instruction book, teacher, autobiographer, novelist, television personality, and board member for the Nashville Songwriters' Association and the Country Music Association.

Hall was born on May 25, 1936, in Tick Ridge, Kentucky, the son of a brick-plant worker. Hall took to words early, writing poetry when he was eight and starting to write songs at age nine. His father was shot in a fishing accident when Hall was 15. To help pay the bills, Hall quit school and went to work in a garment factory. But he also began playing music—at 16 he formed the Kentucky Travelers, a band of bluegrassers who worked their area's school circuit. They also performed on a local radio program. When the band split, Hall stayed on as a deejay. (He had written a jingle for a sponsor, the Polar Bear Flour Company.)

He did an Army stint from 1957 to '61, completing his high school requirements during the period and continuing to write songs, which he'd play for other soldiers. Back in the States, he got a deejay job at station WBLU in Salem, Virginia, and enrolled in Roanoke College to study journalism.

Hall has described a key incident in which a songwriter showed up at the radio station one day, and he and Hall went to Hall's small office for some impromptu music making. "They call it guitar pullin'," Hall said. "You know what that is: I'll sing a song, you pull the guitar away, and the other guy sings a song. I started singing him some songs, and he said, 'Golly, where did you get those songs?' I said, 'I wrote 'em.' He said, 'My God, I'm gonna take those songs to Nashville.' That was it. His name was Harold Postwaite—real weird name. I don't know whatever happened to him, but he brought those songs down and gave 'em to Jimmy Key. And [Key] called me up and said, 'Did you really write these songs? We like 'em, and we're gonna sign you up to a songwriting contract.'

With Jimmy Key's publishing company, New Key, Hall began writing full out. And his songs were soon placed with artists: Jimmy C. Newman and Dave Dudley both scored top 10s with Hall tunes in 1963 and '64, respectively. One year later, Johnny Wright hit Number One country with Hall's "Hello Vietnam." Royalties were soon allowing Hall a comfortable existence doing the work he liked.

Performing was not high on his list of priorities, yet Nashville began indicating interest in his doing just that. No doubt aware that more recordings meant more songs generating royalties, Hall signed with Mercury Records in 1967. His career then shifted gear. He had an initial hit with "I Washed My Face in the Morning Dew" in 1967. One year later, Jeannie C. Riley rode to the top with "Harper Valley P.T.A.," which Hall had written in response to a request for a "tell it like it is" story, coming up with a tale based on that of a woman in his hometown who'd told off a school P.T.A. group for disapproving of the way she raised her child.

Then began Hall's own run of chart winners. "A Week in a Country Jail" was his first Number One as a performer-writer, hitting in 1969. Five top 40 hits followed until his next Number One, "The Year That

Tom T. Hall

Clayton Delaney Died," a song about a recently deceased guitar player who'd been a childhood influence of Hall's. The tune became a Hall signature.

While Hall's pop chart presence was limited, he did reach number 12 in 1973 with "I Love," a country chart-topper that, simply enough, listed the things Hall loves. An established performer by this time, Hall toured extensively with his band, the Storytellers, and racked up television appearances on such programs as "Hee Haw" and "Midnight Special," among many more as time went on.

During this period of musical achievement (five more Number Ones through 1976), Hall penned a book on songwriting, published by Harper and Row. He later began to lean heavily toward prose writing, producing a semi-autobiography, *The Storyteller's Nashville,* in 1979 and the novel *The Laughing Man of Woodmont* in 1982. Serious

TOP ALBUMS

IN SEARCH OF A SONG (Mercury, '71)
THE ESSENTIAL TOM T. HALL (Polygram, '88)

TOP SONGS

A WEEK IN A COUNTRY JAIL (Mercury, '69, 1)
THE YEAR THAT CLAYTON DELANEY DIED
    (Mercury, '71, 1)
(OLD DOGS, CHILDREN AND) WATERMELON WINE
    (Mercury, '72, 1)
I LOVE (Mercury, '73, 1, 12 Pop)
THAT SONG IS DRIVING ME CRAZY (Mercury, '74, 2)
COUNTRY IS (Mercury, '74, 1)
I CARE (Mercury, '74, 1)
FASTER HORSES (THE COWBOY AND THE POET)
    (Mercury, '76, 1)

Additional Top 40 Country Songs: 31

about writers and literature, Hall once told *Newsweek,* "I like to think there was a direct line from *Spoon River Anthology* to *Babbitt* to, God forgive me, 'Harper Valley P.T.A.'"

Hall's chart activity began to settle in the 1980s. But his songs remain durable, having proven effective vehicles for the likes of George Jones, Johnny Cash, Flatt and Scruggs, Burl Ives, Bobby Bare, and a slew of others. Long a member of the Grand Ole Opry, the recipient of a Grammy, and a contributor to humane causes, Hall was honored in 1990 with a chair in creative writing at Middle Tennessee State University established in his name.

GEORGE HAMILTON IV

While most of the major country acts base their careers in the United States, Hamilton made his name primarily in other countries, particularly in Europe. As a result he became the self-styled International Ambassador of Country Music.

Hamilton was the first U.S. country performer to appear in the Soviet Union. He hosted a television program in Canada for a time and recorded a number of songs by that country's Gordon Lightfoot. He worked extensively in England and eventually settled there with his family. And he has recorded and performed with various European groups, including Czechoslovakia's Jiri Brabeck and the Country Beat.

Hamilton began his singular career in rock and roll. Born July 19, 1937, in Winston-Salem, North Carolina, he grew up listening to the music of the singing cowboy Gene Autry, along with traditional country artists like Hank Snow, Hank Williams, and Little Jimmy Dickens. In fact, he began his career with a demo recording of the latter's song "Out Behind the Barn" in the mid-1950s. The demo wasn't released on record, but it came to the attention of Nashville talent scout Orville Campbell, who subsequently introduced Hamilton to rock songwriter J. D. Loudermilk.

Hamilton recorded Loudermilk's "A Rose and Baby Ruth" in 1956, and the record became a major hit, selling over one million copies. But it was a rock rather than a country record, and Hamilton soon became a part of the burgeoning rock scene of the time. He toured with such performers as Buddy Holly and Gene Vincent, appeared on disc jockey Alan Freed's program, and was touted as a new rock idol.

But when his rock career failed to materialize, Hamilton moved to Nashville in the late 1950s and shifted to a country sound. He became a performer at the Grand Ole Opry and was signed by RCA Records, one of the leading country labels.

While Hamilton became something of a success in Nashville, he took an increasingly broad musical approach, by the early 1960s turning to sources from the hootenanny scene of the time. Hamilton was a fan of such folk acts as Bob Dylan and Peter, Paul and Mary, and he incorporated many of their musical ideas into his own music. He also became acquainted with Lightfoot in 1965 and began a long collaboration with the Canadian singer-songwriter. It was his friendship with Lightfoot that pushed Hamilton in a more middle-of-the-road direction. It also drew him into the Canadian musical scene. By the mid-1970s Hamilton had become a fixture there, hosting "North Country," his own television program.

Along the way, Hamilton also began to perform in Europe, initially touring U.S. Army bases on the continent. He made his British debut in 1967 on the BBC program "Country Meets Folk." Over the next few years he became a frequent visitor to England, performing on television and onstage (he appeared in that country's preeminent country music showcase, the annual Country Music Festival at Wembley). In the 1970s he was signed to the British record label Anchor. Using Britain as a base, he has continued to be a presence on the country scene throughout western Europe.

TOP SONGS

BEFORE THIS DAY ENDS (ABC-Paramount, '60, 4)

THREE STEPS TO THE PHONE (MILLIONS OF MILES) (RCA, '61, 9)

IF YOU DON'T KNOW I AIN'T GONNA TELL YOU (RCA, '62, 6)

ABILENE (RCA, '63, *1, 15 Pop*)

FORT WORTH, DALLAS OR HOUSTON (RCA, '64, 9)

TRUCK DRIVING MAN (RCA, '64, 11)

EARLY MORNING RAIN (RCA, '66, 9)

URGE FOR GOING (RCA '67, 7)

BREAK MY MIND (RCA, '67, 6)

SHE'S A LITTLE BIT COUNTRY (RCA, '70, 3)

Additional Top 40 Country Songs: 22

EMMYLOU HARRIS

Emmylou Harris

A traditionalist long before the neotraditional movement; a purveyor of unfettered, straightforward country sound; and the possessor of a distinctively clear and sweet soprano voice, Emmylou Harris has also been called the Queen of Country Rock. Few artists have so comfortably crossed the line between those two genres; for more than 20 years, armed with excellent musical taste and a series of top-flight backup bands, Harris has pointed the way for legions of up-and-coming, tradition-minded artists while carrying the torch of rock-oriented country pioneered by Gram Parsons in the early 1970. "Her great contribution was fusing the sexual primitive thing of rock and the language, poetry, and human storytelling of country," said onetime band member Rodney Crowell in *People.*

Harris is also a noted aficionado of songs and songwriters, filling her repertoire with varied nuggets of American music and imbuing them with country's characteristic simplicity and emotional power. "My main job in life is to find songs and interpret them," she told Robert Hilburn of the *Los Angeles Times.*

The daughter of a Marine pilot and raised mostly in Washington, D.C., suburbs, Harris (b. Apr. 2, 1947, Birmingham, Alabama) grew up listening mainly to folk music—people like Joan Baez, Judy Collins, and Tom Rush. She began playing guitar and singing in public after high school and studied drama at the University of North Carolina. After getting accepted into Boston University's drama program, Harris turned her attention more directly to music and moved to New York to delve into the Greenwich Village folk scene. She was there for two years, meeting musicians, recording a little-heard folk album called *Gliding Bird,* and getting married and having a child.

Harris moved to Nashville briefly, her marriage ended, and she returned to the Washington area. Chris Hillman of the Flying Burrito Brothers heard her sing and mentioned her to his ex-bandmate (and onetime member of the Byrds) Gram Parsons. Months later she was singing and performing with Parsons, an involvement that would continue until his death in 1973 and place her on three seminal country-rock albums: *GP* (1973), *Grievous Angel* (1974), and *Gram Parsons and the Fallen Angels Live 1973.* It would also alter the direction of her

music, leading her away from pure folk and toward a blend of electrified country with strong, folk-influenced lyrics. Essentially this was a perpetuation of Parsons' vision, which she summarized as wanting to "see kids in overalls and black people and all people boogying to country lyrics and digging Charlie Pride and George Jones and Merle Haggard and all those people...because he loved those authentic performers."

Harris launched her solo career after Parsons died, working with his producer Brian Ahern (and marrying him in 1975) and assembling the first edition of what became known, accurately, as the Hot Band. An early lineup included ex–Elvis Presley band members James Burton (guitar), Glen D. Hardin (keyboards), and Emory Gordy (bass) plus John Ware (drums) and Hank DeVito (pedal steel). Subsequent personnel would include such later-to-be-noted players as Rodney Crowell, Albert Lee, Ricky Skaggs, Tony Brown, and Vince Gill.

Harris' first album, 1975's *Pieces of the Sky,* hit Number One country and effectively drew attention to her solo capabilities, as did a cover of the Louvin Brothers'"If I Could Only Win Your Love" that went top five. From that point through the early 1990s, Harris remained a frequent presence on the country charts, tallying 38 top 40 singles, seven of which hit Number One. She also crossed over to pop, with one top 40 song (1981's "Mister Sandman") and six top 40 albums.

Tapping such writers as Buck Owens ("Together Again"), Don Gibson ("Sweet Dreams"), and Delbert McClinton ("Two More Bottles of Wine") and serving as writer of other songs, Harris marked the early part of her career with a series of albums produced by Ahern and issued on Reprise and Warner Brothers Records. *Elite Hotel* (1976), *Luxury Liner* (1977), and *Quarter Moon in a Ten Cent Town* (1978) were key discs from this period.

In 1979, as Nashville leaned toward sweetened country-pop, Harris went in another direction and recorded the bluegrass-flavored *Blue Kentucky Girl,* gaining a Grammy Award (she'd eventually collect six) for Best Country Vocal Performance by a Female. The following year's *Roses in the Snow*—also bluegrass-oriented—led to her being elected the Country Music Association's Female Vocalist of the Year.

Several albums and numerous hits later, Harris split with Ahern and moved to Nashville, soon to marry songwriter and producer Paul Kennerley. 1985's *The Ballad of Sally Rose*—to which Kennerley contributed—proved to be an unusual undertaking, as it involved Harris' writing most of the material. It was followed two albums later by *Trio,* a long-awaited full-album collaboration between Harris and country-pop divas Linda Ronstadt and Dolly Parton, which yielded the Number One "To Know Him Is to Love Him" and three top 10s. Harris' most recent Number One, recorded with Earl Thomas Conley, was 1988's "We Believe in Happy Endings."

In 1990, needing both a musical change and an easing of vocal strain, Harris folded the Hot Band and put together the equally hot but all-acoustic backup group the Nash Ramblers. By this time Harris' new albums were selling less—a result, perhaps, of the influx of young, neotraditional artists whose presence she had helped make possible. But Harris' long-term reputation was solidly in place, carrying with it an audience whose loyalty was not dependent on periodic fluctuations in the marketplace.

FREDDIE HART

Freddie Hart was one of the major country stars of the 1970s. During that decade he scored dozens of hits with his sleek, commercial sound and earnest vocals.

Not that he came to fame quickly. In fact, by the time the '70s rolled down the pike, Hart was approaching middle age. This may have accounted for the mature, pop-tinged quality that made his music widely popular.

Hart was something of a rover in his youth, trying his hand at a number of trades before making his way to the country scene. He was born Fred Segrest on December 21, 1933, in Lochapoka, Alabama, into a family of 15. He began noticing music at age five when his uncle gave him a guitar made from a cigar box.

As he grew older, Hart worked at everything from cotton picking to pipeline laying, everywhere from Texas to New York, all before he reached the age of 20.

After a stint in the Marines, Hart spent time in Los Angeles early in the 1950s, teaching martial arts at

---

TOP ALBUMS

ELITE HOTEL (Reprise, '76)
ROSES IN THE SNOW (Warner, '80)

TOP SONGS

TOGETHER AGAIN (Reprise, '76, *1*)
ONE OF THESE DAYS (Reprise, '76, *3*)
SWEET DREAMS (Reprise, '76, *1*)
TWO MORE BOTTLES OF WINE (Warner, '78, *1*)
BENEATH STILL WATERS (Warner, '80, *1*)
(LOST HIS LOVE) ON OUR LAST DATE (Warner, '82, *1*)

Dolly Parton, Linda Ronstadt, Emmylou Harris:
TO KNOW HIM IS TO LOVE HIM (Warner, '87, *1*)

Earl Thomas Conley and Emmylou Harris:
WE BELIEVE IN HAPPY ENDINGS (RCA, '88, *1*)

Additional Top 40 Country Songs: 30

the L.A. Police Academy. At the same time, he began playing country music with his friend Lefty Frizzell.

By 1953 Hart had decided to become a country soloist. With Frizzell's help he secured a contract with Capitol Records. But for the rest of the decade, Hart's career was disappointing. Switching from Capitol to Columbia Records, he scored a modest hit, "The Wall," in 1959. During the 1960s Hart toured and recorded constantly on various labels, entering the charts a number of times, but not at the highest rankings.

That changed in 1971 when his single "Easy Loving" hit Number One and sold more than a million copies. The song was subsequently named the Song of the Year by the Country Music Association in 1971 and 1972.

"'Easy Loving' was the first contemporary [country] song," Hart said. "It [made] sex a pretty thing. …One line—'one called so sexy looking'—it kind of opened the door for 'Behind Closed Doors,' 'Help Me Make It Through the Night,' that kind of [song]. I guess there have been two hundred songs written from 'Easy Loving.'"

After the success of that record, through the rest of the 1970s, Hart was one of the preeminent performers on the country scene, regularly visiting the chart's top five with such songs as "My Hang-Up Is You" and "Got the All Overs for You (All Over Me)" (both from 1972); "Super Kind of Woman" (1973); "If You Can't Feel It (It Ain't There)" and "The Want-To's" (1974), and a number of others.

Hart's songs were constantly covered by other country artists. "Loose Talk" was recorded by more than 50 performers.

TOP SONGS

EASY LOVING (Capitol, '71, *1*)

MY HANG-UP IS YOU (Capitol, '72, *1*)

BLESS YOUR HEART (Capitol, '72, *1*)

GOT THE ALL OVERS FOR YOU (ALL OVER ME) (Capitol, '72, *1*)

SUPER KIND OF WOMAN (Capitol, '73, *1*)

TRIP TO HEAVEN (Capitol, '73, *1*)

IF YOU CAN'T FEEL IT (IT AIN'T THERE) (Capitol, '73, *3*)

HANG IN THERE GIRL (Capitol, '74, *2*)

THE WANT-TO'S (Capitol, '74, *3*)

THE FIRST TIME (Capitol '75, *2*)

Additional Top 40 Country Songs: 18

Toward the end of the 1970s, Hart's career began to slide. He signed with the much smaller label Sunbird, and the hits evaporated. Hart diversified, spending much of his time investing in a trucking company, breeding bulls, farming, and painting. He established a school for handicapped children in Burbank, California. It was almost as if Hart's country career was a side trip on a long and varied journey.

HIGHWAY 101

"Hard country with a rock and roll backbeat," says drummer Scott "Cactus" Moser of the Highway 101 sound. The act started out as a rarity in country music: a full-time, cohesive quartet fronted by a female singer. The format reflected manager Chuck Morris' original vision of "a band where all the players contributed equally to the music, making it far more powerful than your average female vocalist singing with either hired studio musicians or a group that's hired for the road," as Moser told Holly Gleason of *Country Music Roundup*. Four Number One hits on the *Billboard* country chart in the late 1980s proved his vision potent indeed.

In the original Highway 101 lineup were Paulette Carlson (lead vocal, guitar), Moser, Curtis Stone (bass), and Jack Daniels (lead guitar). All sang.

Carlson (b. Oct. 11, 1953, Northfield, Minnesota) grew up in the small town of Winsted, 50 miles outside of Minneapolis. Her father was a baker. "Dad would always take us fishing and hunting," she says. "Course, he would always have to go to the bar and have a beer . . . and so I'd sing for the guys. . . . I was six, eight years old." After high school, Carlson worked the Minnesota clubs with a number of bands, gathering a following and at one point earning recognition as the Minnesota Female Country Vocalist of the Year.

She moved to Nashville in the late 1970s to further her singing-songwriting career and had rapid good luck, working for about two years with singer Gail Davies and landing a staff songwriter job with Silverline/Goldline Music. She also played Nashville clubs and signed with RCA Records as a soloist, charting with three top 100 country singles in 1983–84. But in the mid-'80s, frustrated with her lack of consistent progress, Carlson took stock and began seeking proper management. That's when her attorney connected her with Chuck Morris, who saw Carlson as fitting well with his vision of a kind of Nashville version of Fleetwood Mac. When she expressed enthusiasm, the two began to turn vision into reality.

Morris contacted Moser (b. May 3, 1957, Montrose, Colorado), an L.A.-based session and road drummer who had played with Johnny Rivers, the Byrds' Chris Hillman, and the Eagles' Bernie Leadon. They also called Curtis Stone (b. Apr. 3, 1950), the son of veteran musician and music publisher Cliffie Stone. Curtis had been playing music from age 10, had been in the house band at North Hollywood's Palomino club, and had spent roughly four

years as a staff writer at MCA, placing his songs with Crystal Gayle, Juice Newton, and others.

Stone, in turn, called guitarist Daniels (b. Oct. 27, 1949, Choktaw, Oklahoma), a studio musician who at age 17 had gone on the road with Freddie Hart and had later worked with Burton Cummings of the Guess Who, among others.

The four musicians met in Denver, and they clicked musically and personally. But the band's sound didn't immediately gel. Their initial recording sessions, for Warner Brothers Records with Paul Worley producing, yielded unsatisfactory, country-pop–flavored results on a song of Stone's titled "Some Fine Love." They tried again on "The Bed

Highway 101

You Made for Me," a tune Carlson had written when she first moved to Nashville. It came out sounding tougher and more straight-ahead, crystalizing the band's sonic identity and yielding a number four country hit in 1987. They rapidly followed it with a debut album, *Highway 101,* and the single "Whiskey, If You Were a Woman," a Wendy Waldman–Bob Morrison composition that charted at number two.

They took to the road, where their polished musicianship attracted fans from across the demographic spectrum. The country music establishment also took notice, especially when the group scored the first of four chart-toppers, "Somewhere Tonight," in late 1987. Three months later they were voted Vocal Group of the Year by the Academy of Country Music, an honor that was seconded by the Country Music Association later that year and repeated by the Academy in 1989.

Two more albums—1988's *Highway 101 2* and 1989's *Paint the Town*—and numerous top 10 chart hits (including three at the very top) took the band to 1990. But Carlson, by that time, had begun refocusing on her solo career. She quit Highway 101, signed with Capitol, and a year later released a solo disc titled *Love Goes On.*

The band replaced her with Nikki Nelson (b. Jan. 3, 1969, Topaz Lake, Nevada), a 22-year-old singer who had performed as a teenager on Nevada's "silver circuit." Within months, Highway 101 had a new album, *Bing Bang Boom,* and a title track positioned at number 14 on the country chart.

But subsequent chart rankings were lower than the group's norm. The Highway 101 path then took

some sharp twists and turns. Jack Daniels left the act in 1992. They switched labels to Liberty Records. Original visionary Morris became their *ex*-manager in mid-1993. And several months later, out of gas and at a dead end, the group disbanded.

FAITH HILL

Her story sounds like the plot from a B movie: The aspiring singer leaves tiny Star, Mississippi, to make it big in Nashville, struggles to survive, gets discovered by accident, and scores a Number One hit with her very first chart single. Faith Hill's story is more complicated than that, but not much, and with a combination of good looks, a good singing voice, and good instincts about songs, she did become an instant success, thanks to her debut Number One smash, "Wild One."

Hill (b. Audrey Faith Perry, Sept. 21, 1967, Jackson, Mississippi) discovered the profit in singing at age five when her family would pay her 50 cents a performance. At age eight she got her own copy of Elvis Presley's *The Legendary Performer: Vol. 2* and got hooked. "I would just hold that album jacket in front of me, stare at his picture, and play the record over and over again," she recalls. Eventually she began performing in public with various choirs and solo at rodeos and fairs.

At 17, Hill went to Meridian, Mississippi, to perform at the Jimmie Rodgers Festival. A band heard her and hired her as their lead singer. Gigging with a group cemented Hill's resolve to try for a career in music, and at 19 she packed up and headed to Nashville.

"I nearly starved to death before a got a job," she says. "I'd tell people I came to town to become a singer, and they wouldn't hire me. I finally started lying and said I was tone deaf and not interested in music and finally got some work." For five years she kept her interest in singing a secret from all of her employers—including singer Gary Morris, who hired her as the receptionist at his publishing company. One day when she thought she was alone in the office, she began singing with the radio at the top of her voice. Her co-worker heard her and tipped off the boss. Recalls Hill: "Gary came to me, and he said, 'Young lady, all I have to say to you is, you need to get out from behind this desk and really start working. You don't need to be doing this.'"

TOP SONGS

WILD ONE (Warner, '93, 1)
PIECE OF MY HEART (Warner, '93, 1)

Hill took her singing out of the closet and on to the stages of showcase clubs like the Bluebird Cafe, where an executive with Warner Brothers Records caught her singing background vocals for a friend. In 1992 she signed with that label and began working on her debut album, *Take Me As I Am.*

Having worked for Gary Morris and, for a time, in Reba McEntire's company, Hill knew the importance of finding good material. She and producer Scott Hendricks came up with some inspired choices, including a dead-on perfect song called "Wild One." It ended up staying at Number One for four weeks in early 1994—helping to make her first album a million seller. She followed it with a remake of Janis Joplin's "Piece of My Heart," an unlikely choice for a country track that nonetheless took Hill back to the top. "I had not heard Janis Joplin's version of the song," says Hill, "only the country version I'd heard on a demo. After I heard Janis' version I said, 'How did we manage to make a country version of that and keep the same attitude?'"

Faith Hill's conspicuous show business entrance provided further proof that country audiences in the mid-'90s were younger than ever—and hungrier than ever for young, energetic country performers.

JOHNNY HORTON

Johnny Horton was known as the Singing Fisherman. During his brief recording career, he reeled in some of the biggest country hits of his time, most notably his signature song, "The Battle of New Orleans."

Horton was born on April 3, 1929, in Tyler, Texas, and grew up learning and loving to fish in the lakes that dotted that region of his state. He attended Baylor University and the University of Seattle and subsequently worked in the fishing industry in Alaska and California. But all the while he was increasingly drawn to his other love: singing.

He combined the two when he assumed the nickname the Singing Fisherman as a performer on Cliffie Stone's television program, "Hometown Jamboree," in California in the mid-1950s. After that, he moved east and joined the "Louisiana Hayride" program in Shreveport, eventually becoming a star of that show.

While his recording career had begun with the Cormac label in 1951, it began to take off in 1956 when he signed with Columbia Records and issued the single "Honky Tonk Man," a top 10 country hit. A hint of the greater success to come occurred when his record "When It's Springtime in Alaska (It's Forty Below)" reached Number One on the country chart in 1959.

Horton's next record, the chart-topping and million-selling "The Battle of New Orleans," made him a national star. While the melody and instrumental track had a country quality (it was based on a traditional bluegrass fiddle tune), the song itself was a novelty of sorts, recounting the tale of the famous battle.

The rest of Horton's hits took a similar approach, with a country and western sound that complemented his trademark husky vocals. First to follow, in 1959, was "Johnny Reb." In 1960 he scored with "Sink the Bismarck," another historical tale, this one about the famed World War II German battleship. That year's "North to Alaska," the theme song of the John Wayne movie of the same title, was another million seller.

Horton's career was tragically cut short on November 5, 1960, when he was killed in an auto crash while driving from Louisiana to a recording session in Nashville.

TOP SONGS

HONKY-TONK MAN (Columbia, '56, 9)
I'M A ONE-WOMAN MAN (Columbia, '56, 7)
THE WOMAN I NEED (Columbia, '57, 9)
ALL GROWN UP (Columbia, '58, 8)
WHEN IT'S SPRINGTIME IN ALASKA (IT'S FORTY BELOW)
   (Columbia, '59, 1)
THE BATTLE OF NEW ORLEANS
   (Columbia, '59, 1, 1 Pop)
JOHNNY REB (Columbia, '59, 10)
SINK THE BISMARCK (Columbia, '60, 6, 3 Pop)
NORTH TO ALASKA (Columbia, '60, 1, 4 Pop)
SLEEPY-EYED JOHN (Columbia, '61, 9)

Additional Top 40 Country Songs: 4

DAVID HOUSTON

avid Houston was only 12 years old when the show business powers-that-be (at least those at the "Louisiana Hayride" radio show in Shreveport) reached a life-altering conclusion: the kid *has* something. Within several years the teenager was a regular on that program. Three decades later he was a man with a legacy: a track record of 61 songs that had entered the country chart, seven of which had reached Number One. While not a major country music trendsetter, Houston ranked high in terms of sheer longevity and the consistent chart-worthiness of his output, showing up on the country listings every year from 1963 to 1981, and one last time in 1989.

Houston (b. Dec. 9, 1938, Bossier City, Louisiana) had been encouraged in his singing by his godfather, Gene Austin, a major singing star of the 1920s (and one of several illustrious names connected with Houston, who was a descendant of Sam Houston and Robert E. Lee). Another who showed interest in Houston was manager Tillman Franks, who came across him through the "Louisiana Hayride" show. Years after that stint, and following a period in which Houston attended and dropped out of college, worked in recording sessions, recorded the unsuccessful single "Sherry's Lips" at Sun studios, and went to work in the insurance business, Franks helped him get a recording contract with Epic Records.

The first release, 1963's "Mountain of Love," made it to number two on the country chart, becoming both Houston's and Epic's first country hit.

There followed a continuous string of top 40s, including the number three "Livin' in a House Full of Love," until a Billy Sherrill–Glenn Sutton composition, "Almost Persuaded," shot to Number One country (24 pop) in 1966. The song served as a springboard for more Houston chart-toppers, earned him a Grammy Award for Best Male Country Performance and another for Best Song, stood as the first top country hit for future powerhouse producer-writer Billy Sherrill, and eventually floated up into the rarefied air of perennial country favorites.

For the next five years, from late 1966 through 1971, Houston was the voice behind a noteworthy chart run: he had 15 consecutive top 10 hits, interrupted only once. Of these, five were consecutive Number Ones, including the Houston–Tammy Wynette duet "My Elusive Dreams" (1967). The song that broke this chain (occurring after three Number Ones) was another Wynette collaboration, 1968's "It's All Over."

This period was capped in 1971 with Houston's induction into the Grand Ole Opry.

Further Wynette duets were not to be. However, between mid-1970 and mid-'74, Houston recorded six pairings with Barbara Mandrell, including the number six country hit "After Closing Time" (1970) and another number six, "I Love You, I Love You" (1973).

Houston's pact with Epic ended in 1976, taking with it his record of high-end chart activity. He signed with the Gusto/Starday label briefly and later moved to Colonial, Elektra, Derrick, and a couple more. In 1989 he barely made it into the top 100 with "A Penny for Your Thoughts Tonight Virginia." Four and a half years later, on November 25, 1993, Houston died of a ruptured brain aneurysm.

TOP SONGS

Mountain of Love (Epic, '63, 2)
Almost Persuaded (Epic, '66, 1, 24 Pop)
With One Exception (Epic, '67, 1)
My Elusive Dreams (Epic, '67, 1)
You Mean the World to Me (Epic, '67, 1)
Have a Little Faith (Epic, '68, 1)
Already It's Heaven (Epic, '68, 1)
Where Love Used to Live (Epic, '68, 2)
Baby, Baby (I Know You're a Lady) (Epic, '69, 1)
A Woman Always Knows (Epic, '71, 2)

Additional Top 40 Country Songs: 35

FERLIN HUSKY

uring his career, Husky assumed various names and personae. Not all of them were successful, but two—the hick satirist Simon Crum and Husky himself—became household names in country music.

Ferlin Husky was born on December 3, 1927, on a farm near the town of Flat River, Missouri. His life story is rife with improbable lore—he constantly invented and reinvented himself. One of the stories has to do with his first guitar, which he got in a trade for a hen. When the hen didn't lay eggs, Husky was forced to give back the guitar.

When he moved to Bakersfield, California, after a wartime stint in the merchant marines at the beginning of the 1950s, Husky changed his name to Terry Preston and became a disc jockey. He also began performing as Preston at that time.

Husky/Preston was soon discovered by Cliffie Stone, who managed Tennessee Ernie Ford and also had the program "Hometown Jamboree." In 1953, Husky was signed—as Ferlin Huskey—to Capitol Records, where he began to record country-pop singles. That same year he teamed with Jean Shepard, singing the latter's ballad "Dear John Letter," which became a major hit.

Using his real name, Husky launched a solo career in 1955 with the moderately successful single "I Feel Better All Over (More Than Anywhere's Else)" and eventually produced a vast number of pop-inflected country hits, including "Gone," "A Fallen Star," "Wings of a Dove," "The Waltz You Saved for Me," and "Just for You."

At the same time, he invented the alter ego Simon Crum, a country philosopher of sorts and a novelty act that Husky signed, separately, to the Capitol label. In 1958, Crum/Husky scored with the feisty comedy record "Country Music Is Here to Stay."

Husky pursued an acting career in the 1950s. It began in 1957 with a guest appearance on the dramatic television series "Kraft TV Theatre." He subsequently appeared in various TV and radio programs and a number of movies, including 1957's *Mr. Rock & Roll* and 1958's *Country Music Holiday* with Zsa Zsa Gabor.

ALAN JACKSON

Singer and songwriter Alan Jackson went to Nashville in the mid-1980s and for four years was turned down by every label in town. Once signed, however, he broke through quickly. His second release hit number three on the country singles chart; his follow-up singles consistently charted in the top five, and his albums sold millions. As flashier performers like Clint Black and Garth Brooks took country music by storm in the early 1990s, the more laid-back Jackson quietly asserted himself as one of the top purveyors of a more traditional sound.

Jackson (b. Alan Eugene Jackson, Oct. 17, 1958, Newnan, Georgia) was the youngest of five children of a Ford auto plant worker. As a child he was exposed to rock and roll and R&B via his sisters' stacks of records and to gospel and country through his parents, who would listen to the radio and watch "Hee Haw" on television. As Jackson got older he discovered George Jones, his major musical influence.

In high school, Jackson sang in choirs and formed an informal duo with a girl he knew in school. Later, a loan officer at a local bank joined up with Jackson in another duo that worked weddings, parties, and occasional club dates. He also formed Dixie Steel, his first band. They played a local circuit that included clubs in nearby Atlanta.

Jackson eventually set his sights on Nashville but felt a small-town boy would have little chance of making it in the big time. An actual move to Music City, in 1985, was triggered by his wife's chance encounter with singer Glen Campbell. Denise Jackson was working as a flight attendant at the time and couldn't resist approaching Campbell in an airport to get some advise for her husband. Glen gave her the number of his publishing company in Nashville and suggested that Alan call them if he was ever in town. "When I got to town, I went to see them right away," Jackson remembers, "and played them a tape of songs I'd written. They thought I was a better singer than a songwriter and couldn't give me a job.

TOP SONGS

Jean Shepard and Ferlin Huskey:
A DEAR JOHN LETTER (Capitol, '53, 1, 4 Pop)
FORGIVE ME JOHN (Capitol, '53, 4)

Ferlin Huskey:
I FEEL BETTER ALL OVER (MORE THAN ANYWHERE'S ELSE) (Capitol, '55, 6)
LITTLE TOM (Capitol, '55, 7)
CUZZ YORE SO SWEET (Capitol, '55, 5)

Ferlin Husky:
GONE (Capitol, '57, 1, 4 Pop)
COUNTRY MUSIC IS HERE TO STAY (Capitol, '58, 2)
WINGS OF A DOVE (Capitol, '60, 1, 12 Pop)
ONCE (Capitol, '66, 4)
JUST FOR YOU (Capitol, '67, 4)

Additional Top 40 Country Songs: 31

Alan Jackson

They were interested but said I needed to get more experience."

Jackson took various day jobs, including a stint in the mail room of the Nashville Network, while he hobnobbed with other writers and worked on improving his writing skills. In 1986, Glen Campbell Music hired him.

While with the Campbell company, Jackson tended to hoard his best material—the songs that didn't mimic other writers or use standard formulas—for himself. "When we began writing, I noticed that there was something very honest and raw about the way he wrote," says Keith Stegall, an early co-writer and Jackson's later record producer. "In the first few meetings that I had with him, I found myself wanting to Nashville-ize his writing. Finally I just realized that it's different, and it's real, and there was no sense in messing with it."

It was his original material and authentic country sound—all packaged in his slender, handsome six-foot-four-inch frame—that attracted the attention of Arista Records' new country division in 1988. The label signed him on as a kind of trial, toes-in-the-country-waters artist. But following the release of his debut album—for which he co-wrote all but one of the songs—and the wide acceptance of the title song, "Here in the Real World," Jackson became the

label's flagship act. He went on to score 16 consecutive top five hits, including 10 Number Ones, between 1990 and the spring of 1995, when "Song for the Life" peaked at number six. Included in that run of hits were "Don't Rock the Jukebox," "Chattahoochee," and a remake of the old Eddie Cochran pop hit "Summertime Blues."

TOP ALBUMS

HERE IN THE REAL WORLD (Arista, '90)
DON'T ROCK THE JUKEBOX (Arista, '91)
A LOT ABOUT LIVIN' (AND A LITTLE 'BOUT LOVE) (Arista, '92)
WHO I AM (Arista, '94)

TOP SONGS

I'D LOVE YOU ALL OVER AGAIN (Arista, '91, *1*)
DON'T ROCK THE JUKEBOX (Arista, '92, *1*)
SHE'S GOT THE RHYTHM (AND I GOT THE BLUES) (Arista, '92, *1*)
CHATTAHOOCHEE (Arista, '93, *1*)
LIVIN' ON LOVE (Arista, '94, *1*)

Additional Top 40 Country Songs: 8

STONEWALL JACKSON

He had the kind of break most aspiring country musicians only dream about. After working a log-trucking business in Moultrie, Georgia, to save enough money for a trip to Nashville to peddle his songs, Stonewall Jackson (b. Nov. 6, 1932, Tabor City, North Carolina) finally hopped in his truck in October 1956 to make the journey. Upon arriving, he gained an audience with Grand Ole Opry founder Judge George D. Hay and the Opry's general manager, W. D. Kilpatrick. They were wowed, and the singer-songwriter achieved the seemingly impossible: becoming a member of the Opry even though he had zero records to his credit.

There was more. Around the same time, Jackson landed a songwriting contract with Wesley Rose, of the Acuff-Rose music publishing firm, and not long thereafter signed a recording agreement with Columbia.

Making this Music City entry all the more remarkable was the extent to which Jackson ultimately proved the bigwigs' instincts to be right on the money.

Stonewall, a descendant of *the* Stonewall Jackson, giant of the Civil War Confederacy, had led the life of an ordinary mortal in spite of his heritage. A longtime plucker and strummer of makeshift guitars, Jackson had started writing songs in earnest while in the Navy, between 1949 and '53. It was when back in the States—starting in 1954—that he'd begun putting aside his pennies for a dream of the big time, doing farming and carpentry along the way.

Two years after his momentous introduction to Nashville and the Opry (where he became a popular regular), Jackson issued his first Columbia single. The song, "Life to Go," took off and went, with relative haste, to the number two spot on the *Billboard* country chart. This softened the market for the assault that was to promptly follow: a major hit on the highest peak of the country chart with "Waterloo," Stonewall's career high point.

With nowhere to go but down, the 26-year-old Jackson managed to do better than just keep afloat; he stayed buoyant on a stream of hits that would flow steadily for 14 years. Of 44 entries to the country hit rankings, 35 made it to the top 40. Eleven of these were in the top 10. Two made it all the way to Number One. And four crossed over to the pop chart.

Jackson's second major chart-shaker, the Number One "B.J. the D.J.," came in 1963. Some top 10s followed, along with a set of lower-ranking singles. These were capped in the mid-'60s with "The Minute Men (Are Turning in Their Graves)" (number 24 country, 1966), Stonewall's musical comment on the period's political and countercultural rumblings—hippies, antiwar demonstrators, and the like. Within a couple of months he was back with more conventional country subject matter, the amusingly titled "Blues Plus Booze (Means I Lose)" (number 12 country, 1966) and "Stamp Out Loneliness" (number five country, 1967).

Thereafter, Jackson's sonic volleys hit somewhat lower-level chart targets, with the exception of the number seven "Me and You and a Dog Named Boo" in 1971. Before finally holding his fire for good, Jackson lobbed out a last one in 1973 and scored a respectable number 41 hit with his lone MGM Records chart entry, "Herman Schwartz."

TOP SONGS

LIFE TO GO (Columbia, '58, 2)

WATERLOO (Columbia, '59, 1, 4 Pop)

WHY I'M WALKIN' (Columbia, '60, 6)

A WOUND TIME CAN'T ERASE (Columbia, '62, 3)

OLD SHOWBOAT (Columbia, '63, 8)

B.J. THE D.J. (Columbia, '63, 1)

DON'T BE ANGRY (Columbia, '64, 4)

I WASHED MY HANDS IN MUDDY WATER (Columbia, '65, 8)

STAMP OUT LONELINESS (Columbia, '67, 5)

ME AND YOU AND A DOG NAMED BOO (Columbia, '71, 7)

Additional Top 40 Country Songs: 25

SONNY JAMES

Sonny James is known as the Southern Gentleman, a name that complements his signature smooth, rich vocals and genteel style. As a recording artist he was immensely popular, residing in the upper reaches of the country charts for nearly three decades and amassing an astonishing 23 Number One records.

James (b. James Hugh Loden, May 1, 1929,

Young Love (Capitol, '56, 1, 1 Pop)
You're the Only World I Know (Capitol, '64, 1)
Behind the Tear (Capitol, '65, 1)
Take Good Care of Her (Capitol, '66, 1)
Need You (Capitol, '67, 1)
I'll Never Find Another You (Capitol, '67, 1)
It's the Little Things (Capitol, '67, 1)
A World of Our Own (Capitol, '68, 1)
Heaven Says Hello (Capitol, '68, 1)
Born to Be with You (Capitol, '68, 1)

Additional Top 40 Country Songs: 53

Hackleburg, Alabama) was raised in a family that played traditional music. By the time he was four years old he was performing with his four sisters in the Loden Family on the radio and onstage. At age seven he took up the fiddle and was later signed to perform on a radio station in Birmingham.

James joined the Army in the early 1950s and was sent to Korea, where he spent most of his time performing for the troops. After his release he was signed by Capitol Records. His 1956 debut single, "For Rent," was moderately successful, but the follow-up, "Young Love," proved to be a country smash, selling over a million copies and crossing over to the pop charts. A third single, "First Date, First Kiss, First Love," hit the top 10 in 1957.

At that point, James' career began to slide. But he rebounded with the pop-oriented single, "The Minute You're Gone," which became a hit in 1963. The success of that record presaged a run on the charts that would make country music history.

It began in 1964 with the record "You're the Only One I Know" and continued until the release of "Here Comes Honey Again" in 1971. During that period, James scored 16 consecutive Number One hits. After he topped the chart in 1972 with "That's Why I Love You Like I Do," he moved to Columbia Records and matched the achievement that same year with "When the Snow Is on the Roses." The run continued through the decade with such records as "Is It Wrong (For Loving You)," "A Little Bit South of Saskatoon," "What in the World's Come Over You," "When Something Is Wrong with My Baby," "You're Free to Go," and a number of others.

Until he was surpassed by Conway Twitty, James held the record for the most Number One country hits.

Along the way, James appeared in various films, most of them minor, including *Second Fiddle to a Steel Guitar, Nashville Rebel* (with Waylon Jennings), *Las Vegas Hillbillies,* and *Hillbilly in a Haunted House* (with Lon Chaney and Basil Rathbone).

He also recorded a 1976 album, *200 Years of Country Music,* that drew on the rich vein of traditional music he had originally performed with his family. Referring to that album, James noted the debt he and others owed to the country artists and idioms that had come before. "We tried to do the original sounds of country that have been so dominant in our industry and made it possible for people such as I to come along with our own styles years later," he said. "For instance, when I did 'The Great Speckled Bird,' I attempted to use the phrasing of Roy Acuff but retain my own style—with his music."

It was just that combination of affectionate derivation and consummate originality that made James a standout in the roster of country's most-noted artists.

WAYLON JENNINGS

In 1994, Waylon Jennings signed a new contract with RCA Records. He had left them 11 years earlier after a two-decade affiliation during which he'd succeeded in changing the way country music was recorded in Nashville and helped redefine the genre. Though once dubbed an "outlaw," Jennings returned to his original label as a modern legend, a unique country voice and the creator of such modern classics as "Only Daddy That'll Walk the Line," "Rainy Day Woman," "Luckenbach, Texas," and "I've Always Been Crazy."

Jennings (b. Wayland Arnold Jennings, June 15, 1937, Littlefield, Texas) says his earliest country influence was the music of Jimmie Rodgers, as sung to him by Jennings' father, a guitar-playing Rodgers fanatic. Young Jennings appreciated Rodgers, but he liked Ernest Tubb more. He was barely out of toddlerhood when he would steal his father's guitar, or even an old broomstick, to mimic Tubb.

Jennings didn't get serious about performing music until he was 13 and began winning local talent contests. By age 14 he had left school and headed to Lubbock, where he ended up becoming a deejay at a radio station that played country and rock and roll.

Waylon Jennings

In Lubbock he met Buddy Holly. "Let me set the record straight," says Jennings. "A lot of people say I was one of the original Crickets. That's not true. Buddy and I were friends, and I was his protégé. He produced a record I cut ["Jole Blon" in 1958]. I was filling in on bass, and he wanted me to work into the show as an opening act, but I was never one of the Crickets. That band on his last tour was a whole different thing."

The "last tour" was the one that took Holly, Ritchie Valens, and the Big Bopper (J. P. Richardson) to Clear Lake, Iowa, in early 1959. It was bitterly cold, and the converted school bus they were traveling in had frozen up a couple of times en route. When Holly decided to charter a plane to fly some of them to the next venue, Jennings gave up his place in the plane to the Big Bopper.

The Bopper died along with Holly and Valens when the plane crashed. "I have a terrible guilt about that, and I'll tell you something I've never told before," said Jennings in 1988 on the Bob Kingsley radio show. "When I gave up my seat on the plane

to the Big Bopper, Buddy came over to me and said, 'Well, you're not going to go on the plane tonight?' and I said, 'No. Bopper wanted to go.' So he says, 'Well I hope your old bus freezes up.' And I shot back, 'Well, I hope your plane crashes.' Imagine how I felt. I was just 20 years old, and I thought I'd caused the accident. It took me two years to get over that before I could get back to making music."

Jennings' first big break as a recording artist came in the early 1960s when he was signed briefly to Herb Alpert's A&M Records. "I didn't stay on A&M very long," he says. "I love Herb Alpert, but he wanted me to sing like Al Martino. I finally told him I couldn't go pop with a mouth full of firecrackers."

Chet Atkins signed him to RCA Nashville, and Jennings scored his first country top 40 in 1965 with "Stop the World (And Let Me Off)."

Jennings quickly grew impatient with the formulaic music and restrictive system in Nashville. He resented having to record four songs a session utilizing the same studio musicians to ensure the music had that "Nashville sound." In 1967 he walked out on the session for a song called "The Chokin' Kind." "I wanted a simple acoustic version like writer Harlan Howard had done on the demo," he claims, "and they insisted on all the instruments, which ruined the

TOP ALBUMS

THIS TIME (RCA, '74)
WANTED: THE OUTLAWS (with Willie Nelson, Jessi Colter, and Tompall Glaser, RCA, '76)
I'VE ALWAYS BEEN CRAZY (RCA, '78)

TOP SONGS

THIS TIME (RCA, '74, *1*)
I'M A RAMBLIN' MAN (RCA, '74, *1*)
LUCKENBACH, TEXAS (BACK TO THE BASICS OF LOVE) (RCA, '77, *1, 25 Pop*)
AMANDA (RCA, '79, *1*)
THEME FROM THE DUKES OF HAZZARD (GOOD OL' BOYS) (RCA, '80, *1, 21 Pop*)

Waylon and Willie:
GOOD HEARTED WOMAN (RCA, '75, *1, 25 Pop*)
MAMMAS DON'T LET YOUR BABIES GROW UP TO BE COWBOYS (RCA, '78, *1*)

Additional Top 40 Country Songs: 75

song. Chet Atkins tracked me down and said, 'Never walk out like that again. I'll keep the boys there until midnight to get the song like you want it.'"

From this first victory in the battle to gain creative control of his music, Jennings went on to win the war. In 1974 he rented the studios of Tompall Glaser to record his *This Man* album and then forced RCA to accept the product, breaking the record company stranglehold that had required nearly every artist to record in company-owned studios. The action made Jennings an "outlaw" within the industry.

He became an outlaw to the rest of the world in 1976 when he, wife Jessi Colter, Willie Nelson, and Tompall Glaser recorded *Wanted: The Outlaws,* the first million-selling album ever recorded in Nashville. In 1977, Jennings released the record that became his biggest country hit and also crossed him over to pop audiences. "Luckenbach Texas (Back to the Basics of Love)," featuring additional vocals from Willie Nelson, stayed at Number One country for six weeks and hit number 25 on the pop chart.

Over the years, Jennings' wild offstage antics with friends Johnny Cash, Willie Nelson, and Kris Kristofferson became the stuff of modern folklore. Jennings has said most of the stories are true, including the one about the 20-year, $1,500-a-day cocaine habit that he quit cold turkey in the mid-1980s.

Through it all, with the lyrical honesty of his material (which includes his own "This Time," "Rainy Day Woman," and "Are You Sure Hank Done It This Way") and with his signature bass-line–powered sound, Jennings managed to leave an indelible imprint on country music. "I brought truth to it," he says. "I brought an edge to the music, taught what the edge was. I borrowed from Buddy Holly to teach them to keep the music in a groove. I gave them that and helped give artists the freedom to realize there's always one more way to do things in the studio, and that's your way. You deserve the right to try it your way at least once."

GEORGE JONES

Estimates range from 100 to 150 original and repackaged albums with his name on them. He's scored nearly 140 top 40 hits, influenced several generations of aspiring singers, and ranks as the favorite country performer of such luminaries as Johnny Cash, Waylon Jennings, James Taylor, Linda Ronstadt, and Bob Dylan. A painfully shy man (much preferring the "show" to the "business" of what he does for a living) whose personal demons have often brought his career to a standstill, George Jones has managed to survive. He remains revered as a brilliant interpreter of traditional country songs and an important contributor to American music some four decades after his country chart debut.

Jones (b. George Glenn Jones, Sept. 12, 1931, Saratoga, Texas) was born near Beaumont, Texas, one of seven children. His father, George Washington Jones, was a jack of all trades, from truck driving to pipe fitting. He was also an alcoholic who often terrorized the family during drunken rages. His mother, Clara, was a teetotaling Pentecostalist who played gospel music on the piano. Young Jones found music to be an avenue of escape from the turmoil at home. Drawn to country music by the songs of Roy Acuff, Bill Monroe, Hank Williams, and Lefty Frizzell, he obtained a Gene Autry guitar and began making music.

George Jones

Jones' earliest audiences were Beaumont bus riders. As a young boy he would get on a bus and sit in the back, where he played and sang his heart out. Bus drivers would let him ride free because he entertained them and their customers. When he wasn't banging away at that guitar on the buses, he played hooky from school and headed off into the woods to practice alone for hours. "I got to the seventh grade but not through it," he explains. "I just didn't care about doing anything but to play and sing."

At 16 he landed his first substantial professional job, performing on the radio with a local act named Eddie and Pearl. Jones continued to perform locally until 1951, when his first marriage broke up and he spent two years in the Marines. He returned to Beaumont in '53 and built his reputation as a club performer. Two local entrepreneurs, Pappy Daily and Jack Starnes, formed Starday Records, and Jones was one of their first acts. "My first recordings for Starday were done in a converted living room, with egg crates for sound baffles," he recalls.

After a few forgettable singles, Starday released Jones' self-penned "Why Baby Why." It became the surprise hit of 1955, and Jones became everybody's "most promising new artist." He had four more top 10s on Starday before moving over to Mercury Records, where he scored his first Number One in 1959 with "White Lightning." "White Lightning" revealed a lighthearted side of Jones that would regularly color such songs as "The Race Is On" and "The Love Bug." But it was on heartfelt country ballads that Jones' true vocal artistry showed through. Able to wrench maximum emotion from a single note of music or syllable of lyric, Jones transformed

many of his performances—including "She Thinks I Still Care," "A Good Year for the Roses," and "He Stopped Loving Her Today"—into unforgettable listening experiences.

Jones sang so convincingly about deep hurt and troubled lives perhaps because of his own life offstage. "It seems like I've been running from something all my life," he once speculated. "If I knew what it was, I could run in the right direction." He had inherited his father's drinking problem and later battled drugs. It cost him marriages, including his storybook union with Tammy Wynette. They married in 1969 as her star was rising, and for a while they were king and queen of country music. They were divorced in 1975 but managed to record a total of 13 top 40 duet hits, including "We're Gonna Hold On" (Number One, 1973) and "Two Story House" (number two, 1980).

In the mid-1980s, Jones' career and life nearly came to an end. In financial trouble, sick, and down to 105 pounds, "I was so low at that point, I thought there was no way back," he says. "I thought I had no chance whatsoever." He came back, with the help and support of his wife, Nancy, and such friends as Merle Haggard and Johnny Cash, to score such hits as "Who's Gonna Fill Their Shoes," "The Right Left Hand," and "I'm a One Woman Man."

In the 1990s, Jones continued to record and tour and inspire up-and-coming country performers.

WYNONNA JUDD

Wynonna Judd has been a top country artist since 1984, when she and her mother, Naomi, debuted as the Judds. In 1992, following the Judds' dissolution, Wynonna launched a solo career with an eclectic, on-the-edge country sound that differed from the roots-oriented music that had made the duet famous.

Wynonna (b. Christina Ciminella, May 30, 1964, Ashland, Kentucky) was the eldest of two children born to Michael and Diana Ciminella (Diana changed her name to Naomi, from her favorite biblical passage; Christina changed hers to Wynonna, an American Indian term for "first born"). The family moved to Los Angeles when Wynonna was four years old, and her parents soon divorced. Brought up by Naomi without much money, Wynonna was still exposed to varied styles of music. "I couldn't afford

---

TOP SONGS

White Lightning (Mercury, '59, 1)

Tender Years (Mercury, '61, 1)

She Thinks I Still Care (United Artists, '62, 1)

Walk Through This World with Me (Musicor, '67, 1)

The Grand Tour (Epic, '74, 1)

The Door (Epic, '74, 1)

He Stopped Loving Her Today (Epic, '80, 1)

Still Doin' Time (Epic, '81, 1)

Yesterday's Wine (with Merle Haggard, Epic, '82, 1)

I Always Get Lucky with You (Epic, '83, 1)

Additional Top 40 Country Songs: 128

to buy Wynonna new records," Naomi explained to *US* magazine, "so I went to the 99 cent record bins and bought her a lot of used blues, R&B, and country records."

They spent several years in California before her mother moved back to Kentucky to get back in touch with their family roots and escape the big-city life. Wynonna was not happy about the move and, at first, hated Kentucky. She was a rebellious child who disliked school. "I felt like a misfit," she says, "until I began to play the guitar and sing." Her voice became her identity and her mother's best hope for her daughter's future.

Influenced by local country and bluegrass performers around Beria, Kentucky, mother and daughter began singing together. They eventually took their talent to Nashville, and began their recording career in 1984. Between 1984 and '91, when Naomi Judd was forced to retire because of ill health, the Judds scored numerous hits on the way to becoming the most successful country duet act in history.

Wynonna Judd thought of retiring, too, but was urged to begin a solo career by her mother and the many Judds fans. "I really didn't feel like going on without mom," Wynonna said, "but singing was so much a part of my life, and I received so much love from the fans, that I decided to keep going." She was further encouraged by the offer of a solo contract with MCA Records and the promise that she could establish her own identity as a performer.

Outside the acoustic-based music of the Judds, Wynonna's tastes embraced eclectic, singing-song-

writing artists like Bonnie Raitt and Karla Bonoff, and her vocal capabilities extended to blues. Those influences and others shaped *Wynonna,* her debut solo album. "I tried to include music that would please my old fans," she says, "but my attitude was that I wanted to please myself. I went completely by gut instinct for the first time in my life."

There was some falling away of Judds followers, and during Wynonna's first year on the road, in 1992, she didn't sell out the venues the mother-daughter duo had always filled. However, any doubt about her future as a solo act disappeared when she scored three consecutive Number One hits—"She Is His Only Need," "I Saw the Light," and "No One Else on Earth"—and her debut album sold over three million copies. Her even more esoteric follow-up, *Tell Me Why,* sold platinum in 1993 and yielded four more top 10 songs.

There were indications, in appearances of her country singles in the lower range of the pop chart, of future crossover potential. "Wynonna has done some major sales numbers and turned on some new listeners," notes her producer, Tony Brown. "She's a great country singer, but she obviously appeals to pop listeners as well."

THE JUDDS

I n the early 1980s, the mother-daughter team the Judds came out of the hills of Kentucky, via Hollywood and Nashville, to capture the hearts of a huge, fiercely loyal following of fans. They had an irresistible combination: a rootsy yet urbane sound, homegrown innocence, big-city sophistication, and the wholesome image of a mother and daughter trying to make it together. Powered by Wynonna's bluesy voice and Naomi's harmonies, they were rarely out of the Number One spot on the country chart during their brief, eight-year collaboration.

Naomi (b. Diana Ellen Judd, Jan. 11, 1946, Ashland, Kentucky) and Wynonna (b. Christina Ciminella, May 30, 1964, Ashland, Kentucky) were born in the same hospital 18 years apart. Wynonna was four years old when the family moved to Los Angeles. Her sister, Ashley, was born shortly before the parents divorced, and Naomi was left to raise two children alone. Naomi took various jobs, from serving as personal secretary of the pop act the Fifth Dimension, to waitressing in a Howard Johnson's

---

TOP ALBUMS

WYNONNA (MCA, '92)
TELL ME WHY (MCA, '93)

TOP SONGS

SHE IS HIS ONLY NEED (Curb/MCA, '92, 1)
I SAW THE LIGHT (Curb/MCA, '92, 1)
NO ONE ELSE ON EARTH (Curb/MCA, '92, 1)
MY STRONGEST WEAKNESS (Curb/MCA, '92, 4)
TELL ME WHY (Curb/MCA, '93, 3)
A BAD GOODBYE (with Clint Black, RCA, '93, 2)
GIRLS WITH GUITARS (Curb/MCA, '94, 10)
ROCK BOTTOM (Curb/MCA, '94, 2)

Additional Top 40 Country Songs: 2

restaurant, to modeling. Finally, after enduring an abusive relationship, Naomi packed up her children and headed back to Kentucky.

They embraced a simple, rural Kentucky lifestyle and began singing together at home for entertainment. The Judds encountered some of their most important musical influences among local hill musicians and were inspired to sing as mother and daughter when they heard a performer named Songbird Yancy and her mother Minnie. Yancy and Minnie taught the Judds their first song, "Kentucky."

Wynonna had sung as a little girl, but when she became a teenager and her voice matured, Naomi knew it was special. After a brief sojourn in Northern California, Naomi decided to move to Nashville to see if she could get something going for Wynonna—or for herself and Wynonna together.

Naomi had become a nurse in Kentucky, and she

TOP SONGS

Mama He's Crazy (RCA, '84, *1*)
Why Not Me (RCA, '84, *1*)
Girls Night Out (RCA, '85, *1*)
Have Mercy (RCA, '85, *1*)
Grandpa (Tell Me 'Bout the Good Old Days) (RCA, '86, *1*)
Rockin' with the Rhythm of the Rain (RCA, '86, *1*)
I Know Where I'm Going (RCA, '87, *1*)
Change of Heart (RCA, '88, *1*)
Young Love (RCA/Curb, '89, *1*)
Let Me Tell You About Love (RCA/Curb, '89, *1*)

Additional Top 40 Country Songs: 13

The Judds

began nursing at a hospital in the Nashville suburb of Franklin. She also began establishing contacts on Nashville's music row. They recorded some material with and without Naomi, but nothing happened.

One of Naomi's patients at the hospital happened to be the daughter of record producer Brent Maher. Naomi eventually gave Maher a crude demo tape of songs, most of which she had written. Maher was immediately impressed. "It was the type of material that intrigued me," he says. "I thought these girls had something between their ears, and there was a whole lot of musicality dying to get out, not to mention Wynonna's voice. It didn't take a rocket scientist to hear the potential of that."

Maher worked with the duo and through an initial deal with Curb Records helped them get an audition with RCA. "March 2, 1983, six o'clock P.M., we walked into a room with seven men and auditioned live," recalls Naomi. "It turned out they were the hierarchy of RCA, and we didn't know it. We wouldn't have been able to open our mouths if we'd known the importance and impact of that moment."

They signed with the label, and after peaking at number 17 in early 1984 with their debut single, "Had a Dream (For the Heart)," the Judds scored eight consecutive Number One hits. The first top song was "Mama He's Crazy." The second, "Why Not Me," became the Country Music Association's Single of the Year, and the Judds were suddenly the hottest act in country music. In all, they scored 23 top 40 songs, of which 20 were in the top 10 and 14 were chart toppers. In the process, they almost single-handedly brought back acoustic-based music to the country charts.

Lyrically, the Judds dealt with bedrock themes of love, home, and family that women understood and men appreciated. That and good timing were crucial elements of their success, according to their former manager, Ken Stilts. "They may not have been as successful as quickly if they hadn't happened at the time Ronald Reagan became president," he says. "The pride of the country was at a pretty low point. Reagan represented a return to traditional family values that a mother and daughter [also] represent."

In late 1991, the Judds dissolved the act. Naomi Judd's diagnosis of chronic liver disease forced her to retire from performing. She has since become an author and lecturer. Wynonna Judd signed with MCA Records and released her first solo single in February 1992.

TOBY KEITH

Toby Keith (b. July 8, 1961, Moore, Oklahoma) began his recording career as part of a bold experiment by Mercury Records. In 1993 they mounted the Triple Play Tour, attempting to simultaneously break three new acts: Keith, Shania Twain, and John Brannen. Shania Twain took two more years to break through; John Brannen is still trying. Toby Keith was an instant success; his debut single, a song he wrote called "Should've Been a Cowboy," was a Number One country hit.

A country traditionalist with a rocking edge, Keith has been noted as a "blue collar poet" for lyrical themes drawn from his rural upbringing and rowdy honky-tonk playing days.

Keith grew up on a six-acre farm not far from Oklahoma City. "My parents and grandparents were Grand Ole Opry kind of people," he recalls. "They loved listening to country music and were always supportive of my music." More than music, Keith was interested in making money and trying to become a pro football player. Right out of high school he worked in the oil fields until the short '70s oil boom went bust. Then he joined the rodeo as a bronco bull tester. All these jobs gave him the time to play semi-pro ball, and he came close to landing a linebacker spot with the old United States Football League.

When he gave up that dream, he turned toward writing and singing music. He formed a garage band, won a talent contest, and hit the honky-tonk circuit around Oklahoma, Texas, and Louisiana. "We played some pretty tough places," says Keith. "Had

TOP ALBUMS

TOBY KEITH (Mercury, '93)
BOOMTOWN (Polydor, '94)

TOP SONGS

SHOULD'VE BEEN A COWBOY (Mercury, '93, *1*)
HE AIN'T WORTH MISSING (Mercury, '93, *5*)
A LITTLE LESS TALK AND A LOT MORE ACTION
  (Mercury, '93, *8*)
WISH I DIDN'T KNOW NOW (Mercury, '94, *2*)
WHO'S THAT MAN (Polydor, '94, *1*)
UPSTAIRS DOWNTOWN (Polydor, '94, *10*)

to fight our way out of a few of them. I remember one place where a fight broke out, and the manager told us not to play until they stopped fighting. Then they turned on us for not playing."

Eventually, Keith and his Easy Money band, performing his original material, became one of the most successful acts in the region. "We bought our own Silver Eagle bus, and we worked as much as 51 weeks out of the year," he claims. Keith wanted more and began making trips to Nashville in the late 1980s. He rustled up some interest in 1990 and cut some sides with a top producer. Trouble was, the producer wouldn't let Keith record his originals. The songs that Keith recorded were not his style, and the project failed. Finally, a mutual friend gave one of Keith's demo tapes to Harold Shedd, the top execu-

tive at Mercury Records. Impressed, Shedd flew to Oklahoma City to catch one of Keith's shows. A contract with the label followed.

After his breakout chart topper, Keith remained in the country top 10 with "He Ain't Worth Missing," "A Little Less Talk and a Lot More Action," and "Who's That Man." His debut album, *Toby Keith,* sold over a million copies, and when Mercury split its roster to establish a sister label, Polydor Records, Toby was chosen to be the new label's flagship artist. He released his second album, *Boomtown,* under that banner.

Toby Keith

SAMMY KERSHAW

In 1990, Sammy Kershaw was in the midst of a self-imposed retirement from the music business, working at remodeling Walmart stores, when he got a call from a friend in Nashville. That call led to an audition with Mercury Records, and a year later, Kershaw's first country chart record, "Cadillac Style," peaked in the top five. He has since established himself as one of country music's most soulful singers and accomplished stage performers.

Kershaw (b. Feb. 24, 1958, Abbeville, Louisiana) had an early—and odd—performing experience at age 10 in a grade school Christmas show. "My teacher knew I liked to sing and asked me if I wanted to sing in the pageant, and I said 'Sure!'" he recalls. "They ended up dressing me in fatigues and a green beret, holding a toy rifle, and I sang Barry Sadler's 'Ballad of the Green Berets.'"

Shortly after that, Kershaw's father fell ill. His mother couldn't afford to buy her son that guitar he wanted. "So my grandfather and I think my uncle might have pitched in, too, to get me one," says Kershaw. "We went down to Western Auto and bought me an old Telstar electric guitar and amplifier. Still have that guitar today."

After his father died, Kershaw's mother thought her wild 12-year-old was headed for trouble. She took advantage of his interest in music and got him a job working as a stagehand for a local band headed by J. B. Perry. Perry picked up on Kershaw's talent and soon made him a part of the band. Until Kershaw turned 18, Perry was a surrogate father and musical mentor. "He was one of the best entertainers I ever met in my life," Kershaw claims, "and he taught me a lot of lessons about the music business along the way.

Some lessons I used, but some that I should have used I didn't." Included in the latter was advice to stay away from too much carousing. After leaving Perry, Kershaw worked in a series of bands in the late 1970s and '80s, including a stint with a popular southern outfit called Blackwater. Living the wilder side of a singer's life cost Kershaw two marriages, by his own admission. It was about to cost him a third when he quit the music business in the late 1980s to concentrate on being a family man. That's when he landed the job of remodeling Walmarts, where he stayed until receiving the call from Nashville.

Kershaw's debut album, *Don't Go Near the Water,* which produced his first hit, drew some criticism that he sounded too much like George Jones—who happened to be Kershaw's idol. (He had befriended Jones in the early 1980s and occasionally appeared with him.) Kershaw admitted the influence, but in follow-up discs he forged a more distinctive personal style.

Over the next few years, Kershaw began to rack up an impressive list of top 10 hits (including "She Don't Know She's Beautiful" and "I Can't Reach Her Anymore")—none of which he wrote. One of the few non-composing singers to emerge in the 1990s, Kershaw has claimed he has no ambition to become a songwriter: "I figure if I keep [the competition] busy writing, they won't want to become singers."

Despite his Cajun heritage (he is a third cousin of Cajun fiddle-playing legend Doug Kershaw), Sammy does very little Cajun music in his show. "Every

Sammy Kershaw

once in a while I might do one, like a song called 'Jolie Blon,' which is sort of Louisiana's national anthem," he says. "There are too many great Cajun musicians back home for me to get into that, because my heart's not in that. My heart's in country music."

TOP ALBUMS

DON'T GO NEAR THE WATER (Mercury, '91)
HAUNTED HEART (Mercury, '93)
FEELIN' GOOD TRAIN (Mercury, '94)

TOP SONGS

CADILLAC STYLE (Mercury, '91, *3*)
SHE DON'T KNOW SHE'S BEAUTIFUL (Mercury, '93, *1*)
HAUNTED HEART (Mercury, '93, *9*)
QUEEN OF MY DOUBLE WIDE TRAILER (Mercury, '93, *7*)
I CAN'T REACH HER ANYMORE (Mercury, '94, *3*)
NATIONAL WORKING WOMAN'S HOLIDAY
    (Mercury, '94, *2*)
THIRD RATE ROMANCE (Mercury, '94, *2*)

Additional Top 40 Country Songs: 5

HAL KETCHUM

Hal Ketchum (b. Apr. 9, 1953, Greenwich, New York) is a drummer turned carpenter turned country singer. He made an attention-grabbing entrance on the country chart in 1991 when he hit number two with the rousing "Small Town Saturday Night." In a world replete with younger, traditional-style singers, he became an important addition to the music as a contemporary country poet with a collection of thoughtful original songs.

Ketchum grew up in upstate New York, on the edge of Adirondack State Park. It was not a bastion of country music, but in the Ketchum household, his father fed him a steady diet of songs by Marty Rob-

TOP ALBUMS

PAST THE POINT OF RESCUE (Curb, '91)
SURE LOVE (Curb, '92)

TOP SONGS

SMALL TOWN SATURDAY NIGHT (Curb, '91, 2)
I KNOW WHERE LOVE LIVES (Curb, '91, 13)
PAST THE POINT OF RESCUE (Curb, '92, 3)
FIVE O'CLOCK WORLD (Curb, '92, 16)
SURE LOVE (Curb, '93, 3)
HEARTS ARE GONNA ROLL (Curb, '93, 2)
MAMA KNOWS THE HIGHWAY (Curb, '93, 8)

Additional Top 40 Country Songs: 4

bins, George Jones, and his dad's favorite, Buck Owens. His grandfather was a violinist who could play Mozart and then kick back and play the Virginia reel at a square dance.

Ketchum started playing drums at age nine and within six years was in an R&B trio that played in local clubs. "I saw a lot of life pass by me between eight and midnight, watching people's relationships develop throughout the night," he remembers.

After high school, he turned his creative energy toward becoming a master furniture builder, pursuing that trade from New York to Florida and, in 1978, settling in the small Texas town of Gruene, which had a very active dance hall and honky-tonk district. Drawn into the local music scene, Ketchum switched from drums to guitar and began writing and singing country songs. He became a fan of such "Texas school" songwriters as Guy Clark and Jerry Jeff Walker, and when he thought his original material was strong enough, he moved to Nashville in 1986. He landed a contract with a music publisher, and in 1989 he recorded an independent album called *Threadbare Alibis*. It was an impressive collection of eclectic songs—impressive enough to bring him to the attention of Curb Records.

Ketchum's debut Curb album, *Past the Point of Rescue*, yielded four top 40 hits (including "Five O'Clock World," a remake of the 1965 number four pop hit written by Ketchum's producer, Allen Reynolds, and recorded by the Vogues).

Set apart from most of his contemporaries by the style of his music, Ketchum further distinguished himself by shunning the normal routine of becoming an opening act for more established artists. "My theory is that the only way to be a headliner is to act like one," he says. "So I found places where I could work, some great old theaters and clubs that hold 1,500 to 2,000 people. I could fill them up, and I knew that everybody in the place came to see me, not somebody else."

He was able to fill bigger venues when his next album, *Sure Love,* brought Ketchum three more top 10 hits, including the title song and the more traditional country tune, "Mama Knows the Highway."

In 1994, Ketchum was inducted into the Grand Ole Opry. He also met his father's idol, Buck Owens. "Buck said to me, 'You've made it,'" Ketchum recalls. "I said, 'What do you mean?' He said, 'When I turn on the radio, I can tell that it's you singing. A unique voice is where it's at.'"

"I think I represent hope for the eclectic, if you will," says Ketchum. "I try to be true to myself artistically. Maybe it says it all about my uniqueness that I'm the member of the Grand Ole Opry from upstate New York."

Hal Ketchum

KRIS KRISTOFFERSON

Kris Kristofferson

One of the most popular and innovative country artists, Kristofferson was a pioneer in opening the music to a wide range of new idioms and fans. He was an "outlaw" years before Willie Nelson and Waylon Jennings settled in Austin, Texas, introducing the Nashville establishment to long hair and beards. And his music blended the traditional musical values of country with the punch of rock and the introspection and intellect of folk.

Kristofferson was born on June 22, 1936, in Brownsville, Texas. The son of an Air Force major general, he moved about constantly with his family. The Kristofferson clan eventually settled in San Mateo, California, and Kris began his study of literature at Pomona College. In between his hours spent on the football and boxing teams, he wrote short stories. In 1958 he was awarded a Rhodes Scholarship and went to England to study the various works of his favorite poet, William Blake, at Oxford University.

During his scholastic year at Oxford, Kristofferson wrote two novels, which were promptly rejected by publishers. At the same time, he began to write songs under the pseudonym Kris Carson.

After college, he joined the U.S. Army and became a helicopter pilot in Germany. He also got married and formed his first band. And he began sending his songs to various music publishers in Nashville.

While on a vacation in Nashville in the mid-1960s, he met Johnny Cash (Kristofferson lore has it that he rented a helicopter, flew to Cash's house, landed in his backyard, and walked up to Cash and gave him a song). Cash encouraged Kristofferson to pursue a songwriting career.

In 1965 he did just that, giving up his marriage and his Army commission and making his way to Nashville. His first job was as a $60-a-week janitor at Columbia Studios (where lore also has it that he once emptied the ashtray of Bob Dylan). To make ends meet, he flew helicopters to offshore oil rigs.

He got a break in 1970 when Roger Miller recorded his ballad "Me and Bobby McGee," which hit Number 12 on the country chart. That same year, Cash recorded a version of Kristofferson's "Sunday Morning Coming Down."

Those songs were included on Kristofferson's 1971 eponymous debut album, which also showcased future country-pop classics "For the Good Times" and "Help Me Make It Through the Night." With the songs' varied musical styles and Kristofferson's long-haired and bearded face on the cover, the album proved to be a watershed of sorts. While rock and folk artists had flirted with country music for years, the reverse had not been the case. Now a country artist was bringing his music to the world of rock and folk.

Kristofferson's fortune and name were secured that same year when "Me and Bobby McGee" became a million-selling hit for Janis Joplin and "Help Me Make It Through the Night" did the same for Sammi Smith.

In demand as a songwriter and performer, Kristofferson appeared at the Troubadour nightclub in Los Angeles and on Cash's television show in 1971. In 1973 he scored his first Number One record with the single "Why Me."

That same year, he married vocalist Rita Coolidge. For a time, in the 1970s, he and Coolidge toured and recorded as a team. But he also increasingly pursued a film acting career that had begun in 1972 with a role in *Cisco Pike*.

TOP ALBUMS

KRISTOFFERSON (Monument, '71)
JESUS WAS A CAPRICORN (Monument, '73)

TOP SONGS

WHY ME (Monument, '73, *1, 16 Pop*)

Waylon Jennings, Willie Nelson, Johnny Cash,
*   Kris Kristofferson:*
HIGHWAYMAN (Columbia, '85, *1*)
DESPERADOS WAITING FOR A TRAIN (Columbia, '85, *15*)
SILVER STALLION (Columbia, '90, *25*)

That new career flourished as the '70s progressed. Kristofferson appeared in *Pat Garrett and Billy the Kid* in 1973 (along with Coolidge, Bob Dylan, and others) and a year later in *Alice Doesn't Live Here Anymore*. Subsequent films included *A Star Is Born* (1976), *Heaven's Gate* (1980), and *Rollover* (1981).

But other aspects of Kristofferson's life began to wane. His recording career took a steady dive, with records such as 1974's "Loving Arms" and "Rain" hitting the lower levels of the country chart. And in 1979 his marriage to Coolidge came to an end.

Kristofferson made a musical comeback in 1985 when he teamed with Willie Nelson, Waylon Jennings, and Johnny Cash in the Highwaymen. The group's debut single, "Highwayman," hit Number One that year, and the trio has continued to be a successful touring and recording act (on and off) into the 1990s, noted for such hits as 1985's "Desperados Waiting for a Train" and 1990's "Silver Stallion."

K.D. LANG

k.d. lang's involvement in country music may have been temporary, a passing phase that bridged the singer's musically eclectic youth and her early-1990s period of stylistic branching out. And during the country phase itself—if indeed just a phase—the reaction of the country establishment may have been a bit standoffish, confronted as it was with an unconventional, makeup-free, boyish bohemian whose off-country approach and extroverted stage act drew such labels as cowpunk and punkabilly. But for many in the country community,

Canadian k.d. lang's arrival on the U.S. national stage in 1987 was important. She supplied "something we've missed in this business for a long time," as Brenda Lee put it. With her rich voice, quirky humor, and knowledge of country tradition (with a special nod to Patsy Cline), lang seemed an ideal link to a new batch of young, sophisticated, "country and eastern" listeners.

Before her country fixation, lang (b. Kathryn Dawn Lang, Nov. 2, 1961, Consort, Alberta, Canada) absorbed music from a variety of sources. Her parents listened to Broadway show tunes. Her older sisters and brother had rock records. lang herself took classical piano lessons as a child, switching to guitar at age 10. She began writing songs early (at age nine sending a set of her lyrics to singer Anne Murray with the message "You have permission to write music to these lyrics"). By 13 she was singing and playing at local social events.

At Red Deer College, lang majored in music while extending her abilities through involvement in a performance art troupe. She also became enamored of country music. "I was getting pretty tired of limitless horizons," she said. "I found the potential of working with country's lyric structure very challenging. A lot of my art friends thought I was kidding, but for me, country was a perfect means to express myself through music."

Around that time she acted in a theater piece, playing a role modeled after early-'60s country-pop singer Patsy Cline. Family members encouraged lang to explore the singer's material. The result was the forging of a deep connection—a very deep connection—felt by lang for Cline. "I think I am the reincarnation of Patsy Cline," she later said in *Pulse*.

lang joined a swing band as lead singer around 1983. When it disbanded, she put together her own country-oriented outfit dubbed the Reclines (as in re-Cline). The members included Ben Mink (who would become her longtime collaborator) on guitar and violin, Gordie Matthews (guitar), Dennis Marchenko (bass), Ted Borowiecki (keyboard, accordion; later replaced by Michael Creeber), and Michel Pouliot (drums). They rapidly attracted attention at live performances in Canada, lang's powerful voice, punkish look, and wild stage routine (she'd been known to sing while assuming the fetal position) seeming to simultaneously celebrate country and send it up.

An initial album, *A Truly Western Experience*, issued on their own Bumstead label, helped spread

TOP ALBUMS

ANGEL WITH A LARIAT (Sire, '87)
SHADOWLANDS (Sire, '88)
ABSOLUTE TORCH AND TWANG (Sire, '89)

TOP SONGS

CRYING (with Roy Orbison, Virgin, '87)
I'M DOWN TO MY LAST CIGARETTE (Sire, '88, *21*)
LOCK, STOCK, AND TEARDROPS (Sire, '88)
FULL MOON FULL OF LOVE (Sire, '89, *22*)
THREE DAYS (Sire, '89)

the word and led to an engagement at New York's Bottom Line. Seymour Stein of Sire Records was there, liked lang's act, and signed her on. By spring 1986 she and the band were in London recording an album with ex-Rockpile guitarist Dave Edmunds at the production helm.

On the market in early 1987, *Angel with a Lariat,* as the disc was titled, entered the *Billboard* country albums chart. But it spun off no singles, in spite of massive media coverage of lang and her showmanship. "My success is based totally on the credibility of the live performances," she concluded.

Radio acceptance increased somewhat for lang's next artifact, a duet with Roy Orbison on a remake of his classic song "Crying" (which earned a Grammy Award for Best Vocal Collaboration). It continued with the release of her follow-up album, the country-history–drenched *Shadowlands* (1988). Veteran Patsy Cline producer Owen Bradley had seen lang perform a Cline tune on "The Tonight Show," and he'd been impressed. At the same time, lang had been trying to interest him in working with her. They finally merged in October 1987 and fashioned 12 tracks of blues- and jazz-infused country, capped with a blending of lang's voice with those of Kitty Wells, Loretta Lynn, and Brenda Lee on a track titled "Honky-Tonk Angels Medley." When it was all over, lang acknowledged that one of her dreams had been realized. "I've worked with the master of the kind of music I've studied, and heard him say, 'You're as good as Patsy Cline,'" she told writer Jack Hurst. Two *Shadowlands* tracks, "I'm Down to My Last Cigarette" and "Lock, Stock, and Teardrops" made the country charts (at numbers 21 and 53, respectively).

lang's next album, *Absolute Torch and Twang,*

marked a return to her own idiosyncratic take on country-tinged sound, with eight of its 12 tracks co-written by lang and Ben Mink and one completely written by lang. Chart activity closely matched that for the previous album, with "Full Moon Full of Love" hitting number 22 and "Three Days" peaking at number 55.

Country radio never did cotton to lang, even though she took a 1989 Grammy Award for Best Country Vocalist (and was voted Best New Female Singer in the 1988 *Rolling Stone* critics' poll and Female Artist of the Decade by the Canadian Academy of Recording Arts and Sciences). Perhaps for that reason, but more likely because of her creative inclinations, lang moved out of country music in 1992 with her *Ingenue* album. "I don't want to be bitter about the country music scene," she told Sheila Rogers of *Musician.* "I did it with respect and with humor. But it's like a love affair. It's over. It's time to move on."

k. d. lang

TRACY LAWRENCE

Tracy Lawrence spent the first couple of years of his career hoping people would stop asking him about the time he was shot during a mugging attempt just before his first album came out. Eventually the nonstop string of top 10 hits that began in 1991 became the real story behind the young singer—who landed a record contract just seven months after arriving in Nashville. He has since established himself as one of the most impor-

Tracy Lawrence

TOP ALBUMS

STICKS AND STONES (Atlantic, '91)
ALIBIS (Atlantic, '92)
I SEE IT NOW (Atlantic, '94)

TOP SONGS

STICKS AND STONES (Atlantic, '91, 1)
TODAY'S LONELY FOOL (Atlantic, '92, 3)
ALIBIS (Atlantic, '93, 1)
CAN'T BREAK IT TO MY HEART (Atlantic, '93, 1)
MY SECOND HOME (Atlantic, '93, 1)
IF THE GOOD DIE YOUNG (Atlantic, '94, 1)
I SEE IT NOW (Atlantic, '94, 2)

Additional Top 40 Country Songs: 3

tant '90s-born artists, with proof resting in an impressive set of Number One country songs.

Lawrence (b. Jan. 27, 1968, Atlanta, Texas) had just turned four when his family moved from Texas to Foreman, Arkansas, where he was raised by his mother and stepfather. Musically curious at age two, he would sit with his mother as she played stacks of Glen Campbell and Charley Pride records. He wrote a song at age four, "about a 17-year-old girl I liked that lived down the street," he says. His first organized musical experience was blowing trumpet in grade school and junior high bands. At 17 he played country music with various local groups. After two years of college he spent two years with a band whose music ran the gamut. "They literally went from George Jones' 'He Stopped Loving Her Today' to rapping 'Bust a Move,' with some Lynyrd Skynyrd and ZZ Top thrown in the middle," he claims.

In 1990, Lawrence struck out on his own and headed to Nashville. He arrived in the fall, supporting himself mostly by entering and winning talent contests at local clubs. He began to frequent all the known music industry hangouts and had luck in networking with the right people, including writers Randy Boudreau, Kim Williams, and Hank Cochran. A contract with Atlantic Records materialized quickly.

It was in mid-1991, just before his first album, *Sticks and Stones,* was to be released, that he and a lady friend were accosted in a hotel parking lot and Lawrence was shot four times. Remarkably, Lawrence made a full recovery. The album's title song, which he helped write, made it to the country chart peak.

All four singles from *Sticks and Stones* reached the top 10, but Lawrence didn't return to the top of the chart until the release of his highly successful sophomore album, *Alibis.* It yielded four consecutive Number One hits, including the title song and "If the Good Die Young."

Lawrence made an appearance in the 1994 movie *Maverick* and received a bonus when his song from the movie soundtrack, "Renegades, Rebels and Rogues," hit the top 10.

Two years into his career, Lawrence became a kind of role model for up-and-coming young performers who achieve rapid success. To cash in on the demand for Lawrence, his managers worked him so hard early on that they nearly burned him out. In 1993, Lawrence dissolved his management agreements and took control of his own career. Since then, other stars such as Clint Black, Lorrie Morgan, and Doug Stone have followed suit. "I think that was a good lesson for a young singer to learn," says Lawrence. "For the first two years I was a success, but I wasn't enjoying myself, and I was so tired I wasn't doing my best onstage. Now I take the time I need to be my best and enjoy life with my family."

Lawrence's third album, *I See It Now,* was released in late 1994, and the title song reached number two on the country chart.

BRENDA LEE

N ear the start of her career, Brenda Lee became known to the rock and roll and country worlds as Little Miss Dynamite. At four feet, eleven inches, Lee was, in fact, little. And with her string of hits and exuberant personality, Lee also proved to be dynamite over the course of a musical career that spanned more than three decades.

Lee was born Brenda Mae Tarpley on December 11, 1944, in Lithonia, Georgia. She grew up quickly. At age four she began singing the songs of Hank Williams on local television programs in Nashville. At six, she won her first talent contest. At a subsequent contest in 1956 she came to the attention of country great Red Foley, who invited her to become

Brenda Lee

a part of his "Ozark Jubilee" television show. Her appearance on that program attracted the attention of Decca Records, which offered Lee a contract that same year.

Her 1956 debut record, a version of Hank Williams' classic song "Jambalaya," failed to chart. But when "One Step at a Time" rose to number 15 country in 1957, she was on her way.

"She was so small," said legendary country producer Owen Bradley about Lee early in her career. "The thing that got me was how confidant she was." Perhaps it was that confidence that gave Lee the ability to make several startling career moves. The first was away from country music.

It began with her next single of 1957, the bouncy "Dynamite," which became a minor hit on the pop charts. With the follow-up, "Sweet Nuthin's," Lee was catapulted into the upper ranks of the burgeoning rock and roll scene. She went to Number One in 1960 with both "I'm Sorry" and "I Want to Be Wanted." From 1960 to 1966, Lee scored 21 top 40 hits on the pop charts, five of which were million-selling singles.

During her 1960s heyday, Lee was on top of the pop world. She got a fan letter from Elvis Presley. She performed before the Queen of England. And the opening act for her early '60s tour of Germany was a then-obscure Liverpudlian quartet called the

TOP SONGS

One Step at a Time (Decca, '57, *15*)
Nobody Wins (MCA, '73, *5*)
Sunday Sunrise (MCA, '73, *6*)
Wrong Ideas (MCA, '74, *6*)
Big Four Poster Bed (MCA, '74, *4*)
Rock On Baby (MCA, '74, *6*)
He's My Rock (MCA, '75, *8*)
Tell Me What It's Like (MCA, '79, *8*)
The Cowgirl and the Dandy (MCA, '80, *10*)
Broken Trust (MCA, '80, *9*)

Additional Top 40 Country Songs: 9

Beatles. "When I came back to the States, I tried to get Decca to sign them, but they weren't interested," Lee told *USA Today* in 1991.

After the release of 1966's "Coming On Strong," Lee's pop career began to decline. Like other rock stars before her—Jerry Lee Lewis being one of the most notable—Lee turned to her country roots. She started slowly, in 1969, with "Johnny One Time," which hit number 50 on the country charts. Subsequent singles, such as "If This Is Our Last Time" and "Always on My Mind," were also modest hits into 1972.

In 1973, Lee's country career finally blossomed when "Nobody Wins" hit number five. That single was the start of a notable run on the country chart, with Lee amassing 16 top 40 hits over the next 12 years. They included 1973's "Sunday Sunrise," 1974's "Rock on Baby" and "Big Four Poster Bed," and 1980's "Broken Trust."

Along the way, Lee sang with two of country's leading performers. In 1983 she and Willie Nelson had a number 43 chart hit with their duet "You're Gonna Love Yourself (In the Morning)," and in 1984 she and George Jones hit number 15 with "Hallelujah, I Love You So."

Lee appeared on stage, screen, and radio. She acted in the film *Smokey and the Bandit 2* and hosted a syndicated radio program, "Brenda Lee's Country Profile." As the director of the Country Music Association, Lee also spent much of her time publicizing the country music scene.

Active at the dawn of the 1990s, Lee said, "The big thrill for me is to still be in the business, being accepted and still doing it." That "big thrill" is well deserved, given Lee's accumulated sales of some 100 million records.

JOHNNY LEE

A longtime featured vocalist at Gilley's honky-tonk in Pasadena, Texas, Johnny Lee gained national fame—and Number One hits—when that nightclub became the focus of the 1980 film *Urban Cowboy.*

He grew up in the 1950s on a dairy farm in the east Texas town of Alta Loma. When not milking cows, young Lee (b. John Lee Hamm, July 3, 1946, Texas City) would absorb and emulate the sounds of Elvis Presley, Jerry Lee Lewis, Chuck Berry, and the

---

TOP SONGS

LOOKIN' FOR LOVE (Full Moon, '80, *1, 5 Pop*)
ONE IN A MILLION (Asylum, '80, *1*)
PICKIN' UP STRANGERS (Full Moon, '81, *3*)
PRISONER OF HOPE (Full Moon, '81, *3*)
BET YOUR HEART ON ME (Full Moon, '81, *1*)
HEY BARTENDER (Full Moon, '83, *2*)
THE YELLOW ROSE (Warner, '84, *1*)
YOU COULD'VE HEARD A HEART BREAK (Warner, '84, *1*)

Additional Top 40 Country Songs: 12

Tater Pete country music radio show. "I'd go out there and sing my heart out," he says, "hold me a concert for them cows, I guess."

By the time he was in high school, others were listening. The Future Farmers of America band at Santa Fe High brought him in as a singer in time to win a local talent contest and a statewide competition. From that group he formed Johnny Lee and the Road Runners, and they played area high school dances.

When the band broke up, Lee joined the Navy and shipped off to Vietnam, where he did some playing on the guided-missile cruiser the U.S.S. Chicago. Back in the States four years later, he bummed around California for a while, considered becoming a police officer, and then, feeling the pull of show business, made his way back to Texas. He played briefly in a trio called the Jesters and rustled up the odd day job and nighttime club date.

He'd long been a fan of singer Mickey Gilley and aimed to work with him. On one occasion in 1968, Lee drove to a club in Pasadena where Gilley was playing. "I got up my nerve and went over and said, 'Hey, Gilley!'" recalls Lee. "He turned around and said, 'Hey, how are you doing?' I said, 'You remember me, don't you? I did a job with you in Galveston, Texas, must have been a year or so ago.' . . . And he said, 'Oh, yeah, yeah, I remember.' But I'd never met him before in my life." Lee asked if he could sit in and sing a song, and Gilley let him. "I stayed up there a while," Lee says. "And I came back a couple of times, and the first thing you know, he offered me a job." The careers of the two remained intertwined for many years thereafter. When Gilley opened his later-to-become-famous nightclub in Pasadena in 1971, Lee stayed with him, becoming a regular singer with the house band.

At the same time, Lee pursued a recording career. He signed with ABC/Dot Records in the mid-'70s and issued the modestly successful single "Sometimes" (number 59). Six more chart-worthy releases, popular on Texas radio, carried Lee into 1978.

It looked as if he'd be permanently relegated to regionality when Gilley's club was chosen as the main setting for the 1980 John Travolta film *Urban Cowboy*. Lee appeared in the film and recorded a song, "Lookin' for Love," that was used on the soundtrack. "Lookin'" became a smash crossover hit, topping the *Billboard* country singles chart and reaching number five in the pop Hot 100.

Urban Cowboy brought on a wave of national interest in western sounds and style, and Lee—a man in the right place at the right time—rode it like one of those mechanical bulls depicted in the film. He wasted little time in opening his own club, Johnny Lee's, down the road from Gilley's. "We'll have Johnny Lee belt buckles," he predicted, "Johnny Lee beer, Johnny Lee panties, Johnny Lee shirts, the whole bit."

The ride carried him a decent way into the realm of national celebrity. For a healthy half a decade he remained chart-viable, scoring four more Number One hits and 11 more top 40s. He married actress Charlene Tilton of TV's "Dallas." But the marriage ended, the hits stopped, and for a spell in the mid-1980s, Lee had no record label.

Curb Records picked him up in 1989 and new singles were issued, but Johnny Lee—at least through the mid-1990s—was not to reexperience heady, bucking-bronco glory of the *Urban Cowboy* kind.

JERRY LEE LEWIS

Jerry Lee Lewis is, and probably forever will be, known primarily as one of the founding fathers of rock and roll. What is less known is that he is also one of the more enduring country performers, his career in country lasting far longer and producing far more hits than his somewhat brief but crucial involvement in rock.

Born on September 29, 1935, in Ferriday, Louisiana, Lewis spent his youth soaking up the rich musical brew of the South. His parents sang at the local Assembly of God, and they imbued in him a love of gospel. Along with his cousin (and future country star) Mickey Gilley, he also listened to the hillbilly

---

TOP SONGS

WHOLE LOT OF SHAKIN' GOING ON (Sun, '57, *1, 3 Pop*)

GREAT BALLS OF FIRE (Sun, '57, *1, 2 Pop*)

YOU WIN AGAIN (Sun, '57, *2*)

WHAT'S MADE MILWAUKEE FAMOUS (HAS MADE A LOSER OUT OF ME) (Smash, '68, *2*)

SHE STILL COMES AROUND (TO LOVE WHAT'S LEFT OF ME) (Smash, '68, *2*)

TO MAKE LOVE SWEETER FOR YOU (Smash, '68, *1*)

SHE EVEN WOKE ME UP TO SAY GOODBYE (Sun, '69, *2*)

THERE MUST BE MORE TO LOVE THAN THIS (Mercury, '70, *1*)

WOULD YOU TAKE ANOTHER CHANCE ON ME (Mercury, '71, *1*)

CHANTILLY LACE (Mercury, '72, *1*)

Additional Top 40 Country Songs: 39

---

music of the 1930s and '40s that was evolving into country. And as a teenager he frequented clubs and roadhouses of the South, listening to and learning the ways of the black blues and R&B musicians.

At the same time, he learned to play the piano, which he'd taken up at age nine. By 15, he was performing, reportedly making his stage debut at a local Ford dealership.

In 1956 Lewis signed a contract with the soon-to-be-legendary Sun label. His first record was a version of a country song, Ray Price's "Crazy Arms," that didn't register in rock.

But in mid-1957, Lewis'"Whole Lot of Shakin' Going On" shook the rock world with quake-like power. "Great Balls of Fire" did it again at the end of the year. Both singles became defining classics of the rock era. And with his wild antics onstage and off and his trademark piano-pounding acrobatics, Lewis himself became one of the icons of rock and roll. Ironically, both records were even bigger hits on the country chart, topping it while hitting numbers three and two, respectively, on the pop listings.

When Lewis released "Breathless" in 1958, the single promptly went to seven pop and—true to form—four on the country chart. Lewis, it seemed, could do no wrong.

But just as his career began to peak, Lewis suddenly could do no right. During a tour of Great Britain in 1958, word leaked out that he had married his 13-year-old second cousin, Myra (the daughter of his bassist). The scandal ruined his rock career.

In the late 1960s, Lewis made a comeback—but in country music rather than rock and roll. He had flirted with country during the late 1950s and the early '60s, scoring minor hits with versions of "What'd I Say" in 1961 and "Cold Cold Heart" in 1964 (apart from his late-'50s megahits). But in 1968 he returned to the charts in a big way with four top five singles, including "To Make Love Sweeter for You," which hit Number One at the beginning of 1969.

From that point on, Lewis' country career eclipsed his rock activity in years and hits. Over the succeeding two decades, he scored such top 40 country singles as "One Has My Name (The Other Has My Heart)," "There Must Be More to Love Than This," "Chantilly Lace," and "Middle Age Crazy," among many others.

The title of the latter reflected Lewis' life as much as his music. The former rock and roll madman of the 1950s grew even crazier as he got older. His life was filled with various and sundry tragedies and controversies. In 1973 he was arrested for waving a derringer at the gates of Elvis Presley's Memphis home, demanding to see and speak with the King.

He shot his bass player at one point, ran his Rolls Royce into a ditch at another. He sparred with the tax authorities (and won). He lost two sons and two (of five) wives along the way. And he nearly died at several points, of various illnesses. The public didn't call him the Killer for nothing.

But Lewis remained a defining figure of his time, a pop icon. In 1989 he released the single "Never Too Old to Rock 'n' Roll," a record that seemed to sum up his role in rock and country music.

LITTLE TEXAS

L ittle Texas debuted in 1991 with the top 10 "Some Guys Have All the Love." They provided some of the surest evidence that country audiences were skewing younger demographics. Heavy metal in look, with shoulder-length hair, sometimes shirtless and leather-togged, Little Texas caught on with a contemporary country sound that borrowed as much from the Beatles as Bob Wills. They steadily became one of the most important acts of the 1990s by helping to broaden country's listenership.

Longview, Texas, high school buddies Duane Propes (b. Dec. 17, 1966, Houston, Texas; bass and vocals) and Porter Howell (b. June 21, 1964, Houston; lead guitar and vocals) played together in local bands in the early 1980s. By 1985, they had moved to Nashville to attend Belmont College. Tim Rushlow (b. Oct. 6, 1966, Oklahoma City; lead vocals, guitar, mandolin) moved to Nashville from Arlington, Texas, in 1986 and hooked up with Dwayne O'Brien (b. July 30, 1963, Ada, Oklahoma; guitars and vocals), who had arrived in 1987. Brady Seals (b. Mar. 29, 1969; keyboards and vocals) and Del Gray (b. May 8, 1968; drums and vocals) were both from the Hamilton, Ohio, area and had worked together in local bands before heading to Nashville. By 1988, Propes and Howell were performing with Rushlow and O'Brien when Seals and Gray joined them to complete the band.

That same year, they got a development deal with Warner Brothers Records and went into the studio to record some demos. "We listened to these songs and said, 'Man, this is not working, these songs aren't us,'" says Propes. "The label put us on the road and said, 'We want you to become a band, get to know yourselves, and find an attitude and a sound.'"

So began three years of dues paying in "every dive hole in America" as they honed their sound and writing skills. By 1991 Warner Brothers was impressed by their progress and put them into the studio to record their debut album. They had once dubbed themselves Possum Flat, "for all the flattened critters we'd see on the road," they explained. Their official name was derived from an area near Nashville that had once been known as Little Texas because of all the rough and rowdy honky-tonks that lined that stretch of the highway during the 1930s and '40s.

Their first single, "Some Guys Have All the Love," reached number eight. An accompanying video established their image: it opened with close-up scenes of their flashy cowboy boots walking across the screen and then revealed their entire, rock-outfitted figures. Their next few releases dipped in and out of the top 10 as country radio held back from fully embracing their hybrid concept. But with subsequent videos and an increasingly popular, very energetic concert presentation, Little Texas moved ahead.

The 1993 release of their second album, *Big Time,* solidly established them as a hit act when the CD's first single, "What Might Have Been," hit number two. They followed it with the high-impact track "God Blessed Texas" and the Number One single (their first), "My Love."

Tim Rushlow had sung lead vocals on most of their hits, but Brady Seals was the voice heard on "My Love." Seals (the cousin of pop and country star Dan Seals and country songwriter Troy Seals) left Little Texas a few months after the success of "My Love" to begin a solo career. He was replaced

TOP ALBUMS

FIRST TIME FOR EVERYTHING (Warner, '91)
BIG TIME (Warner, '93)
KICK A LITTLE (Warner, '94)

TOP SONGS

SOME GUYS HAVE ALL THE LOVE (Warner, '91, 8)
YOU AND FOREVER AND ME (Warner, '92, 5)
WHAT MIGHT HAVE BEEN (Warner, '93, 2)
GOD BLESSED TEXAS (Warner, '93, 4)
MY LOVE (Warner, '94, 1)
KICK A LITTLE (Warner, '94, 5)
AMY'S BACK IN AUSTIN (Warner, '94, 4)

by keyboardist and fiddle player Jeff Huskins (b. Apr. 26, 1966) of Arlington, Texas.

Big Time was certified platinum just before the summer 1994 release of their third album, *Kick a Little.*

PATTY LOVELESS

Patty Loveless

Patty Loveless is a Kentucky coal miner's daughter who made good, just like her cousins Loretta Lynn and Crystal Gayle. With her powerful, traditional country voice, Loveless was prominent among female artists who emerged in the 1980s.

Loveless (b. Patricia Ramey, Jan. 4, 1957, Pikeville, Kentucky) grew up the seventh of eight children in a family that fell on hard times when her father fell ill and eventually died of black lung, the coal miner's disease. An extremely shy and introspective child, she enjoyed singing but would only perform for family and guests from behind the closed door of the kitchen. Her older brother Roger Ramey got her on stage when she was 12 and became her mentor and promoter.

At age 13, Loveless and her brother began to make trips to Nashville. They met Porter Wagoner and Dolly Parton, who encouraged Loveless to sing; Parton's writing inspired her to begin creating her own songs. "Between 14 and 16 I wrote 30," says Loveless. "Porter and Dolly were friends and advisors to me up until I was 18."

Loveless came to the attention of the Wilburn Brothers, who were trying to find the right girl to replace Loretta Lynn. She worked with the Wilburns just long enough to fall in love and elope with their drummer, Terry Lovelace. He formed a rock band, and Patty spent the next seven years singing rock and roll music.

By the mid-1980s her marriage was failing, and she was feeling the urge to return to her country roots. She contacted her brother, who agreed to try once again to promote her as a country recording artist. They recorded a demo of songs that included some of her original material. Ramey took it to the MCA Records offices, where he managed to intercept producer and MCA chief Tony Brown in a corridor. "He insisted I listen to this tape," says Brown. "So I told him I'd listen to one song—half a song—and that's it. Once I heard that voice I listened to the whole tape and told him not to let anybody else in town hear it."

With her married name of Lovelace modified to Loveless, she signed with MCA in 1985. The first singles included a song, written when she was 17, called "I Did." A debut album, *Patty Loveless,* soon appeared and yielded two more singles—"After All" and "You Saved Me"—that hovered just under the top 40 mark.

Loveless' sophomore album, *If My Heart Had Windows,* proved her breakthrough. The title tune reached top 10 in 1988, followed by the number two performance of a Steve Earle composition titled "A Little Bit in Love." The way was paved for album three, which contained both a wide range of material and her first two Number One songs, "Timber, I'm Falling in Love" and "Chains."

In 1989, Loveless delivered a key performance with her brilliant, high-harmony background vocals on Vince Gill's "When I Call Your Name." The song became the Country Music Association's Single of the Year in 1990, and Gill correctly cited her singing as essential to its success.

In 1992, feeling that MCA was too heavily laden with top female acts (including Reba McEntire, Wynonna Judd, and Trisha Yearwood), Loveless moved over to Epic Records. With her husband, Emory Gordy, Jr., as her producer (he had co-produced her early sessions on MCA), she created such high-impact hits as "Blame It on Your Heart" and "How Can I Help You Say Goodbye."

"I recorded songs that were kind of sassy and middle of the road," says Loveless of her overall con-tribution to country. "But I think it is very important to keep the traditional sound alive in country music, and I hope that I played a part in that."

LYLE LOVETT

Blues-tinged and jazz-inflected while country-based and Texas-born, Lyle Lovett's sound brought stylistic variety to Nashville in the late 1980s. Lovett also shook the rafters a bit with his distinctly unconventional image and skewed variations on age-old country themes. While neotraditionalists wore cowboy hats and crooned about losers, boozers, and broken hearts, Lovett sported an unruly, sky-high pompadour; favored suits in bohemian black; and sang of "redneckness" as a disease and of warped, loaded-pistol solutions to romantic conflict. An apparent one-man country emissary to the pop left field, Lovett was, in the combined words of pundits, a "postpunk cowboy" with "the tallest hair in Nashville," purveying a cosmopolitan, "uptown down-home sound."

"I view what I'm doing as a continuation of a non-Nashville tradition that includes the Eagles, Jackson Browne, James Taylor, and John Prine," Lovett said in the *New York Times.* He also drew inspiration from "Texas-school" songwriters Guy Clark and Townes Van Zandt. "They really knew how to present their point of view in a song," he told the *Chicago Tribune*'s Lynn Van Matre. "They don't mince words, they say what they mean, and they don't seem to worry if one of their songs is going to get on the radio."

Lovett (b. Nov. 1, 1956) was raised on property that had been in his family since the 1840s in a town north of Houston called Klein, named after his great-great-grandfather. As he grew up, so did Houston, placing him in mixed urban and rural surroundings that would have an impact on his songwriting. When young he played some guitar and had a high school band with members of the Future Farmers of America. But it wasn't until college that he began seriously delving into music. While working toward degrees in journalism and German at Texas A&M University he wrote songs and and played solo in local hangouts.

In the early 1980s Lovett performed as much as he could, targeting songwriter showcase clubs rather than places that would require him to play others'

TOP ALBUMS

If My Heart Had Windows (MCA, '88)
Honky Tonk Angel (MCA, '89)
On Down the Line (MCA, '90)
Only What I Feel (Epic, '93)

TOP SONGS

A Little Bit in Love (MCA, '88, 2)
Timber, I'm Falling in Love (MCA, '89, 1)
Chains (MCA, '90, 1)
Blame It on Your Heart (Epic, '93, 1)
How Can I Help You Say Goodbye (Epic, '94, 3)

Additional Top 40 Country Songs: 12

Lyle Lovett

hits. From venues in Houston, Austin, and Dallas, he branched out to cities in other parts of the country. A break came his way in 1983 when he wrote a song for, and appeared in, the CBS-TV movie "A Bill of His Own." Another occurred when he performed in September 1983 at a festival in Luxembourg and met a band from Phoenix called J. David Sloan and the Rogues. They hit it off, and in the summer of the following year, he and the band convened in Scottsdale, Arizona, and recorded 18 Lovett songs. Four were included on a demo that Lovett brought along when he traveled to Nashville to sing on an album by friend and fellow songwriter Nanci Griffith. Some well-connected people—including ASCAP's Merlin Littlefield and songwriters Jom Rooney and Guy Clark—heard Lovett's tape and were impressed. Through Rooney, Lovett connected with Criterion Music and cut a publishing deal. Through Clark, the tape made its way to MCA vice president of A&R Tony Brown. A contract with MCA/Curb Records followed.

Released in 1986, his debut album, *Lyle Lovett,* produced four top 40 country hits and attracted wide attention. Singled out by critics was "God Will," a song with a lyrical twist that exemplified

Lovett's ability to come up with wry reworkings of country clichés and subject matter.

The follow-up disc, 1987's *Pontiac,* offered enough sonic variety for MCA/Curb to begin promoting Lovett to non-country radio formats. On country, he scored another four chart entries, three of them in the top 40. "She's No Lady (She's My Wife)" proved the most discussed, its sardonic take on marriage neatly dovetailing with the theme of another track, "L.A. County," in which a jilted man plans to bring a gun when he attends his ex-lover's wedding.

Lovett assembled and went on the road with an 11-piece outfit whose name served as the title of his third album, *Lyle Lovett and His Large Band* (1989). Its facility with swing jazz and R&B—providing superb backing for Lovett's understated, blues-edged vocals—set the band apart. It also gave new life to the question of whether Lovett was producing anything resembling mainstream country, a question that appeared to be answered by his diminishing presence on the country singles chart.

Lovett's subsequent moves seemed to take him further toward the pop center. In 1991 he joined a set of rock luminaries on the Grateful Dead tribute album *Deadicated.* He had a featured role in the acclaimed Robert Altman film *The Player.* Lovett's 1992 disc *Joshua Judges Ruth* was his first to be recorded in Los Angeles. And in June 1993 he married actress Julia Roberts, a mating that seemed destined to become material for one of his songs when it ended in early 1995—nearly six years after his last chart entry, "If I Were the Man You Wanted."

TOP ALBUMS

LYLE LOVETT (Curb/MCA, '86)
PONTIAC (Curb/MCA, '87)
LYLE LOVETT AND HIS LARGE BAND (Curb/MCA, '89)
JOSHUA JUDGES RUTH (Curb/MCA, '92)
I LOVE EVERYBODY (Curb/MCA, '94)

TOP SONGS

COWBOY MAN (Curb/MCA, '86, 10)
GOD WILL (Curb/MCA, '87, 18)
WHY I DON'T KNOW (Curb/MCA, '87, 15)
GIVE BACK MY HEART (Curb/MCA, '87, 13)
SHE'S NO LADY (Curb/MCA, '88, 17)

Additional Top 40 Country Songs: 2

LORETTA LYNN

Loretta Lynn is a country legend with a life straight out of a movie script; in fact, it became a script for the film *Coal Miner's Daughter,* which was based on Lynn's autobiography. Alone— and with her singing partner, Conway Twitty—Lynn created a body of work that virtually defined country music.

She was born in Butcher Hollow, Kentucky, on April 4, 1934. And true to the song (and book and film), her father, Melvin Webb, was indeed a coal miner for the Van Lear mines. Loretta sang in church and at various local shows and events in her youth, which was cut short when she got married at age 13 to Oliver "Doolittle" Lynn in January 1948.

Her musical career didn't get started until the 1950s, when she and Lynn and their brood moved to Custer, Washington, where she formed a group with her brother, Jay Lee Webb. At the end of the decade she signed a contract with Zero Records and in 1960 released her debut record, "I'm a Honky Tonk Girl."

Lynn and her husband promoted the single by driving from one radio station to the next in their beat-up Mercury sedan. "We didn't know anything about releasing a record, but we tried our best," noted Lynn in her autobiography. "Doolittle had a hobby of photography at the time, so he made up a picture of me. We mailed out 3,500 copies of the record and my picture and sent them to every radio station we could find." "I'm a Honky Tonk Girl" eventually hit number 14 on the country chart.

The record's success gained the attention of the Wilburn Brothers, who recruited Lynn and her group as part of their tour in 1960 (Lynn would continue to tour with the Wilburns until 1968). The Wilburns encouraged Lynn to move to Nashville, which she did in 1960, subsequently securing a contract with Decca Records.

In 1962, Decca released the single "Success," which proved to be as good as its title, peaking at number six. From there, Lynn's popularity began to build steadily. In 1966 she scored her first Number One hit with "Don't Come Home A'Drinkin' (With Lovin' on Your Mind)." It was the first of many chart-topping songs, including "Fist City," "Coal Miner's Daughter," "One's on the Way," "Rated 'X,'" "Love Is the Foundation," and "Out of My Head and Back in My Bed."

As the hits rolled out, the awards did as well.

TOP SONGS

DON'T COME HOME A'DRINKIN' (WITH LOVIN' ON YOUR MIND) (Decca, '66, 1)

FIST CITY (Decca, '68, 1)

WOMAN OF THE WORLD (LEAVE MY WORLD ALONE) (Decca, '69, 1)

COAL MINER'S DAUGHTER (Decca, '70, 1)

ONE'S ON THE WAY (Decca, '71, 1)

RATED "X" (Decca, '72, 1)

LOVE IS THE FOUNDATION (MCA, '73, 1)

TROUBLE IN PARADISE (MCA, '74, 1)

SOMEBODY SOMEWHERE (DON'T KNOW WHAT HE'S MISSIN' TONIGHT) (MCA, '76, 1)

SHE'S GOT YOU (MCA, '77, 1)

Additional Top 40 Country Songs: 56

Loretta Lynn

Lynn was voted Female Vocalist of the Year by the Country Music Association in 1967, 1972, and 1973. In 1972 she became the first female artist to be named Entertainer of the Year by the CMA.

She was also honored four years in a row, from 1972 to 1975, as one-half of the Vocal Duo of the Year, with Conway Twitty. That duo was one of the most successful partnerships in country history. Their debut record, "After the Fire Is Gone," topped the chart in 1971. Over the next decade, they collected five Number One singles, along with seven other records that made the top 10. Lynn's vocal fire and feistiness were the perfect foils for Twitty's earnestness, and they merged in an original sound.

At times, their partnership seemed almost too convincing. "I'm always getting letters from Conway's fans who say I'm responsible for breaking up his marriage," Lynn wrote. "Those fans hear Conway and me singing on our records, or they know we're partners in a talent agency. But that's the only way we're partners."

The success of the 1980 film *Coal Miner's Daughter* (in which actress Sissy Spacek portrayed Lynn and won a Best Actress Oscar for her stirring performance) brought Lynn's life and music to the mass public, extending her legend far beyond the traditional country boundaries. And while her presence at the top of the charts began to fade somewhat, she continued to issue hits on a steady basis, reaching the top 40 11 times during the rest of the decade with such songs as "Pregnant Again" (Lynn has six children).

In 1988, Lynn was elected to the Country Music Hall of Fame.

ROSE MADDOX

As the singer with the Maddox Brothers and Rose, the self-styled Most Colorful Hillbilly Band in the Land, Rose Maddox contributed to some of the wildest pre-rockabilly country sounds of the 1940s and early '50s. She continued on her own in later years, scoring top 40 hits and delving into bluegrass and gospel.

In 1933, Rose (b. Roseea Arbana Brogdon, Dec. 15, 1926, Boaz, Alabama) and the rest of the Maddox family (including siblings Cal, Cliff, Don, Fred, and Henry) migrated from Alabama to California's San Joaquin Valley, where they faced a future of

working as crop pickers. They were saved from it in 1937 when the Maddox brothers convinced a local furniture company to sponsor them on a country show on KTRB radio in Modesto. Rose, then 10 years old, was brought in to sing. The act took off, doing radio and playing in West Coast nightspots up until 1941, when the brothers were drafted into the service for World War II.

After the war, the act picked up where it had left off, now sporting spangled cowboy attire designed by Nathan Turk and blending high-spirited humor with over-the-top versions of country favorites played with electric guitar, stand-up bass, mandolin, and fiddle. Their first sides were recorded for the 4-Star label. They switched to Columbia in 1951, and before ceasing operation in 1956 they performed as regulars on KWKH-Shreveport's "Louisiana Hayride" and once on the "Grand Ole Opry."

Rose stayed on Columbia until 1959, when she signed with Capitol and proceeded to issue 13 top 40 country hits through 1964. The most successful was 1962's "Sing a Little Song of Heartache" (number three), followed by some duets with Buck Owens, including "Mental Cruelty" and "Loose Talk," both in 1961. Rose's brothers continued to accompany her on disc, notably the 1960 album *The One Rose*, which featured remakes of such Maddox Brothers and Rose favorites as "Philadelphia Lawyer" and "Sally Let Your Bangs Hang Down." A gospel album was cut for Capitol in that same year. In

---

TOP ALBUMS

MADDOX BROTHERS AND ROSE, 1946–1951, VOL. 1 (Arhoolie, '76)
ROSE MADDOX SINGS BLUEGRASS (Capitol, '62)

TOP SONGS

KISSING MY PILLOW (Capitol, '61, *14*)
I WANT TO LIVE AGAIN (Capitol, '61, *15*)
CONSCIENCE, I'M GUILTY (Capitol, '61, *14*)
SING A LITTLE SONG OF HEARTACHE (Capitol, '62, *3*)
LONELY TEARDROPS (Capitol, '63, *18*)

Buck Owens and Rose Maddox:
MENTAL CRUELTY (Capitol, '61, *8*)
LOOSE TALK (Capitol, '61, *4*)
WE'RE THE TALK OF THE TOWN (Capitol, '63, *15*)

Additional Top 40 Country Songs: 5

1962, she recorded *Rose Maddox Sings Bluegrass,* on which she was accompanied by ex–Bill Monroe fiddler Don Reno, guitarist Red Smiley, and Bill Monroe himself.

Maddox kept working over the years, performing live and recording such albums as *A Beautiful Bouquet* (with backing by Vern Williams and his band) and *Queen of the West,* on which she was joined by Merle Haggard and—on several tracks—Emmylou Harris. Maddox was still active in the 1990s.

BARBARA MANDRELL

As the title of one of her biggest hits suggests, Barbara Mandrell might have been country when country wasn't cool. But with her pop-oriented sound, sleek vocals, and glitzy persona, Mandrell was one of the artists whose crossover success made country cool to the public at large.

Mandrell was born December 25, 1948, in Hous-

Barbara Mandrell

ton, Texas. Raised mostly in Los Angeles, Mandrell was a prodigious musical talent who reportedly learned to play a number of instruments before she could read. By age 11 she was performing onstage, notably at the Showboat Hotel in Las Vegas; she also made her television debut on the program "Town Hall Party." When she was 13 she toured with Johnny Cash. And by the time she was in her middle teens she was playing piano, saxophone, bass, guitar, and banjo and singing with her father's group, the Mandrells.

After signing to the Mosrite label in the mid-'60s and releasing the record "Queen for a Day," she and her family moved to Nashville. She signed a contract with Columbia in 1969 and began pursuing a career that was aimed primarily at the country market. But even in her fledgling days on the country scene, Mandrell sang music that had potential to cross over.

In 1969 her first Columbia single, a version of Otis Redding's soul ballad "I've Been Loving You Too Long," became a hit on the country chart. On subsequent singles she continued in the soul vein with renditions of such classics as "Do Right Woman—Do Right Man" and Joe Tex's "Show Me." She had her first top 10 hit in 1971 with the single "Tonight My Baby's Coming Home."

Switching labels from Columbia to ABC/Dot in 1975, she maintained a chart presence with "Married But Not to Each Other" and "Woman to Woman," among many other songs. And with 1978's "Sleeping Single in a Double Bed" she hit Number One for the first time.

It wouldn't be her last. Her version of "(If Loving You Is Wrong) I Don't Want to Be Right" reached Number One in 1979, as did "Years." In 1981 she rose to the top again with "I Was Country When Country Wasn't Cool," which became one of her signature songs.

With that record and others of the time, Mandrell began redefining her sound and musical approach. The pop and soul inflections of her initial hits were combined with a slicked-up country feel that made Mandrell's records a crossover success with a fan base that far exceeded that of more traditional country artists. Along with such artists as Kenny Rogers, Larry Gatlin, and Anne Murray, Mandrell transformed traditional country into a pop-oriented product that was broadly appealing.

But she remained the darling of the country set. In 1980 and 1981, she was voted the Entertainer of the Year by the Country Music Association.

Mandrell shrewdly translated her recording success into activity in other entertainment media. In the 1980s she starred in her own television series along with her sisters Irlene and Louise. On those programs, Mandrell and her sisters expanded their act, playing a wide range of instruments, singing everything from pop and country to gospel, and performing comedy and dance. During the same period, Mandrell debuted as an actress in the television movie "Burning Rage."

But Mandrell's success was curtailed in 1984 when she nearly died in an auto crash. She spent weeks in the hospital with a concussion and other injuries. By 1985, however, she was back with a new television movie, a television special with Roy Acuff, and a new set of country hits.

KATHY MATTEA

In 1983, Kathy Mattea (b. June 21, 1959, Cross Lanes, West Virginia) scored a number 25 hit with her first chart record, "Street Talk." That generated some talk on the streets of Nashville, because it was extremely difficult for new female artists to get a serious shot at a recording career back then, much less score such a significant hit. Indeed, Mattea found it difficult to surpass it at first and didn't land in the country top 10 until 1986. But from that point on, she remained in the front lines of country performers, gaining a reputation as a roots-oriented artist of impeccable taste and musical integrity with such chart-topping songs as "Eighteen Wheels and a Dozen Roses" and "Come from the Heart."

Raised in the southern coal fields of West Virginia, Mattea sang and played guitar through high school before heading off to West Virginia University at Morgantown.

In college, Mattea fell in with a musical group called Pennsboro. "We used to hang out on the porch of this house we rented and picked and sang for hours," she recalls. "I really got turned on to bluegrass and acoustic music." Shortly after she turned 19, Mattea left West Virginia with Pennsboro's lead singer and headed for Nashville. Her friend lasted a short time and returned home, leaving Mattea with a decision. "I thought about breaking and running, too," she says, "but something told me I had to at least give it a good try before I gave up." Mattea held various jobs, including tour guide at the Country Music Hall of Fame. It was her demo singing and a stint on the road backing up Bobby Goldsboro that brought her to the attention of Mercury Records, who signed her to a contract in early 1983.

Her top 25 first single was followed by the release of *Kathy Mattea* in early 1984. That album and its follow-up, *From My Heart,* netted Mattea four top 40 songs, but her career didn't break open until 1986 and the release of *Walk the Way the Wind Blows.* Full of relationship-oriented songs, it

Kathy Mattea

TOP ALBUMS

WALK THE WAY THE WIND BLOWS (Mercury, '86)
UNTASTED HONEY (Mercury, '87)
WALKING AWAY A WINNER (Mercury, '94)

TOP SONGS

LOVE AT THE FIVE & DIME (Mercury, '86, 3)
GOIN' GONE (Mercury, '87, 1)
EIGHTEEN WHEELS AND A DOZEN ROSES
   (Mercury, '88, 1)
COME FROM THE HEART (Mercury, '89, 1)
BURNIN' OLD MEMORIES (Mercury, '89, 1)
SHE CAME FROM FORT WORTH (Mercury, '90, 2)
WALKING AWAY A WINNER (Mercury, '94, 3)

Additional Top 40 Country Songs: 20

helped define her style with the number three debut single, "Love at the Five & Dime," and the top 10 title tune. Those were the first two of 15 consecutive top 10 hits, which also included the Number One "Goin' Gone" and "Eighteen Wheels and a Dozen Roses," the latter a smash that became the Country Music Association's Single of the Year for 1988.

Mattea's life and career were enriched by her marriage to songwriter Jon Vezner. "He made me happier than I've ever been, and he lets me see some of his best stuff before anybody else," says Mattea. One he let her see was a touching composition inspired by his elderly grandparents and written with Don Henry. Mattea's recording of that tune, "Where've You Been," stopped climbing the chart at number 10, but it won Song of the Year honors from both the Country Music Association and the Academy of Country Music.

Mattea entered the 1990s buoyed enough by her success to release an "artistic" album that she hoped would work commercially. Critically acclaimed, *Time Passes By* yielded two top 10 songs, but eventually the album cost her momentum at country radio. The next releases from the disc dropped her out of the top 10 for the first time in five years. At a time when country music was dealing with an influx of popular new artists, male and female, Mattea was nearly shoved aside, releasing two songs in 1993 that failed to make the top 40.

She turned things around dramatically in early 1994 with a strong and commercially viable album, hitting number three on the chart with the first single and title song, "Walking Away a Winner."

McBRIDE AND THE RIDE

"**W**hen our first album came out, we were hyped as the next big whatever," said singer-bassist Terry McBride to *Tune-In*'s Sandy Adzgery. "So when the first record didn't chart, I was crushed."

Another single failed from McBride and the Ride's first album, 1990's *Burnin' Up the Road,* and the much-touted trio—which also included guitarist Ray Herndon and drummer Billy Thomas—seemed headed for early oblivion. But with three subsequent hits, the Ride held on and eventually hit its stride, establishing itself as a purveyor of straight-ahead country overlaid with tight, Poco-like vocal har-

McBride and the Ride

monies, fronted and largely conceived by McBride himself.

McBride's father was Dale McBride, a regionally popular Texas performer who scored some minor chart hits in the 1970s. Terry (b. Sept. 16, 1958, Austin, Texas) grew up in Lampasas, Texas, surrounded by Dale's sound. "On his days off he'd have the top pickers, these great pickers, over at the house, just pickin' and playin', workin' out some new tunes on a day off," McBride told writer Jay Saporita, "and for me, *shoot,* it was like Disneyland." Dale started Terry on guitar at age five. By his teens, Terry was playing in a country band. After high school graduation he joined his father on the road for three years of club work and paying dues.

After that he served two years as bassist in Delbert McClinton's band and—working out of Austin—forged a career playing with such others as Stevie Ray Vaughn and David Allan Coe.

It was during that period that McBride began paying regular visits to Nashville in the hope of getting his songs recorded. One contact, MCA Nashville president Tony Brown, took note of McBride's multiple singing-songwriting-playing abilities and in June 1989 invited McBride to join a band he was assembling. The other members were session players that Brown knew: Herndon, formerly of J. David Sloan and the Rogues, the band that backed Lyle Lovett on his breakthrough demos; and Thomas, drum veteran of stints with Vince Gill, Emmylou Harris, Rick Nelson, and others. With McBride singing leads, supplying much of the material, and playing bass, the band meshed.

"We were brought together for our musicianship—our ability to play," McBride told Adzgery. "It wasn't until later that we realized the harmonies were going to play such an important role." Singing in three parts, McBride, Herndon, and Thomas created a sound for which the Ride became noted, heard prominently on "Can I Count on You," the song that put the group on track. On the second album, *Sacred Ground,* they focused on harmony more intently and succeeded in placing two songs, "Going Out of My Mind" and McBride's "Just One Night," in the top five of the country chart. The record's title song, co-written by Kix Brooks of Brooks & Dunn, climbed to number two.

That was the Ride's high point. A follow-up album fared less well. When it became time to prepare an album number four in 1994, the label suggested some changes. The band name became Terry McBride and the Ride. Gone were Herndon and Thomas; in were replacements; McBride was shuffled further to the front. Songs came more from outside the band. "I had to be really diplomatic," McBride said to Deborah Price of *Country Song Roundup,* "and take a look at my career and say, 'Do I want to be an artist who writes all his songs just for the sake of writing them and let people know I'm a writer? Or do I want to be an artist who has hits because there's some great songs to record out there other than my own?' And that's the stand that I've taken."

Still, the band was unable to generate momentum with a new album. In 1995, while preparing yet another album, Terry McBride and the Ride were dropped from MCA Records.

TOP ALBUMS

Burnin' Up the Road (MCA, '90)
Sacred Ground (MCA, '91)

TOP SONGS

Can I Count on You (MCA, '91, *15*)
Sacred Ground (MCA, '92, *2*)
Going Out of My Mind (MCA, '92, *5*)
Just One Night (MCA, '92, *5*)
Love on the Loose, Heart on the Run
    (MCA, '93, *3*)
Hurry Sundown (MCA, '93, *17*)

Additional Top 40 Country Songs: 2

CHARLY McCLAIN

At the beginning of the 1970s, country music seemed content with the female stars who began careers in the 1960s (Loretta Lynn, Tammy Wynette, Dolly Parton, Barbara Mandrell). By the mid-'70s it was time to give a few new women a shot, and Reba McEntire and Charly McClain were among those who managed to break in. McClain first entered the country charts in 1976 but didn't reach the top 40 until 1978. Two years later she began a period of consistent top 10 hitmaking that marked her as one of the most important acts of the early '80s.

Charlie McClain

McClain (b. Charlotte Denise McClain, Mar. 26, 1956, Jackson, Tennessee) was raised in Memphis and got into organized music at age nine, when she joined her brother's band. In her teens, McClain's main reason for performing was to help keep her family intact. "My father had been ill when I was young, and I did music to please him," she remembers. "Later, when my parents seemed ready to divorce, their interest in helping me with my career gave them a reason to stay together." What fueled her ambition for a national career was her success on a regional radio show out of Memphis called the "Mid-South Jamboree," where she began appearing as a regular at age 17. By 20 she had scored a record contract in Nashville and chalked up a low-charting first single with "Lay Down" on Epic Records.

It took a couple more years to find the right combination of record producer and songs. In 1978 she cracked the top 40 with "Let Me Be Your Baby" (number 13). That was followed by "That's What You Do to Me," marking her first visit to the top 10 (peaking at number eight). Her next was "Men," which reached number seven in 1980. It was an important song, bolstering McClain's cultivated image of wholesome sexiness that appealed to the men in her audience without alienating female fans.

Her first Number One hit came in early 1981 with "Who's Cheatin' Who," and for the next several years she remained in the upper reaches of the charts. Between 1981 and '84 she collected nine of her 14 top 10s, including two duet hits with Mickey Gilley, "Paradise Tonight" (Number One) and "Candy Man" (number five).

Country stardom led McClain to appearances in the television shows "Hart to Hart," "Fantasy Island," and "CHiPs." It also brought her to the attention of a TV actor with ambitions to become a singer. She married former "One Life to Live" star Wayne Massey in 1984. He had charted a few songs in the early 1980s, and in 1985 he signed with McClain's label. That year, McClain and Massey entered the country chart twice, duetting on "With Just One Look in Your Eyes" (number five) and "You Are My Music, You Are My Song" (number 10).

Early in 1985, McClain had scored a Number One on her own with "Radio Heart." Following that song and the duets with Massey, her career began to fade. In 1988 the two switched to Mercury Records but couldn't resurrect either of their recording careers. McClain seemed resigned to that fact. "I think once you have peace with yourself," she said of her contented married life, "no matter what happens in your daily life or career you have the strength to handle it, accept it, and go on." By the end of the 1980s, McClain had settled down to a quieter life in the couple's Memphis-area home.

TOP ALBUMS

GREATEST HITS—CHARLY MCCLAIN (Epic, '82)
TEN YEAR ANNIVERSARY: THEN AND NOW (Epic, '87)

TOP SONGS

WHO'S CHEATIN' WHO (Epic, '80, *1*)
SURROUND ME WITH LOVE (Epic, '81, *5*)
SLEEPIN' WITH THE RADIO ON (Epic, '81, *4*)
THE VERY BEST IS YOU (Epic, '81, *5*)
DANCING YOUR MEMORY AWAY (Epic, '82, *3*)
PARADISE TONIGHT (with Mickey Gilley, Epic, '83, *1*)
RADIO HEART (Epic, '85, *1*)

Additional Top 40 Country Songs: 20

NEAL McCOY

Neal McCoy

Singer Charley Pride always promised to "pass it on," to help some worthy newcomer along. Neal McCoy was one that Pride passed it on to, when he discovered him and helped him get a record contract in 1987. One of country music's most in-demand live performers, McCoy asserted himself in the mid-1990s as a hit recording act as well.

McCoy (b. Hubert Neal McGauhey, Jr., July 30, 1958, Jacksonville, Texas) grew up in a musical family. His sister played various instruments, and his father and mother both sang. (McCoy's mother is from the Philippines, giving McCoy the distinction of becoming the first singer of Philippine descent to become a country star.) "In our house I learned every style of music imaginable, from gospel to jazz and rock," McCoy says. In college he played in garage bands and joined a gospel quartet.

His break came after he moved to Longview, Texas, where he worked a day job in a shoe store (and became known as the "singing shoe salesman" because of his habit of singing while he stocked the store shelves). He entered a talent contest at a Dallas club called the Bell Star. McCoy didn't win the contest, but one of the judges was a representative from Charley Pride's management company. Impressed, they took McCoy on as a client. He began opening Pride's shows, and Pride and company guided him to a contract with 16th Avenue Records. He had changed his last name from McGauhey to McGoy, and that's the name that appeared on his first chart record in 1988.

He changed his name again in 1990 when he signed with Atlantic Records as McCoy.

The move to Atlantic came after a series of low-charting 16th Avenue releases. Several more years passed before Atlantic began to see results, which started with "Where Forever Begins," McCoy's first top 40 hit, in 1992. In an era when country performers had just one or two chances to prove themselves, it was a tribute to McCoy's talent that the label had remained patient. "It wasn't Neal's fault," admitted Atlantic chief Rick Blackburn. "We simply hadn't found the right songs for him to sing."

When he wasn't scoring hits, McCoy sustained his career by building a reputation as a charismatic and musically eclectic stage performer. McCoy often stole the show as an opening act and earned standing ovations without a hit song to his credit. "I did have some acts who didn't want to hire me again to open for them," he confesses.

In 1993, he reached number 26 with the song "Now I Pray for Rain." The next release, "No Doubt About It," became his first Number One hit. He followed it with "Wink," another chart-topper and one of the biggest hits of 1994, assuring McCoy's place as a top act of the 1990s. "I had a lot

of fans stick with me for a long time before I gave them hits," he says, "so it was a good feeling to finally break through."

REBA McENTIRE

It took Reba McEntire nearly seven years (from her first chart record in 1976, "I Don't Want to Be a One Night Stand") to collect her first Number One, "Can't Even Get the Blues," in early 1983. It had been a slow rise from obscurity to prominence, but by the beginning of the 1990s, thanks to a constant flow of top 10 and Number One hits and her ability to evolve as a performer without alienating her fans, she had become the most popular and successful female artist in country music.

McEntire (b. Reba Nell McEntire, Mar. 28, 1954, Chockie, Oklahoma) is one of four children born to a rodeo rider named Clark McEntire. She received her first musical training from her mother, Jackie, who kept her children occupied during long trips to rodeo events by teaching them to sing songs. At one event in Cheyenne, Wyoming, a then five-year-old Reba planted herself in the lobby of the hotel and belted out the chorus of "Jesus Loves Me." A cowboy put a nickel in her hand, and McEntire had earned her first money as a singer.

As a teenager, McEntire and her younger sister, Susie, began singing background harmonies with their older brother, Pake, in a trio called the Singing McEntires. The family act performed together for several years hoping someday to land a recording contract. Those plans changed in 1974 when McEntire sang the national anthem at the National Rodeo Finals in Oklahoma City. Singer-songwriter Red Steagall heard that performance and helped her land a solo recording contract with Mercury Records in Nashville. "Reba first refused to go to Nashville without her brother and sister," her mother remembers, "but we decided it was better one of them got their foot in the door so they could help the others along later." (Eventually, McEntire did help her brother land a recording contract with RCA Records. Between 1986 and '88 Pake McEntire collected five top 40 hits. Susie McEntire toured briefly with her sister and later started a gospel and country recording career under her married name of Susie Luchsinger.)

In 1984, after scoring just six top 10 songs in

TOP ALBUMS

No Doubt About It (Atlantic, '94)
You Gotta Love That (Atlantic, '95)

TOP SONGS

Where Forever Begins (Atlantic, '92, 40)
Now I Pray for Rain (Atlantic, '93, 26)
No Doubt About It (Atlantic, '94, 1)
Wink (Atlantic, '94, 1)
For a Change (Atlantic, '94, 3)

Reba McEntire

seven years with Mercury Records, McEntire switched to the MCA label, and her career soon broke wide open. Beginning with "How Blue," a Number One in early 1985, through "Is There Life Out There," a top song in 1992, McEntire scored 24 consecutive solo top 10 hits, including 14 chart-toppers. During this period her total album sales topped 20 million, she took four Country Music Association Female Vocalist of the Year awards, and was the CMA's Entertainer of the Year for 1986.

McEntire doesn't regret the slow but steady growth of her career. "If I had gone right to the top like some of these singers are doing today, I couldn't have handled it," she says. "I wasn't ready, and I'd have been out of the business and doing laundry and washing dishes."

McEntire entered the 1990s as the reigning queen of country music. She has maintained her position since by "constantly reinventing herself," as *Billboard* magazine's Ed Morris once noted. McEntire began pushing against the boundaries of country music with more pop-oriented production on such songs as "Sunday Kind of Love," "Walk On," and "For My Broken Heart." Her stage show became increasingly flashy, featuring huge sets, multiple costume changes, video screens, and dancers. In spite of critics who claimed she had somehow forsaken country music, McEntire insisted she simply gives her fans what they want. "I'm in constant contact with my fans," she says. "I talk to them after every show. I pay attention to my fan club members and the letters we get in the mail. I take my cues from them, and if I go too far they tell me." McEntire is also one of the few top country stars who maintains

close contact with country radio programmers. She phones them to personally determine how her music is perceived by radio and the listening public.

Part of McEntire's charm, and perhaps even the secret to her success, is that she remained remarkably unaffected, self-effacing, and honest about her accomplishments. "I absolutely brought nothing into this fracas," she states. "I learned, I drained everybody's brain, I watched, I studied, and then I contributed, but I brought absolutely nothing in. I was a totally ignorant hick from Oklahoma. Thanks to all the teachers [Loretta Lynn, Dolly Parton, Barbara Mandrell, and others] that I have been able to work with and be associated with, I have become a pretty good singer and pretty knowledgeable person about the music business. Hopefully I have improved one or two techniques, hopefully I have inspired a few children, and the most important thing is, I hope and pray that I have been a positive role model."

TIM McGRAW

Growing up, Tim McGraw was good at sports like his baseball star father, Tug McGraw (pitcher with the New York Mets and the Philadelphia Phillies), but he was better at singing and playing the guitar. McGraw moved to Nashville in 1989 and debuted with an album, *Tim McGraw*, and three chart singles that failed to reach the top 40. His second album, *Not a Moment Too Soon*, was released not a moment too soon, because it contained a pair of career-making hits that helped drive the album to multiplatinum status, establishing McGraw as a top country artist.

McGraw was born on May 1, 1967, in Delhi, Louisiana, the product of a summertime romance between his mother and then minor-league player Tug McGraw. Tim McGraw didn't know who his real father was until he was 12 and didn't establish a relationship with him until he turned 18. In school he was known as Tim Smith, using his stepfather's last name. "My stepdad was a trucker, and when I was five or six years old, he used to take me on long runs with him to Texas," McGraw recalls. "He loved country music and played it all the time in the truck. I'd sit there in the seat with him singing along with those country songs at the top of my lungs."

As a teenager, McGraw excelled in football and baseball, and it looked like he would follow his birth

---

TOP SONGS

CAN'T EVEN GET THE BLUES (Mercury, '82, *1*)

HOW BLUE (MCA, '84, *1*)

SOMEBODY SHOULD LEAVE (MCA, '85, *1*)

WHOEVER'S IN NEW ENGLAND (MCA, '86, *1*)

ONE PROMISE TOO LATE (MCA, '87, *1*)

CATHY'S CLOWN (MCA, '88, *1*)

YOU LIE (MCA, '90, *1*)

FOR MY BROKEN HEART (MCA, '91, *1*)

IS THERE LIFE OUT THERE (MCA, '92, *1*)

DOES HE LOVE YOU (with Linda Davis, MCA, '93, *1*)

Additional Top 40 Country Songs: 44

Tim McGraw

father's path into professional sports. By the time he got into Northeast Louisiana University, knee injuries slowed his athletic career, and his interest turned toward making music. He got a guitar and began performing locally as a solo act, singing the songs of his biggest influences, Merle Haggard, Charley Pride, Mel Street, and Keith Whitley. It wasn't long before he quit school and headed to Tennessee.

He says he arrived in Nashville as naive as anybody who ever went there. He began to frequent a couple of so-called "writer hangouts" to start networking. "I blew a good part of my grubstake buying drinks for guys who I thought were well-connected writers but who were just like me, struggling to get noticed," he laments. After that, he worked day jobs and began performing anywhere he could around town while he learned the ropes. One of his peers and fellow strugglers was Tracy Lawrence, whose success in 1991 inspired McGraw to stay the course. Eventually, McGraw recorded demo tapes that he circulated in Nashville. He also sent one to Tug McGraw, who happened to be friends with an executive at Curb Records. Tug gave his friend the tape, and Curb became interested enough to help young McGraw record another demo just for them. On the basis of that tape, the label signed him up.

After the lackluster performance of his first album, McGraw's fortune turned somewhat on controversy with the release of the first song from the second album. The tune, "Indian Outlaw," came out in early 1994 and contained some tongue-in-cheek references to Native American stereotypes ("wigwams" and "beating on tom-toms" among them). A few Indian activists protested, and the resulting news coverage connected with the protest was credited with helping the song make it into the top 10.

TOP ALBUMS

TIM MCGRAW (Curb, '92)
NOT A MOMENT TOO SOON (Curb, '93)

TOP SONGS

INDIAN OUTLAW (Curb, '94, 8)
DON'T TAKE THE GIRL (Curb, '94, 1)
DOWN ON THE FARM (Curb, '94, 2)
NOT A MOMENT TOO SOON (Curb, '94, 1)

The follow-up song, "Don't Take the Girl," became McGraw's first country Number One. "I was glad to have the second hit with a more serious song," he says. "'Indian Outlaw' was just an innocent, feel-good song, so I felt validated after 'Don't Take the Girl.'"

McGraw's place as one of the most important acts to emerge in the 1990s was confirmed with the release in 1994 of "Down on the Farm" (number two) and "Not a Moment Too Soon," the latter spending two weeks at Number One in early 1995.

ROGER MILLER

Roger Miller

In many ways, Roger Miller was pure country. He had a cornpone sense of humor. His vocal twang was as thick as a Tennessee thicket. His music was always simple and straightforward. But in the 1960s, Miller created a body of songs that transcended their country roots and became vastly popular in the cultural mainstream.

Miller was born on January 2, 1936, in Fort Worth, Texas. He was raised mostly in the small town of Erick, Oklahoma, where it is said that he gave his first performance at age five at his uncle's one-room schoolhouse.

But from the start, Miller seemed to know that there was more to life than the proverbial sticks. "I grew up not wanting to pull cotton or milk cows," he told writer Vernell Hackett of *American Songwriter* magazine in 1988. "I wanted to write songs and be in the music business. There was something magic about the music business."

He spent a year as a ranch hand and, later, served three years with the U.S. Army in Korea. But after he was discharged, he made his way to Nashville to ply his songwriting trade. That trade didn't materialize right away. He spent a year as a bellhop at Nashville's Andrew Jackson Hotel.

But by the mid-'50s, Miller had begun making a name for himself in the music business. At the time he wrote about 150 songs that were recorded by the likes of George Jones, Ernest Tubb, and others. In 1958, Miller finally hit it big when his song "Invitation to the Blues" became a hit for Ray Price.

By 1960 he had a contract of his own with RCA. He had modest hits at the start of the decade with songs like "You Don't Want My Love" and "When Two Worlds Collide," which were respectable, if hardly noteworthy, fare.

But in 1964, Miller began a run on the charts that would make him one of the biggest country artists of the decade. The first hit, "Dang Me," was a lively bit of hokum pulled straight out of country vaudeville. But it also had a lithe pop sensibility that appealed to the mainstream record-buying public.

As the 1960s progressed, Miller hit the charts

TOP SONGS

When Two Worlds Collide (RCA, '61, 6)
Dang Me (Smash, '64, 1, 7 Pop)
Chug-A-Lug (Smash, '64, 3, 9 Pop)
King of the Road (Smash, '65, 1, 4 Pop)
Engine Engine #9 (Smash, '65, 2, 7 Pop)
Kansas City Star (Smash, '65, 7, 31 Pop)
England Swings (Smash, '65, 3, 8 Pop)
Husbands and Wives (Smash, '66, 5, 26 Pop)
Walkin' in the Sunshine (Smash '67, 7)
Little Green Apples (Smash, '68, 6, 39 Pop)

Additional Top 40 Country Songs: 21

again and again with that same winning combination of wry wit and immediately hummable, hook-laden melodies. "Kansas City Star," "Chug-a-Lug," "King of the Road," "You Can't Roller Skate in a Buffalo Herd," and a host of others had the whole country singing and smiling along. "I don't know what makes a good songwriter," Miller said at one point, "except a good heart and a little intelligence." In his biting, tongue-in-cheek songs from the '60s, Miller displayed both.

While Miller recorded mostly his own songs he also recognized talent in others. He was one of the first artists to record a song written by the fledgling Kris Kristofferson. In 1969, Miller's version of Kristofferson's "Me and Bobby McGee" hit number 12 on the country charts—preceding Janis Joplin's chart-topping version by a year.

Toward the end of the 1960s, however, Miller's career began to decline. While he continued to record, the hits stopped coming for the most part. And he increasingly spent time overseeing his hotel chain, named after one of his hits, King of the Road. He did make a comeback of sorts when he recorded the 1982 album *Old Friends* with Ray Price and Willie Nelson.

Miller, who had previously written songs for the film *Waterhole 3* and a version of *Robin Hood* by Walt Disney, moved in a new direction in the middle 1980s when he agreed to write the score for the splashy 1985 Broadway musical *Big River*. Based on the writings of Mark Twain, *Big River* became a big hit and won seven Tony awards, including those for best musical and outstanding score.

It would be the last great hurrah in Miller's career. He died on October 25, 1992.

RONNIE MILSAP

Ronnie Milsap claims that his blindness was more of a blessing than a curse, since if he'd been sighted he might have done other things with his life and not concentrated on music. A case can also be made that he would have found his way into a music career anyway. A musically gifted, classically trained multi-instrumentalist, Milsap had an ingrained feel for country music that brought him a total of 35 Number One hits in 16 years, making him one of the greatest country stars of all time.

Milsap (b. Jan. 16, 1946, Robbinsville, North Carolina) was raised in the Smoky Mountains of North Carolina near the Tennessee border. Blinded by congenital glaucoma, Milsap experienced the world through his ears. The first music he heard was the gospel music at revival tent meetings and the bluegrass generated by local pickers. At age six, he was sent away to the state school for the blind. It was there that his aptitude for music was discovered, and he was enrolled in their musical training program. He studied classical piano and violin and was good enough to have gone on to concert performing. But as a teenager he became curious about nonclassical music, and he was once kicked out of the music department of his school when he was caught pounding out some Jerry Lee Lewis tunes when he was supposed to be practicing Beethoven and Bach compositions.

In the early 1960s he turned down a scholarship to study law at Emory University and became involved in the music scene in Atlanta. In 1965 he was signed to Scepter Records as an R&B artist, and

Ronnie Milsap

he scored a number five soul chart hit with "Never Had It So Good." "My R&B career was cut short when my publicity picture was circulated and the soul stations found out I was a blue-eyed white guy," Milsap claims. "Legend has it that one of our promoters tried to convince some stations to play my music by telling them I was blind and had been told by people that I was a black and that I didn't know I was white."

Milsap later drifted to Memphis, where he became a popular club performer and session musician. He played piano on recordings for Petula Clark, Dionne Warwick, and Elvis Presley, including some memorable keyboard work on the King's "Kentucky Rain."

By the early 1970s, Milsap had moved to Nashville and begun appearing at Roger Miller's King of the Road club. He soon had several offers to record country music. He signed to Warner Bros., staying there briefly before landing at RCA Records in 1973. That year his first country chart single, "I Hate You," hit the top 10. A year later he scored his first Number One with a song written by Eddie Rabbitt called "Pure Love." From that point on, every RCA release up until 1992 went top 10—an incredible total of 48—with most of them hitting Number One. The list includes such Milsap classics as "(I'm a) Stand by My Woman Man," "It Was Almost Like a Song," "Only One Love in My Life," "Smoky Mountain Rain," and "(There's) No Gettin' Over Me," a song that hit top five on the pop chart. In 1993, Milsap left RCA to record with Liberty Records.

TOP SONGS

PLEASE DON'T TELL ME HOW THE STORY ENDS
(RCA, '74, 1)

DAYDREAMS ABOUT NIGHT THINGS (RCA, '75, 1)

IT WAS ALMOST LIKE A SONG (RCA, '77, 1, 16 Pop)

MY HEART (RCA, '80, 1)

SMOKY MOUNTAIN RAIN (RCA, '80, 1, 24 Pop)

(THERE'S) NO GETTIN' OVER ME (RCA, '81, 1, 5 Pop)

ANY DAY NOW (RCA, '82, 1, 14 Pop)

LOST IN THE FIFTIES TONIGHT (IN THE STILL OF
THE NIGHT) (RCA, '85, 1)

DON'T YOU EVER GET TIRED (OF HURTING ME)
(RCA, '88, 1)

A WOMAN IN LOVE (RCA, '89, 1)

Additional Top 40 Country Songs: 43

Milsap confesses to loving all forms of music, from rock to the classics, and includes examples of all of his musical influences in his popular stage show. Asked why he settled on country, he replies, "There's too much of those all-day singing picnics on the grounds, too much of getting up and singing for the foot-washing Baptists that I did as a kid, and there's too much country music and bluegrass in my blood to ignore it. Even if I had gone on to success as a soul singer or something else, I'd have had to return at some point to country, where my heart is."

BILL MONROE

He's the Father of Bluegrass, a patriarch of country music, and a venerated figure in American cultural history. Professionally active for more than 60 years, Bill Monroe led the Blue Grass Boys, a style-setting entity that showcased his mandolin playing and unique, high tenor vocal. The group—and Monroe—influenced generations of country musicians while providing on-the-job training to an elite roster of virtuosos, including Lester Flatt, Earl Scruggs, Vassar Clements, Mac Wiseman, and Bill Keith.

It was with ample justification that the U.S. Senate adopted a resolution in 1986 honoring Monroe as "a force of signal importance in our time."

He was born on a farm in Rosina, Kentucky, on September 13, 1911. Monroe's poor eyesight kept him at a distance from typical boyhood sports activities, but he gravitated toward music under the influence of his mother, Malissa (a singer, accordionist, and fiddle player), and his uncle Pen, a fiddler. Two older brothers, Charlie and Birch, played guitar and fiddle, respectively. At 10, Bill took up the mandolin.

After his mother and father died, Monroe lived with Pen. For a time he played guitar behind his uncle at local square dances and social events. (Monroe has credited his square dance days with teaching him the value of "thinking about the other man"— setting the rhythm and tempo to please the dancers. "You have to really know how to dance yourself to understand how it should be played," he told writer Peter Guralnick.) Another early influence was a black blues guitarist named Arnold Shultz, a local virtuoso about whom little is known.

At 18, Monroe followed his brothers Charlie and Birch to Indiana, where for five years he divided his

Bill Monroe

time between working day jobs (he washed barrels at the Sinclair oil refinery) and playing music with his brothers. At one point they were hired as square dancers for the "WLS Jamboree" road show. Monroe also performed on the "WLS Barn Dance" radio program.

In 1934, Birch quit just when the act secured the sponsorship of the Texas Crystals Company, a laxative manufacturer. Now a duo, the Monroe Brothers began making a name via live shows and radio broadcasts in Iowa, Nebraska, and the Carolinas.

The Victor Company took notice and wooed the not instantly receptive duo. "Back in my young days," Monroe told Guralnick, "you'd have heard people on record, you know, but you kind of shunned a lot of that stuff yourself." Finally convinced, they recorded for the first time in February of 1936. One of the resulting 10 sides, "What Would You Give in Exchange," became a hit. For the next two years the brothers waxed some 60 tracks.

The two split in 1938. Charlie formed a success-

ful group, the Kentucky Pardners (in which Bill's voice-and-mandolin role would eventually be played by Lester Flatt). Bill undertook to forge a new style, an instrumentally challenging music that would blend the old-time tunes of his Uncle Pen days with the blues. "I built it around my mandolin," Monroe says, "and I was going to put the high, lonesome sound in it, the hard drive to it, and play the melody where it would have a feeling in it."

Monroe assembled a group and named it the Kentuckians, then the Blue Grass Boys. They debuted on the WSM "Grand Ole Opry" radio program in October 1939—an occasion cited by some as the birthdate of bluegrass. Through the World War II years—even during a hiatus in record manufacturing due to shortage of shellac—the Blue Grass Boys steadily gained popularity with their regular Saturday night "Grand Ole Opry" broadcasts.

In 1944, guitarist-vocalist Lester Flatt joined the group, followed by ace banjoist Earl Scruggs. With Chubby Wise on fiddle and Howard Watts (a.k.a.

Cedric Rainwater) on bass, the classic Blue Grass Boys lineup was in place. Through 1948 they defined the bluegrass style, with mandolin, fiddle, and banjo playing leads; guitar holding down the rhythm; and high, clear voices covering the melody. Country hits (on Columbia Records) were scored—"Kentucky Waltz" and "Footprints in the Snow" among them—and tours were undertaken, notable for the huge circus tent that the band would set up in each small town in which they performed.

Flatt and Scruggs left to form their own group (eventually surpassing Monroe in breadth of fame). With a revamped band, Monroe entered a new phase in which he switched to Decca (later MCA) Records and penned what he called his "true true songs": evocative numbers like "Uncle Pen" and "Memories of Mother" and such classic instrumentals as "Rawhide," "Roanoke," and "Pine Country Breakdown."

Monroe held on through the 1950s and the birth of rock and roll, recording his first album, *Knee Deep in Bluegrass,* in 1958 and attracting a new, young audience of folk music enthusiasts as the 1960s dawned. His continued commercial viability—and that of bluegrass in general—was given a boost in the mid-'60s when Monroe initiated the first of what would be an annual, heavily attended bluegrass event: the Bill Monroe Bean Blossom Festival.

Following his induction into the Country Music Hall of Fame in 1970, Monroe continued to spend 150 to 200 days a year on the road with various editions of the Blue Grass Boys. In 1985 he recorded the Emory Gordy, Jr.–produced album *Bill Monroe and Stars of the Bluegrass Hall of Fame,* cited as "quite possibly the best bluegrass record ever made" by *Country Music* magazine. More albums followed, including *Bluegrass '87* and 1988's *Southern Flavor.*

A Lifetime Achievement Grammy Award was bestowed on Monroe in 1993.

JOHN MICHAEL MONTGOMERY

John Michael Montgomery debuted on the *Billboard* country chart in 1992. At first he was dubbed a Garth Brooks clone, due to similarities in their features, dress, and voice. The comparisons quickly faded when Montgomery drew on a lifetime of performing experience to establish his own country style and amass his own following of fans with a series of Number One hits.

Montgomery (b. Jan. 20, 1965, Danville, Kentucky) was raised in the Lexington, Kentucky, suburb of Nicholasville. His father, Harold, was a country performer who took a run at a recording career in the 1970s. "Back then my father was singing country rock stuff and did pretty good," says Montgomery. "He put out a song back in '75 or '76 that got him on the Grand Ole Opry, which was the thrill of his life."

When the elder Montgomery gave up trying to make it on the national music scene, he put his whole family in a country band, including his wife on drums and his two young sons. "What I remember at five years old was my mom and dad being on stage with some other musicians, and to me it was like a game," Montgomery says. "I think one of the first songs that I did was 'Nighttime Friends and Daytime Lovers' by Kenny Rogers. I was about six years old then."

He remained in the Montgomery family troupe until he was 17, at which point he and his brother, Eddy, struck out to form their own band. A few years later, Montgomery fronted another outfit called Erly Tymz and became the headlining act at a popular Lexington club called Austin City Saloon.

In 1991, after making a couple of exploratory visits to Nashville, Montgomery concluded he would

---

TOP ALBUMS

BILL MONROE AND STARS OF THE BLUEGRASS HALL OF FAME (MCA, '88)

THE ESSENTIAL BILL MONROE (1945–1949) (Sony, '91)

TOP SONGS

KENTUCKY WALTZ (Columbia, '46, 3)

FOOTPRINTS IN THE SNOW (Columbia, '46, 5)

SWEETHEART, YOU DONE ME WRONG (Columbia, '48, 11)

WICKED PATH OF SIN (Columbia, '48, 13)

LITTLE COMMUNITY CHURCH (Columbia, '48, 11)

TOY HEART (Columbia, '49, 12)

WHEN YOU ARE LONELY (Columbia, '49, 12)

SCOTLAND (Decca, '58, 27)

Additional Top 40 Country Songs: 1

have to move there to land a record contract. As it turned out, Nashville came to him. "A man named Estel Sowards brought another singer into the club to hear some of my original songs," John Michael recalls. "He was hoping to get this other singer a record deal, but when he heard my show he took me aside that night and said he thought he could get me a contract. He had contacts at Atlantic Records who came up to the club to see me, and I ended up getting signed."

Montgomery first entered the chart with "Life's a Dance," the title song of his debut album and a number four hit in early 1993. He followed it with a smash ballad, "I Love the Way You Love Me," that spent three weeks at Number One. His second album, *Kickin' It Up*, came out in late 1993, and in early '94 he scored a huge hit with "I Swear," a song that stayed at Number One for four weeks. It was

TOP ALBUMS

LIFE'S A DANCE (Atlantic, '92)
KICKIN' IT UP (Atlantic, '93)
JOHN MICHAEL MONTGOMERY (Atlantic, '94)

TOP SONGS

LIFE'S A DANCE (Atlantic, '92, *4*)
I LOVE THE WAY YOU LOVE ME (Atlantic, '93, *1*)
I SWEAR (Atlantic, '93, *1*)
BE MY BABY TONIGHT (Atlantic, '94, *1*)
IF YOU'VE GOT LOVE (Atlantic, '94, *1*)
I CAN LOVE YOU LIKE THAT (Atlantic, '95, *1*)
SOLD (THE GRUNDY COUNTY AUCTION INCIDENT)
(Atlantic, '95, *1*)

John Michael Montgomery

then covered by the pop R&B group All-4-One, and their version spent 11 weeks at Number One on the pop chart. "I was really pleased to see that happen," Montgomery claims, "to see that country music has become so popular that songs like 'I Swear' and Dolly Parton's 'I Will Always Love You' are getting covered by other formats."

Montgomery continued to score big hits with "Be My Baby Tonight" and "If You've Got Love," both from his second album, plus "I Can Love You Like That" (also covered by All-4-One) and "Sold (The Grundy County Auction Incident)" from his self-titled third album.

By the middle of 1995, Montgomery's albums had reached sales of over six million.

MELBA MONTGOMERY

Melba Montgomery was a queen of country duets. While she had hit records of her own, it was her work with George Jones, Charlie Louvin, and others that made her name and secured her place on the charts of the 1960s and '70s.

Montgomery was born on October 14, 1938, in Iron City, Tennessee. Her father taught music at a Methodist church in Florence, Alabama, where Montgomery spent most of her youth. She began to sing as a child and also learned to play guitar and fiddle.

Montgomery's music career got its start when her family moved to Nashville in the 1950s. With a group that included her brothers, she made the finals of a 1958 talent contest.

Their performance in the contest came to the attention of Roy Acuff, who recruited Montgomery as a vocalist in his group the Smoky Mountain Boys. Montgomery spent four years with Acuff's group. But in 1962 she decided to pursue a solo career, gaining a contract with United Artists.

The label paired her with George Jones, and the duo hit the charts in 1963 with the single "We Must Have Been Out of Our Minds." Jones had an ornery earnestness that complemented Montgomery's pop-tinged sincerity, and the two subsequently became a team of sorts while pursuing their individual careers.

Montgomery had a hit of her own in 1963 with

the single "Hall of Shame." But she continued her collaboration with Jones until 1967, scoring several hits on the charts in the process. During that period she also recorded an album with Gene Pitney.

Switching labels to Capitol Records, Montgomery hooked up with a new vocal partner, Charlie Louvin, with whom she enjoyed a number of hits during the 1970s. She also began to work with Pete Drake, with whom she collaborated when she moved to Elektra Records in the mid-'70s. Primarily a rock label, Elektra was attempting to expand into country, and Montgomery was one of the artists involved in that move. The result was a series of albums and singles that were similar in sound to the country-rock of the 1970s.

With her long, straight hair and sculpted face, Montgomery represented a new look in country music. At the time, most country female vocalists were more "traditional" in appearance, which is to say they favored big hairdos and rather garish stage costumes. With her jeans and white shirts, Montgomery had a look that was more in line with the country rockers of the '70s.

In 1974 she topped the charts with "No Charge," a talking ballad that was as sincere as it was sentimental. An album of the same title was also released and showcased Montgomery's crossover sound.

A number of moderately successful songs took Montgomery through the next few years. A downward trend on the country chart was broken twice,

TOP ALBUMS

BABY YOU'VE GOT WHAT IT TAKES (Capitol, '71)
NO CHARGE (Elektra, '74)
DON'T LET THE GOOD TIMES FOOL YOU (Elektra, '75)

TOP SONGS

WE MUST HAVE BEEN OUT OF OUR MINDS
    (United Artists, '63, 3)
WHAT'S IN OUR HEART (United Artists, '63, 20)
LET'S INVITE THEM OVER (United Artists, '63, 17)
BABY, AIN'T THAT FINE (Musicor, '66, 15)
SOMETHING TO BRAG ABOUT (Capitol, '70, 18)
NO CHARGE (Elektra, '74, 1, 39 Pop)
DON'T LET THE GOOD TIMES FOOL YOU
    (Elektra, '75, 15)

Additional Top 40 Country Songs: 9

by "Don't Let the Good Times Fool You" (number 15, 1975) and the pop-tinged "Angel of the Morning" (number 22, 1977), which had a folk-rock sound. But as the 1980s began, Montgomery declined as a hitmaking force in pop and country music.

GEORGE MORGAN

Called the Candy Kid, thanks to his 1949 Number One debut single, "Candy Kisses," George spent 30 years on the *Billboard* country singles chart. A smooth, emotive vocalist, he was among the many talented artists who joined the Grand Ole Opry in the late 1940s and early '50s, when it consolidated its position as the leading country music showcase.

Morgan (b. June 28, 1925, Waverly, Tennessee) grew up in Barberton, Ohio. He attended the University of Akron and then served in the U.S. Army during World War II. Afterward, he performed with bands and sang on the radio in Ohio before obtaining regular work on the WWVA "Jamboree" radio program in Wheeling, West Virginia, in the late 1940s.

A demo tape brought Morgan to the attention of the Grand Ole Opry. He joined it in 1948 and in the same year landed a recording contract with the Columbia label.

Morgan's first single, the original composition "Candy Kisses," debuted on the country chart in early 1949. It took Morgan all the way to Number One and attracted the attention of several other performers, including Elton Britt and Red Foley, who scored top 10 hits with their own versions in the same year.

As it happened, Morgan arrived and peaked in one short stretch of time: 1949 was the single most successful year of his career, chart-wise. During it he reached the top 10 with six singles and the top 20 with another. Of these, the number four "Room Full of Roses" also showed up on the pop chart, making it Morgan's only crossover single.

At 1949's end, Morgan abruptly dropped off the charts, not to return until two and a half years later, when the aptly titled "Almost" came within one point of reaching the top. Thereafter, his chart activity was spotty, peaking with "I'm in Love Again" (number three, 1959) and "You're the Only Good

Thing (That's Happened to Me)" (number four, 1960), his last major hit.

Part of the problem was the rise of both rock and roll and the pop-oriented Nashville Sound, challenging the traditional country approach that Morgan favored. Still, he held on as a Grand Ole Opry regular and was among the artists who weathered the commercial storm by banding together and performing in package shows in the mid-1950s.

After many years with Columbia Records, Morgan shifted to Starday in 1967. Five chart singles resulted, of which two—1967's "I Couldn't See" and 1968's "Sounds of Goodbye"—were in the top 40. With Stop Records in 1968–69 he scored two more top 40 hits: "Like a Bird" and "Lilacs and Fire."

Continuing his label hopping, Morgan moved over to Decca, then MCA, yielding 1973's number 21 "Red Rose from the Blue Side of Town" and several other minor chart entries. Meanwhile, he served for a time as president of the Association of Country Entertainers (ACE), an organization that started in 1974 as a reaction to country's increasing "pop" orientation, the ACE's purpose being to "preserve the identity of [traditional] country music."

In his last year, Morgan shifted labels yet again, this time to 4-Star. At the age of 50, having just released a new album (and undoubtedly planning to maintain his usual busy performance schedule), Morgan died of a heart ailment at Nashville's Baptist Hospital on July 7, 1975.

His daughter Lorrie made her own debut on the country chart four years later. By 1990 she had a Number One hit of her own.

TOP SONGS

CANDY KISSES (Columbia, '49, 1)
PLEASE DON'T LET ME LOVE YOU (Columbia, '49, 4)
RAINBOW IN MY HEART (Columbia, '49, 8)
ROOM FULL OF ROSES (Columbia, '49, 4, 25 *Pop*)
CRY-BABY HEART (Columbia, '49, 5)
I LOVE EVERYTHING ABOUT YOU (Columbia, '49, 4)
ALMOST (Columbia, '52, 2)
(I JUST HAD A DATE) A LOVER'S QUARREL (Columbia, '53, 10)
I'M IN LOVE AGAIN (Columbia, '59, 3)
YOU'RE THE ONLY GOOD THING (THAT'S HAPPENED TO ME) (Columbia, '60, 4)

Additional Top 40 Country Songs: 13

LORRIE MORGAN

Lorrie Morgan has been connected to country music literally all of her life. The youngest daughter of Grand Ole Opry star George Morgan, she first sang on the Opry at age 13. She grew up to become one of the leading female artists of the 1990s, reaching the top of the charts with such songs as "Five Minutes" and "What Part of No."

Morgan (b. Loretta Lynn Morgan, May 27, 1959, Nashville) showed early on that she was a chip off the block. "I was just a little girl when my sister would hold a flashlight and shine it on me like a spotlight so I could put on shows for the family in the living room," she recalls. Morgan loved growing up in the business, finding great country personalities like Loretta Lynn or Minnie Pearl sitting on her family's front porch. She also enjoyed hanging out at the Grand Ole Opry when her father went there to perform, but she was petrified the first time she sang

on the stage of the old Ryman Auditorium. "I don't remember anything but a big pole that held up the balcony," she says. "I just fixed a stare on that pole and don't remember seeing anything else until I walked off stage and my father said I had done good." She continued to perform on the Opry periodically with other "Opry brats" who appeared there, including a young Marty Stuart (a member of Lester Flatt's band) and Steve Wariner (a then-teenaged member of Dottie West's band). At 24, Morgan became one of the youngest members of the Grand Ole Opry, following in the footsteps of her late father.

Morgan first recorded in 1979 for ABC/Hickory Records and then MCA Records. She describes this early attempt as an uncomfortable experience, claiming that she was being advised to put forth a more contemporary image and disassociate herself from the Grand Ole Opry. "It was a time when traditional country music wasn't as important as it is now," she explains. "I got a reputation of being hard to

Lorrie Morgan

deal with, but I wasn't about to turn my back on an institution that I loved and that had been such an important part of my life."

From 1984 to '88, Morgan bided her time between record contracts by opening for George Jones, singing backup vocals on the Grand Ole Opry, and appearing on Ralph Emery's early morning TV show.

In 1986 she met and married Keith Whitley, a rising star on RCA Records. Morgan says that her own efforts to get a new contract were thwarted by her "familiarity." "I was perceived as that 'local' girl they see around town," she claims. "Everybody was looking past me to see what new female act was coming in town from outside." Morgan finally signed her own RCA contract in 1988 and scored a number 20 hit in early '89 with her debut RCA single, "Trainwreck of Emotion." In April of that year she released "Dear Me," a song that would become her first top 10 hit. That breakthrough was marred in May 1989 by Keith Whitley's sudden death from alcohol poisoning.

Afterward, Morgan rededicated herself to her career and began to string together an impressive list of hits on RCA and later on BNA Entertainment, RCA's sister label.

Interestingly, while Morgan remains a defender of country tradition, as her career progressed she seemed to follow Reba McEntire's example by establishing a dual image: singing pop-sounding material like "Something in Red" and then scoring a big hit with a traditional-sounding song like "What Part of No." It's a role she sees as providing a "direct link to country music's past while helping it progress."

TOP SONGS

DEAR ME (RCA, '89, 9)

OUT OF YOUR SHOES (RCA, '89, 2)

FIVE MINUTES (RCA, '90, 1)

HE TALKS TO ME (RCA, '90, 4)

WE BOTH WALK (RCA, '91, 3)

A PICTURE OF ME (WITHOUT YOU) (RCA, '91, 9)

EXCEPT FOR MONDAY (RCA, '91, 4)

WATCH ME (BNA, '92, 2)

WHAT PART OF NO (BNA, '92, 1)

HALF ENOUGH (BNA, '93, 8)

Additional Top 40 Country Songs: 4

GARY MORRIS

From the top of the country charts to the stage of the New York Shakespeare Festival, with side trips to the set of the television show "Dynasty," Gary Morris has been there, done that. One of the major stars of country in the 1980s, Morris has had a varied career as a vocalist and entertainer.

Born in 1949 in Fort Worth, Texas, Morris spent his teen years singing with his church choir and learning to play the guitar. In high school he was also an athlete who excelled in football. He eventually opted for a musical career, and at the end of the 1960s he formed a trio. They performed in Denver for several years but failed to gain any attention or success.

Discouraged, Morris decided to pursue a solo career and went back to Fort Worth in the mid-'70s. It was there that he met songwriter Lawton Williams, the composer of the Bobby Helms hit "Fraulein." With Williams' encouragement, Morris began singing and performing as a solo act.

When he performed at the White House before President Carter in 1978, Morris came to the attention of MCA Records in Nashville. He was subsequently signed to a contract, but success continued to elude him.

The White House connection would again serve Morris' career well. In 1980 he headed back to Nashville and pitched his songs to producer Norro Wilson of Warner Bros. Records. "It was crazy the way I was signed," Morris later explained to writer Kip Kirby in 1984. "I'd done a lot of campaigning for Jimmy Carter in his race for the presidency. After he won, Carter invited me to perform at a White House reception he was hosting for the Country Music Association. Norro was there. Two years later, when I came into his office to pitch my tape, he remembered me and signed me on the spot."

From that point on, Morris' career began to flourish. He hit the top 10 with a series of records that included "Headed for a Heartache," "Velvet Chains," and "The Love She Found in Me," the top five record that finally gained him a broad range of fans.

As the decade unfolded, Morris continued his run on the country charts. He had a hit in 1984 with "You're Welcome Tonight," a duet with country siren Lynn Anderson. And he topped the charts in 1985 with the record "Baby Bye Bye."

Gary Morris

But these hits proved to be merely the starting point of Morris' wide-ranging career in entertainment. In 1985 he starred with Linda Ronstadt in a production of the opera *La Boheme* as part of the New York Shakespeare Festival. And based on that performance, he was subsequently recruited as a co-star of "Dynasty II: The Colbys," one of the hit television prime-time soap operas of the day.

The public attention that Morris gained from that series fueled his recording career, and as the decade unfolded he scored more hits, including "Lasso the Moon" and "I'll Never Stop Loving You." In 1987, Morris assumed the lead role of Jean Valjean in the Broadway production of the smash hit musical *Les Miserables*, gaining the role after competing against 50 other actors. "I can't tell you how excited I am about doing [*Les Miserables*]," Morris said in 1988 to writer Eda Galeno. "It's a stretch for me in another direction. I like doing those kinds of things."

Into the 1990s, Morris continued to explore new spheres of expression. In 1991 he made his debut as a director with a video for the hit record "One Fall Is All It Takes," which employed a unique series of watercolor special effects superimposed over landscapes of Colorado and Tennessee. And in 1992 he taped four 60-minute television specials as part of the TNN cable network, hosting musical tours of Estonia, Hungary, Slovakia, and Russia.

MICHAEL MARTIN MURPHEY

"**W**ildfire" introduced Michael Murphey to the mainstream pop audience in 1975, about seven years before his sound spread like wildfire into the country music realm. Along the way he became known as a musical purveyor of southwestern Americana, a man on a mission to bring the "western" back into country and western music.

Murphey (b. March 14, 1945) spent the first 20 years of his life in Dallas, Texas. "I grew up on family farms and ranches in Texas and Arkansas where my grandfathers and my uncle ran cattle," he told writer Jack Hurst. "There was a lot of music sung while they were working." At 16, guitar in hand, Murphey made his professional performing debut at a coffeehouse in Dallas. He spent two years at North

TOP ALBUMS

Faded Blue (Warner, '81)
Second Hand Love (Warner, '84)

TOP SONGS

The Wind Beneath My Wings (Warner, '83, *4*)
Why Lady Why (Warner, '83, *4*)
Baby Bye Bye (Warner, '84, *1*)
I'll Never Stop Loving You (Warner, '85, *1*)
Makin' Up for Lost Time (The Dallas Lovers' Song) (Warner, '85, *1*)
100% Chance of Rain (Warner, '86, *1*)
Leave Me Lonely (Warner, '86, *1*)
Another World (Warner, '87, *4*)

Additional Top 40 Country Songs: 15

Texas State University studying speech and drama and then packed his bags for California.

In Los Angeles in the late 1960s, Murphy studied literature at UCLA and played honky-tonks and folk clubs at night. Through fellow Texan Mike Nesmith, recently hired as one of the Monkees, Murphey got signed as a songwriter for Screen Gems. For several years he cranked out scores of songs, placing them with Kenny Rogers, the Nitty Gritty Dirt Band, and Flatt and Scruggs, among others. He formed an act called the Lewis and Clark Expedition with Owen "Boomer" Castleman (Murphey used the pseudonym Travis Lewis), issuing one low-charting pop single, "I Feel Good (I Feel Bad)," in 1967.

In the early 1970s, Murphey spent time in Austin amid a burgeoning country "outlaw" scene. It was while playing at a club called the Rubaiyat that Murphey was heard by a patron named R. A. Caldwell, a housepainter and repairman. The enthusiastic Caldwell advised Murphey to start issuing records and said he was going to help make it happen. "And I said, 'Right,'" recalls Murphy. "Here I am stuck in Texas, there is really nothing going on, and I'm being told by a repairman that he's going to make a star out of me."

According to Murphey, Caldwell hitchhiked to Nashville and got a job painting the house of producer Bob Johnston. One day he cornered Johnson in his kitchen and told him, "There's a guy playing in Dallas tonight that I want you to go hear, and I'll pay for your plane flight." Johnston took him up on the deal, says Murphey, "got on the plane that afternoon with the housepainter . . . came into the club that night. As a result of that I ended up going to Nashville to make a record."

The record was Murphey's first solo album, *Geronimo's Cadillac,* the title track of which took him to the top 40 of the pop chart.

Three years later, Murphey hit it big with "Wildfire," a song "that evoked that childhood dream of wanting to escape on horseback," he said. A number three pop hit, it placed him in the middle of the country-pop singer-songwriter mainstream.

Nashville, which had previously ignored Murphey's music, took an interest in 1976. From that year until 1982, Murphey placed six moderately successful singles on the country chart. By 1982 Murphey had released nine albums—including the soundtrack for *Hard Country,* a film he'd scripted—and scored four top 40 pop hits, establishing himself as an artist of consistent quality.

His role in country changed dramatically in 1982, when he went to Number One with the single "What's Forever For." The Country Music Association named him (ironically) Best New Artist. For years thereafter, Murphey regularly placed songs in the country top 10, while his pop presence diminished.

By the early 1980s residing in Taos, New Mexico, Murphey turned increasingly toward the history, lore, and culture of the Old West as a source of inspiration. He performed concerts with a symphony orchestra, mixing his own songs with the western-themed works of such "classical" composers as Aaron Copland and Ferde Grofé. He also initiated the West Fest, an annual celebration of the American West.

Murphey's fourteenth album, *Americana,* spun off his second Number One hit, "A Long Line of Love." The follow-up discs *River of Time* and *Land of Enchantment* put several more songs in the country top 10.

Traditional western music became Murphey's exclusive focus on three albums in the 1990s (*Cowboy Songs Vol. I, Cowboy Christmas Songs Vol. II,* and *Cowboy Songs III—Rhymes of the Renegades*) that included such chestnuts as "Happy Trails to You," "Red River Valley," and "Home on the Range," along with similarly themed contemporary material.

TOP ALBUMS

BLUE SKY—NIGHT THUNDER (Epic, '75)
MICHAEL MARTIN MURPHEY (Liberty, '82)
AMERICANA (Warner, '87)

TOP SONGS

WHAT'S FOREVER FOR (Liberty, '82, *1, 19 Pop*)
STILL TAKING CHANCES (Liberty, '82, *3*)
A FACE IN THE CROWD (with Holly Dunn,
    Warner, '87, *4*)
A LONG LINE OF LOVE (Warner, '87, *1*)
I'M GONNA MISS YOU, GIRL (Warner, '87, *3*)
TALKIN' TO THE WRONG MAN (with Ryan Murphey,
    Warner, '88, *4*)
FROM THE WORD GO (Warner, '88, *3*)

Additional Top 40 Country Songs: 13

ANNE MURRAY

Canadian Anne Murray was at the forefront of a trend, starting in the late 1960s, in which country music and pop came together in a successful new musical blend. Over the course of the

Anne Murray

next two decades, Murray often walked the tightrope between country and pop, to much acclaim and some controversy, selling millions of records along the way.

Murray (b. June 20, 1946, Springhill, Nova Scotia) did not come quickly to music in general or country music in particular. The only sister in a family of five brothers, Murray grew up loving sports.

She also trained as a classical vocalist during her youth and reportedly never listened to country music until she had begun her musical career.

That career had to wait a while as Murray obtained a bachelor's degree at the University of New Brunswick and began a career as a physical education instructor on Canada's Prince Edward Island. But while teaching she also began to sing at local shows and events. After a year as a teacher, she was signed by Capitol Records of Canada.

Her debut record, "Snowbird," was released in 1970 and became an international hit on the pop charts. With its winsome pop sensibility and lilting country-tinged refrains, the record brought Murray fans of both pop and country. It provided Murray with an opportunity to express herself in both genres, which she proceeded to do over the course of the rest of her career. In fact, she would eventually win Grammy Awards as Best Female Vocalist in both the country and pop categories.

At times, Murray's refusal to be limited musically caused her problems with the press and fans. But she pursued her own course nonetheless. When she was accused of abandoning country music in 1988, she told writer Jack Hurst, "There've been people who've said [vocalist] Kathy Mattea has filled a hole I left when I decided I didn't want to sing country songs anymore. That's garbage. I never said I didn't want to sing country songs anymore. I just needed a break, a change. I've always said I like to sing different kinds of music. I didn't want to be pigeonholed."

Murray's eclectic taste in music was obvious in her choice of songs. Her debut album, 1968's *Snowbird*, featured material by the likes of Bob Dylan, Dino Valenti, and Jose Feliciano. Her second album, *Anne Murray*, included songs by Carole King and Burt Bacharach.

After the initial success of "Snowbird," Murray's wide-ranging career and broad fan base proceeded to grow. In the 1970s, she became a star of Glen Campbell's television show on CBS, which secured her position as one of the top pop artists of the time. During that decade and the next, Murray hit the country and pop charts on a steady basis with such hits as "Cotton Jenny," "He Thinks I Still Care," "A Little Good News," and scores of others. Again, her wide range of musical tastes was apparent;

from the country-sweet sound of the 1978 hit "You Needed Me" to a pop-inflected version of the Monkees' hit "Daydream Believer," Murray covered various musical bases and was successful in each.

While Murray's career slowed somewhat in the 1980s and '90s, she continued to be a celebrity of some note. In 1989 her hometown honored her with the opening of the 4,000-square-foot Anne Murray Center, a museum that includes memorabilia from her career. Something of a hero in her native country, Murray has won 22 Juno Awards (the Canadian equivalent of the Grammies).

WILLIE NELSON

Willie Nelson's recording and songwriting career spans four decades. He's written such country classics as "Crazy" and "Night Life," recorded such seminal albums as *Red Headed Stranger* and *Wanted: The Outlaws*, and scored 81 top 40 country hits—all on the way to becoming an American music icon and a country legend in his own time.

Nelson (b. Willie Hugh Nelson, Apr. 30, 1933, Fort Worth, Texas) grew up in Abbott, Texas. He was raised by his paternal grandparents after his mother deserted the family when Nelson was just six months old. His grandparents had learned music through mail-order courses and passed it on to Nelson and his sister Bobbie. Nelson was six years old when they got him a Stella guitar. He was just 10 when he joined his first group, a Bohemian polka band. At 13, he started his own band.

After earning his musical stripes in the rough and rowdy honky-tonks along Fort Worth's infamous Jacksboro Highway, where they saw at least one good fight a night, Nelson followed a brief deejay career to Oregon. While in the Northwest, he financed his first recording session in 1956, cutting a song called "No Place for Me."

He moved to Houston in the late 1950s, where his songwriting improved. On one of his first songs, "Family Bible," he sold the rights cheap just to buy groceries. "I sold it to Paul Buskirk; Claude Grey, a country singer; and Walt Breland," Nelson says. "Took all three of them to get together $50." Later he sold "Nightlife"—destined to become a country standard—for just $150. "I used the money to buy an old car that took me to Nashville," he recalls. "I eventually got the rights to that one back."

In Nashville he began to score big as a writer: "Crazy" was a number two hit for Patsy Cline in 1962, and "Hello Walls" topped the chart in 1961 for Faron Young. Nelson's 1961 composition "Funny How Time Slips Away" has since been recorded over 80 times.

In 1962, Nelson was signed to Liberty Records and promptly scored two top 10 hits: "Willingly" and "Touch Me." But instead of taking off, he was only moderately successful, remaining out of the top 10 until scoring a Number One hit in 1975 with "Blue Eyes Cryin' in the Rain." That song came from Nelson's innovative concept album *Red Headed Stranger*. "I didn't know what a concept album was," he admits. "I didn't know *Red Headed Stranger* was a concept album until somebody said to me, 'That's a nice concept album,' and I said, 'Oh, really?' and they said, 'Yes, it tells a nice story.'" In 1976, Nelson experienced his first million-seller: the album *Wanted: The Outlaws*, recorded with Waylon Jennings, Jessi Colter, and Tompall Glaser.

The legend of Willie Nelson grew as he continued to release hit albums and hit songs through the late 1970s and '80s, including "Georgia on My Mind," "On the Road Again," and perhaps the biggest country hit of the 1980s, "Always on My Mind." Throughout this period he recorded memorable duets with artists as diverse as Leon Russell, Dolly Parton, Merle Haggard, Ray Charles, and Julio Iglesias along with a successful series of albums with Johnny Cash, Waylon Jennings, and Kris Kristofferson.

As impressive as his recording career is, Nelson may ultimately be best remembered for his songwriting—and perhaps also best known *through* his song-

Willie Nelson

TOP ALBUMS

RED HEADED STRANGER (Columbia, '75)
STARDUST (Columbia, '78)
ALWAYS ON MY MIND (Columbia, '82)

TOP SONGS

BLUE EYES CRYING IN THE RAIN (Columbia, '75,
   1, 21 Pop)
MY HEROES HAVE ALWAYS BEEN COWBOYS
   (Columbia, '80, 1)
ON THE ROAD AGAIN (Columbia, '80, 1, 20 Pop)
ALWAYS ON MY MIND (Columbia, '82, 1, 5 Pop)
TO ALL THE GIRLS I'VE LOVED BEFORE
   (with Julio Iglesias, Columbia, '84, 1, 5 Pop)
LIVING IN THE PROMISELAND (Columbia, '86, 1)
NOTHING I CAN DO ABOUT IT NOW (Columbia, '89, 1)

Additional Top 40 Country Songs: 74

writing. "I write 99 percent from my own experience," he says, "and if somebody wanted to know my story, it's pretty much there in the songs I write." It's a long story, given the total of 900 songs it's estimated he's written.

During the 1990s, Nelson, like many of his peers, began to find it difficult to score big chart records as a younger generation of stars came in. He remained philosophical about the change: "This is a business that goes in cycles and phases and stages, and no one can be that productive forever. I get a run at it every now and then, Waylon Jennings gets a run at it, Garth Brooks, George Strait, all these guys are getting their run at it, but nobody stays hot forever. I don't think anybody would want to, really—there's too much pressure involved in that. When my stuff is selling, well, that's great; when it's not, that's great, too, because somebody is in there, and usually whoever's there needs it and deserves it. Things happen the way they're supposed to."

JUICE NEWTON

A hard-working club-circuit veteran with a label-resistant voice and sound, Juice Newton (b. Judy Kay Newton, Feb. 18, 1952, Lakehurst, New Jersey) experienced an extended

burst of fame in the 1980s marked by major pop-to-country crossover hits in the early part of the decade and a focus on country in the latter half.

Newton's country involvement came relatively late. Growing up in Virginia Beach, Virginia, she listened mostly to rhythm and blues records. When given a guitar by her mother at the beginning of high school, she delved into folk music.

In northern California, where she attended Foothill College in Los Altos Hills, she met guitarist-songwriter Otha Young, and the two began performing on the bar circuit. (During her early years, Newton also worked as an arc welder, a waitress, and a car wash attendant.)

It was the quality of her voice that led her to country. "When I came to California from Virginia, I thought I was a folk singer," she told writer Holly Gleason. "But the people out there said, 'No, you have an accent. You must be a country singer.' I didn't mind what they said, but I was a little surprised. Then from that time on, though, I had a direction. I was able to make a living."

Newton and Young formed the band Silver Spur and took it to Los Angeles to try for the brass ring. Amid a burgeoning country-rock scene spearheaded by the Eagles, the country-tinged mix played by Silver Spur quickly found receptive ears—and a recording contract—at RCA Records.

The 1975 debut disc, *Juice Newton and Silver Spur,* contained "Love Is a Word," which became a minor country hit. But subsequent records (four albums—one on RCA, three on Capitol) attracted little attention apart from some middle-ranking country chart singles.

With the 1981 release of *Juice* on Capitol came national exposure. The songs "Angel of the Morning" and "Queen of Hearts" both reached the top five of the *Billboard* Hot 100 pop chart and the top 40 of the country listings. "The Sweetest Thing (I've Ever Known)"—a remixed version of a track on the '75 *Silver Spur* album—became Newton's first of four country chart-toppers. The album went platinum, and expert voices began touting Newton as the next big thing in the music business.

The next album, 1982's *Quiet Lies,* brought Newton two more crossover hits and a Grammy Award for Best Country Vocal Performance, Female. ("I didn't get to be there when it was handed out," she says, "'cause I was stuck in traffic doing an interview.")

Maintaining a professional and personal partnership with Young, Newton toured and recorded steadily (now on RCA) during the mid-1980s. The 1985 release *Old Flame* proved her commercial peak—and marked a move away from the pop chart. Three of the tracks, including the Newton–Eddie Rabbitt duet "Both to Each Other (Friends & Lovers)," reached Number One country. Three others —"Old Flame," "Cheap Love," and "What Can I Do with My Heart"—made the top 10.

But follow-ups didn't match that performance. A personal breakup with Young ensued (although the work relationship continued). Several albums were issued (including 1987's more straight-country *Emotion*, with its singles "First-Time Caller" and "Tell Me True"). In 1989, her recording agreement with RCA came to an end.

"When Love Comes Around the Bend" (number 40, 1989) marked the end of Newton's chart run, although her voice seemed destined to return to the foreground. "There are people, honestly, who feel that I'm much too raw, I'm just not refined in my

TOP ALBUMS

JUICE (Capitol, '81)
OLD FLAME (RCA, '85)

TOP SONGS

THE SWEETEST THING (I'VE EVER KNOWN)
   (Capitol, '81, *1, 7 Pop*)
BREAK IT TO ME GENTLY (Capitol, '82, *2, 11 Pop*)
YOU MAKE ME WANT TO MAKE YOU MINE (RCA, '85, *1*)
HURT (RCA, '85, *1*)
OLD FLAME (RCA, '86, *5*)
BOTH TO EACH OTHER (FRIENDS & LOVERS)
   (with Eddie Rabbitt, RCA, '86, *1*)
CHEAP LOVE (RCA, '86, *9*)
TELL ME TRUE (RCA, '87, *8*)

Additional Top 40 Country Songs: 9

Juice Newton

singing," she said in 1985. "I'm not concerned about that. . . . The sound of my voice, the way I say the word, whether or not it's sharp or flat . . . if it gets the feeling, then I've accomplished my goal."

NITTY GRITTY
DIRT BAND
• • • • • • • • • • • • • • • •

Over the course of its long career, the Nitty Gritty Dirt Band has created music in a vast and vastly varied range of American musical idioms, from folk and bluegrass to country and rock, with other styles and genres tossed in along the way.

But it was the group's 1973 album, *Will the Circle Be Unbroken,* a historic collaboration of such legends as Roy Acuff, Doc Watson, and others, that laid the groundwork for their career in country music.

The group was formed in 1966 in Long Beach, California, by Bruce Kunkel and Jeff Hanna, both of whom played guitar and instruments like the washtub bass, comb, and kazoo. They were joined by Jimmy Fadden (harmonica, kazoo), Ralphy Barr (kazoo, bass, and guitar), Les Thompson (mandolin, kazoo, and vocals), and John McEuen (banjo).

From the very start, the group's creative philosophy was based on a sheer love and affection for all sorts of music. "Above all, I think we're all fans of music as well as people who make their livings playing it," Hanna said in 1988. "That's why we all got into music in the first place, and it's certainly the reason that we've stayed in it after all these years."

Originally, the group called itself the Illegitimate Jug Band (because it didn't have a jug player). But its music had the good-timey feel of other groups, like the Lovin' Spoonful, that blended folk and its various offshoots with such typically American forms as ragtime, blues, and country. Unlike those groups, however, the NGDB was primarily a folk outfit that played its music on acoustic instruments.

The NGDB's debut album appeared in 1967 and created a minor stir in the emerging psychedelic rock scene of the West Coast. Into the '70s, the group had a few modest hits with "Mr. Bojangles," "House at Pooh Corner," and others.

But in 1973 the group moved more in a country direction when it released the album *Will the Circle be Unbroken.* A lavish three-record set, *Circle* came

with the NGDB backing some of the most illustrious country stars of all time, including Acuff, Watson, Merle Travis, Earl Scruggs, and Mother Maybelle Carter. The album was a watershed, introducing a new generation of country and rock fans to the songs of their musical forebears, even as it brought old-time fans into contact with the music of long-haired rock youth—which the NGDB was, in look if not in sound. (Acuff himself, in an interview with the Nashville newspaper the *Tennessean,* noted that "they are very nice boys, and they certainly knew what they were doing [in the studio].")

From a musical standpoint, *Circle* proved just how much rock and folk and country music had in common. The all-acoustic album was something of a musical melting pot, with the NGDB adding its eclectic range of idioms and styles to the distinctive images of the country masters.

As the decade unfolded, the NGDB continued to focus on country music, while also adapting it to rock. But while other participants in the country-rock movement—like the Eagles, Jackson Browne, and others—became vastly popular, the NGDB was merely a cult act.

In 1976 the group's name was shortened to the Dirt Band, and in 1978 the group scored a minor hit on the rock charts with "In for the Night."

But it wasn't until the 1980s that the group—which had subsequently reinstated the name Nitty Gritty Dirt Band—began to achieve any sort of substantial success. Fittingly, it came on the country

---

TOP ALBUMS
• • • • • • • • • • • •

THE NITTY GRITTY DIRT BAND (Liberty, '67)
WILL THE CIRCLE BE UNBROKEN (United Artists, '71)

TOP SONGS
• • • • • • • • • •

LONG HARD ROAD (THE SHARECROPPER'S DREAM) (Warner, '84, *1*)
I LOVE ONLY YOU (Warner, '84, *3*)
HIGH HORSE (Warner, '85, *2*)
MODERN DAY ROMANCE (Warner, '85, *1*)
HOME AGAIN IN MY HEART (Warner, '85, *3*)
BABY'S GOT A HOLD ON ME (Warner, '87, *2*)
FISHIN' IN THE DARK (Warner, '87, *1*)
I'VE BEEN LOOKIN' (Warner, '88, *2*)

Additional Top 40 Country Songs: 11

Nitty Gritty Dirt Band

charts with such songs as "Shot Full of Love" and "Dance Little Jean." Then the NGDB enjoyed their greatest run of chart success. Beginning in '84 with their first Number One, "Long Hard Road (The Sharecropper's Dream)," they racked up 15 consecutive top 10 country hits, including such memorable Number Ones as "Modern Day Romance" ('85) and "Fishin' in the Dark" ('87). Their crowning achievement was *Will the Circle Be Unbroken Vol. 2.* Released in 1988, the two-record set earned them two Grammy Awards (Best Bluegrass Recording and Best Country Performance by a Vocal Duo or Group) and won CMA Album of the Year honors as well.

MARK O'CONNOR

A virtuoso performer on guitar, mandolin, and violin, Mark O'Connor had a major impact on country music in the 1980s and '90s. As a session musician he's played on over 450 recordings (earning credit—along with such other players as

Ricky Skaggs and Charlie Daniels—for putting the fiddle back into country music in the 1980s). As a leader he's issued the notable albums *The New Nashville Cats, Heroes,* and *Fiddle Concerto for Violin and Orchestra.* Chet Atkins, the dean of country instrumentalists, calls him one of the greatest musicians he's ever met.

O'Connor (b. Aug. 5, 1961, Seattle, Washington) grew up in a home full of classical music. His parents recognized their son's musical ability early and gave him classical and flamenco guitar lessons. At age 10, he won a classical guitar competition at the University of Washington. He won even though his heart wasn't in it, because he had already discovered the fiddle. "Doug Kershaw was the first fiddle hero I had," he says. "I was eight years old when I saw him on the 'Johnny Cash Show,' and he really floored me. After seeing his performance I begged for a fiddle, I begged for three years until I finally got one." (Before his twelfth birthday he had also mastered mandolin, banjo, steel-string guitar, and dobro.) "In a year and a half I had learned 200 fiddle tunes," he claims. "I recorded an album in Nashville at age 12 and appeared on the Grand Ole Opry with Roy Acuff. The next year I won the International Grand Master's Fiddle Championships." By the time he entered high school, he had recorded four albums. After high school, he played guitar with the David Grisman Quintet and, with them, toured with his greatest violin hero, Stephane Grappelli.

In 1983, O'Connor moved to Nashville at a time when fiddle had all but disappeared from the songs he heard on country radio. "I'd listen for three hours and maybe hear one tune that had fiddle on it," he says.

That soon changed. O'Connor became an in-demand, triple-scale session musician, playing on every major singer's albums and hundreds of others. He also recorded three jazz and new-age–style albums of his own for Warner Bros. during the 1980s. In 1990, he cut back on his session work to put together *The New Nashville Cats,* a monumental project featuring 53 of the top pickers in Nashville, including Ricky Skaggs, Steve Wariner, and Vince Gill. A single called "Restless" became a top 25 hit, and the album earned O'Connor a Grammy Award.

He followed up in 1993 with *Heroes,* which included violin duets with artists as diverse as Grappelli, Johnny Gimble, Charlie Daniels, Byron Berline, Pinchas Zukerman, and Vassar Clements.

O'Connor became known for his ability to display dazzling technique without forfeiting bluegrass and country authenticity, as evidenced by his intricate versions of classics like "Orange Blossom Special." He went on to combine his love of country fiddle and mastery of classical violin. With a $25,000 grant, he composed a "Fiddle Concerto for Violin and Orchestra," trying it out with various orchestras around the United States before recording and releasing it in 1995.

TOP ALBUMS

THE NEW NASHVILLE CATS (Warner, '91)
HEROES (Warner, '93)
FIDDLE CONCERTO FOR VIOLIN AND ORCHESTRA
  (Warner, '93)

TOP SONG

RESTLESS (with Vince Gill, Ricky Skaggs, Steve
  Wariner, Warner, '91, 25)

Mark O'Connor

OAK RIDGE BOYS

One of the few current country acts that can trace its origins back half a century, the Oak Ridge Boys began in the mid-1940s as a local country-gospel group that provided entertainment for the scientists who moved to Oak Ridge, Tennessee, to develop the atomic bomb. After World War II the quartet disbanded a couple of times only to have new members take up the name. They remained a gospel act until 1977, when they released a decidedly non-gospel, country record called "Y'All Come Back Saloon." Through the late 1970s, '80s, and early '90s they were the dominant country quartet, scoring 17 Number One songs, including the country-to-pop crossover smash "Elvira."

The group that began performing for the atomic scientists in Oak Ridge was originally called the Country Cut-Ups. They soon renamed themselves the Oak Ridge Quartet. In 1959, the group moved to Nashville and in 1964 became the Oak Ridge Boys. By 1973 the membership that became the country

quartet was in place. Baritone William Lee Golden (b. Jan. 12, 1935, Brewton, Alabama) joined in 1964; lead singer Duane Allen (b. Apr. 29, 1943, Taylortown, Texas) joined in 1966; bass singer Richard Sterban (b. Apr. 24, 1943, Camden, New Jersey) came in 1972; and tenor Joe Bonsall (b. May 18, 1948, Philadelphia) was on board in 1973.

In the early 1970s the Oak Ridge Boys became increasingly progressive by gospel standards, taking their music more toward country and dressing and acting less conservatively than their peers. It raised gospel eyebrows, but it also gained them more fans. In 1973, they got their first taste of the country chart when they joined Johnny Cash and June Carter on a record called "Praise the Lord and Pass the Soup." That resulted in a contract with Columbia Records and another minor country chart record in 1976 called "Family Reunion." They were trying to walk the fence between country and gospel, hoping to maintain their gospel fan base, and nearly went bankrupt in the process.

In 1977 they decided to go for broke and signed with ABC/Dot Records as a country act. Their first

Oak Ridge Boys

release for the label, "Y'All Come Back Saloon," did alienate many of their gospel fans, but compensation came when the song hit number three on the chart. That began an unbroken string of 14 top 10s through 1982, including the group's first Number One, "I'll Be True to You," and their most successful song, "Elvira," a 1981 Number One country, number five pop hit and the Country Music Association's Single of the Year.

With that song, their skilled four-part vocal harmony, and an increasingly energetic, pop-style show, the Oak Ridge Boys developed into a major touring act. Along the way they began tapping into younger audiences several years before doing so became a country trend. "We attracted the traditional country fans," says Joe Bonsall, "but their kids were starting to flock to our shows, and they were really digging what we were doing."

Through the 1980s, the members developed their distinct images and personal styles. Bonsall was the sports-loving, karate-kicking free spirit. Allen became the leader and the group's resident fashion plate. Richard Sterban remained the vocal anchor and the most conservative member. Golden turned inward and became fascinated with the simple life of mountain men. He let his hair and beard grow, took to sleeping on buffalo skins, and wore buckskin costumes. Eventually, his idiosyncrasies caused the other members to vote him out of the group. Golden was replaced by Oaks backup band member Steve

---

TOP ALBUMS

OAK RIDGE BOYS HAVE ARRIVED (MCA, '79)
FANCY FREE (MCA, '81)
BOBBIE SUE (MCA, '82)

TOP SONGS

LEAVING LOUISIANA IN THE BROAD DAYLIGHT
　　(MCA, '79, 1)
ELVIRA (MCA, '81, 1, 5 Pop)
FANCY FREE (MCA, '81, 1)
BOBBIE SUE (MCA, '82, 1)
AMERICAN MADE (MCA, '83, 1)
IT TAKES A LITTLE RAIN (TO MAKE LOVE GROW)
　　(MCA, '87, 1)
NO MATTER HOW HIGH (MCA, '89, 1)

Additional Top 40 Country Songs: 33

Sanders (b. Sept. 12, 1953, Richland, Georgia) in 1987.

The Oak Ridge Boys entered the 1990s looking over their shoulders at an influx of younger acts and, like many of their contemporaries, finding it tougher to compete. "I'm just proud that we have always studied the business," says Duane Allen. "We love the new kids and know that they wouldn't be having success on radio if they hadn't done something viable enough to deserve it. We're just going to give it all we have, and we're doggone happy that we're still around."

K.T. OSLIN

K.T. Oslin was born country in the South, but she had a longer career in New York City as a Broadway singer and dancer than she did in Nashville as a country singer-songwriter. It wasn't until the late 1980s that she accomplished the next to impossible: launching a successful country recording career at age 45.

Oslin (b. Kay Toinette Oslin, May 15, 1941, Crossitt, Arkansas) was raised in Mobile, Alabama. After her father died when she was just five, the family moved to several cities before settling in Houston, the place she considers her home. She wasn't surrounded by a lot of music, but Oslin was a child with a keen imagination. She would play alone, creating elaborate scenarios full of many characters and playing all the parts. "Artistically, I just did the normal kid things like taking dance lessons," she explains.

She didn't get serious about music until she met singer-songwriter Guy Clark through an old high school buddy, David Jones. "In the winter of '62, we formed a trio and began singing folk songs at a Houston Club called the Jester," Oslin recalls. "We did that for a couple of years."

After that, she got involved in local musical theater productions. In 1966 her ticket out of Houston was earning a spot in the chorus of the national touring company of *Hello Dolly*, starring Carol Channing. "When I got the job the stage manager said, 'I hired you simply because of your slightly belligerent attitude,'" says Oslin. "I hit the road and then stayed with the show when it went to New York."

For the next several years she appeared in revivals of such Broadway shows as *West Side Story* and *Promises, Promises*. She also supported herself by writing and singing jingles and appearing in TV commercials. Then, on a trip down south in the mid-'70s, she went into the washroom of a roadside cafe. Scribbled on a wall was a graffiti message: "I ain't never going to love nobody but Cornell Crawford." "I said, that sounds like a country song title," Oslin recalls. "So I raced home and wrote my first country song: 'Cornell Crawford.'"

In 1978 her friend Guy Clark invited her to visit him in Nashville to sing background vocals on some of his songs. While there, she made connections that resulted in a brief recording contract with Elektra Records. In '81 she had a minor hit with a song called "Clean Your Own Tables," then she returned to New York.

Oslin visited Nashville briefly in 1984 to try to connect as a songwriter but returned to New York once again. Finally, in 1986, she decided to go all out for a country music career. She borrowed $7,000 from her aunt to pay for her own showcase performances in Nashville. It was a gutsy move for a woman in her mid-40s at a time when the youth movement in country music was in full swing, but it worked, gaining her a recording contract with RCA Records. In 1987 she hit number 40 with a run-of-the mill country song called "Wall of Tears." It was her second release, an original song, that broke her career open: "'80s Ladies" hit number seven and became an instant anthem for women of all ages. She followed that with more insightful original songs like "Do Ya'," "Hold Me," and "Hey Bobby."

From 1987 to 1990 she was one of the hottest

K. T. Oslin

TOP ALBUMS

'80s Ladies (RCA, '87)
Love in a Small Town (RCA, 88)
This Woman (RCA, '89)

TOP SONGS

'80s Ladies (RCA, '87, 7)
Do Ya' (RCA, '87, 1)
I'll Always Come Back (RCA, '88, 1)
Hold Me (RCA, '88, 1)
Hey Bobby (RCA, '89, 2)
The Woman (RCA, '89, 5)
Come Next Monday (RCA, '90, 1)

Additional Top 40 Country Songs: 4

acts in country music on radio and on tour. Ultimately, though, the touring and the politics of the music industry "got to her," as she explains it. "I never loved the road. I had done that in an earlier career." In 1992 she quit touring and put her recording career on hold indefinitely.

Oslin's impact on country music, even if over a brief period, was enough to earn her the Country Music Association Female Vocalist of the Year award in 1988 plus three Grammies. She proved to be an eloquent spokesperson for the female point of view, yet wrote songs that appealed almost equally to men, offering clues as to how their actions affected the women in their lives. She once concluded, "The older I get, the more I wonder how we ever get together, men and women. We are totally different creatures."

BUCK OWENS
....

Hard-driving, twang-guitar–powered country music was what Buck Owens spawned in the 1960s, spearheading the Bakersfield Sound—a California-based resurgence of honky-tonk music in the wake of the more heavily produced and sweetened Nashville Sound. With 21 Number One country hits to his credit—and an astonishing total of 74 songs in the country top 40—Owens made his music a major country force. Enroute, he led the style-setting band the Buckaroos; drew rock and R&B influences into country; sported a signature red, white, and blue guitar during the countercultural 1960s; and in general, did it all his own way—influencing generations of performers in the process.

The Depression-era Dust Bowl served as the backdrop of his childhood in Sherman, Texas, where he was born Alvis Edgar Owens on August 12, 1929. Tough circumstances propelled his family westward in 1937, and they stopped and stayed in Mesa, Arizona. Owens dropped out of school and worked to help the family, picking crops and eventually hauling fruit between Mesa and California's San Joaquin Valley. He also picked up some guitar chords from his mother and began playing in local honky-tonks. Married at 18, he and his wife, Bonnie (later a hitmaker in her own right), played in Mac's Skillet Lickers and were heard on the local "Buck and Britt" radio show.

In 1951, Buck and Bonnie moved to Bakersfield. "I didn't want to dig ditch, buck hay bales, and do all that hot old dusty, dirty, long-hours work," says Owens. "I didn't want to be cold, and I didn't want to be hungry. Never wanted to do that again." Aiming to do music instead, he formed a band called the Schoolhouse Playboys, in which he played guitar and occasional sax and trumpet. He also landed a gig as lead guitarist and sometime singer with keyboardist Bill Woods and his Orange Blossom Playboys.

Years of regular work in smoky, dimly lit clubs—mixing country with Little Richard with (as Owens described it) "mambos and sambas and tangos"—honed his skills to a sharp edge. Others took notice, and Owens found himself in demand, picking guitar leads behind singer Tommy Collins and playing on records for Sonny James, Wanda Jackson, and Tennessee Ernie Ford. He made a couple of stabs at recording as a front man, including a rock and roll single called "Hot Dog," which he waxed on the small Pep label under the pseudonym of Corky Jones. "We didn't want to alienate or upset what few country disc jockeys there were," says Owens, "because I remember the thing, 'Oh, that guy's trying to be rock and roll'—that was the kiss of death as far as country boys go."

The doorway to fame opened when Capitol Records signed Owens as a solo artist in 1957. Within two years he was on the country chart with the number 24 "Second Fiddle," preceding a run of top 10 hits—many penned by Owens—that would continue for some 15 years. "Under Your Spell Again" began it at number four in 1959. Duets with Rose Maddox on "Mental Cruelty" and "Loose Talk" hit in 1961. "Act Naturally" (written by Johnny Russell and Voni Morrison) took him to the ultimate chart peak in 1963 (and the Beatles covered it two years later).

In 1960, Don Rich (born Don Ulrich) joined Owens as a Telecaster guitar player, starting what would be a long musical association. When Tom Brumley added his wailing steel-guitar licks in 1963, it solidified the signature sound of the Owens backup group, dubbed the Buckaroos (reportedly by fellow Bakersfield Sound founder Merle Haggard).

Starting in 1965 with the Number One hit "Buckaroo," the Buckaroos' moniker appeared alongside the name Buck Owens on the labels of the act's records, which included such Owens classics as "Together Again," "I've Got the Tiger by the Tail,"

TOP ALBUMS
....

LIVE AT CARNEGIE HALL (Country Music Foundation, '89)

THE BUCK OWENS COLLECTION (1959–1990) (Rhino, '92)

TOP SONGS
....

ACT NATURALLY (Capitol, '63, 1)

LOVE'S GONNA LIVE HERE (Capitol, '63, 1)

TOGETHER AGAIN (Capitol, '64, 1)

I'VE GOT A TIGER BY THE TAIL (Capitol, '65, 1, 25 Pop)

WAITIN' IN YOUR WELFARE LINE (Capitol, '66, 1)

SAM'S PLACE (Capitol, '67, 1)

TALL DARK STRANGER (Capitol, '69, 1)

STREETS OF BAKERSFIELD (with Dwight Yoakam, Capitol, '88, 1)

Additional Top 40 Country Songs: 66

Buck Owens

"Tall Dark Stranger," and a cover of Chuck Berry's "Johnny B. Goode."

Owens capitalized on his recording success by developing a business concern, Buck Owens Enterprises. Over time he became owner of a music publishing firm, a management and booking agency, a recording studio, and some radio stations. In 1966 he began hosting a syndicated television program, "The Buck Owens Ranch Show."

The wacky country TV series "Hee Haw" first went on the air in 1969, and Owens was recruited as a host. He would continue in that role—sharing it with guitarist Roy Clark—through the mid-1980s. The exposure was massive—which Owens began to view as a possible detriment to his chart dominance. "If you want to be a big record act...you sure as hell don't want TV exposure, because it removes the mystique," he told writer Laura Deni in 1975.

Signed to Warner Bros. Records in 1976, Owens cut records that lacked the innovative vitality of his classics (the death of Rich in 1974 was a contributing factor). Chart rankings began dipping to below-40 levels.

By 1980 he'd had enough, and with his business interests to tend to, he retired from active musical duty. "The old adage about 'leave 'em wanting more' is one thing that I live by," Owens says. "In 1979 the hard, cold facts [were] that I could not compete with pop-country."

That might have been the end of the story had late-'80s neotraditionalist Dwight Yoakam not dedicated his first album to Owens and had such other '80s country luminaries as Emmylou Harris, Highway 101, and the Desert Rose Band not openly acknowledged his influence. At the Country Music Association's thirtieth-anniversary TV special in 1988, Owens came out of retirement to sing a duet with Yoakam on the song "Streets of Bakersfield." The duo repeated the performance on disc, racking up another Number One hit for Owens—16 years after his previous chart-topper—and renewing interest in the hardscrabble sound he pioneered.

"Let's face it," Owens says, "my songs are not syrupy; they haven't got a lot of molasses poured on them. People have called me a honky-tonk singer... I worried about that, 'cause I used to think that a honky-tonk was a place outside of town where a man went to do his wife wrong....[Now] I like the word *honky-tonk*....If someone now talks about me being a honky-tonk singer, I think that's a good description."

DOLLY PARTON

Country music abounds with rags-to-riches stories, but few artists started on a lower rung and climbed higher in the entertainment world than Dolly Parton. With a combination of singing and songwriting talent, a flamboyant look, and good business sense, she built a huge country career, first as a partner with Porter Wagoner and then on her own with hit songs like "Jolene," "Coat of Many Colors," "9 to 5," and "I Will Always Love You."

Parton (b. Dolly Rebecca Parton, Jan. 19, 1946, Sevier County, Tennessee) was one of 12 children raised in poverty near Sevierville, Tennessee. "Being poor is something I am neither proud of nor ashamed of," Parton revealed in her autobiography. "Poverty is something you don't realize when you're in it. Not if you are a kid with a head full of dreams and a house full of loving family." Parton doesn't remember when she learned to read, but she read everything she could get her hands on and became the first person in her family to graduate high school. It was in the books she read that she learned about faraway places and fantasy worlds. Her dreams of a glamorous life and show business began then.

Both sides of her family were musical. The performing was done mostly in churches or on back porches, and nobody but Parton had ever dreamed of taking music beyond their county. She was just a small child when she started writing little songs and simple fun-filled stories that she sang for the family. "One of my uncles recognized my talent and ambition," she says. "He started working with me, and at age 10 I started getting paid to sing on local radio and television stations."

At age 12 her chutzpah showed itself when her uncle took her to Nashville. She talked her way backstage at the Grand Ole Opry and then talked singer Jimmy C. Newman into letting her sing. "I told him I just had to sing that night, because I had told my whole family to listen, that I was going to sing on the Opry," she remembers. At age 15, she made another trip to Nashville. Producer Buddy Killen took an interest in her and made a record that was released on Mercury, "but nothing came of that one," she says. She realized that she would have to move to Nashville and did just that soon after her high school graduation.

She starved for the first couple of years, then landed a writing deal and began recording for Mon-

Dolly Parton

ument Records, scoring two top 40 hits for them in 1967: "Dumb Blonde" and "Something Fishy." That same year, she replaced singer Norma Jean on Porter Wagoner's television show, beginning a partnership with Wagoner that would continue until 1974. She moved over to RCA Records in 1968, scored her first top 10 in '70 with her version of "Mule Skinner Blues," and collected her first Number One in early '71 with her original composition "Joshua." Parton's songs were often deeply personal, like "Coat of Many Colors," written about a coat her mother had made for her out of pieces of cloth and rags and that she had worn to school only to be ridiculed by other students.

From 1967 to '80, Parton and Wagoner sang 20 top 40 duets, including 14 top 10 hits. Parton broke away from Wagoner in 1974, but to let Wagoner know how she felt about him and all he had done for her, she wrote the song "I Will Always Love You." A future classic, that song reached Number One three times, in three different decades. Parton took it to Number One twice, first in 1974 and then in '82. Ten years later, Whitney Houston's performance of the song was included on the soundtrack of the film *The Bodyguard,* and it became a monster pop hit.

There were other memorable Parton collaborations, including several songs with Kenny Rogers (the crossover Number One "Islands in the Stream" among them) and a superb collection of songs

recorded with Linda Ronstadt and Emmylou Harris, issued on the 1987 album *Trio.*

As a soloist, Parton scored such crossover pop hits as "Here You Come Again" and "9 to 5." She became an American entertainment icon through her music, her own national TV show, and starring roles in films like *The Best Little Whorehouse in Texas, 9 to 5,* and *Steel Magnolias.* She also opened Dollywood, a very successful East Tennessee theme park.

Honest and sincere to a fault, Parton remained forthcoming about her life and claimed to have no regrets about her career, even when her moves toward the pop world and movies drew criticism from country purists. "I never ever left country music," she said. "I just took it with me."

JOHNNY PAYCHECK

"I've always been an outlaw, ever since I was a kid," Johnny Paycheck once said. "An outlaw is just someone who does things his own way, right or wrong." Doing it "his way," singer-guitarist-writer Paycheck—who's undergone several name changes, from the given Donald Eugene Lytle to Donny Young to John Austin Paycheck to Johnny PayCheck (with a capital C)—has careened through a life that begs for a film treatment, or immortalization in a lengthy dirge with a title like "The Ballad of Johnny Paycheck." He's had ups, downs, fade-outs, comebacks, and more than a few gritty visits to the country chart—most memorably with the 1977 Number One hit "Take This Job and Shove It."

Lost memories and conflicting reports have long since blurred the details of Paycheck's history. He was born in Greenfield, Ohio—a town 40 miles out of Columbus—on May 31, 1937 (or 1938 or 1941). He showed musical ability early, picking up guitar at age six and entering talent contests by nine. Within several years he was already doing things "his way": "I left home when I was about 15 years old," he told writer Daniel Cooper. "I was riding freight trains, bumming around the country; I was a gypsy." Several years later he joined the Navy, where an altercation with a superior officer brought Lytle a sentence in the brig.

Following release, he drifted into Nashville. By this time, he was accomplished enough a performer to attract music industry notice. He played bass briefly with Porter Wagoner's band and served time

TOP SONGS

JOSHUA (RCA, '70, *1*)

JOLENE (RCA, '73, *1*)

I WILL ALWAYS LOVE YOU (RCA, '74, *1*)

HERE YOU COME AGAIN (RCA, '77, *1, 3 Pop*)

IT'S ALL WRONG BUT IT'S ALL RIGHT
    (RCA, '78, *1, 19 Pop*)

9 TO 5 (RCA, '80, *1, 1 Pop*)

ISLANDS IN THE STREAM (with Kenny Rogers,
    RCA, '83, *1, 1 Pop*)

WILDFLOWERS (with Emmylou Harris and
    Linda Ronstadt, Warner, '88, *6*)

PLEASE DON'T STOP LOVING ME (with Porter
    Wagoner, RCA, '74, *1*)

ROCKIN' YEARS (with Ricky Van Shelton,
    Columbia, '91, *1*)

Additional Top 40 Country Songs: 70

as a tenor vocalist with Faron Young's Country Deputies, Ray Price's Cherokee Cowboys, and George Jones' Jones Boys. From 1958 to '61, under the name Donny Young, he recorded four unsuccessful singles for Decca, followed by two for Mercury.

A&R man Aubrey Mayhew heard Lytle/Young on a demo in 1964 and excitedly set up a record label, Hilltop, for the exclusive purpose of releasing singles of the vocalist. Now named Johnny Paycheck, after a boxer he admired, he hit number 26 on the country chart with a cover of the Buck Owens song "A-11."

When Hilltop folded one top 40 hit later, Paycheck and Mayhew joined forces to create the Little Darlin' label in 1966. That year saw Paycheck's fortunes improve. Two of his compositions—"Apartment #9" and "Touch My Heart"—were hits for Tammy Wynette (her first) and Ray Price, respectively. As a soloist he hit with "The Lovin' Machine" (number eight) and launched a run of rough-hewn tunes with titles like "Motel Time Again" and "(It Won't Be Long) And I'll Be Hating You" that served as a darker flip side of the honky-tonk sound rippling through country airwaves in the 1960s (and a humorous side: the first album, depicting a dapper, formally dressed Paycheck on the cover, was titled *Johnny Paycheck at Carnegie Hall* even though the record had no connection whatever to the prestigious concert venue).

Little Darlin' folded, and Paycheck dropped out—and reportedly down—scraping by in San Diego and Los Angeles for an extended spell, "bumming off the streets and working clubs for beer," he admitted.

Johnny Paycheck

Producer Billy Sherrill helped pull him back, offering a contract with Epic Records. Starting with "She's All I Got"—a number two hit in 1971—Paycheck entered a new career phase marked by increased popularity and a shifting on-disc identity. Through 1976 he was an interpreter of love songs—"Mr. Lovemaker" being a high-charting example. Then, starting with the 1976 album *11 Months and 29 Days* (the title referring to a prison sentence), he assumed the tailor-made role of country "outlaw," playing it through the top 10 hit "I'm the Only Hell (Mama Ever Raised)" and his career topper, "Take This Job and Shove It," which struck a chord among disgruntled workers everywhere. Along with some George Jones collaborations on "Mabellene" and "You Better Move On," Paycheck went on to cut such image-cultivating titles as "The Cocaine Train," "Drinkin' and Drivin'," "Fifteen Beers," and "D.O.A. (Drunk on Arrival)" before reaching the end of his time with Epic in 1982.

A period of label hopping followed, commencing with three minor chart singles on AMI Records and including the well-regarded 1976 album *Modern Times* on Mercury, which yielded the top 40 Paycheck composition "Old Violin." On December 19,

TOP SONGS

THE LOVIN' MACHINE (Little Darlin', '66, 8)

SHE'S ALL I GOT (Epic, '71, 2)

SOMEONE TO GIVE MY LOVE TO (Epic, '72, 4)

MR. LOVEMAKER (Epic, '73, 2)

SONG AND DANCE MAN (Epic, '73, 8)

SLIDE OFF OF YOUR SATIN SHEETS (Epic, '77, 7)

I'M THE ONLY HELL (MAMA EVER RAISED) (Epic, '77, 8)

TAKE THIS JOB AND SHOVE IT (Epic, '77, 1)

FRIEND, LOVER, WIFE (Epic, '78, 7)

MABELLENE (Epic, '78, 7)

Additional Top 40 Country Songs: 28

1985, about a week after the third AMI single entered the chart, Paycheck was involved in a shooting in a small bar in Ohio. He was charged with aggravated assault and eventually given a sentence of up to nine and a half years in prison.

Released in 1991 with a commuted sentence, Paycheck embarked on a mission to replicate his success of the late 1970s. His most recent chart singles at the time, all ranking in the low range of the top 100 in the late 1980s, were three tellingly titled songs: "I Grow Old Too Fast," "Out of Beer," and "Scars."

"He's just a raw talent," Aubrey Mayhew told writer Cooper, "a raw, magnificent talent, that if he were a different person, and that talent could have been developed, he would have had no equal in this industry."

CARL PERKINS

Carl Perkins was never much of a country star. And only for a short time, during his heyday in 1956, was he a rock idol. But with the hit record "Blue Suede Shoes" and his signature rockabilly sound, Perkins created a mix of country and rock that influenced both for generations.

Perkins' sound came directly from his personal background. Born on April 9, 1932, in Lake City, Tennessee, Perkins grew up in poverty in a family of sharecroppers. Raised on a plantation farm where he and his family were the only white workers, Perkins came under the spell of black music, particularly the blues and gospel. At the same time, he began listening to country music on the radio.

The result was Perkins' distinctive distillation of those forms into a singular musical sound. At age 13, as lore has it, Perkins built his own guitar out of a cigar box and a broom handle and promptly won a talent contest singing a self-penned song, "Movie Magg." He was soon performing at local dances with his brothers Jay and Clayton as the Perkins Brothers Band.

When Perkins heard Elvis Presley's hit "That's All Right Mama" (a version of a song by Arthur Crudup), he made the decision to audition for the man who had discovered and produced Presley, Sam Phillips. While Phillips was impressed, he first signed Perkins to the Flip label, a subsidiary of the famous Sun Records that he had founded. He also refused to record any of Perkins' rock material, instead encour-

aging his new artist to stick with country songs. Thus, Perkins recorded his old song "Movie Magg" in 1955, along with the slightly rockabilly-inflected "Gone Gone Gone." Both languished on the charts.

But when Presley moved from Sun to RCA Records in 1956, Phillips decided to build Perkins into the "next Elvis." He did that with "Blue Suede Shoes." Released in March 1956, "Blue Suede Shoes" topped the country, R&B, and pop charts simultaneously, selling more than one million copies in the process. It was the first rockabilly song in history to score on the charts, and it became a signature hit of the rock era.

Just as Perkins' career was rising, it was cut short on March 21 of that year when he was injured in a car wreck while on his way to perform on the nationally televised "Perry Como Show." By the time he had recovered from his injuries, months later, Perkins' time as a budding rock hero had passed. At the end of the year, he recorded as part of the legendary Million Dollar Quartet along with

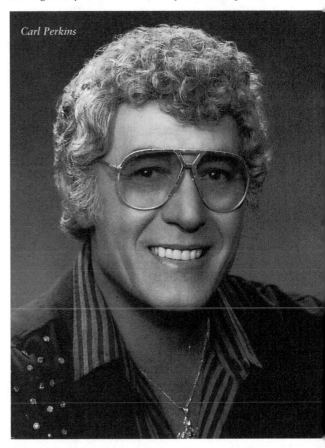

Carl Perkins

Presley, Jerry Lee Lewis, and Johnny Cash. But rock fans didn't seem to care about him or his music anymore.

But Perkins wasn't bitter. In the Colin Escott and Martin Hawkins book *Sun Records,* he was quoted as saying, "Elvis had the looks on me. The girls were going for him for more reasons than music. Elvis was hitting them with sideburns, flashy clothes . . . there was no way of keeping him from being the man in that music."

With his career in rock on the wane, Perkins moved to Columbia Records and a more country-inflected sound in 1958. He had a few modest hits, "Pink Pedal Pushers" and "Pointy Toe Shoes" among them, but he was not embraced by the rock public. At the end of the decade he joined Cash's show as a sideman, where he plied his trade for a number of years. He then wandered musically, recording a 1970 album with NRBQ and, later in the decade, attempting a comeback in Britain with the solo album *Ol' Blue Suede's Back.*

A hero of the British Invaders of 1964, Perkins was feted by them in later years. In 1982 he performed on a track of the Paul McCartney album *Tug of War.* In 1985, Ringo Starr and George Harrison were part of a star-studded commemoration on British television of the thirtieth anniversary of the release of "Blue Suede Shoes." And in 1987, Perkins was inducted into the Rock and Roll Hall of Fame.

While Perkins was primarily a rock figure, many of his songs—including "Matchbox," "Honey Don't," and "Everybody's Trying to Be My Baby"—bridged the musical gap between rock and country. And as interpreted by various groups, most notably the Beatles, these songs brought country sound to a vast new generation of musicians and fans.

TOP SONGS

BLUE SUEDE SHOES (Sun, '56, *1, 2 Pop*)

BOPPIN' THE BLUES (Sun, '56, *7*)

DIXIE FRIED (Sun, '56, *10*)

YOUR TRUE LOVE (Sun, '57, *13*)

PINK PEDAL PUSHERS (Columbia, '58, *17*)

COUNTRY BOY'S DREAM (Dollie, '66, *22*)

SHINE SHINE SHINE (Dollie, '67, *40*)

RESTLESS (Columbia, '69, *20*)

COTTON TOP (Columbia, '71)

BIRTH OF ROCK AND ROLL (America, '86, *31*)

WEBB PIERCE

Wearing colorfully embroidered suits, his name emblazoned on his guitar, and later boasting a matching pair of silver-dollar–inlaid Pontiac convertibles and a mansion with a guitar-shaped swimming pool, Webb Pierce was the prototypical flamboyant country superstar, wallowing in excess.

He earned it. Pierce's country impact was immense. Starting with his first three *Billboard* chart singles—all Number Ones—in 1952, Pierce blazed a trail of 96 country hits through 1982. As a vocalist, he was distinctive, emotive, and versatile. As a torch-carrying honky-tonker in the Hank Williams tradition he was also innovative, the first to absorb pedal-steel guitar into mainstream country song. Along the way, he gave a boost to such up-and-comers as Mel Tillis, Charlie Pride, and Faron Young.

He was born on August 8, 1926 (some sources say 1921), in West Monroe, Louisiana, and learned to play music while growing up on his father's farm. At 16 he landed a regular 15-minute slot on a local Monroe radio station.

Following a stint in the Army in the late 1940s, Pierce moved to Shreveport and combined working at the local Sears—where he started as a delivery boy and moved up to men's department manager—with performing music on the side. The goal was to play on KWKH radio's "Louisiana Hayride" show, and in 1950 he became a cast member. He issued a couple of recordings around this time, including "Hayride Boogie"—recorded with the Tillman Frank band on Pierce's own Pacemaker Records (formed with "Hayride" chief Horace Logan)—but none took off.

Signing with Decca in 1951, Pierce soon began outputting singles. His 1952 debut, "Wondering," climbed all the way to Number One, signaling the arrival of a potential major hitmaker. He followed up in that same year with "That Heart Belongs to Me" and "Back Street Affair," both chart-toppers and the latter a future honky-tonk standard (and the inspiration for a Kitty Wells answer song, "Paying for That Back Street Affair").

In September of that eventful year, Pierce graduated from the "Hayride" to the Grand Ole Opry.

Of the 13 Number One hits that he would eventually amass, the next several were standouts: "There Stands the Glass" (1953) has been singled out as a definitive honky-tonk drinking song; on "Slowly" (1954), Pierce introduced the sliding, swelling sound of pedal-steel guitar (played by Bud Isaacs), subsequently to become one of country's key sonic components; Pierce's 1955 cover of Jimmie Rodgers' "In the Jailhouse Now" stayed on top of the country chart for nearly half a year. All of these songs—and those that followed—proved that Pierce was indeed a major hitmaker.

Also an able businessman, Pierce wisely retained publishing rights to his own material, forming Cedarwood Music in 1954 with Jim Denny, former Opry manager. The firm became a significant publisher, its stable of writers eventually including Mel Tillis, whom Pierce met in 1957 and tapped for his own recording material. Pierce scored a number of hits with Tillis tunes, including his last Number One, 1957's "Honky Tonk Song."

Pierce's main hitmaking years were the 1950s and early '60s. The arrival of the heavily produced and sleekened Nashville Sound and the onslaught of Presley-led rock and roll ultimately pushed Pierce (and others) aside. He gamely worked some rock into his sound—notably on 1956's "Teenage Boogie" (a reworking of his early "Hayride Boogie") and "Bye Bye Love" (charting at the same time as the Everly Brothers' version, only lower)—but couldn't sustain a dominant chart presence after around 1964.

He kept charting, though, up until Decca dropped him in 1972. Afterward he signed with the Plantation label and scored two minor hits in 1975 and '76. By that time, flush with wealth, he'd opened his sumptuous Oak Hill, Tennessee, estate to the public as a tourist attraction, even building a tour-bus ramp on his property.

TOP SONGS

Wondering (Decca, '52, 1)
That Heart Belongs to Me (Decca, '52, 1)
Back Street Affair (Decca, '52, 1)
It's Been So Long (Decca, '53, 1)
There Stands the Glass (Decca, '53, 1)
Slowly (Decca, '54, 1)
In the Jailhouse Now (Decca, '55, 1)
I Don't Care (Decca, '55, 1)
Love, Love, Love (Decca, '55, 1)
Honky Tonk Song (Decca, '57, 1)

Additional Top 40 Country Songs: 70

In 1982, Pierce fan Willie Nelson sang a duet with Pierce on a remake of "In the Jailhouse Now." It was Pierce's last chart entry. He died on February 24, 1991, after a bout with cancer.

ELVIS PRESLEY

Elvis Presley was the king of rock and roll. But central to his reign was the way in which he mixed black music—R&B, gospel, and the blues—and the melodic, vocal, and instrumental signatures of country music and forged a revolutionary new style. It was a sound that would ultimately popularize both forms and make Presley one of the most successful performers of the century.

Elvis Aaron Presley was born on January 8, 1935, in a modest, two-room house in Tupelo, Mississippi. His parents were poor but very religious, and the young Presley originally sang gospel music in church. He also listened to country music on the radio, and his interest in the music became more involved when, at age 11, he was given a guitar for his birthday by his father (his Uncle Vester taught Presley a few basic chords). That same year, he won a talent contest at the state fair singing a rendition of "Old Shep."

But it was in Memphis (where his family moved when he was 13) that Presley would finally meet his destiny. In 1954 he went to the fledgling Sun Studios to make a personal recording of the country song "My Happiness" as a birthday present for his mother. The recording came to the attention of the studio's owner, Sam Phillips, who subsequently signed Presley to a contract. Phillips teamed Presley with bassist Bill Black and guitarist Scotty Moore, and the three began recording. Presley's debut single, "That's All Right Mama," was a supercharged version of an R&B song by Arthur Crudup.

While Presley's music would evolve in many directions during the course of his career, it was the approach used on his Sun recordings that would set the stage for rock and roll. The sound itself was a revamped version of traditional country and hillbilly music. The notes and rhythms of Black's bass had about them the kick of bluegrass and the flow of western swing, while Moore's phrasings were a bluesy reinterpretation of Merle Travis. To all of this Presley added vocals that spanned the range of American popular idioms, from the adenoidal stylings of Hank Williams to the fevered displays of

Elvis Presley

the blues and gospel artists and the svelte posturings of the '40s pop stars.

In 1955, Presley's career began to develop and expand. That year he was signed by manager "Colonel" Tom Parker, who bought out his Sun contract and negotiated a deal with gigantic RCA Records. But even as his rock and roll roots were growing, Presley's country connections continued to be an important facet of his career. One of his first major media performances was on the legendary country radio program "Louisiana Hayride" in 1955. That year he also appeared at the traditional bastion of country music, the Grand Ole Opry. And Presley had scored his first chart hit in July 1955, when the single "Baby Let's Play House" made the top 10 on the *Billboard* country chart.

But it was in 1956 that Presley's career grew exponentially. His RCA debut single, "Heartbreak Hotel," went to the top of the chart and, in a definitive manner, gave birth to the rock and roll era. With his tousled locks and swiveling hips and his singular sound, Presley conquered the world of popular music.

During his 21-year career, Presley became the biggest-selling artist in the history of music. He had an astonishing 67 top 20 hits in the singles charts with literally scores of others making the top 100. He also had 38 top 20 albums, again with numerous others making the charts. In the process, he sold hundreds of millions of records.

And what records! "Jailhouse Rock," "Hound Dog," "Love Me Tender," "All Shook Up," "Dont' Be Cruel," and others virtually defined the sound and musical imagery of rock and roll. And Presley's appearances onstage and on such television programs as "The Ed Sullivan Show" were cultural watersheds, the points at which the emerging teen movement and its records, fashions, fads, and trends overwhelmed the culture at large.

The initial, revolutionary phase of Presley's career was brief. It was interrupted in 1958 when he was drafted into the U.S. Army. And by the time he reemerged in 1960, the excitement and energy of the '50s rock that he had created and symbolized was gone—as was, for the most part, the exhilaration of Presley's music and career. While he continued to be enormously successful in terms of record sales, Presley increasingly subverted his music to a succession of dreary, exploitative teen movies, which also provided the bulk of his musical output. He made a brief comeback with a wondrous television special in 1968. But soon, he degenerated into a cultural cliché, a bloated and excessive travesty who played to the lowest common denominator of his fans. He died on August 16, 1977, at his fabled Memphis mansion, Graceland.

TOP SONGS

I Forgot to Remember to Forget (Sun, '55, *1*)
Heartbreak Hotel (RCA, '56, *1, 1 Pop*)
I Want You, I Need You, I Love You
  (RCA, '56, *1, 1 Pop*)
Don't Be Cruel (RCA, '56, *1, 1 Pop*)
Hound Dog (RCA, '56, *1, 1 Pop*)
All Shook Up (RCA, '57, *1, 1 Pop*)
(Let Me Be) Your Teddy Bear (RCA, '57, *1, 1 Pop*)
Jailhouse Rock (RCA, '57, *1, 1 Pop*)
Moody Blue (RCA, '76, *1, 31 Pop*)
Way Down (RCA, '77, *1, 18 Pop*)

Additional Top 40 Country Songs: 41

RAY PRICE

"In 1956, I took the music of the day, rhythm and blues and country music, and made some changes by new chord progressions, raised the brass, lowered the steel, and got started."

So said Ray Price in the Dallas *Times Herald* in 1972, 16 years after he hit Number One with "Crazy Arms" and launched what would be one of the lengthiest and most successful recording careers in country music.

A master of the smooth, mellow croon, Texan Ray Price melded the western swing influence of Bob Wills with a honky-tonk style picked up from Hank Williams and took the result—along with later heavily orchestrated material—straight to the pop mainstream.

Born on January 12, 1926, in Perryville, Texas, and raised in Dallas, Noble Ray Price wanted to be a veterinarian at first. But while studying at North Texas Agricultural College in the late 1940s he became more involved in singing. His recording career began when a guitarist-songwriter friend requested that Price sing with him at an audition. It led to a contract for Price—but not the friend—with Bullet Records. In 1949 a Price song, "Jealous Lies," became his first single.

Price aimed to get with a larger label, and an incident in 1951 helped him. He was hanging out at Jim Beck's Dallas studio on a day when Lefty Frizzell—a country newcomer at the time—was booked to record four songs for Columbia. Frizzell, it turned out, only had three songs. "He came running to me," says Price. "He says, 'Can you write me one real quick?' and he says, 'You only got so many minutes.' I said, 'Man, what are you talking about?' He said, 'Write me one.' 'Well, OK, I'll try.' And I went to the other side of the studio, and about 15 minutes later I took one to him and said, 'This is the best I could do,' and he recorded it. And it sold a couple million records. It's called 'Give Me More, More, More (Of Your Kisses).'" The song was a Number One hit for Frizzell.

On March 15, 1951, Columbia signed Price. A year later, Price issued the singles "Talk to Your Heart" and "Don't Let the Stars Get in Your Eyes," both top 10 hits.

Living in Nashville by that time, Price befriended hitmaker Hank Williams, touring and at one point sharing a house with him (and through him gaining entry to the Grand Ole Opry). When Williams died,

in 1953, Price worked with his backup band, the Drifting Cowboys. Then, in 1954, he formed his own group he called the Cherokee Cowboys (whose alumni over the years would include such later stars as Willie Nelson, Johnny Paycheck, and Roger Miller).

Number One hits eluded Price—until he came across an appealing tune called "Crazy Arms." "I was real fortunate," says Price. "I ran into a disc jockey in Tampa, Florida, and he said, 'I've got a song on a small label I want you to hear.' And I listened to it, and I said, 'Hey, I like that—that's a hit.' And I took it in and I recorded it and came up with a new sound. . . . I came up with a new beat with the drums and a new beat with the bass, and we started what is basically the basic country sound today. 'Cause when I went to Nashville there were no drums."

The influential, shuffle-rhythmed sound of "Crazy Arms"—which crossed over to the pop chart—led to "My Shoes Keep Walking Back to You," "City Lights," and other chart-topping artifacts of Price's honky-tonk heyday, a period that established his place in country history.

Controversy accompanied Price's subsequent move to country-pop, in which he supplemented the Cherokee Cowboys with swelling, sweeping sym-

Ray Price

TOP SONGS

I'LL BE THERE (IF YOU EVER WANT ME)
(Columbia, '54, 2)

CRAZY ARMS (Columbia, '56, 1)

I'VE GOT A NEW HEARTACHE (Columbia, '56, 2)

MY SHOES KEEP WALKING BACK TO YOU
(Columbia, '57, 1)

CITY LIGHTS (Columbia, '58, 1)

THE SAME OLD ME (Columbia, '59, 1)

FOR THE GOOD TIMES (Columbia, '70, 1, 11 Pop)

I WON'T MENTION IT AGAIN (Columbia, '71, 1)

SHE'S GOT TO BE A SAINT (Columbia, '72, 1)

YOU'RE THE BEST THING THAT EVER HAPPENED
TO ME (Columbia, '73, 1)

Additional Top 40 Country Songs: 70

phonic strings. First heard on his early gospel material, the approach brought Price a secular chart hit with "Danny Boy" in 1966. "The reason that I did the other [orchestrated] sound was to broaden the scope of country music," claims Price. "It allowed a lot of people to listen to it that wouldn't listen to it if it wasn't dressed up a little bit more sophisticated." At the time, a number of purists accused him of deserting country.

"None of them understood me, or they didn't know what to do with me," he says. "They were great people, but I was just something they didn't understand." But the sound was successful, taking 1970's "For the Good Times" to Number One, yielding more chart-toppers, and making Price a frequent guest at symphonic "pops" concerts across the United States.

With occasional nods to his old style, Price remained a presence on the country chart through 1989.

CHARLEY PRIDE

The first, and only, black country superstar, Charley Pride arrived on the scene smack in the middle of the civil rights movement of the 1960s. He avoided being labeled the token black country artist through a long and astoundingly successful career, scoring over 50 top 10 hits that include "Is Anybody Goin' to San Antone" and

"Kiss an Angel Good Mornin'." He's regarded as one of the best ever to sing a country song.

Pride (b. Mar. 18, 1938, Sledge, Mississippi) was raised in rural Mississippi, one of 11 children. Everybody in the family contributed to making a living by picking cotton, something he did alongside his brothers and sisters until he was 17. At night the family would listen to the broadcasts of the Grand Ole Opry, and Charley grew to love country music. "I loved it so much I wanted to sing it," he says, "even when my people were asking me, 'Why do you want to sing their [white people's] songs?'" But what he wanted more than anything as a young man was to play professional baseball. He made significant headway in that direction, starting in the Negro American League and then, in 1961, playing briefly for the Los Angeles Angels.

When he wasn't playing ball, Pride held various day jobs and sang country music in honky-tonks at night. One of his jobs was at a Montana smelting plant in 1963. Pride sang at the Helena, Montana, Civic Center on a show that included country greats Red Sovine and Red Foley. Pride's version of Hank Williams' "Lovesick Blues" impressed them, and they suggested he go to Nashville and record a demo. Pride took them up on the offer, and his demo tape landed him a contract with RCA Records.

Label executive Chet Atkins feared country radio and audiences wouldn't give Pride a chance if they promoted him as a black singer. Pride didn't sing country music with a black or R&B flavor to his voice; he just sounded like a traditional country singer. Still, to avoid any initial negative reaction, RCA released his first records without accompanying them with publicity photos, billing him as Country Charley Pride. By the time the public knew he was black he had scored three consecutive top 10 hits and was on his way.

Over the years, Pride managed to keep race from being an issue. "I came along during the height of the bus boycotts," he once said. "People always ask me about race, but if I got off into those things, I would cease to be an entertainer. I'd become Charley Pride the activist."

Pride scored his first Number One in 1969 with "All I Have to Offer You (Is Me)." In all, Pride amassed an astounding 29 chart-topping songs, including his biggest hit—and a crossover success at number 21 on the pop chart—"Kiss an Angel Good Mornin'." For years, Pride was RCA's top-selling act, and he ranks today as one of the biggest sellers

Charley Pride

in the history of the label. His industry honors include Male Vocalist and Entertainer of the Year Awards from the Country Music Association and three country Grammy Awards.

In spite of his success, in 1986 Pride felt he was no longer a priority with RCA and asked to be released. He signed with independent 16th Avenue Records and continued recording and touring.

Pride's achievements are all the more significant in light of the continuing difficulty black performers have in finding country acceptance, recent artists such as Dobie Gray and, more recently, Cleve Francis notwithstanding. Yet Pride remains modest. "Even though I appreciate the fame and adoration, I remember I used to pick cotton," he says. "Even then I felt like I was somebody. I have the same feet, hands, and heart like everyone else. I'm just blessed with a good voice."

TOP SONGS

(I'm So) Afraid of Losing You Again (RCA, '69, 1)
I Can't Believe That You've Stopped Loving Me
   (RCA, '70, 1)
I'm Just Me (RCA, '71, 1)
Kiss an Angel Good Mornin'
   (RCA, '71, 1, 21 Pop)
It's Gonna Take a Little Bit Longer (RCA, '72, 1)
She's Too Good to Be True (RCA, '72, 1)
Honky Tonk Blues (RCA, '80, 1)
Never Been So Loved (In All My Life) (RCA, '81, 1)
Mountain of Love (RCA, '81, 1)
Night Games (RCA, '83, 1)

Additional Top 40 Country Songs: 50

EDDIE RABBITT

Eddie Rabbit

One of the biggest country-pop crossover artists of the 1970s and '80s, Eddie Rabbitt hit the charts consistently with a sleek, middle-of-the-road sound that won fans even as it was derided by country music purists. But his musical status notwithstanding, Rabbit was one of the first artists in the country field to make the music a staple of the pop charts and, as such, was partially responsible for the movement of country into the musical mainstream.

Tellingly, Rabbitt (né Edward Thomas) was born not in the hollows of Tennessee but in the canyons of Brooklyn, New York, on November 27, 1941. His father was an accordionist and fiddler who encouraged Rabbitt to pursue a career in music.

Rabbitt learned to play guitar at age 12. He was introduced to the instrument by his scoutmaster, Tony Schwickrath, a country singer from New Jersey who performed under the name Texas Bob Randall. As Rabbitt recounts it, "On one of our hikes he pulled out a guitar and started playing some Johnny Cash and Bob Wills tunes. It was my first time to hear a guitar up close, and I was fascinated."

By the mid-'60s, Rabbitt was performing in various clubs in the New York–New Jersey area and recording on the Columbia and 20th Century Fox labels to no success.

He moved to Nashville in 1968 and went to work as a songwriter with the Hill and Range music publishing company for $37.50 a week. He immediately scored a hit with "Working My Way Up from the Bottom," which was recorded by Roy Drusky and made number 33 on the country chart. He also frequented the music clubs with other struggling songwriters like Kris Kristofferson and Larry Gatlin. Mostly, after gaining his initial success, he settled into the day-to-day struggle for survival—and attention—in the busy Nashville scene.

"Boy, this is gonna be easy," Rabbitt said later of his thoughts about his first songwriting hit. "But it wasn't easy. I soon found out that Nashville is where all the best musicians in the world gather, and I was in competition with every one of them."

While his career as a performer was developing, Rabbit continued to write songs that were hits for others artists. In 1970 he wrote "Kentucky Rain," which became the fiftieth gold record by Elvis Presley. When his song "Pure Love," recorded by Ronnie Milsap, topped the charts in 1973, Rabbitt was offered a contract of his own with Elektra Records.

His career as a performer soon eclipsed that of his songwriting days. He scored his first Number One in 1975 with "Drinkin' My Baby (Off My Mind)" and later hit with "Two Dollars in the Jukebox," two rollicking honky-tonk songs from his second album, *Rocky Mountain Music*. By 1977 he was one of the major figures in country music. That year he was voted Best New Artist by *Country* magazine.

TOP SONGS

DRINKIN' MY BABY (OFF MY MIND) (Elektra, '76, *1*)
YOU DON'T LOVE ME ANYMORE (Elektra, '78, *1*)
I JUST WANT TO LOVE YOU (Elektra, '78, *1*)
EVERY WHICH WAY BUT LOOSE (Elektra, '78, *1, 30 Pop*)
SUSPICIONS (Elektra, '79, *1, 13 Pop*)
GONE TOO FAR (Elektra, '80, *1*)
DRIVIN' MY LIFE AWAY (Elektra, '80, *1, 5 Pop*)
I LOVE A RAINY NIGHT (Elektra, '80, *1, 1 Pop*)
STEP BY STEP (Elektra, '81, *1, 5 Pop*)
SOMEONE COULD LOSE A HEART TONIGHT
    (Elektra, '81, *1, 15 Pop*)

Additional Top 40 Country Songs: 29

And he was named Best New Artist of the Year by the Country Music Association in 1978.

Rabbitt proved popular to broad audiences by scoring a number of hits on the pop charts as well as the country charts. Over the course of his career he won more than 20 BMI awards as a country songwriter and more than a dozen in the pop category.

He topped the charts three times in 1978, his hits including "Every Which Way But Loose" (which was also the theme of a Clint Eastwood movie). On this record and others, Rabbitt created a sound that was as smoothed-out and homogenized as it was accessible to a wide range of country and non-country fans. His 1980 hit "I Love a Rainy Night" topped the pop charts, as did his 1982 duet with Crystal Gayle, "You and I."

But while he was one of the major stars of country, Rabbitt was often dismissed by purists as a pop performer. In 1990, Rabbitt responded to this when he told writer Jack Hurst, "I'm continually having to reestablish myself in this country business. Even though I've had 20-something country number one records, I still have a hard time convincing a lot of these people in the Country Music Association and the Academy of Country Music that I love country music."

Rabbitt's success was an important development in the commercial evolution of country music. Despite criticism, Rabbitt was, in fact, winning a new generation of fans for country music. If such records as "Step by Step" and "Drivin' My Life Away" were as much pop as they were country, they nonetheless created a market for the music that was much larger than in the past. Along with Gayle, Kenny Rogers, and certain other artists, Rabbitt was setting the stage for the influx of country artists onto the national pop scene that would become a dominant musical trend in the 1980s and '90s.

EDDY RAVEN

"**S**omething I've wanted to do for a long time is marry the Cajun music with the island influence, the steel drums and everything, without making the music traditional."

Eddy Raven's stated goal is to be expected from someone who grew up in the musical melting pot of southern Louisiana. What's surprising is how long it took him to reach it. Intervening years were spent learning the ropes in the Nashville music industry,

Eddy Raven

building a reputation as a reliable songwriter and hitmaking recording artist.

As a teenager, Edward Garvin Futch (b. Aug. 9, 1944) bounced between Lafayette and coastal Georgia and absorbed the sounds of country (through his father's taste for Roy Acuff), rock, Cajun music, and rhythm and blues. He cut his teeth playing with bands like the Rockin' Cajuns, the Boogie Kings, the Glades, the Swing Kings, and the pre-fame blues brothers, Johnny and Edgar Winter. While doing a radio show out of Baxley, Georgia, Eddy was heard by a rep for the local Cosmo label and offered a shot at recording. In 1960, at age 16, he was the proud possessor of a solo single, "Once a Fool," the label of which gave his name as Eddy Raven.

Back in Lafayette he resubmerged himself in the surrounding sonic stew, working at a music store and sound studio called La Louisiane through whose doors passed Dr. John, Professor Longhair, and several of the area's significant others. It was there that Raven recorded his own first album, *That Cajun Country Sound,* in 1969.

Through Cajun-country singer Jimmy C. Newman—who'd heard the disc—Raven connected with

Nashville's Acuff-Rose music publishing firm and was signed as a writer. His first efforts were hits for country stalwart Don Gibson and Jeannie C. Riley. Follow-ups clicked for Randy Cornor, Connie Smith, and Acuff himself. Raven seemed headed for behind-the-scenes writing success.

But Acuff-Rose's Don Gant moved to ABC Records and signed Raven as a solo artist, freeing the singer locked inside the pensman. Eight singles charted, starting with "The Last of the Sunshine Cowboys," but none cracked the top 10.

Raven the recording artist label-hopped from ABC to Monument to Dimension to Elektra, where in 1981 he issued *Desperate Dreams,* produced by Jimmy Bowen. It yielded "She's Playing Hard to Forget," giving Raven that cherished first top 10 single. Around that time, the Oak Ridge Boys scored a hit with Raven's "Thank God for Kids." Feeling flush, Raven took a break, took stock, and hopped labels yet again—this time to RCA.

The creative control granted him by that company bore fruit: Raven's first RCA chart single, 1984's "I Got Mexico," was also his first chart-topper. It gave way to a six-year run of top 10 hits, of which two—1988's "I'm Gonna Get You" and "Joe Knows How to Live"—provided Cajun and Caribbean hints of sonic exotica yet to come.

By now a confident creator of widely popular material, Raven made a move to a new label, Universal, where he was finally given license to explore the full range of his favored styles. Describing the resulting album, *Temporary Sanity,* as containing

"the kind of stuff with the rollicking good-time feel, what I call my electric Cajun band music," he shot to the top yet again with the steel-drum–powered "Bayou Boys," trailed at lower rankings by "Islands" and "Zydeco Lady."

By the very next year—true to Raven form—he was with another record company.

COLLIN RAYE

Singer Collin Raye (b. Floyd Collin Wray, Aug. 22, 1959, DeQueen, Arkansas) put out four low-charting records in the 1980s, two as part of the Wray Brothers Band and two more under the name the Wrays (recording with his brother Scott), but both acts failed to break through. In the 1990s he adjusted the spelling of his last name and emerged as a solo artist, rising to prominence in early 1992 with a huge ballad hit called "Love Me." Since then, he's become a consistent hitmaker and one of the most dynamic live performers in country music.

Raye found the inspiration for his career in his home. His mother, Lois Wray, was a regional country star and once shared the stage at a big fair with Johnny Cash, Jerry Lee Lewis, Carl Perkins, and Elvis Presley. "She taught me how to sing harmony," recalls Raye, "and my dad was a bass player, he taught me how to do that." Raye and his brother Scott started performing early. "I remember doing it when I was very small, maybe four or five years old," Raye says. "We did the Lion's Club minstrel show in DeQueen, a talent show. My brother was six or seven, and he could pick. He played guitar real well—not just chords: he picked. We dressed alike, and we wore cowboy hats, and they did give me a tambourine to bang on."

While Raye's early musical experience was country-oriented, he and his brother played rock as teenagers, Collin fronting his own bands and his brother playing guitar. They moved to Oregon in 1980 and began performing a sort of outlaw brand of country music with Eagles-style harmonies. Raye billed himself as "Bubba Wray" when an incarnation of that group, the Wray Brothers Band, charted in 1983 and again in '85 on independent record labels.

They thought they had made it when Mercury Records in Nashville picked them up in 1986. They came close in '87 as the Wrays, hitting number 48

TOP ALBUMS

RIGHT HAND MAN (RCA, '86)
TEMPORARY SANITY (Universal, '89)

TOP SONGS

I GOT MEXICO (RCA, '84, 1)
YOU SHOULD HAVE BEEN GONE BY NOW (RCA, '85, 3)
SOMETIMES A LADY (RCA, '86, 3)
SHINE, SHINE, SHINE (RCA, '87, 1)
I'M GONNA GET YOU (RCA, '88, 1)
JOE KNOWS HOW TO LIVE (RCA, '88, 1)
IN A LETTER TO YOU (Universal, '89, 1)
BAYOU BOYS (Universal, '89, 1)

Additional Top 40 Country Songs: 18

with "You Lay a Lotta Love on Me." Caught up in label politics, they gave up on Nashville, and the brothers went their separate ways. Brother Scott went back to Oregon, while Raye settled in Reno, Nevada. For the next five years, Raye established himself as a successful lounge act and honed his skills as a live performer.

He was playing the casinos when he was seen by some California-based record producers. They recorded a demo of his songs that led to his signing with Epic Records in 1990.

In the summer of 1991, Raye hit number 29 with his first release. His second was a strong ballad called "Love Me," which put him on the map when it stayed at Number One for three weeks in early '92. Afterward, he was a regular visitor to the top 10, most notably with ballads like "In This Life" and "Little Rock."

"I got such a reputation as a balladeer that it was hurting my live show," claims Raye. "People were expecting me to be just a stand-up-at-the-mike, low-energy guy. I'm just the opposite; I kick it and rock it on stage." He moved to counter the image with energetic hits like "That's My Story."

Raye's versatility and experience became distinct advantages over younger artists who were scoring hit records but had no seasoning as stage performers to back them up. "When I step on stage I'm completely confident that I can give a good show," Raye says. He also made a point to record albums he felt would appeal to everybody in his audience on some level. "You take any hundred country fans, and they're

Collin Raye

going to like something on my album very much. They may hate five or six tracks, but they're going to love three or four tracks on it. That's what I try to do: throw a wide loop with my music."

TOP ALBUMS

ALL I CAN BE (Epic, '91)
IN THIS LIFE (Epic, '92)
EXTREMES (Epic, '93)

TOP SONGS

LOVE ME (Epic, '91, 1)
EVERY SECOND (Epic, '92, 2)
IN THIS LIFE (Epic, '92, 1)
SOMEBODY ELSE'S MOON (Epic, '93, 5)
THAT WAS A RIVER (Epic, '93, 4)
THAT'S MY STORY (Epic, '93, 6)
LITTLE ROCK (Epic, '94, 2)

Additional Top 40 Country Songs: 1

JERRY REED

With his odd assortment of hats, his chiseled face, and his raspy twang of a voice, Jerry Reed came to epitomize the ornery, rascally, down-home good ole boy that is at the core of the country music ethos. But during his career, these often obscured the fact that Reed was an able songwriter and performer and one of the finest guitarists on the country scene.

Reed (Jerry Hubbard) was born on March 20, 1937, in Atlanta, Georgia. In his teens he worked by day in a cotton mill and by nights performed at the local bars and honky-tonks. In those days—the 1950s—Reed was as much a rocker as a country musician. In fact, when he landed a record contract in 1955, his producer, Bill Lowery, encouraged him to try his hand at rockabilly. "I was too young to be making records," Reed recounted later. "I didn't know what to do."

While Reed had little success with the rockabilly approach, he did write "Crazy Legs," a song that was recorded by Gene Vincent in 1956. But after this initial flirtation with the music business, Reed joined the military and did not reemerge until the beginning of the 1960s.

In 1962 he settled in Nashville and began pursuing a career as a songwriter and performer. Securing a contract with Columbia Records he scored two hits that year with "Goodnight, Irene" and "Hully Gully Guitars."

He also began to work as a session guitarist and became known for his instrumental prowess. In 1965, Chet Atkins signed Reed to a contract with RCA Records. Inspired by his session gigs, Reed wrote "Guitar Man," which became a modest hit in 1967. The next year, Reed's status grew when Elvis Presley recorded his own version of the song along with "U.S. Male," another Reed original.

From the later 1960s into the '70s, Reed's own records began to appear on the charts with increasing consistency. These included "Tupelo Mississippi Flash" (dedicated to Presley), "Are You from Dixie?" and "Talk About the Good Times," among others, each of which came with Reed's wry down-home approach.

But it was the 1970 hit "Amos Moses" that sent Reed's career into its most successful phase. The record became a top 10 hit on the pop charts and established Reed's name outside his traditional country base. The hits also won Reed a 1970 Grammy Award for Best Country Male Vocal Performance and a nomination by the Country Music Association for Instrumentalist of the Year.

"Amos Moses" became such a broad-based hit that Reed was invited to become a cast member on the "Glen Campbell Goodtime Hour" television series. His performances on that show made him a national celebrity, which he translated into new hits on the charts.

Those hits—particularly 1971's "When You're Hot, You're Hot"—were infused with Reed's infectious personality and rollicking wit, which he in turn parlayed into an acting career.

It began with a dare, made by a friend in 1974, that prompted Reed to audition for a co-starring role in the Burt Reynolds movie W.W. and the Dixie Dancekings. Reed got the part. He subsequently appeared in such Reynolds films as Gator (1976), Smokey and the Bandit (1977), and Smokey and the Bandit II (1980). In the 1980s, Reed also starred with Claude Akins in the television series "Nashville 99."

Although his new career increasingly drew time and attention away from his touring and recording schedule, Reed remained musically active in the 1970s and '80s. He recorded albums with Chet Atkins that were fine instrumental efforts. And he also continued to enjoy hits, including 1978's "(I Love You) What Can I Say" and 1982's "She Got the Goldmine (I Got the Shaft)."

Reed eventually became less active on the charts and in the movies while continuing to record and tour.

TOP ALBUMS

ME AND CHET (RCA, '74)
THE UPTOWN POKER CLUB (RCA, '75)

TOP SONGS

ARE YOU FROM DIXIE (CAUSE I'M FROM DIXIE TOO) (RCA, '69, 11)
WHEN YOU'RE HOT, YOU'RE HOT (RCA, '71, 1, 9 Pop)
KO-KO JOE (RCA, '71, 11)
LORD, MR. FORD (RCA, '73, 1)
EAST BOUND AND DOWN (RCA, '77, 2)
(I LOVE YOU) WHAT CAN I SAY (RCA, '78, 10)
SHE GOT THE GOLDMINE (I GOT THE SHAFT) (RCA, '82, 1)
THE BIRD (RCA, '82, 2)

Additional Top 40 Country Songs: 28

JIM REEVES

So popular was the velvet-voiced Jim Reeves during his '50s and '60s heyday that after he died, other singers scored major hits by recording "duets" with his old vocal tracks.

Internationally embraced—more so than most other country records—Reeves' music evolved from a straight-country honky-tonk style to the more polished and broadly accepted Nashville Sound, yielding scores of hits, many of which crossed over to pop.

Reeves (b. Aug. 20, 1924, Galloway, Texas) was brought up on a farm by his mother. He developed early interests in music (picking up guitar by age six) and especially baseball. An athletic scholarship took him to the University of Texas, and for a while it appeared that pro baseball would be his calling. But after quickly dropping out of college, working in a Houston shipyard, and playing ball in the East Texas League, he sustained a foot injury that prompted a career reassessment.

Reeves' appealing speaking voice landed him an announcer position at KGRI radio in Henderson, Texas. He would remain there for several years, moving up to program director, occasionally singing over the air, and performing music in clubs in the surrounding region. In 1949 he released his first record, for the local Macy label.

Action picked up when he was hired as an announcer on KWKH radio in Shreveport, home of the popular "Louisiana Hayride" show. A subsequent record deal with the Abbott label produced a 1953 Number One hit, "Mexican Joe," which helped Reeves become a regular musical performer on the "Hayride." "Bimbo," his Number One follow-up, sealed his popularity.

RCA Records took notice and in 1955 bought out his Abbott contract. In that same year, Reeves joined the Grand Ole Opry.

Early RCA tracks, such as "Yonder Comes a Sucker" and "According to My Heart," were not far removed in tone from the no-frills honky-tonk country purveyed by Hank Williams, Lefty Frizzell, Ray Price, and others of the era. But with the threatening arrival of rock and roll, changes were in the wind. To keep current—and also to appropriately cushion

his low, resonant voice—Reeves began stripping away defining country instruments like fiddle and steel guitar and fashioning a warmer, more pop-oriented sonic setting. The first major hit with this approach was 1957's "Four Walls," a crossover success at Number One country and number 11 pop. A year later, Reeves reached number two with "Blue Boy," another crossover and the inspiration for the name of his backup band, the Blue Boys. With 1959's "He'll Have to Go," a monster hit at Number One country and number two pop, Reeves' mass appeal was firmly established.

Tours in the late 1950s and early '60s to Europe, South Africa, and elsewhere were greeted with enthusiasm, providing vast new audiences for Reeves' records. Reeves spoke out on the value of distributing country music internationally, even writing an article on the subject for *Billboard* magazine.

But the article didn't come out until November 1964, three and a half months after Reeves' single-engine aircraft went down in a rainstorm outside of Nashville, ending his life on July 31, 1964.

Three years later, Reeves was elected to the Country Music Hall of Fame.

Reeves' records would continue to become hits for two decades thereafter. An immediate six Number One singles followed his death, and 28 posthumous releases made the top 40. In 1979 and '80 Deborah Allen scored three top 10s with songs in which she dubbed her voice over old Reeves recordings. Odder still, in 1981 two hits were created by electronically combining the voices of Reeves and the late Patsy Cline on "Have You Ever Been Lonely (Have You Ever Been Blue)" and "I Fall to Pieces."

RESTLESS HEART

It is the dream, no doubt, of every session musician who toils in the trenches of the Nashville studio scene: to step out of the studio and into the spotlight and become a star. In 1984, five session musicians chucked the scene and formed a group of their own, Restless Heart, that became one of the bigger country acts of the decade.

The group began to coalesce at the beginning of the 1980s when guitarist Greg Jennings (b. Oct. 2, 1954, Oklahoma City, Oklahoma) and accounting professor–songwriter Tim DuBois teamed up in Nashville. While Jennings began assembling the rest

Restless Heart

TOP ALBUMS

RESTLESS HEART (RCA, '85)
WHEELS (RCA, '86)
BIG DREAMS IN A SMALL TOWN (RCA, '88)
FAST MOVIN' TRAIN (RCA, '90)

TOP SONGS

THAT ROCK WON'T ROLL (RCA, '86, 1)
I'LL STILL BE LOVING YOU (RCA, '86, 1, 33 Pop)
WHY DOES IT HAVE TO BE (WRONG OR RIGHT)
  (RCA, '87, 1)
WHEELS (RCA, '87, 1)
BLUEST EYES IN TEXAS (RCA, '88, 1)
A TENDER LIE (RCA, '88, 1)

Additional Top 40 Country Songs: 15

of the group, DuBois became its financier and producer. Soon, keyboardist Dave Innis (b. Apr. 9, 1959, Bartlesville, Oklahoma), vocalist Larry Stewart (b. Mar. 2, 1959, Padukah, Kentucky), drummer John Dittrich (b. Apr. 7, 1951, West Orange, New Jersey), and bassist Paul Gregg (b. Dec. 3, 1954, Altus, Oklahoma) came on board, and Restless Heart became a reality. "This band is a culmination of something that all five of us, each in his own way, has wanted to do," Stewart said at the time. "Each of us really had it in his heart to be part of a band."

From the start, the musicians set out to create a sleek, pop-oriented sound that would conform to the "new country" music of such crossover performers as Alabama, Eddie Rabbitt, and others. It was an approach that was becoming increasingly successful on the country scene of the time, and it would prove just as viable for Restless Heart.

Their 1985 debut album, *Restless Heart*, yielded four top 40 country singles: "Let the Heartache

Ride," "I Want Everyone to Cry," "(Back to the) Heartbreak Kid," and "Til I Loved You."

Restless Heart then began a touring schedule that brought it to most of the major country markets, with the group opening for such established acts as Alabama, Glenn Frey, and Juice Newton. The live concert exposure, in conjunction with the radio airplay generated by the debut album, pushed Restless Heart to the foreground of the country scene.

Their smash sophomore album, *Wheels,* increased the momentum in 1986. With the release of that record, Restless Heart began a run on the country chart that would include six straight Number One singles, starting with "That Rock Won't Roll" and ending with "A Tender Lie" from the 1988 album *Big Dreams in a Small Town.*

Restless Heart accomplished all this with a sound that combined the boisterous vocals of Stewart and flowing vocal harmonies from the rest of the group with crisp, studio-clean musicianship. It kept them in the top five of the charts through the end of the decade with such songs as "Big Dreams in a Small Town" and "Fast Movin' Train." But crossover success proved to be elusive. Of the group's country Number Ones, only its 1986 single "I'll Still Be Loving You" hit the pop top 40.

As the 1990s began, problems surfaced within the group. Stewart departed in 1992 to pursue a solo career. In 1993, Innis did the same. Gregg, Dittrich, and Jennings hired two new musicians, and the group managed to roll on. Ironically, it was during this period that the group scored its first crossover hit, reaching both the country and pop top 20 with the single "When She Cries" in 1992.

With the exception of two other country hits in 1993, Restless Heart receded from the charts and the touring scene in the mid-1990s. The group was released from its record contract with RCA in 1994.

CHARLIE RICH

C alled the Silver Fox because of his snowy white hair, Charlie Rich sang a soulful brand of country tinged with blues and a touch of jazz. Originally signed by Sun Records' Sam Phillips as a session musician (and seen by Phillips as one of the few acts who might rival Elvis Presley), Rich managed to miss out on mass popularity for some 20 years from the time he began playing professionally.

TOP ALBUMS
....

BEHIND CLOSED DOORS (Epic, '73)
THERE WON'T BE ANYMORE (RCA, '74)
VERY SPECIAL LOVE SONGS (Epic, '74)

TOP SONGS
....

BEHIND CLOSED DOORS (Epic, '73, 1, 15 Pop)
THE MOST BEAUTIFUL GIRL (Epic, '73, 1, 1 Pop)
THERE WON'T BE ANYMORE (RCA, '73, 1, 18 Pop)
A VERY SPECIAL LOVE SONG (Epic, '73, 1, 11 Pop)
I DON'T SEE ME IN YOUR EYES ANYMORE (RCA, '74, 1)
I LOVE MY FRIEND (Epic, '74, 1, 24 Pop)
SHE CALLED ME BABY (RCA, '74, 1)

Additional Top 40 Country Songs: 24

When he finally did hit, it was with a mainstream "country-politan" sound that appealed to country fans while frequently crossing over to pop.

Rich (b. Dec. 14, 1932, Colt, Arkansas) grew up on his father's farm and as a youth gained exposure to the blues, gospel, and country music. He played jazz in a group called the Velvetones while serving in the Air Force. A later attempt at farming gave way to an overriding interest in a music career.

It was while playing at a Memphis club called the Sharecropper that that he was heard by Sun Records musician Bill Justis (sax player on the 1957 hit instrumental "Raunchy") and brought into the Sun fold. His activities at the label were many: singing behind Johnny Cash, pounding the piano behind Jerry Lee Lewis, recording some singles of his own. He had some success there as a songwriter, penning the pop single "Break-Up" for Lewis and "The Ways of a Woman in Love," a crossover hit for Cash at number two country and 24 pop. But nothing else clicked for him at Sun, with one exception: the single "Lonely Weekends," a number 22 chart entry.

He moved to RCA's Groove subsidiary, cutting tracks under the aegis of executive-guitarist-producer Chet Atkins, including an original called "There Won't Be Anymore." Still nothing clicked.

By 1965, Rich was at Smash, a spinoff of Mercury, where he charted pop with "Mohair Sam" then switched labels again, to Hi Records.

Rich's shift in fortunes occurred when he signed with Epic to work with producer Billy Sherrill, whom he'd met at Sun. Their first singles all hit mid-

Charlie Rich

dle ranks of the country chart until "I Take It On Home" made number six. Then in 1973 he broke through with "Behind Closed Doors," a Number One country, number 15 pop hit that finally brought Rich his hard-earned recognition, including three awards from the Country Music Association (Best Male Vocalist, Single of the Year, and Album of the Year—for *Behind Closed Doors*) and a Grammy Award for Best Male Vocalist. That paved the way for the most successful song of Rich's career, the crossover Number One "The Most Beautiful Girl."

The gates opened for a flood of Rich hits, starting with three consecutive chart-toppers in 1973. One of them was "There Won't Be Anymore," the song he'd recorded with Atkins at RCA. Once Rich hit, his former label cashed in by releasing many of the tracks from his RCA days. Another was "She Called Me Baby," which hit Number One in 1974, about 10 years after it was recorded.

Rich's Epic singles—all in the top 40—took him through the rest of the decade, during which he was voted CMA Entertainer of the Year in 1974 (and caused a stir at the next year's awards ceremony by setting fire to the certificate for the new Entertainer of the Year, John Denver). His final hit with that label was "On My Knees," a duet with Janie Fricke.

After releasing a few mildly successful singles on United Artists, Rich retreated from high-profile musical activity. In addition to a 1992 comeback album, *Pictures and Paintings,* he remains audible in early and later incarnations on a number of reissues and compilations.

Rich died on July 25, 1995, due to a blood clot in his lung.

MARTY ROBBINS

Marty Robbins symbolized the "western" in country western music, particularly in such signature hits as "El Paso." But over the course of his 30-year career, he was also a major rockabilly star and a romantic pop balladeer who reached audiences all over the world.

Robbins' background established the "western" end of his musical direction. Born on September 26, 1925, in Glendale, Arizona, he grew up in the desert. He was a big fan of Gene Autry, and he wanted, at one point, to become a singing cowboy. He was taught western lore by his grandfather, Texas Bob Heckle, a musician who had also been a traveling medicine man.

After a stint in the Navy, Robbins returned to Phoenix and began to pursue a musical career, per-

forming at local clubs and dances. From there he graduated to local radio and television programs, eventually securing a show of his own called "Western Caravan." In 1952, one of his guests on the show was Little Jimmy Dickens. Impressed by Robbins' vast repertoire of cowboy stories and songs, Dickens advised his record company, Columbia, to sign the young musician.

While Robbins' debut record, "Love Me or Leave Me Alone," was a modest success, his third effort, "I'll Go On Alone," hit the country top 10 in 1953, and he was on his way. That same year, he joined the Grand Ole Opry, where he would become a fixture for the next three decades.

But Robbins' career took a surprising turn in 1954 when he recorded his own version of Arthur Crudup's "That's All Right Mama" (the song that had also been recorded that year by fledgling rock star Elvis Presley). The Presley connection estab-

Marty Robbins

lished Robbins with the emerging rockabilly movement, with which he would remain associated for the remainder of the decade, charting repeatedly with such crossover hits as "Singing the Blues" and "White Sport Coat" and such romantic songs as "Teenage Dream."

He reestablished himself as a country and western star in 1959, when he dominated the charts with "El Paso," his signature hit and the first record by a country artist to win a Grammy Award. While succeeding in the pop arena in the 1960s with "Devil Woman," "Ruby Ann," and other singles, Robbins increasingly concentrated on country, topping the charts again and again with such records as "Begging to You," "I Walk Alone," and "My Woman, My Woman, My Wife." In 1976 he invoked the sound and style of the biggest hit of his career when he recorded "El Paso City."

In fact, one of Robbins' greatest attributes was his ability to be successful in various styles of music while retaining his western persona. From such rockabilly hits as "A White Sport Coat," to the cowboy songs, to such romantic ballads as "You Gave Me a Mountain," Robbins proved to be remarkably versatile and elastic in his musical sensibilities. His success in these disparate genres was also significant in that it drew new audiences to country music at a time when that music was still primarily confined to a relatively narrow fan base.

Along the way, he pursued an acting career, appearing in such films as *The Gun and the Gavel, Buffalo Gun,* and *The Badge of Marshall Brennan.* These films accentuated his public image as one of the kings of country and western music.

TOP SONGS

I'LL GO ON ALONE (Columbia, '52, 1)
SINGING THE BLUES (Columbia, '56, 1, 17 Pop)
A WHITE SPORT COAT (AND A PINK CARNATION) (Columbia, '57, 1, 2 Pop)
THE STORY OF MY LIFE (Columbia, '57, 1, 15 Pop)
JUST MARRIED (Columbia, '58, 1, 26 Pop)
EL PASO (Columbia, '59, 1 Pop)
DON'T WORRY (Columbia, '61, 1, 3 Pop)
DEVIL WOMAN (Columbia, '62, 1, 16 Pop)
RUBY ANN (Columbia, '62, 1, 18 Pop)
BEGGIN' TO YOU (Columbia, '63, 1)

Additional Top 40 Country Songs: 71

Robbins also flirted with a career as a racing car driver. On his 1961 album *Devil Woman,* Robbins shared the cover with a photo of a (devil) woman and his stock car.

Robbins was perhaps most visible over the years through his tenure at the Grand Ole Opry. For years, he closed the Opry shows with a performance that was liberally sprinkled with his stories, songs, and wry wit. Robbins was the last artist to perform at the Ryman Auditorium, the original home of the Opry, and the first to perform at its new stage at Opryland.

Robbins had a history of heart problems dating back to 1970, when he was forced to undergo surgery. He died of a heart attack on December 8, 1982. In 1983 he was inducted into the Country Music Hall of Fame.

JIMMIE RODGERS

To understand why Jimmie Rodgers came to be remembered as the Father of Country Music, consider this: before singer-songwriter-guitarist Rodgers arrived on the scene in 1927, country music consisted mainly of rural string bands—with names like the Skillet Lickers, the Hill Billies, the Possum Hunters, and the Clod Hoppers—whose show business impact was relatively minor. With Rodgers, in his heyday a phenomenally popular recording artist (self-promoted as the Singing Brakeman and America's Blue Yodeler), country music came to the fore as a major entertainment force, essentially remaining one from then on.

The sound and style of his output not only drew audiences but changed the substance of country music. His signature "blue yodel"—expressed in 13 "Blue Yodel" recordings—neatly brought together so-called hillbilly music and the blues, a fusion that would justify Rodgers' election to the Rock and Roll Hall of Fame 53 years after his death. Rodgers' recordings employed a variety of accompaniments, from Hawaiian guitar players to jazz bands (Louis Armstrong recorded with him on "Blue Yodel No. 9") to Mexican-American musicians, prefiguring the melting pot of musical styles that country would eventually become. Adding lyrics that ranged from sentimental to bawdy to intensely personal and that connected with the lives of a largely rural southern constituency, Rodgers forged an art of the culture hero that became the model for generations of musicians to come. Ernest Tubb, Gene Autry, Lefty Frizzell, Hank Snow, Bill Monroe, and Merle Haggard are but a few who built on the foundation that Rodgers laid down.

Born in Meridian, Mississippi, on September 8, 1897, James Charles Rodgers was raised by his railroad worker father. While similar employment was in his future, the young Rodgers began turning toward music, listening to the blues and gospel and folk songs, singing and picking up guitar and banjo, and winning a local talent contest at age 12. Three years later, already feeling the urge to move that would remain with him through life, he ran away from home and began a lengthy period of itinerancy, playing pickup gigs with traveling shows and wherever people would listen and doing railroad work to fill in the financial gaps.

In 1924 he learned that he'd contracted tuberculosis, a death sentence at the time, though years remained before it would become debilitating. That illness led Rodgers to curtail his physical labor and focus on music with greater determination.

In Asheville, North Carolina, in 1927 he hooked up with a band he called the Jimmie Rodgers Entertainers, working with them only a short time before learning that the Victor Talking Machine Company, represented by Ralph Peer, was about to record local talent in Bristol, Tennessee. Rodgers made his way there with the Entertainers in August. His group split from him in Bristol, but Rodgers managed to make his initial recordings there anyway (as did the Carter Family, making Victor's Bristol sessions key in the history of country music). The result was a hit: a song called "The Soldier's Sweetheart" reached number nine on the popularity chart of the day. An emboldened Rodgers was then invited to record again in November at Victor studios in New Jersey. Within four months the first of his "Blue Yodels," this one subtitled "T for Texas," was a massive seller and a national hit at number two on the chart—commercially, Rodgers' peak recorded moment.

One his way, but with not much time to live, Rodgers made the most of the next several years. He began promoting himself relentlessly, cultivating a public image as the Singing Brakeman and capturing the imagination of the Depression-ridden American public with songs that drew from his experience on the rails. He traveled and toured widely, performed in vaudeville and in tent shows, broadcast over radio (at one point, every week on WTFF out of Washington, D.C.), and made a short 1929 film called *The Singing Brakeman* in which he performed several songs.

From 1929 to 1933, Rodgers recorded 111 songs, standouts of which include "Muleskinner Blues" (covered in the late 1930s by Bill Monroe), "In the Jailhouse Now" (which Webb Pierce recorded in 1955 and again in 1982, scoring a Number One hit the first time), "Waiting for a Train" (a number 14 hit for Rodgers in 1929), and "T.B. Blues."

Rodgers gained wealth and enjoyed it fully while he could, building his "Blue Yodeler's Palace" home and purchasing expensive cars—a sharp contrast to the hand-to-mouth existence he had only recently left behind.

But the money ran out—as did his time. Rodgers' final days were spent in New York City recording new music even while weak from illness. On May 26, 1933, two days after completing the sessions, he died in New York's Taft Hotel.

Jimmie Rodgers was inducted into the Country Music Hall of Fame in 1961.

TOP ALBUMS

FIRST SESSIONS (Rounder, '91)
ON THE WAY UP (Rounder, '91)

TOP SONGS

THE SOLDIER'S SWEETHEART (Victor, '27)
BLUE YODEL (T FOR TEXAS) (Victor, '28)
THE BRAKEMAN'S BLUES (Victor, '28)
BLUE YODEL NO. 3 (Victor, '28)
WAITING FOR A TRAIN (Victor, '29)
ANNIVERSARY MODEL (BLUE YODEL NO. 7) (Victor, '30)
ROLL ALONG, KENTUCKY (Victor, '32)
IN THE JAILHOUSE NOW (RCA, '55, 7)

JOHNNY RODRIGUEZ

A long with his counterpart, Freddy Fender, Johnny Rodriguez is a Chicano performer who became a major star of country music. In fact, the background and lives of these musicians have much in common, while their music is different in personality and feel.

Like Fender, Rodriguez was born in a Texas border town, where he grew up listening to rock and roll. His Tex-Mex background, like that of Fender, would add a new range of musical flavors to country music and draw to it a new range of fans.

Rodriguez was born on December 10, 1952, in Sabinal, Texas, about 90 miles from the Mexican border. The second of nine children, he grew up surrounded by traditional Mexican music. He was given his first guitar by his brother Andres at age seven. In high school he formed his own rock band, which performed at various local clubs and dances.

Rodriguez's rise to musical success came by way of an odd route. In his teens, he was arrested for stealing and barbecuing a goat. While in jail, he sang songs and came to the attention of a police officer, who encouraged him to audition for Happy Shahan. Shahan owned Alamo Village, a local resort in Bracketville, Texas, and he hired Rodriguez as a stunt rider and singer. In 1971, Tom T. Hall and

Johnny Rodriguez

Bobby Bare heard Rodriguez and suggested that he come to Nashville to pursue a country music career.

Rodriguez heeded their advice and in 1971 moved to Nashville, where he joined Hall's band, the Storytellers. Hall, who was signed to Mercury Records, urged the label to sign his new protégé, which it did that same year.

Rodriguez's debut record, "Pass Me By," made the top 10 in 1972, hinting at the success that was to come. It came quickly—with his next record, in fact—when "You Always Come Back (To Hurting Me)" topped the charts in 1973.

Rodriguez moved to the front line of '70s country performers. He hit Number One regularly with such songs as "That's the Way Love Goes," "I Just Can't Get Her Out of My Mind," and "Just Get Up and Close the Door" and scored numerous other chart hits. His sleek, pop-inflected sound and image differed from that of the more traditional Fender, but both maintained an edge of rock and roll in their music. Much younger than Fender (who was born in 1937), Rodriguez also attracted a teen fan base, becoming something of a sex symbol in the process.

But there were problems on the horizon. Starting in the 1980s, his records began to languish on the charts, and his career declined. But in 1983, Rodriguez invited producer Richie Albright to work with him, and a new series of records, including such songs as "Foolin'," hit the top 10. After that comeback, however, Rodriguez was unable to match the success of his '70s heyday.

TOP SONGS

You Always Come Back (To Hurting Me)
   (Mercury, '73, *1*)
Ridin' My Thumb to Mexico (Mercury, '73, *1*)
That's the Way Love Goes (Mercury, '73, *1*)
Dance with Me (Just One More Time)
   (Mercury, '74, *2*)
We're Over (Mercury, '74, *3*)
I Just Can't Get Her Out of My Mind
   (Mercury, '75, *1*)
Just Get Up and Close the Door (Mercury, '75, *1*)
Love Put a Song in My Heart (Mercury, '75, *1*)
I Couldn't Be Me Without You (Mercury, '76, *3*)
I Wonder If I Ever Said Goodbye (Mercury, '76, *2*)

Additional Top 40 Country Songs: 24

Kenny Rogers

KENNY ROGERS
•••••••••••••••••••••••

As successful as Kenny Rogers was in the country field in the late 1970s and 1980s—to the tune of 20 Number One hits—he was also an immensely popular crossover artist, responsible for such high-ranking singles as 1980's "Lady" and 1983's "We've Got Tonight" and "Islands in the Stream." What held country listeners' attention during his pop-oriented outings was his voice: rich, husky, rough-edged yet warm-sounding, and instantly recognizable in any sonic environment.

Considering his early years, it's not surprising that Rogers (b. Kenneth Donald Rogers, Aug. 21, 1938) crossed musical boundaries. He has claimed that when growing up in Houston, Texas, his favorite performers were Ray Charles, Sam Cooke, and other R&B artists. After scoring a regional hit called "Crazy Feeling" with his high school band the Scholars and then enrolling in the University of

Houston, he played bass in a jazz group, the Bobby Doyle Trio, and sang harmony in a vocal quartet called the Lively Ones.

Adding folk music to the mix, he sang with the New Christy Minstrels for a time in the mid-'60s. With several of the group's members he broke off in 1967 to form the First Edition, a pop outfit and Rogers' first major stab at making it in the recording industry. Reprise Records signed them.

Not quite bubblegum but certainly geared for ear-catchiness, the Edition's first chart single was 1968's number five pop "Just Dropped In (To See What Condition My Condition Was In)." The group stayed in, posting another top 40 entry with its follow-up, "But You Know I Love You." Rogers, getting much of the attention, then became the nominal (and actual) front man for a run of nine charting singles, three of which put him on the country chart for the first time (one, "Ruby, Don't Take Your Love to Town," a Mel Tillis composition).

Rogers made the leap to solo status in 1975,

keeping his Edition manager, Ken Kragen, but moving to a new label, United Artists, and beginning what would be a fruitful five-year alliance with producer Larry Butler. First out was the country top 20 "Love Lifted Me" (also 97 pop), followed by two respectably successful singles. Then, starting with the crossover tune "Lucille"—Number One country, number five pop—Rogers scored a string of seven chart-topping songs and launched what would be a nonstop, lengthy run of hits, most in the top 10.

"Lucille" also brought him the first of many industry awards, in this case a Grammy and several from the Country Music Association. His fourth Number One, 1978's "The Gambler," led to two Grammies, three CMA awards, and two from the Academy of Country Music and spawned a series of "Gambler" made-for-TV movies in which Rogers appeared. The parent album, *The Gambler,* went platinum.

Rogers, interested in varying the settings for his voice, found great success over the years in a number of different vocal and production collaborations. With Kim Carnes (also a onetime Christy Minstrel) he cut "Don't Fall in Love with a Dreamer" (three country, four pop, 1980). Pairing with Dottie West he scored three Number Ones between 1978 and 1981. Rogers switched to Liberty Records in 1980 and worked with producer-writer (and, at the time, Commodores member) Lionel Richie on "Lady," a monster crossover hit in 1980. With pop hitmaker Sheena Easton he duetted on the Bob Seger composition "We've Got Tonight." And following a lucrative move to RCA, Rogers scored his second crossover Number One singing with Dolly Parton on "Islands in the Stream" from the album *Eyes That*

See in the Dark, a collection of songs written for Rogers by the Bee Gees. Rogers' ultimate collaboration may have been his 1985 participation in the U.S.A. for Africa benefit recording of "We Are the World" alongside Michael Jackson, Richie, Bruce Springsteen, and 41 other leading pop stars.

By 1985 Rogers was fading from the pop chart but still going strong in country, hitting the top with Ronnie Milsap in 1987 on "Make No Mistake, She's Mine" and pairing with Anne Murray, Holly Dunn, and Dolly Parton in later efforts.

LINDA RONSTADT

As much a rock star as a country singer, Linda Ronstadt was a major artist, in the 1970s, in both genres. The Queen of Country Rock, she had hits on the pop and country charts and played a pivotal role in forging a sound that drew on the best of both musical worlds.

Ronstadt was born on July 15, 1946, in Tucson, Arizona, where she grew up listening to Mexican and country music. At one point, in high school, she flirted with the idea of pursuing a musical career when she formed a group, the Three Ronstadts, with her sister and brother. But as she said later, "It [Tucson] was so boring. All there was were cows and cactus." So in 1964 she moved to Los Angeles.

The next year, Ronstadt again tried her hand at music when she formed the folk-rock group the Stone Poneys. This time her efforts paid off, with the group eventually scoring a rock hit in 1967 with its version of Michael Nesmith's "Different Drum."

Ronstadt disbanded the group in 1969 to pursue a solo career that drew from more country-inflected sources. The 1969 album *Hand Sown, Home Grown* and 1970's *Silk Purse* came with the instrumental work of some of the finest musicians in Los Angeles and Nashville. But it was the group that Ronstadt formed in 1971—with future Eagles Glenn Frey, Don Henley, Randy Meisner, and Bernie Leadon—that put her and her new sound on the musical map.

That sound emerged on the 1971 album *Linda Ronstadt,* which included a rendition of the classic "I Fall to Pieces" and the contributions of such country-rock pioneers as fiddler Gib Guilbeau and pedal-steel guitarist Sneaky Pete Kleinow. As the '70s progressed, the sound evolved into an exciting composite of styles.

TOP SONGS

LUCILLE (United Artists, '77, *1, 5 Pop*)

DAYTIME FRIENDS (United Artists, '77, *1, 28 Pop*)

LOVE OR SOMETHING LIKE IT (United Artists, '78, *1, 32 Pop*)

THE GAMBLER (United Artists, '78, *1, 16 Pop*)

SHE BELIEVES IN ME (United Artists, '79, *1, 5 Pop*)

YOU DECORATED MY LIFE (United Artists, '79, *1, 7 Pop*)

COWARD OF THE COUNTY (United Artists, '79, *1, 3 Pop*)

LADY (Liberty, '80, *1, 1 Pop*)

WE'VE GOT TONIGHT (Liberty, '83, *1, 6 Pop*)

ISLANDS IN THE STREAM (Liberty, '83, *1, 1 Pop*)

Additional Top 40 Country Songs: 40

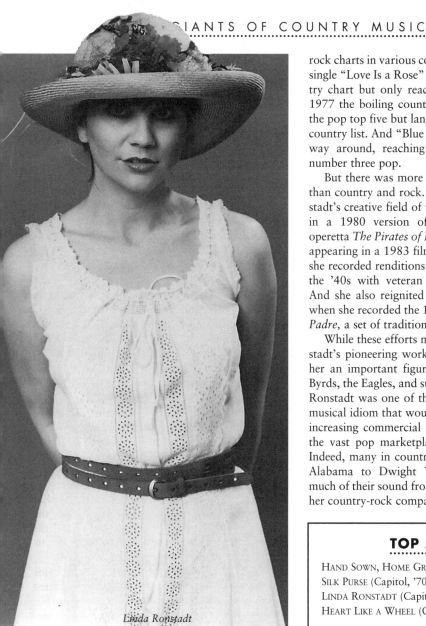

Linda Ronstadt

rock charts in various configurations. Thus her 1975 single "Love Is a Rose" hit number five on the country chart but only reached number 63 in rock. In 1977 the boiling country rocker "It's So Easy" hit the pop top five but languished at number 81 on the country list. And "Blue Bayou" was a success all the way around, reaching number two country and number three pop.

But there was more on Ronstadt's musical mind than country and rock. As her career evolved, Ronstadt's creative field of vision expanded. She starred in a 1980 version of the Gilbert and Sullivan operetta *The Pirates of Penzance* on Broadway (later appearing in a 1983 film version). In the mid-1980s she recorded renditions of various torch songs from the '40s with veteran bandleader Nelson Riddle. And she also reignited her love of Mexican music when she recorded the 1987 album *Canciones de Mi Padre,* a set of traditional Mexican songs.

While these efforts met with success, it was Ronstadt's pioneering work in country rock that made her an important figure in music. Along with the Byrds, the Eagles, and such figures as Gram Parsons, Ronstadt was one of the major architects of a new musical idiom that would contribute, in turn, to the increasing commercial success of country music in the vast pop marketplace of the 1980s and '90s. Indeed, many in country's newer generation—from Alabama to Dwight Yoakam and others—drew much of their sound from the music of Ronstadt and her country-rock compatriots.

TOP ALBUMS

Hand Sown, Home Grown (Capitol, '69)
Silk Purse (Capitol, '70)
Linda Ronstadt (Capitol, '71)
Heart Like a Wheel (Capitol, '74)

TOP SONGS

I Can't Help It (If I'm Still in Love with You) (Capitol, '74, *2*)
When Will I Be Loved (Capitol, '75, *1, 2 Pop*)
Love Is a Rose (Asylum, '74, *5*)
Blue Bayou (Asylum, '77, *2, 3 Pop*)
To Know Him Is to Love Him (Warner, '87, *1*)
Telling Me Lies (Warner, '87, *3*)

Additional Top 40 Country Songs: 9

Singles like 1975's "When Will I Be Loved" and 1976's "That'll Be the Day" came with the melodic and vocal inflections of country music but also with the energy and expressive ebullience of rock.

Along the way, Ronstadt collaborated with country artists. In 1976 she recorded "The Sweetest Gift," a duet with Emmylou Harris. In 1986 she and Harris teamed with Dolly Parton to record an album, *Trio,* that yielded the Number One hit "To Know Him Is to Love Him."

Meanwhile, her solo records hit the country and

SAWYER BROWN

Sawyer Brown still ranks as one of the biggest acts to launch a career as winners of the television talent show "Star Search." From that win in 1984, they landed a Nashville recording contract, and a year later they scored a Number One hit with "Step That Step." Over the next decade they sometimes struggled to become consistent chart hitters while evolving into one of the most exciting and sought-after touring acts in country music.

The band came together in 1981 when Mark Miller (lead singer, b. Oct. 25, 1958, Dayton, Ohio) and Gregg Hubbard (keyboards, b. Oct. 2, 1960, Apopka, Florida) arrived in Nashville after attending college together in Central Florida. They hooked up with Bobby Randall (lead guitar, b. Midland, Michigan) and Jim Scholten (bass, b. Apr. 18, 1952, Bay City, Michigan), who had recently arrived from Michigan. They met Joe Smyth (drums, b. Sept. 6, 1957, Portland, Maine) when all but Miller became the backup band for singer Don King. "I was writing for Don's publishing company and just traveled with the band as guitar tuner and road crew," Miller explains.

During the tour with King the group became friends, and they decided to stay together after King quit actively pursuing his recording career. "We didn't know anybody else in town," says Miller. "Bobby and I had talked about forming our own bands, so we just kept what we had together, and I joined in as lead singer." They called themselves Savannah and began touring the southern regional club circuit performing as many as 300 dates in one year. Along the way they ran into so many other bands named Savannah that they renamed themselves after Sawyer Brown Road, a street in the Bellvue area of Nashville.

In late 1983 they auditioned for "Star Search" and after several weeks of performances won a first prize of $100,000 in early '84. That brought them to the attention of Curb Records, who signed them to a contract. Curb became a silent partner when the group signed on with Capitol Records and hit number 16 with their first release, "Leona," later that year. The band then scored three top 10s in 1985, including their self-penned first Number One, "Step That Step." After that, their chart success became more sporadic. Most of their records landed somewhere in the middle of the top 40, but once every couple of years they would hit the top 10, notably with the songs "This Missin' You Heart of Mine" and "The Race Is On."

What never wavered was Sawyer Brown's success performing live. With a high-energy, youth-oriented show sparked by Mark Miller's lead vocals and athletic jumps and dances on stage, they continually ranked high on the list of top concert draws. That helped keep their album sales up and kept their record label patient about their moderate success on the charts.

In 1991, as they matured as writers and performers, their songs seemed to finally sync up with country radio. Beginning with "The Walk" (number two, 1991) they enjoyed a succession of top 10 hits stretching into 1995. "I was 23 years old when I wrote 'Step That Step,'" explains Miller, "and it sounds like a kid would've thought of that, and I was a kid. Ten years later your focus changes, your life and view of life changes. Our music changed with us and our audience."

In 1992, guitarist Randall left the group to host a cable TV talent show called "Be a Star." He was replaced by guitarist Duncan Cameron (b. July 27, 1956, Utica, New York).

Sawyer Brown remained successful at the box office, expanding their onstage dynamics with the inclusion of such low-key later hits as "The Dirt Road" and "Thank God for You." From the mid-1980s into the '90s Sawyer Brown symbolized the youth movement in country music, proving that younger country fans would support an alternative to the neotraditionalist performers proliferating at the time.

TOP ALBUMS

THE BOYS ARE BACK (Capitol, '89)
THE DIRT ROAD (Curb/Capitol, '91)
CAFE ON THE CORNER (Curb, '92)
OUTSKIRTS OF TOWN (Curb, '93)

TOP SONGS

STEP THAT STEP (Capitol, '85, 1)
BETTY'S BEIN' BAD (Capitol, '85, 5)
THE WALK (Curb/Capitol, '91, 2)
THE DIRT ROAD (Curb/Capitol, '91, 3)
SOME GIRLS DO (Curb/Capitol, '92, 1)
THANK GOD FOR YOU (Curb, '93, 1)

Additional Top 40 Country Songs: 21

Sawyer Brown

EARL SCRUGGS

He's the Paganini of bluegrass banjo—one of country music's top virtuosos. As a member of Bill Monroe's Blue Grass Boys in the late 1940s, Earl Scruggs helped define the bluegrass style and established the banjo as one of its lead instruments. As half of the acclaimed duo Flatt and Scruggs for two decades, he brought the intricate, energy-infused bluegrass sound to the attention of mass audiences.

Earl Eugene Scruggs was born on January 6, 1924, in Flintville, North Carolina. "I just grew up around banjo," he claimed. Scruggs picked up the region's standard banjo styles and at the age of 12 began experimenting with the more complex three-finger picking approach that would become his signature. "I was just sitting around," he said, "not especially conscious of what I was doing, when all of a sudden I noticed I was picking with three fingers. My mother encouraged me to go beyond the usual two-finger style."

After graduating from high school and working for a spell in a factory making parachutes (during World War II), Scruggs landed a gig playing in Knoxville with John Miller and his Allied Kentuckians.

In the mid-1940s he auditioned for, and was hired by, singer-mandolinist Bill Monroe and his Blue Grass Boys, an act whose modernized string-band music had been attracting attention on the Grand Ole Opry. Scruggs' banjo brought a new texture to Monroe's bluegrass—"almost as much a part of making the band sound different as putting an electric instrument into the band," Scruggs told Jim Hatlo in *Country Musicians*. It raised the music's excitement level, and with the guitar and voice of Lester Flatt, the bass of Howard Watts (a.k.a. Cedric Rainwater), and the fiddle playing of Chubby Wise—the "classic" Blue Grass Boys lineup—it helped shape the hard-driving, "high, lonesome" sound that Monroe had in mind.

Scruggs left Monroe in 1948 and joined Flatt in putting together the Foggy Mountain Boys, a state-of-the-art bluegrass band whose membership over time would include Rainwater, guitarist-vocalist Mac Wiseman, fiddler Jim Shumate, and dobro player Josh Graves.

Starting out on Mercury Records, Flatt and Scruggs and the Foggy Mountain Boys issued initial singles like "Foggy Mountain Breakdown" and "Pike Mountain Breakdown." They later moved to Columbia Records, starred in their own radio show (sponsored by the Martha White Flour company), and joined the Grand Ole Opry. Their first record on the *Billboard* country chart was the top 10 " 'Tis Sweet to Be Remembered" in 1952, which they followed with 19 other hits through 1968.

In the late 1950s and early '60s, Flatt and Scruggs attracted the attention of young, northern, folk-oriented audiences and drew raves from the national media. The *Saturday Review* described their show as "one of the most exciting and fascinating experiences in all of American folk music." Scruggs, in particular, earned high marks from the not-traditionally-country crowd. The *New York Times* noted his "heavily syncopated style that sharply accents the melodic line to make it stand out in a shower of notes. Moving at gasping tempos, it is dominated by a brilliant technical shine." Critic Pete Welding placed Scruggs' playing "at the very core of the bluegrass approach."

The act went on to crack the national mass market with its 1962 Number One hit performance of "The Ballad of Jed Clampett" (from the television series "The Beverly Hillbillies") and the inclusion of

---

TOP ALBUMS

Bill Monroe:
THE ESSENTIAL BILL MONROE (1945–1949) (Sony, '91)

Flatt and Scruggs:
AT CARNEGIE HALL (Columbia, '62)

Earl Scruggs Revue:
EARL SCRUGGS REVUE (Columbia, '72)

TOP SONGS

Flatt and Scruggs:
'TIS SWEET TO BE REMEMBERED (Columbia, '52, 9)
CABIN ON THE HILL (Columbia, '59, 9)
GO HOME (Columbia, '61, 10)
THE BALLAD OF JED CLAMPETT (Columbia, '62, 1)
PEARL, PEARL, PEARL (Columbia, '63, 8)
PETTICOAT JUNCTION (Columbia, '64, 4)

Earl Scruggs Revue:
I COULD SURE USE THE FEELING (Columbia, '79, 30)

Additional Top 40 Country Songs: 9

"Foggy Mountain Breakdown" in the 1968 film *Bonnie and Clyde*.

As the popularity of rock music increased in the 1960s, Flatt and Scruggs moved apart. Scruggs was more inclined than Flatt to try different music and change with the times, resulting in the act's top 20 hit "California Up Tight Band" in 1967 and a cover of Bob Dylan's "Like a Rolling Stone" in 1968. But the duo finally split in 1969.

Scruggs organized the electrified Earl Scruggs Revue in the 1970s, bringing together his sons Gary (bass) and Randy (guitar), fiddler Vassar Clements, dobroist Josh Graves, and drummer Jody Maphis (replaced by Steve Scruggs). They issued several Columbia albums and placed three songs on the country chart, including the top 30 "I Could Sure Use the Feeling," before Scruggs pulled back from active duty.

In 1985, the Flatt and Scruggs act was inducted into the Country Music Hall of Fame.

DAN SEALS

Dan Seals was a moderately successful rock and roller for 15 years before he recognized his true musical calling. When he finally returned to his country roots in the 1980s, he became one of the most popular stars of the day, scoring 11 Number One hits in the later half of the decade.

Seals (b. Feb. 8, 1948, McCamey, Texas) literally grew up with country music. His family, which hailed from Tennessee, had a strong musical background, and his father was a guitarist who performed with the various country stars who toured western Texas. At the early age of four, Dan began performing in the family band along with brother Jim (who would later enjoy success with the rock duo Seals and Crofts).

While in high school, Dan turned to rock and roll, forming the band Southwest F.O.B. (Freight on Board) in 1967 with his friends John Ford Coley and Shane Keister. Recording on the GPC label, they had a modest chart hit the following year with "Smell of Incense."

Disbanding Southwest F.O.B., Seals and Coley moved to Los Angeles, eventually securing a contract with Atlantic Records as the duo England Dan and John Ford Coley. During the 1970s they were stars of a sort, scoring the number two pop hit "I'd Really Love to See You Tonight" and such lower-charting ones as "Nights Are Forever Without You" and "We'll Never Have to Say Goodbye Again."

But Seals eventually became dissatisfied with rock, and in 1982 he relocated from Los Angeles to Nashville, where he began to pursue a career as a country artist. The move proved to be inspired. From the start, Seals was a success, reaching the top 20 on the country charts with the single "Everybody's Dream Girl" in 1983. Over the succeeding two years, Seals consolidated his name and rock-inflected sound on records like "After You" and "You Really Go for the Heart."

But it was in 1985 that his country career began to soar. The single "Meet Me in Montana," a duet with Marie Osmond, topped the chart in July (Seals and Osmond were subsequently honored as the Vocal Duo of the Year by the Country Music Association). In October, on his own, Seals hit Number One again with "Bop," which was later named Single of the Year by the CMA.

From that point on, Seals was unstoppable. From 1985 to 1990, he scored an impressive total of 11 Number One country hits—almost all of them consecutive—with such songs as "Everything That Glitters (Is Not Gold)," "I Will Be There," "One Friend," and "Love on Arrival."

But just as quickly as success had come, it began to fade. New songs like "Bordertown" and "Mason Dixon Line"—though similar to Seals' hits of the '80s—languished on the charts, apparent victims of changing times and changing tastes.

TOP SONGS

MEET ME IN MONTANA (Capitol, '85, *1*)

BOP (EMI America, '85, *1*)

EVERYTHING THAT GLITTERS (IS NOT GOLD) (EMI America, '86, *1*)

YOU STILL MOVE ME (EMI America, '86, *1*)

I WILL BE THERE (EMI America, '87, *1*)

THREE TIME LOSER (EMI America, '87, *1*)

ONE FRIEND (Capitol, '87, *1*)

ADDICTED (Capitol, '88, *1*)

BIG WHEELS IN THE MOONLIGHT (Capitol, '88, *1*)

LOVE ON ARRIVAL (Capitol, '90, *1*)

Additional Top 40 Country Songs: 9

RICKY VAN SHELTON

H e came in on the second mid-'80s wave of country traditionalists, right after the one that had delivered Randy Travis and Dwight Yoakam. Ricky Van Shelton possessed a clear, compelling voice that propelled him into the foreground in 1987, bolstered by 15 consecutive top 10 hits, of which 10 went all the way to Number One.

Shelton (b. Jan. 12, 1952, Danville, Virginia) was raised in what he describes as a wide spot in the road called Gritt, Virginia. Both his parents worked in cloth mills and attended the Pentecostal Holiness Church. "My daddy played guitar and could sing real good and always sang in church," Shelton says. "In that church they made more music than preaching. I was in that church a lot and sang there at a very early age—three or four years old. They used to set me up on the altar and I would sing. I just thought that was what little kids did." Shelton was just a little bit older when he made his first money as a singer. He would wait until the postman arrived at the local store, then run up to him and sing him a song, and the man would reward Shelton with a quarter every time.

By the time he entered his teens he'd begun strumming his first guitar, but the music he liked was being made by the Beatles and Rolling Stones, not Haggard and Jones. It was an older brother that turned him on to country music. Shelton was 15

Ricky Van Shelton

when his brother bribed him to join his country band by letting Shelton drive his new Ford. After accompanying his brother to play at dozens of fish fries, small clubs, and backwoods jam sessions, Shelton grew to love country and bluegrass music. "One night we stopped by this old mountain store," he recalls. "In the back room there were three or four old guys playing fiddles. They were just having a great time playing 'Turkey in the Straw.' They were doing it for the sheer love of making that music, and I was soon having a great time right along with them."

From 1975 to 1978, Shelton made exploratory trips to Nashville but was unable to make any solid connections. He didn't return until 1985, when his

---

TOP ALBUMS

WILD-EYED DREAM (Columbia, '87)
LOVING PROOF (Columbia, '89)
RVS III (Columbia, '90)

TOP SONGS

I'LL LEAVE THIS WORLD LOVING YOU
    (Columbia, '88, *1*)
FROM A JACK TO A KING (Columbia, '89, *1*)
LIVING PROOF (Columbia, '89, *1*)
I'VE CRIED MY LAST TEAR FOR YOU (Columbia, '90, *1*)
ROCKIN' YEARS (with Dolly Parton, Columbia, '91, *1*)
I AM A SIMPLE MAN (Columbia, '91, *1*)
KEEP IT BETWEEN THE LINES (Columbia, '91, *1*)

Additional Top 40 Country Songs: 14

wife Bettye provided him an opportunity to go to Music City to stay. Bettye got a job as the personnel manager at a Nashville company, earning enough of a salary to support them both and allow Shelton to concentrate on his career.

In Nashville, the Sheltons befriended a local newspaper reporter who had contacts at Columbia Records. He helped Shelton set up a showcase performance for the label, and Columbia signed him up. Within two weeks they had him in the studio, where Shelton, who had never recorded before, impressed his record producer and the session pickers by nailing each song on the first or second take.

He reached number 27 in early 1987 with his first single, "Wild-Eyed Dream." He followed up with a number seven, "Crime of Passion," and scored his first Number One the next time out with "Somebody Lied." Everything he released from 1987 to early '92 hit the top 10, and he became a platinum-selling album artist.

In addition to the original material he interpreted so well, Shelton put his own stamp on some memorable remakes of such songs as "Life Turned Her That Way" (number 11 for Mel Tillis in 1967), "From a Jack to a King" (number two for Ned Miller in 1963), and "Statue of a Fool" (Number One for Jack Greene in 1969).

Shelton has also written a series of books for children called *Tales from a Duck Named Quacker,* released the 1992 gospel album *Don't Overlook Salvation,* and earned recognition as the Country Music Association's Male Vocalist of the Year in 1989.

SHENANDOAH

Discovered playing in a club in Muscle Shoals, Alabama, in 1986, the five-man band Shenandoah launched their recording career when they signed with Columbia Records. They struggled at first but struck a chord with songs like "Mama Knows," "The Church on Cumberland Road," and "Sunday in the South" and lead singer Marty Raybon's convincing delivery, finally establishing themselves as one of the top country acts to emerge in the late 1980s.

Columbia Records first came across the band in 1985, when producer Rick Hall was given seed money to record acts with potential in the Muscle Shoals area. One of Hall's cohorts, Robert Byrne,

---

TOP ALBUMS

THE ROAD NOT TAKEN (Columbia, '89)
EXTRA MILE (Columbia, '90)

TOP SONGS

MAMA KNOWS (Columbia, '88, 5)
THE CHURCH ON CUMBERLAND ROAD
    (Columbia, '89, 1)
SUNDAY IN THE SOUTH (Columbia, '89, 1)
TWO DOZEN ROSES (Columbia, '89, 1)
NEXT TO YOU NEXT TO ME (Columbia, '90, 1)
ROCK MY BABY (RCA, '92, 2)
IF BUBBA CAN DANCE (I CAN TOO) (RCA, '94, 1)
SOMEWHERE IN THE VICINITY OF THE HEART (with
    Alison Krauss, Liberty, '95, 7)

Additional Top 40 Country Songs: 11

---

had been watching the progress of the house band at a local club called MGM. They recorded seven sides on the group and sent the tape to Nashville, and Columbia soon signed the band to a contract. They had no name at the time, and when the label suggested Shenandoah, they took it.

The original members of the MGM house band were drummer Mike McGuire (b. Dec. 28, 1958, Hamilton, Alabama), keyboardist Stan Thorn (b. Mar. 3, 1959, Kenosha, Wisconsin), and guitarist Jim Seales (b. Mar. 20, 1954, Hamilton, Alabama). Ralph Ezell (b. June 26, 1953, Union, Mississippi) replaced the original bass player, and Marty Raybon (b. June 26, 1953, Sanford, Florida) replaced the original lead vocalist. The key to the band's sound was Raybon, who had been lured away from his efforts to start a solo career in Nashville by the promise of steady work. "I had gotten down to eating nothing but potatoes," he says, "so I thought maybe it was time to try something else." Starting out as a loose-knit group primarily interested in furthering each other's individual careers, especially Raybon's ambition to become a solo artist, they had become a unit after a year and a half together and developed a band personality. It made sense to stay together when the offer came from Columbia.

Their first single failed to reach the top 40. The second, "Stop the Rain," made it to number 28. The third, "She Doesn't Cry Anymore," hit the top 10. From that point on, the band scored one hit after

another—10 consecutive top 10 hits between 1989 and '91, including the chart-topping songs "Two Dozen Roses" and "Next to You Next to Me." Shenandoah was on such a roll, it appeared that nothing could stop them. But something nearly did.

Their career ran into a roadblock in late 1990 when they were hit with multiple copyright infringement suits over the name Shenandoah. They ended up acquiring the right to the name, but not before they were forced into bankruptcy and had to sue their record label.

By 1992, they had moved over to RCA Records. A number two hit, "Rock My Baby," helped them regain momentum.

In 1994, Shenandoah switched to the Liberty label and continued to hit the top 10. Early the following year, Stan Thorn left the group to explore jazz music. While surprised, the band made no immediate move to replace Thorn with a new, full member.

Shenandoah credits their success to filling a small void in country music. They were a progressive country band in their harmonies and instrumentation, but their material was characterized by heart-

felt, positive messages. "Our stuff is wholesome," says Raybon. "Family values were a dominant part of what we stand for. We never wanted to go back and listen to our material and feel ashamed of what we recorded."

T.G. SHEPPARD

He was born William Neal Browder, later made a record as Brian Stacy, and finally settled on the pseudonym T.G. Sheppard in time to see it printed on the labels of 14 Number One middle-of-the-road country hits from 1974 to 1986.

Sheppard (b. July 20, 1944, Humboldt, Tennessee), whose mother was a piano teacher, picked up piano and guitar during childhood. At 16 he moved to Memphis, performed with a band led by guitarist Travis Wammack, and recorded for Sonic Records with a group called the Embers. In the early 1960s he used the Stacy pseudonym on the nationally ignored Atlantic Records single "High School Days."

Deterred, he gave up performing and wound up working as a promotion man in Memphis for RCA and then for his own company, Umbrella Productions.

He had been at it for a while when a song called "Devil in the Bottle," written by Bobby David, came to his attention after having been rejected by a number of music executives. He recorded a demo of "Devil," sold Motown's Melodyland subsidiary on the tune, and released it—featuring himself as the singer under the name T.G. Sheppard—in 1974. Early in '75 it became a Number One country hit. He quickly followed it with "Tryin' to Beat the Morning Home," which he co-wrote. When it, too, climbed to the top, the foundation was set for Sheppard's future as one of the 1980s' leading purveyors—alongside Kenny Rogers, Eddie Rabbitt, and others—of mainstream country pop.

Sheppard consolidated his success when he moved to Warner Brothers Records in 1977 and began working with producer and Tree Publishing executive Buddy Killen. Following two top 20 and four top 10 singles, Sheppard began an impressive run of 11 Number One hits, interrupted only by the number six "Smooth Sailin'" in 1980 and the number 12 "Without You," a remake of Nilsson's 1972 Number One pop hit. Sheppard's most successful song was 1981's "I Loved 'Em Every One," which did well on both the country and pop charts.

The run was broken in 1984 by the number 12 "Make My Day," a duet with actor Clint Eastwood from his film *Sudden Impact*.

Sheppard cut a mildly successful duet, "Home Again," with Judy Collins in 1984. Soon after, he switched to Columbia, where seven top 10 hits and a smattering of others took him comfortably into the 1990s.

RICKY SKAGGS

One of two artists (George Strait the other) credited with sparking the neotraditionalist movement that dominated country music in the middle to late 1980s and early '90s, Ricky Skaggs (b. July 18, 1954, Cordell, Kentucky) began hitting big in 1981 with bluegrass-spiced, traditional country songs like "You May See Me Walkin'" and "I Don't Care." It was a remarkable achievement in a more pop-oriented era, and he followed it by becoming one of the dominant forces in country music into the 1990s.

A child prodigy, Skaggs demonstrated an ability to pick out recognizable tunes on a mandolin when he was just three, and he had conquered the instrument by age five. He was that age in 1959 when a crowd in Martha, Kentucky, asked him to get up at a Bill Monroe concert and he obliged, playing a song called "Ruby" on Monroe's mandolin. By the time he was 10 he could play any country instrument with strings on it. He became a local sensation, playing at the town band shell and in various bluegrass festivals and eventually gaining enough recognition to get booked on the Flatt and Scruggs television show. "That was my first paid music job," Skaggs recalls. "I got $52.50 for that TV performance."

His father recognized the value of his son's talent by promoting and protecting it. "I never got to play any sports like football or baseball," says Skaggs. "My father was afraid something bad would happen to my hands."

Skaggs was greatly influenced by the Stanley Brothers, as was his close friend Keith Whitley. They had been playing some together and knew all of the Stanley Brothers material, a fact that inspired Ralph Stanley to hire them both for his Clinch Mountain Boys band after his brother Carter died. Skaggs was just 15 at the time, and he credits his years with Ralph Stanley with teaching him how to be a professional musician.

From there, Skaggs joined a Washington, D.C., act called the Country Gentlemen, a progressive group credited with creating the "newgrass" movement by pushing the boundaries of bluegrass. Next

---

TOP SONGS

DEVIL IN THE BOTTLE (Melodyland, '74, *1*)

TRYIN' TO BEAT THE MORNING HOME
    (Melodyland, '75, *1*)

LAST CHEATER'S WALTZ (Warner, '79, *1*)

I'LL BE COMING BACK FOR MORE (Warner, '79, *1*)

DO YOU WANNA GO TO HEAVEN (Warner, '80, *1*)

I FEEL LIKE LOVING YOU AGAIN (Warner, '80, *1*)

I LOVED 'EM EVERY ONE (Warner, '81, *1, 37 Pop*)

PARTY TIME (Warner, '81, *1*)

ONLY ONE YOU (Warner, '81, *1*)

FINALLY (Warner, '82, *1*)

Additional Top 40 Country Songs: 29

CAL SMITH

Largely unsung, but more than able to sing, Cal Smith (b. Calvin Grant Shofner, Apr. 7, 1932, Gans, Oklahoma) proved it on the 1974 single "Country Bumpkin," a Number One hit and the Country Music Association's Song of the Year. He kept at it until he'd amassed 36 songs on the country chart over a period between 1967 to 1986, an impressive record that never quite kept him in the uppermost ranks of country recording artists, commercially. Vocally, he's been ranked with the best.

Smith spent his early youth in Oklahoma and after age 11 lived in Oakland, California. In the beginning stage of his career he worked as a deejay at KEEN radio in San Jose, performed on the "California Hayride" television program, and played in clubs.

A turning point came in 1962 when he was asked to join Ernest Tubb's Texas Troubadours, a job that put him in the role of singer and rhythm guitarist. He stayed with Tubb into 1968, all the while acquiring vocal expertise and knowledge of the musical ropes.

Smith signed with Kapp Records in the mid-'60s and began issuing solo singles. Nine of them charted between 1967 and 1970, but only one, "Drinking Champagne," made it to the country top 40.

Switching to Decca, Smith scored his first major hit—at number four—with "I've Found Someone of My Own." Two singles later, his interpretation of "The Lord Knows I'm Drinking," penned by hit-making artist Bill Anderson, topped the chart.

It was while recording an album for MCA that

he joined another progressive bluegrass outfit, J. D. Crowe and the New South, and later put together his own band, Boone Creek. But it took him until 1977, the year he joined Emmylou Harris' Hot Band, to get into mainstream country music.

Over the years, Skaggs had appeared on several albums, from Stanley Brothers and Emmylou Harris records to his own disc on the Sugar Hill label. He was ready for the big time when he moved his Sugar Hill contract over to Epic Records in 1981. His first single for Epic, "Don't Get Above Your Raising," hit number 16. He reached the top 10 with his next release, "You May See Me Walkin'." Then, beginning with his first top song, "Crying My Heart Over You," Skaggs scored 10 Number One hits between 1982 and '86, including "Heartbroke," "Honey (Open That Door)," and "Uncle Pen" (a song written and first recorded by Bill Monroe).

During the 1980s, Skaggs often toured with a briefly successful family recording act called the Whites that included his wife, Sharon White.

Skaggs was best appreciated live. He always surrounded himself with superb musicians, but he'd steal the show during extended instrumental breaks, displaying his prowess on the guitar, mandolin, fiddle, and the mandocaster (a five-string, electric cross between a Telecaster guitar and a mandolin, that Skaggs helped popularize). The high point of his career came in 1985, when his chart success and the reputation of his band led to Skaggs being named Entertainer of the Year by the Country Music Association.

Smith became aware of "Country Bumpkin," a story song—written by Don Wayne—chronicling the relationship of the title character and his more worldly bride. Smith liked it so much he recorded it and made it the title song of the album.

The follow-up, "Between Lust and Watching TV," rose no higher on the *Billboard* chart than number 11, but "It's Time to Pay the Fiddler" came next and made it to Number One.

Smith spent his remaining time in the spotlight without major hits, though top 40 chart rankings were the rule through 1977. At that point, with songs like "Throwin' Memories on the Fire," "Bits and Pieces of Life," and "Too Many Irons in the Fire," Smith began fading from view, and by the end of 1982 he was on to other endeavors.

One disc, the number 75 "King Lear," brought him back for a wink in mid-1986.

CARL SMITH

Carl Smith was one of the most durable country stars of all time. From the 1950s through the latter part of the '70s he logged hits on the country charts in every year but one. In the process he sold more than 15 million records.

Smith was born on March 15, 1927, in Maynardsville, Tennessee. As lore would have it, he sold flower seeds to earn money to buy his first guitar. In the 1940s he began to make a name for himself on radio, originally with WROL in Knoxville, Tennessee, and later at WSM in Nashville.

His appearances on the latter brought him to the attention of Columbia Records and led to a contract with the label in 1950—the same year he joined the Grand Ole Opry. Smith debuted on the country charts with his second record, "Let's Live a Little" (number two in 1951). He went on to win top male vocalist honors in various country music polls.

At the time he also married June Carter (the future wife of Johnny Cash). Smith and Carter's daughter, Carlene, would become a star of country and rock and roll in the 1980s.

With his traditional style and down-home feel, Smith was a country mainstay during the 1950s, recording such hits as "(When You Feel Like You're in Love) Don't Just Stand There" and "Are You Teasing Me." In 1957 he toured as part of the Phillip Morris Country Music Show troupe.

TOP SONGS

LET'S LIVE A LITTLE (Columbia, '51, 2)
LET OLD MOTHER NATURE HAVE HER WAY
  (Columbia, '51, 1)
(WHEN YOU FEEL LIKE YOU'RE IN LOVE) DON'T JUST
  STAND THERE (Columbia, '52, 1)
ARE YOU TEASING ME (Columbia, '52, 1)
TRADEMARK (Columbia, '53, 2)
HEY JOE! (Columbia, '53, 1)
BACK UP BUDDY (Columbia, '54, 2)
LOOSE TALK (Columbia, '54, 1)
THERE SHE GOES (Columbia, '55, 3)
WHY, WHY (Columbia, '57, 2)

Additional Top 40 Country Songs: 59

Smith's burgeoning country fame led to his being drawn, in the 1960s, into a new career as a host for television music shows. In 1961 he starred in "Four Star Jubilee," a nationally televised program on ABC. Later in the '60s, "Carl Smith's Country Music Hall" ran for five years on Canadian television (it was also syndicated in the U.S.). Smith also appeared in two films, *The Badge of Marshall Brennan* and *Buffalo Guns.*

By the end of the 1960s, Smith's lengthy run of top 40 hits had subsided. But he continued to record prolifically. While a newer generation of country stars began making its mark, Smith maintained a place in the business, hitting the singles chart 17 times in the 1970s.

By the latter part of that decade Smith had begun to tire of the business. In 1977 he retired from country music, eventually settling on his 500-acre ranch near Franklin, Tennessee, with his wife Goldie Hill (whom he married in 1957). He returned, briefly, to the music business in the 1980s to record an album of his greatest hits.

CONNIE SMITH

Considered by many to be among the most talented country singers, Connie Smith (b. Constance June Meadows, Aug. 14, 1941, Elkhart, Indiana) maintained a very visible presence on the country popularity charts for 15 years starting in the mid-1960s.

Her powerful, deeply emotional vocal delivery had its roots in the heartland values of her midwestern birthplace. Born to an Indiana carpenter, she spent her youth in West Virginia and then Ohio, growing up in a family of 14 children. Exposed to Grand Ole Opry radio broadcasts, she gravitated naturally to singing and playing guitar. She sang in her high school and then became more active as a performer, eventually appearing on the "Saturday Night Jamboree" television program in Huntington, West Virginia.

But marriage and motherhood interrupted her musical activities. She became a housewife for a while (a role for which she was not unsuited, once telling writer Jack Hurst, "I'd a lot rather have somebody brag on my supper than my new record").

Encouraged by her husband, she played at a talent show outside Columbus, Ohio, in 1963. Star performer Bill Anderson heard her there and became interested. Smith cut a demo tape, which found its way, through Anderson, to several important sets of ears in Nashville. Chet Atkins heard the tape, and in 1964 he helped Smith get a contract with RCA Records. That same year, her first single, the Anderson-penned "Once a Day," received a smash-hit welcome, reaching the top of the *Billboard* country chart and drawing accolades as the Country Music Association's Song of the Year.

Suddenly an acclaimed new arrival, Smith worked steadily for the RCA label over the next eight years, outputting a more traditionally country brand of music than the sleek Nashville Sound permeating Music City at the time. This was Smith's peak run, fueled by an impressive 10 top five hits and some 16 others, appearances on such widely viewed television showcases as "The Jimmy Dean Show" and "The Lawrence Welk Show," and induction into the Grand Ole Opry.

Along the way she cut numerous albums—there would eventually be dozens—that supplemented traditional country fare (including an album of Bill Anderson songs) with material that reflected the powerful commitment to Christianity that would increasingly come to the foreground in her work.

A shift to Columbia Records in 1973 kept the hits coming, including the top 10 chart singles "Ain't Love a Good Thing" (1973) and "('Til) I Kissed You" (1976). Compared to the RCA releases, however, these records achieved generally lower levels of public acceptance, as reflected in chart rankings.

By the time she changed over to Monument Records—in 1977—Smith's commercial glory days were over, although her spiritual glory days were on the increase. Gospel-oriented music became a main focus, as did her family.

Smith was off the charts by 1980. She receded from the front lines of country music, although she remained a member of the Grand Ole Opry and signed briefly with Epic Records, issuing the single "A Far Cry from You" in 1985.

SAMMI SMITH

Sammi Smith has as much in common with the torch singers of the 1940s as she does with her female counterparts in country music. With her simmering and emotionally charged vocals, Smith has a soulful sound that has set her apart while also hampering her country recording career. One of the first artists to have a major hit with a Kris Kristofferson song—1970's "Help Me Make It Through the Night"—Smith was subsequently encumbered with an "outlaw" image that virtually barred her from the top ranks of the country roster.

Smith was born on August 5, 1943, in Orange, California, and grew up mostly in Oklahoma City. By age 12 she was singing in local clubs, where she eventually came to the attention of Oklahoma songwriter Gene Sullivan. With his encouragement, Smith subsequently met Luther Perkins of the Tennessee Three, who suggested she move to Nashville.

TOP SONGS

Once a Day (RCA, '64, *1*)

Then and Only Then (RCA, '65, *4*)

If I Talk to Him (RCA, '65, *4*)

Nobody But a Fool (Would Love You) (RCA, '66, *4*)

Ain't Had No Lovin' (RCA, '66, *2*)

The Hurtin's All Over (RCA, '66, *3*)

Cincinnati, Ohio (RCA, '67, *4*)

Burning a Hole in My Mind (RCA, '67, *5*)

I Never Once Stopped Loving You (RCA, '70, *5*)

Just One Time (RCA, '71, *2*)

Additional Top 40 Country Songs: 29

After doing so in the late 1960s she met Johnny Cash, who helped her to secure a recording contract with Columbia Records.

Her initial recordings were modest successes, with her debut, "So Long, Charlie Brown, Don't Look for Me Around," hitting number 69 on the country chart and three follow-up releases hovering in the middle level of that list. In 1970, Smith changed record labels, moving from Columbia to Mega, and immediately struck gold.

The release of "Help Me Make It Through the Night"—a track from her debut album, *He's Everywhere*—transformed Smith into one of the major stars in country music. A crossover hit, the record topped the country chart, hit number eight in the pop Hot 100, and in the process sold more than two million copies. Mega, banking on this success, subsequently changed the album title to that of the single and rereleased it.

"Help Me Make It Through the Night" not only put Smith on the map but also boosted Kristofferson, making him one of the most in-demand songwriters of the day.

While his career would continue to flourish, however, Smith's began to wane almost immediately. Following "Then You Walk In," a number 10 single in 1971, her releases would prove to be commercial disappointments.

She made a comeback of sorts in 1975 when "Today I Started Loving You Again" hit number nine. And when she began recording on the Elektra label in the middle '70s, she flirted with the possibility of crossing over to country-rock. During that period she became associated with the "outlaw" movement led by Willie Nelson and Waylon Jennings and centered in Austin, Texas.

But all of this merely served to distance Smith from the country mainstream. By the 1980s she was a marginal figure, at least in commercial terms. Still a passionate vocalist—and one known for bringing a distinctive sound to country music—Smith logged two more minor hits in 1985 and '86, "You Just Hurt My Last Feeling" and "Love Me All Over," and then dropped off the chart.

HANK SNOW

A precision vocalist, a fine guitar player, and a composer of classic songs, Hank Snow ranks among country music's leading legends. As the Singing Ranger (a nod to his lifelong inspiration, Jimmie Rodgers, the Singing Brakeman) Snow first entered the *Billboard* country chart—and the public consciousness—in 1949, and he stayed there through his election to the Country Music Hall of Fame 30 years later.

At the height of his fame he was a vast distance from the depths of poverty he endured when young. Snow (b. Clarence Eugene Snow, May 9, 1914, Liverpool, Nova Scotia, Canada) left home at age 12 after suffering abuse at the hands of his stepfather. He did what he could to survive—door-to-door selling, physical labor—and eventually scraped together enough money to buy a guitar. It was while working as a cabin boy in the merchant marines that Snow first heard the voice and songs of Rodgers, and he became hooked. Back in Nova Scotia and propelled toward a music career, he began playing professionally under the name Hank the Yodeling Ranger (another nod to Rodgers, a.k.a. America's Blue Yodeler).

The next 15 years were spent establishing a reputation as one of Canada's top country musicians. He started in clubs and by 1934 had a radio show of his own on CHNS in Halifax. Within two years he was signed to Victor in Canada. First records had him yodeling on songs like his own "Lonesome Blue Yodel" as he endeavored to copy his hero. But over time he began developing his own style, a lower

TOP ALBUMS

He's Everywhere / Help Me Make It Through the Night (Columbia, '70)
Mixed Emotions (Elektra, '76)

TOP SONGS

Help Me Make It Through the Night (Mega, '70, 1, 8 Pop)
Then You Walk In (Mega, '71, 10)
I've Got to Have You (Mega, '72, 13)
The Rainbow in Daddy's Eyes (Mega, '74, 16)
Today I Started Loving You Again (Mega, '75, 9)
Loving Arms (Elektra, '77, 19)
What I Lie (Cyclone, '79, 16)
Cheatin's a Two Way Street (Sound Factory, '81, 16)

Additional Top 40 Country Songs: 12

voice, and a new image as the Singing Ranger. (His reverence for Rodgers wouldn't lessen, however: he would one day cut an album of Rodgers tunes and name his own son Jimmie Rodgers Snow.)

Snow longed to break into the United States market, and in the mid-'40s he began to do so. Initial attempts may have felt like promises unkept. He landed a stint on the "WWVA Jamboree" radio show in Wheeling, West Virginia, and in 1946 made his way to Hollywood—with band and performing horse, Shawnee, in tow. But it didn't work out, and he returned to Canada.

Another stab at the U.S. was more successful, starting with work at KRLD radio in Dallas. When RCA Records released his single "Marriage Vow" in late 1949—credited, as would be most of his records through the mid-'50s, to Hank Snow (the Singing Ranger) and His Rainbow Ranch Boys—it hit number 10 on the *Billboard* Best Seller chart. Ernest Tubb, meanwhile, helped Snow get on the Grand Ole Opry, which turned into a membership when Snow scored a 21-week Number One hit with his song "I'm Moving On."

From that point on—helped by the reinforcement of two follow-up chart-toppers, "The Golden Rocket" and "The Rhumba Boogie"—Snow was a mainstay on the country charts. Sixty-five of his songs reached the top 40 through 1974. Twenty-seven of them made it to the top five. Seven hit Number One. Several of his hits, including "Let Me Go, Lover!" and "(Now and Then There's) A Fool Such as I" (covered by Elvis Presley in 1959), became standards. "I'm Moving On," for example, was a number 40 pop hit for Ray Charles in 1959.

TOP SONGS

I'M MOVING ON (RCA Victor, '50, *1*)
THE GOLDEN ROCKET (RCA Victor, '50, *1*)
THE RHUMBA BOOGIE (RCA, '51, *1*)
THE GOLD RUSH IS OVER (RCA, '52, *2*)
LADY'S MAN (RCA, '52, *2*)
I DON'T HURT ANYMORE (RCA, '54, *1*)
LET ME GO, LOVER! (RCA, '54, *1*)
I'VE BEEN EVERYWHERE (RCA, '62, *1*)
NINETY MILES AN HOUR (DOWN A DEAD END
    STREET) (RCA, '63, *2*)
HELLO LOVE (RCA, '74, *1*)

Additional Top 40 Country Songs: 55

The arrival of rock and roll in the mid-'50s (a movement in which Snow had played a role, having included a fledgling Elvis Presley on one of his tours) found Snow turning to the country-pop Nashville Sound under the aegis of his RCA producer, Chet Atkins. With Atkins he also cut an instrumental album, *Reminiscing,* in 1964, adding to the smattering of non-vocal discs he had previously issued, a rarity for instrumentally skilled country singers.

In the late 1960s and early '70s, Snow's recorded output proved somewhat less chart-worthy than previous successes—until he abruptly returned to Number One in 1974 with "Hello Love" (which was subsequently used as the theme song for Garrison Keillor's "Prairie Home Companion" radio show).

Following his Hall of Fame induction, Snow ended his 44-year association with RCA Records, having released a total of over 100 albums. Also a member of the RCA Records Country Music Hall of Fame (apparently insufficient reason to extend his tenure with the label) and the Nashville Songwriters Hall of Fame, Snow remained part of the Grand Ole Opry and continued to perform, when not ensconced in his Rainbow Ranch home in the Nashville suburbs surrounded by career memorabilia and a collection of guitars.

JOE STAMPLEY

Joe Stampley began his career as a rock and roller in the 1950s, and by the time the '80s rolled around he had become a honky-tonk man. In between, mostly in the 1970s, Stampley (sometimes with his duo partner, Moe Bandy) made a name as one of the more popular artists in country music.

Born on June 6, 1943, in Springhill, Louisiana, Stampley grew up listening to the music of Hank Williams. But with the emergence of Elvis Presley, Jerry Lee Lewis, and other earth-shakers in the 1950s, Stampley became a fan of rock and roll. He took his excitement several steps further, recording a number of singles for the legendary rock labels Imperial and Chess in 1959.

While those discs failed on the charts, Stampley continued rocking undeterred, eventually hitting the pop charts in the 1960s as a member of the Uniques with the singles "Not Too Long Ago" and "All These Things."

Joe Stampley

TOP SONGS

SOUL SONG (Dot, '72, *1*)
BRING IT ON HOME (TO YOUR WOMAN) (Dot, '72, *7*)
I'M STILL LOVING YOU (Dot, '73, *3*)
TAKE ME HOME TO SOMEWHERE (Dot, '74, *5*)
ROLL ON BIG MAMA (Dot, '75, *1*)
ALL THESE THINGS (Dot, '76, *1*)
RED WINE AND BLUE MEMORIES (Dot, '78, *6*)
IF YOU'VE GOT TEN MINUTES (LET'S FALL IN LOVE)
     (Dot, '78, *6*)
DO YOU EVER FOOL AROUND (Dot, '78, *5*)
JUST GOOD OL' BOYS (Columbia, '79, *1*)

Additional Top 40 Country Songs: 35

But by the late '60s his interests were turning back to the country music he had grown up with in his youth. Moving to Nashville in 1969, he signed a contract with Dot Records and became a songwriter for Gallico Music.

He began emerging as a country artist early in the 1970s. Initial releases were moderate hits, two songs charting at numbers 74 and 75 and a third, "If You Touch Me (You've Got to Love Me)," shooting up to number nine. Then he reached the top in 1972 with "Soul Song." Over the course of the rest of the decade he would score hits on a steady basis, topping the charts again in 1975 with "Roll on Big Mama" and in 1976 with "All These Things." In 1976 he had more hits than any country artist that year, making the charts eight times: four on Dot and four on his new label, Epic Records.

"Every time I put out a new record, [Dot] would release one of my old tracks," Stampley said later. "This meant I kept having two records competing with each other. Sometimes this meant that neither would make the top ten, or, in one case, an old song, 'All These Things,' went to number one while my new release didn't. It was a little frustrating."

While his career continued to flourish in a solo context, Stampley decided to try a new approach. In 1979 he teamed with the Texas honky-tonk vocalist Moe Bandy. The result was an immediate success, with the rolling debut release, "Just Good Ol' Boys," reaching Number One. Stampley and Bandy were named the Vocal Duo of the Year by the Country Music Association in 1980.

Over the next six years, the duo hit the charts nine times. The records were a rollicking bunch, from boisterous numbers like "Boys Night Out" to novelty items like "Where's the Dress," a parody about Boy George of the pop group Culture Club.

Along the way, Stampley released more recordings of his own. While none of them topped the charts, they maintained Stampley's position as a consistent country hitmaker. He also continued to vary his musical output. In addition to his honky-tonk outings with Bandy, Stampley recorded such straight country songs as "When You Were Blue and I Was Green," rockers like his version of the 1967 Van Morrison hit "Brown Eyed Girl," and soul-inflected numbers like "If You Don't Know Me by Now."

By 1989, the hits had dried up. It was the end of one of the more eclectic and musically intriguing chart runs in country music.

THE STATLER BROTHERS

Unique four-voice harmony, warm and clever humor, and original songs that summon feelings of nostalgia for America's small-town past all made the Statler Brothers massively popular among a largely conservative, mainstream audience in the 1970s and '80s. Called "one of country music's best—and funniest—acts" in *Billboard* magazine, the Statlers are the recipients of a staggering array of music awards and the creators of 62 hit songs, four of which climbed to Number One.

A long-running act, the Statlers began as childhood friends. Harold Reid (bass, b. Aug. 21, 1939), Don Reid (lead, b. June 5, 1945), Philip Balsley (baritone, b. Aug. 8, 1939), and Lew DeWitt (tenor, b. Mar. 8, 1938) grew up together in Staunton, Virginia. All but Don began singing as a group in 1955,

joined by fourth member Joe McDorman. At first they sang gospel and called themselves the Four Stars, later changing to the Kingsmen. By 1960, Don Reid had replaced McDorman, completing the group's key lineup. Within several years they'd taken the name the Statler Brothers (having become aware of several other groups called the Kingsmen) from the brand name on a box of tissues.

In 1964 they landed a job performing with the Johnny Cash Show, and with Cash's help they joined Columbia Records' roster of artists.

Following initial poor record sales, the Statlers scored a number two hit with DeWitt's "Flowers on the Wall" (a million seller that also brought in two Grammy Awards) and from then on would not stray from the *Billboard* chart. Meanwhile, they continued working with Cash, which they would do on tour through 1972 and on television as part of his regular ABC series.

A move to the Mercury label in 1970 brought new momentum, starting with the number nine "Bed

The Statler Brothers

of Rose's," the title reflecting a penchant for word-play also demonstrated three years earlier on "You Can Have Your Kate and Edith, Too." (More wacky humor was behind the Statlers' creation of *Alive at Johnny Mack Brown High School,* an album record-ed under the name Lester "Roadhog" Moran and the Cadillac Cowboys.) Within two years, during which they released the memorable hits "Do You Remember These" and "The Class of '57," the Statlers had begun collecting a set of awards that would eventually include eight Vocal Group of the Year honors from the Country Music Association, some 25 awards from *Music City News,* and several American Music Awards.

With 1978's "Do You Know You Are My Sun-shine," the Statlers reached the top of the country chart for the first time. It would also be the last for the group's original lineup. DeWitt, taken ill, was replaced in 1982 by Jimmy Fortune. The choice of new member was a good one: he would write all three of the group's remaining Number One hits. (DeWitt went on to record a 1985 solo album before passing away on August 15, 1990.)

The 1980s proved a period of peak popularity for the group as they collected rave reviews, vast concert audiences, and their highest-charting hits. But they weren't the only active vocal group in country music. Competition came from both Alabama and the Oak Ridge Boys, and by the late '80s the Statlers were experiencing slippage on the charts. The number six

"More Than a Name on the Wall" reasserted their viability somewhat in 1989, as did their 1990s tele-vision series on the Nashville Network. To this day, even with an absence of chart hits, Statler Brothers records continue to sell in large quantities.

Apart from providing decades of acclaimed enter-tainment, the Statlers left a permanent mark by bringing vocal groups from the country background to up-front headlining status. "When we started out," said Harold Reid to Kip Kirby in *Billboard,* "you didn't find country groups being asked to host network television shows or participating in comedy skits or getting their own specials. We didn't see no reason why we couldn't, though, so we just went right on ahead and did it."

RAY STEVENS

Mention the name Ray Stevens and other names immediately come to mind: "Ahab the Arab," "Harry the Hairy Ape," "Gitarzan." These novelty hits made Stevens' name in the music business and culture of the 1960s. But from that decade on, Stevens was also active on the country scene, recording a wide range of traditional songs along with new novelty items.

Stevens (b. Ray Ragsdale, Jan. 24, 1939, Clarks-dale, Georgia) began his study of music in the late 1950s at Georgia State University, and during the next four years he began releasing records of his own songs. One of them, "Jeremiah Peabody's Poly Unsaturated Quick Dissolving Fast Acting Pleasant Tasting Green and Purple Pills," was a modest hit in 1961.

Encouraged by that success, Stevens moved to Nashville, where he pursued a career as a producer, instrumentalist, and songwriter, outputting a collec-tion of wacky recordings that would leave an indeli-ble imprint on the pop chart. (Stevens is still considered the number one novelty artist of the past 30 years.)

During the 1960s he became a frequent guest on television's "Andy Williams Show," and in 1973 and '74 he performed on the program "Music Country."

The later show reflected his move into conven-tional country music in the late 1960s. It began with his 1969 version of "Sunday Morning Coming Down," which hit number 55. From there, Stevens used his familiar vocals to distinctly country ends on

---

TOP ALBUMS

THE BEST OF THE STATLER BROTHERS (Mercury, '75)
THE BEST OF THE STATLER BROTHERS, VOL. 2
 (Mercury, '80)

TOP SONGS

FLOWERS ON THE WALL (Columbia, '65, *2, 4 Pop*)
DO YOU REMEMBER THESE (Mercury, '72, *2*)
I'LL GO TO MY GRAVE LOVING YOU (Mercury, '75, *3*)
DO YOU KNOW YOU ARE MY SUNSHINE
 (Mercury, '78, *1*)
OH BABY MINE (I GET SO LONELY) (Mercury, '83, *2*)
ELIZABETH (Mercury, '83, *1*)
MY ONLY LOVE (Mercury, '84, *1*)
TOO MUCH ON MY HEART (Mercury, '85, *1*)

Additional Top 40 Country Songs: 51

such middle-of-the-road hits as 1970's "Everything Is Beautiful" (which topped the pop chart) and 1971's "Turn Your Radio On" (number 17 country, 63 pop).

But Stevens' feisty sense of humor remained as potent as ever. In 1974 he released the novelty song "The Streak," a crossover hit at Number One pop and number three country. It seemed that no matter how hard Stevens tried to gain an audience for his conventional songs, it was always the novelty material that charmed the public at large.

But that changed, temporarily, in 1975 with the release of his version of the Erroll Garner classic "Misty." The record climbed high on both the country and pop charts and won a Grammy Award for Best Arrangement Accompanying a Vocalist.

In the mid-1970s, Stevens displayed his varied tastes in music with versions of the 1975 Joe Cocker rock ballad "You Are So Beautiful" and the 1925 Paul Whiteman classic "Indian Love Call." At the same time, his witty, cornball side continued to emerge. In 1977, recording as the Henhouse Five Plus Two, he issued a novelty version of the Glenn Miller hit "In the Mood" and over the next 15 years released "I Need Your Help Barry Manilow," "People's Court," and "It's Me Again, Margaret."

Following his last major hit, 1980's number seven "Shriner's Convention," Stevens steadily descended from the charts' upper reaches with such characteristically nutty titles as "Would Jesus Wear a Rolex," "Working for the Japanese," and "Power Tools."

Add 3 lines here to text. Add 3 lines here to text. Add 3 lines here to text. Add 3 lines here to text. Add lines here to text. Add 3 lines here to text.

TOP SONGS

Turn Your Radio On (Barnaby, '70, 17)

The Streak (Barnaby, '74, 3, 1 Pop)

Misty (Barnaby, '75, 3, 14 Pop)

You Are So Beautiful (Warner, '76, 16)

Honky Tonk Waltz (Warner, '76, 27)

Be Your Own Best Friend (Warner, '78, 36)

Shriner's Convention (RCA, '80, 7)

Night Games (RCA, '80, 20)

One More Last Chance (RCA, '81, 33)

Written Down in My Heart (RCA, '82, 35)

Additional Top 40 Country Songs: 6

DOUG STONE

This former diesel mechanic was discovered singing in a Georgia club back in 1988 by a woman who promised to get him a Nashville record contract within a year. She delivered, and Doug Stone delivered a top five hit in 1990 with his first release, "I'd Be Better Off in a Pine Box." Through the mid-1990s, each subsequent release reached the top 10 or higher as Stone developed into one of country music's top ballad singing stars.

Stone (b. Doug Brooks, June 19, 1956, Atlanta, Georgia)—who changed his name to avoid confusion with Garth Brooks—was raised in various small communities near Atlanta by a family with a split personality. His mother was artistic, a singer and guitar player who once pursued a country music career. His father was a practical man, a diesel mechanic who wanted his children to learn practical trades. Doug's folks inevitably split up, and the boys stayed with their father, because he seemed better suited to teaching them something that could make them a steady living.

Doug was in constant conflict, because he shared his mother's dream to be an entertainer. As a little boy she had taught him how to play guitar, even getting him up on stage at age seven to perform before the headliner, Loretta Lynn. Doug loved making music, and he got his first experience in the studio as a session drummer when he was just 11 years old. "On the first take I started improvising," he says. "The producer told me not to do that, but they ended up using the take where I had played what I felt, so I felt pretty good about myself at a young age."

Stone delved deeper into the music world. At age 15 he moved into an old motor home on his father's property and built the first of several home recording studios he would create over the years, where he practiced singing and writing. To make a living he and his father and brother worked in a diesel repair shop together. "I never thought dad could turn me into a mechanic," Stone claims, "but damned if I didn't become a good one. I hated it, but I was good at it, and it paid well." In the evenings he returned to his passion, making music in his recording studio, often waking up with his head on the mixing board. One such occasion provided a turning point when he woke up to the sound of a voice playing back. "I said, 'Hey this guy sounds good,' then I realized it

Doug Stone

was my own voice I was listening to. That was a revelation because I never thought I had what it takes to be a singer until that happened."

Stone became a popular performer in a triangle of communities, Carrollton, Newnan, and Marietta, but for all his dreams of becoming a recording act, he had never made a serious run at Nashville until he was discovered by Phyllis Bennett while singing in the Newnan Veterans of Foreign Wars club in 1988. Signed to Epic Records in '89, he debuted on the chart in the spring of '90 and soon gained wide popularity with his solid, country tenor voice and easygoing charm as a stage performer.

In April of 1992, at the height of his success, Stone fell ill after a concert in Colorado and had to undergo triple bypass heart surgery. Just 35 at the time, he was able to recover quickly and return to his career, scoring new chart hits and investing his performances with new vitality. "After coming that close to death, all I want to do is have a good time," he said. "I don't want to hurt anybody, do anything wrong, just have a good time. That's come through in my shows, because after that, I hit the stage just a ball of energy."

Of key importance to Stone was that his music

communicate something to his listeners. He once admitted wanting to be remembered "as a singer who made people say, 'Hey, he's saying what I want to say.' I've had people tell me they've taken my songs to the person they love and said, 'Now this is what I really mean.' I always take that as a compliment."

TOP ALBUMS

DOUG STONE (Epic, '90)
I THOUGHT IT WAS YOU (Epic, '91)
FROM THE HEART (Epic, '92)
MORE LOVE (Epic, '93)

TOP SONGS

IN A DIFFERENT LIGHT (Epic, '91, *1*)
A JUKEBOX WITH A COUNTRY SONG (Epic, '91, *1*)
TOO BUSY BEING IN LOVE (Epic, '92, *1*)
WHY DIDN'T I THINK OF THAT (Epic, '93, *1*)
I NEVER KNEW LOVE (Epic, '93, *2*)
ADDICTED TO A DOLLAR (Epic, '94, *4*)

Additional Top 40 Country Songs: 10

GEORGE STRAIT

George Strait

George Strait is one of the few cowboy-hat–wearing country stars who actually spent time in the saddle as a working cowboy. As a singer, he first hit the top 10 in 1981 with "Unwound." What unwound after that was an amazing success story that saw him gain credit (along with Ricky Skaggs) for spearheading the neo-traditionalist movement in the mid-1980s and '90s and, in his case, inspiring many more "hat acts." A country megastar, Strait scored high chart rankings with remarkable consistency and collected nearly 30 Number One country hits.

Strait (b. May 18, 1952, Poteet, Texas) was raised in Pearsall, Texas, by a schoolteaching father who also worked the ranch that had been in the family nearly a hundred years. When George was young his mother deserted the family, taking his sister with her and leaving his father to raise two boys alone. Life consisted of the family staying in Pearsall during the week, then traveling to the ranch on weekends to run fences and round up and vaccinate a few cows. As a teenager, George began to fool around with music. "Just a few garage bands, but nothing serious," he explains. "I always knew I wanted to sing, but never thought it was a possibility until I entered the service."

Strait enlisted in the Army in 1971, and he was stationed in Hawaii in '73. The base commander

there wanted to start an Army-sponsored country band. "That really appealed to me," says Strait, "so I bought a cheap old acoustic guitar, learned three chords, got me a bunch of Hank Williams sheet music, and went to town." The Army band performed as Rambling Country, and they used the name Santee for the gigs they played off-base and out of uniform.

Strait returned home in 1975, and to fulfill his father's wish that he get an education, he entered Southwest Texas State University at San Marcos. While studying toward a degree in agriculture education he formed the core of his Ace in the Hole band.

A couple of fruitless overtures toward Nashville left Strait ready to stop trying. Then, in 1979, a fellow Texan and former MCA Records employee named Erv Woolsey hired Strait and his band to play at his club in San Marcos. Woolsey was soon on the phone to MCA Nashville, and Strait was soon working on his debut album.

TOP ALBUMS

STRAIT COUNTRY (MCA, '81)
STRAIT FROM THE HEART (MCA, '83)
OCEAN FRONT PROPERTY (MCA, '87)
BEYOND THE BLUE NEON (MCA, '89)
PURE COUNTRY (MCA, '92)

TOP SONGS

FOOL HEARTED MEMORY (MCA, '82, *1*)
THE CHAIR (MCA, '85, *1*)
LOVE WITHOUT END, AMEN (MCA, '90, *1*)
EASY COME EASY GO (MCA, '93, *1*)
THE BIG ONE (MCA, '94, *1*)

Additional Top 40 Country Songs: 41

Following the number six success of "Unwound," Strait reached only number 16 with "Down and Out," his second release. But the third, "If You're Thinking You Want a Stranger," hit number three and opened the door to Strait's extended residence in the top 10.

In 1982, "Fool Hearted Memory" became the first of Strait's more than two dozen Number One country hits, a list that includes "The Chair," "Ocean Front Property," "Love Without End, Amen," and "If I Know You." Most of his hits were solid country, but in his live show—backed by one of the best road bands in the business—Strait broadened the focus to include such sounds as western swing.

In the 1990s, Strait was one of the few veteran acts that remained undaunted by the influx of hot new performers like Garth Brooks, many of whom—including Brooks—viewed him as a role model. An intensely private man who does fewer interviews than any major country act, Strait came out of his shell in 1992 to promote and star in the movie *Pure Country,* the soundtrack album of which yielded four hits and helped to keep him in the country forefront.

Strait has managed to achieve a kind of country star nirvana. His career continues to grow, in spite of the fact he dedicates only six months of each year to recording and touring while spending the rest of his time sequestered back home in Texas, riding and roping and spending time with his family.

MARTY STUART

He began as a child prodigy, a multi-instrumentalist, and a member of bluegrass legend Lester Flatt's band, and he went on to work with Johnny Cash. Marty Stuart, active as a soloist in the 1990s and with the hits to prove it, remains a living link to great artists and influential styles of the country music past dating back to the late 1960s.

He can trace his musical heritage all the way to a great-great-grandfather who played fiddle to calm his fellow rebel troops in the trenches during the Civil War. Stuart (b. John Marty Stuart, Sept. 30, 1958, Philadelphia, Mississippi) began his performing career at age 11, singing gospel music at tent meetings with a family act called the Sullivans. A year later, his father took him to a bluegrass festival

in Indiana, where he made friends with Lester Flatt's mandolin player. The fellow was very impressed with the 12-year-old's guitar and mandolin playing. A few months later, Flatt's band played near Philadelphia, and Stuart was invited to meet Flatt. "I think Lester was impressed with my picking," Stuart remembers. "I think what most impressed him was that I knew so many of his songs. Anyway, we hit it off right away."

Flatt offered to make the young sensation part of his band, assuring Stuart's parents he'd be well taken care of. For the next seven years, Stuart got paid for a musical education money could not have bought. He met and performed with the great ones of the time, appearing often at the Grand Ole Opry and

Marty Stuart

learning lessons from the Master, as Stuart refers to Flatt. And he learned about more than just music. "One day in 1972," recalls Stuart, "at a concert in Glasgow, Delaware, Lester pointed out a couple of real old fellows that were coming toward the bus, and he said, 'Those people used to come see me and Earl Scruggs when we were in Bill Monroe's band in 1945. They've been coming to my shows ever since. That's what country fans are about; they're loyal.' That's the best lesson I ever learned—to take care of your fans." Stuart played with Flatt up until his death in 1979.

That year, Stuart helped produce a memorial album to Flatt, asking Johnny Cash to participate. Cash not only became Stuart's friend but also hired him to play in his band. In 1982, Stuart produced an acoustic album on Sugar Hill Records that included Cash on vocals along with such prominent pickers as Doc and Merle Watson and Earl Scruggs.

Stuart began a solo career with Columbia Records in 1985. He was part of an ambitious plan to simultaneously promote a number of hot new acts, including Sweethearts of the Rodeo. Stuart went for a sort of revved-up, rocking country style, and at first it looked like he might catch on. But after his debut single, "Arlene," hit number 19, none of his follow-ups matched even that moderate success. Three years later, he found himself without a label and in search of his true identity as a vocalist. "Actually, I was faking it back then," Stuart confesses. "I had never been the front man, so I really had to learn how to be a singer *after* I got a deal."

Stuart got a second chance when MCA Records signed him in 1989. A remake of an old Johnny Cash song, "Cry, Cry, Cry," got him back in the top 40. In '90 he broke into the top 10 for the first time with "Hillbilly Rock." His cause was furthered by songs he'd co-written with Paul Kennerly during his time between labels. Their collaboration provided his next two top 10s, "Little Things" and "Tempted."

During this period, Stuart and Travis Tritt became close friends. In 1992 they mounted a highly successful co-tour dubbed the No Hats Tour (poking fun at a portion of their neotraditional competition) and scored a pair of top 10 duet hits.

A country traditionalist and proud of his deep musical roots, Stuart once said he wanted to be remembered as "the kid who lucked out when he was very young, got a start with one of the masters of country music, and it caught fire inside of him. The guy that went on and lived his life as a crusader and a warrior for country music, one who always was trying to write a song as good as 'Today I Started Loving You Again' and believed in country music until they put him away."

DOUG SUPERNAW

He emulated fellow Texan Willie Nelson when, after three years in Nashville trying to get noticed, Doug Supernaw returned to the Lone Star State, put a band together, and made such a name for himself locally that Nashville noticed him there. Signed to a contract in 1992, he soon made his mark with top 10 hits like "Reno" and his first Number One, "I Don't Call Him Daddy."

Supernaw (b. Sept. 26, 1960, Bryan, Texas) grew up in Houston, the son of a Texaco Oil research scientist. The only music he was exposed to growing up was whatever came over the radio. With nobody pushing him toward music, he was as surprised as anybody in the family when he wrote two songs at age eight, one called "Virginia" and another titled "Hurricanes and Window Panes." "I've been writing songs ever since," he says.

Although he continued to make music as a hobby, and was encouraged when he placed second in a big Houston radio talent contest, his main focus through high school was sports.

He went to college on a golf scholarship. He even quit college to attend the Professional Golf Association pro qualifying school, but when he didn't qual-

---

TOP ALBUMS

TEMPTED (MCA, '90)
THIS ONE'S GONNA HURT YOU (MCA, '92)

TOP SONGS

HILLBILLY ROCK (MCA, '90, 8)
TEMPTED (MCA, '91, 5)
THE WHISKEY AIN'T WORKIN' (with Travis Tritt, Warner, '91, 2)
BURN ME DOWN (MCA, '92, 7)
THIS ONE'S GONNA HURT YOU (FOR A LONG, LONG TIME) (with Travis Tritt, MCA, '92, 7)

Additional Top 40 Country Songs: 11

TOP ALBUM

RED AND RIO GRANDE (BNA, '93)

TOP SONGS

RENO (BNA, '93, 4)
I DON'T CALL HIM DADDY (BNA, '93, 1)
RED AND RIO GRANDE (BNA, '94, 23)

Additional Top 40 Country Songs: 1

ify for the pro tour, he lost heart. "I just figured I didn't want to do it as much as the guys like Tom Kite," he says. "That's when I realized that music was what I really wanted to do."

In 1987 he moved to Nashville and began writing for a publishing company. A couple of years later, thinking he was ready for a recording career, he mounted a full-blown showcase for some music industry executives. When that failed, he folded his tent and returned to Texas. "Truth is I wasn't quite ready," he admits. "I had taken somebody else's advice and got up in clothes I wouldn't have worn,

Doug Supernaw

and sang songs that weren't really me. I wouldn't have signed me to a deal either back then."

Once back in Texas, Supernaw set out to establish himself as a performer. He put together a band called Texas Steel that soon made a name for itself as a hot dance band, becoming the top group at a Tyler, Texas, club called the Oil Palace. Supernaw ended up opening for most of the major acts that came through the area, and after revisiting Nashville periodically, he finally landed a contract with BNA Entertainment.

Supernaw's first single failed to reach the top 40, but he rectified that with his high-charting second release, "Reno," a song he wrote with his band. He followed up in 1993 with the Number One "I Don't Call Him Daddy," a heartfelt ballad that revealed Supernaw's unique strength as a performer. "I'm not technically the best singer around," he says, "but I can put as much feeling into a song as anybody."

In 1994 his record label reorganized, causing Supernaw to switch to Giant Records early the following year.

HANK THOMPSON

One of the kings of western swing, Hank Thompson enjoyed a career that in chart durability and longevity had few equals in the world of country music. With his Brazos Valley Boys band he had songs on the country chart in five decades (from the 1940s to the '80s), and his sound and music influenced several generations of country musicians.

He was born Henry William Thompson on September 3, 1925, in Waco, Texas. In his youth he learned to play the harmonica, and he won several local talent contests. By the time he reached his teens he had also taught himself to play the guitar and, billing himself as Hank the Hired Hand, had landed a job on a WACO radio program (sponsored by one of the flour companies that did so much for country music during its fledgling years).

Thompson's blossoming music career was curtailed in 1943 when he joined the Navy. Upon his discharge three years later, he entered Texas University, later studying at Southern Methodist University and Princeton. Then, back in Waco, he returned to music and resumed his recording career. Gaining another radio program, he formed his band, the Bra-

zos Valley Boys, and secured a contract with the local Globe label. In August 1946, he and his band released their debut record, "Whoa Sailor," which became a regional hit.

That record came to the attention of Tex Ritter, who encouraged Capitol Records to sign Thompson in 1948. The result was a recording relationship that would go on for 18 years and yield 37 charting hits.

"Humpty Dumpty Heart" reached number two on the country chart in 1948. Notable follow-ups included a new version of "Whoa Sailor" (released in 1949) and "Soft Lips." Thompson's signature records—and the peak of his career—came in the years 1952 and '53 when "The Wild Side of Life," "Rub-A-Dub-Dub," and "Wake Up, Irene" all hit Number One.

But Thompson's musical career had barely begun. Over the course of the next four decades he and his band would become an institution in country music, touring and recording almost constantly, winning music polls on a perennial basis, and defying musical trends and fads with their time-honored sound. In 1966, Thompson left Capitol and began a career as a solo artist for the Warner label. But over succeeding years he would re-form the Brazos Valley Boys again and again to further consistent success as a hit-making recording act.

Even as the western swing sound declined in popularity in the 1960s and '70s, Thompson continued to score hits with such records as "He's Got a Way with Women" (1967), "I've Come Awful Close" (1971), "The Older the Violin, the Sweeter the Music" (1974), and the song that carried him into his fifth decade on the charts, 1980's "Tony's Tank-

TOP SONGS

HUMPTY DUMPTY HEART (Capitol, '48, *2*)
THE WILD SIDE OF LIFE (Capitol, '52, *1*)
WAITING IN THE LOBBY OF YOUR HEART
  (Capitol, '52, *3*)
RUB-A-DUB-DUB (Capitol, '53, *1*)
WAKE UP, IRENE (Capitol, '53, *1*)
THE NEW GREEN LIGHT (Capitol, '54, *3*)
WILDWOOD FLOWER (Capitol, '55, *5*)
DON'T TAKE IT OUT ON ME (Capitol, '55, *5*)
THE BLACKBOARD OF MY HEART (Capitol, '56, *4*)
SQUAWS ALONG THE YUKON (Capitol, '58, *2*)

Additional Top 40 Country Songs: 48

Mel Tillis

Up, Drive-In Cafe." Thompson's final chart entry—as of this writing—came with "Once in a Blue Moon" in 1983.

Among his other accomplishments, Thompson was the first country artist to record in the hi-fi and stereo formats. His western swing sound—along with that of Bob Wills and the Texas Playboys—became the musical foundation for numerous later groups, most notably Asleep at the Wheel. And his very longevity as an artist secured him a significant place in the history of country music and helped gain him membership, as of 1989, in the Country Music Hall of Fame.

MEL TILLIS
• • • • • • • • • • • • • • • •

Best known in the 1990s as the famous father of Pam Tillis and the King of Branson, Missouri, Mel Tillis made his reputation as one of country music's great singer-songwriters and storytellers in a career that spanned five decades. He wrote such classics as "Detroit City" and "Ruby, Don't Take Your Love to Town" and recorded such big hits as "I Ain't Never," "Coca Cola Cowboy," and "Southern Rains." Several times voted Country Music Association Comedian of the Year, and once

TOP SONGS

HEART OVER MIND (Kapp, '70, 3)

THE ARMS OF A FOOL (MGM, '71, 4)

I AIN'T NEVER (MGM, '72, 1)

SAW MILL (MGM, '73, 2)

MIDNIGHT, ME AND THE BLUES (MGM, '74, 2)

GOOD WOMAN BLUES (MCA, '76, 1)

HEART HEALER (MCA, '77, 1)

I BELIEVE IN YOU (MCA, '78, 1)

COCA COLA COWBOY (MCA, '79, 1)

SOUTHERN RAINS (Elektra, '80, 1)

Additional Top 40 Country Songs: 57

Entertainer of the Year, he's done well for a man with a severe, lifelong stuttering problem.

Tillis (b. Lonnie Melvin Tillis, Aug. 8, 1932, Tampa, Florida) was raised in Pahokee, Florida, the son of a baker. He was just three when he began to stutter after coming down with malaria. "I also had a friend, LeRoy English, who stuttered," Tillis says, "and I honestly don't know whether I started stuttering from being around LeRoy so much or from the malaria. I think it's a bit of both." In a way, his affliction was responsible for his career as an entertainer. "I became a cutup in school," says he. "I was always coming out with these ad-libs, because I didn't stutter when I ad-libbed, only when I had to get up and say something in class or read something. The kids loved it when I had to stand up and read something. It would take so long for me to get through it, the class would end before it was their turn."

It was in school that one of his teachers discovered that he didn't stutter when he sang, and that when he sang, it sounded real good. "When I'm in front of the microphone, I become Mel Tillis the singer, almost like another person, and that person doesn't stutter," he explains.

Tillis made his first public appearance as a singer in 1948 when he entered a local talent contest. In 1951 he joined the Air Force to become a pilot. His request for flight school was turned down, he was told, "because the Air Force doesn't need any stuttering pilots." He spent the bulk of his time in the service as a baker, but while stationed in Okinawa, he formed a band called the Westerners that performed in local clubs.

After the service he went to Nashville. When he

was turned down as a recording artist, he landed a $50-a-week writing job. In addition to the Grammy-winning Bobby Bare hit "Detroit City" and Kenny Rogers and the First Edition's "Ruby, Don't Take Your Love to Town," Tillis eventually scribed such hits as Brenda Lee's "Emotions" and Charley Pride's "Snakes Crawl Out at Night."

His own recording career began in 1958 when he hit number 24 with "The Violet and a Rose." Tillis made the top 40 consistently after that, but he didn't break into the top 10 until "Who's Julie" peaked at number 10 in early 1969. From that year to 1972, the top 10s mounted up until he scored his first Number One with "I Ain't Never."

Tillis scored the bulk of his biggest hits during the 1970s. He also saw his popularity spread through appearances on late-night talk shows and in the popular films *W.W. and the Dixie Dancekings* (1975) and *Smokey and the Bandit II* (1980). He remained an important recording act through 1988, when he collected his last top 40 record with "You'll Come Back (You Always Do)."

By the 1990s, Tillis had given up trying to compete on the chart and moved the focus of his career to a theater in Branson, Missouri. One of the first to cash in on his past popularity, Tillis has made millions each year he's been in Branson.

Happy to move over to make room for his daughter Pam, who broke through in the early 1990s, Tillis looks back on an impressive career-long accumulation of nearly 60 albums and 67 top 40 hits.

PAM TILLIS

She inherited a lot from her father, Mel Tillis, including abundant singing and songwriting ability and a sense of humor. She also was blessed with the desire to be an entertainer, and after a shaky start in the mid-1980s she came on strong as one of country's top female vocalists with such hits as "Maybe It Was Memphis," 'When You Walk in the Room," and "Mi Vida Loca."

Growing up, Pamela Tillis (b. July 24, 1957, Plant City, Florida) had a love-hate relationship with her father's career. She loved what he did for a living, but she resented how much his career deprived her of time with him. "I figured once that by the time I was 18 I had spent a collective total of three years in his presence," she says. Some of the time he spent

Pam Tillis

with her was memorable. "I was eight years old when he got me up on the stage of the Grand Ole Opry along with some other kids to sing with him. I was so nervous my leg started twitching like Elvis, the shaking kind of traveled up my body to my mouth, and I was half expecting people to say, 'Look, she's just like him, her lips flutter!'" Tillis was painfully shy and felt like an ugly duckling in school. She remembers being melancholy, making up sad songs that she would sing to herself and then starting to cry. Then, like her father, she compensated by

acting up and was voted the funniest kid in her fourth grade class.

Through junior high and high school, Tillis wrote songs and performed occasionally, but she didn't get really turned on to music until she was 19. "I went out on tour with dad so I could get to know him better, and I did get a better appreciation of what he did for a living and why he did it," she says. "But the two little songs he let me get up and do weren't much fun. I wanted to do an hour and a half."

Her father never directly helped start her recording career, but the name helped open the door to her first record contract in 1984 with Warner Bros. In her early 20s she had experimented with rock music, working in a band and in a duo with rock singer Ashley Cleveland. Not surprisingly, her first country releases had a decidedly rockabilly edge.

Five low-charting singles later, Tillis left Warner in 1987 and concentrated on writing. Her songs, increasingly reflecting her country roots, were cut by the likes of Suzy Bogguss, Highway 101, Ricky Van Shelton, and Conway Twitty. During this time she met and started writing with her future husband, Bob Di Piero.

Tillis got another chance to record when offered a contract with Arista Records. In early 1991 her first single for the label, "Don't Tell Me What to Do," hit the top five. The debut album, *Put Yourself in My Place,* yielded two more top 10s, "One of Those Things" and a high-impact, career-affirming ballad called "Maybe It Was Memphis."

In 1992 she released her second Arista album, *Homeward Looking Angel,* followed by two more top 10s. Finally, in 1994, she scored her first Number One hit with "Mi Vida Loca" from the album *Sweetheart's Dance*

Proud to have made it on her own terms, Tillis remained cognizant that her experiences as the daughter of Mel Tillis provided a framework for her career. "I grew up listening to the early country music," she recalls. "Lying in bed at night I would hear the demos my dad would bring home. I was with him at the old Grand Ole Opry and met all

those great artists, and I absorbed that part of country music. . . . At the same time I've been a real open person. I love jazz, R&B, rock, and bluegrass, and I like to think I'm a bridge between the old and the new."

AARON TIPPIN

Almost too country for country when he arrived on the scene in late 1990, Aaron Tippin practically willed his career into existence with his sharply written working-man anthems, good ol' boy kickers, and honky-tonk ballads. In spite of constant resistance to his hard-core country vocals from many key urban country radio stations, he managed to collect top 10 hits like "You've Got to Stand for Something" and "There Ain't Nothin' Wrong with the Radio" on his way to becoming a platinum-selling act.

Tippin (b. July 3, 1958, Pensacola, Florida) was raised on a farm in Blue Ridge, South Carolina, near Greenville. His father was a former jet pilot instructor turned commercial aviator who farmed their 110 acres on the weekends with the family's help. "In my growing up days I did all kinds of farmhand work," says Tippin. "I raised two champion show hogs for the 4-H club. The sow ended up over 500 pounds before she became pork chops."

Tippin fell in love with traditional country music when he was 13. He and a friend were looking for eight-track tapes to play, and found his father's stash of Hank Williams recordings. "We plugged a tape in and just had a ball laughing and making fun of the music," he confesses. "But I kept on playing that tape, played it all night, and before the night was over I had fallen in love with it; I was sunk."

He kept the fixation through high school, when liking country music wasn't cool even in a rural community. "I was just an arrogant redneck," he says, "and I'd drive up to school in my Jeep with the top down and Loretta and Conway blaring."

Making music was not Tippin's first love; flying airplanes was. He was just four years old when his father propped him up and gave him the controls of a DC-3. By 16 he had soloed, and by 19 he had a multiengine license to fly commercially. "I was headed toward a career in the airlines when the economy went sour," he recollects, "so I gave up the idea of a flying career and turned to music."

TOP ALBUMS

PUT YOURSELF IN MY PLACE (Arista, '90)
HOMEWARD LOOKING ANGEL (Arista, '92)
SWEETHEART'S DANCE (Arista, '94)

TOP SONGS

DON'T TELL ME WHAT TO DO (Arista, '90, 5)
MAYBE IT WAS MEMPHIS (Arista, '91, 3)
SHAKE THE SUGAR TREE (Arista, '92, 3)
LET THAT PONY RUN (Arista, '93, 4)
SPILLED PERFUME (Arista, '94, 5)
WHEN YOU WALK INTO THE ROOM (Arista, '94, 2)
MI VIDA LOCA (Arista, '95, 1)

Additional Top 40 Country Songs: 2

Aaron Tippin

In the late 1980s he concluded that songwriting was his ticket to Nashville. In '88 he landed a factory job working the night shift at a rolling mill in Russellville, Kentucky, some 50 miles from Music City. He commuted each day to Nashville looking for a publishing deal. Finally a gospel song he wrote intrigued Opryland Music enough to hire him. Then one of his demo tapes got to the head of RCA Records, whose first response was, "Who is this hillbilly singing these demos?"

RCA signed him to a contract in 1990, and in most ways he was a dream artist. His writing was rock-solid, he had tons of down-home personality, and in addition to the interesting fact that he was a pilot, Tippin was a serious, sometimes pro, bodybuilder who looked great. The only problem was that he sounded hard-core country in the way he talked and sang. Slicker-sounding fellows like Clint Black and Garth Brooks were the heavy hitters at the time, and the label wasn't sure if all of country radio would go for him.

Luck was on their side when they released his first single, "You've Got to Stand for Something," in late 1990. It coincided with the Gulf War in Iraq, and the message of the song was tied in with the job of the American troops in the Persian Gulf. That patriotic sentiment helped drive it to number six on the chart.

After two subsequent lackluster releases, Tippin released a fun, nonsensical tribute to his old Toyota wagon named Daisy, the one that had taken him back and forth from Nashville to Russellville.

TOP ALBUMS

YOU'VE GOT TO STAND FOR SOMETHING (RCA, '90)
READ BETWEEN THE LINES (RCA, '92)
CALL OF THE WILD (RCA, '93)

TOP SONGS

YOU'VE GOT TO STAND FOR SOMETHING (RCA, '90, 6)
THERE AIN'T NOTHING WRONG WITH THE RADIO
    (RCA, '92, 1)
I WOULDN'T HAVE IT ANY OTHER WAY (RCA, '92, 5)
MY BLUE ANGEL (RCA, '93, 7)
WORKING MAN'S PH.D (RCA, '93, 7)
I GOT IT HONEST (RCA, '94, 15)

Additional Top 40 Country Songs: 2

"There Ain't Nothing Wrong with the Radio" stayed at Number One for three weeks in the spring of 1992, putting Tippin on the map to stay. (Interestingly, his record label later reported that in spite of his success and big record sales they still had to work hard with each release to convince some radio stations to play him.)

Tippin never compromised his style. "I can't sing any other way than I do," he says, "and I know what the people want to hear from me." He continued to succeed with songs like "Working Man's Ph.D." and the ballad "My Blue Angel," which he says sold enough copies of his second album, *Read Between the Lines,* to move it from gold to platinum.

MERLE TRAVIS

H e's noted for many important contributions to country music, not the least of which is the guitar style that bears his name. Travis picking, a technique in which the thumb plays alternating bass strings while fingers pluck melodies or chords, heavily influenced Chet Atkins and a generation of other guitar masters, from Doc Watson and Jerry Reed to Scotty Moore and Duane Eddy. Add that to Merle Travis' fame as the composer of the 1955 megahit "Sixteen Tons," his various other talents, and his colorful personality, and you end up with a character who was tailor-made for the Country Music Hall of Fame.

The guitar style evolved primarily in western Kentucky, where Travis (b. Nov. 29, 1917, Rosewood, Kentucky) spent his childhood. Traceable to African-American blues players, the fingerpicking technique passed—in one of several evolutionary threads—from little-known guitarist Arnold Shultz (who also influenced Bill Monroe) to Muhlenberg County thumbpick pioneer Kennedy Jones and Lester English and then to two coal miners named Mose Rager and Ike Everly—friends of Travis' coal miner father.

"My dad was a five-string banjo picker," Travis said in a *Guitar Player* interview. "He used his fingers on some tunes, but he just called it 'knockin' the banjo.' Later the college kids named it everything: clawhammer, drop-thumb, frailing. . . . Then there was a couple of fellas around town that played a lot of guitar. They played blues with a thumbpick. So I followed them around and learned to pick from them."

The two—Rager and Everly—taught Travis well. In 1936, Travis' picking began to attract attention in its own right, gaining him work with a succession of bands that included the Tennessee Tomcats and influential fiddler Clayton McMichen and his Georgia Wildcats. By 1937, Travis was a member of the Drifting Pioneers, with whom he would spend a number of years working on WLW radio in Cincinnati.

Those years laid down Travis' career foundation. His sound traveled the airwaves to many receptive ears (including those of a teenaged Chet Atkins, who set out to copy him). He also met a collection of musicians, several of whom—singer-banjoist Grandpa Jones and the Delmore brothers, Alton and Rabon—joined him in WLW broadcasts as the Brown's Ferry Four. With Jones he recorded in 1943 as the Sheppard Brothers—the first artists to cut sides for Syd Nathan's fledgling King label in Cincinnati.

World War II and a brief stint in the Marines intervened, but by mid-1944 Travis was back, and heading west. He settled in Los Angeles and embarked on what would be his most productive period. At first he worked live dates and small-label sessions with a variety of bands, many of which played western swing, and he managed to land bit parts in some movie westerns. He also became involved with Capitol Records as a session musician; by 1946 he was signed to the label as a recording artist.

Travis' first release, "Cincinnati Lou," was a number two chart hit with a flip side, "No Vacancy," that peaked at number three. The follow-up, "Divorce Me C.O.D.," took him to Number One.

It was later in that year—1946—that producer Lee Gillette nudged Travis to record a collection of rustic folk songs. Feeling he didn't know any, Travis ended up writing some himself, including a ballad about coal mining. "'Sixteen Tons,' I just threw that thing together; I had to make an album. It's nothing to it," he told *Guitar Player.* "I started thinking about an old saying around the mines. You know, people are always in debt. I heard my brother say, 'Hell, I can't afford to die. I owe my soul to the company store." With the revised line "Saint Peter don't you call me 'cause I can't go / I owe my soul to the company store," that song—and its parent album, the four-disc, 78 rpm *Folk Songs of the Hills*—arrived without fanfare in 1947.

That year, Travis returned to Number One on the country chart with "So Round, So Firm, So Fully Packed," another original. Months later he repeated the achievement with the composition "Smoke!

Smoke! Smoke! (That Cigarette)" on a recording by labelmate Tex Williams.

Travis' chart tenure was short but sweet—four more top 10 hits, two in the top 20, and out.

That was in 1949. But activity continued, including involvement with Cliffie Stone's "Hometown Jamboree" television program out of Pasadena, where he met a pre-fame Tennessee Ernie Ford. The meeting was providential. In 1955, by which time Ford was a national figure with his own NBC-TV series, Ford decided to record a song he'd performed on the "Jamboree." It was the mining ditty "Sixteen Tons," and it became a massive crossover hit, topping both the country and pop charts and focusing national attention on Travis' songwriting skill.

Meanwhile, Travis had been visible to film audiences through a role in *From Here to Eternity* (1953) as a soldier singing "Re-Enlistment Blues." In 1955 he revisited the country chart with "Wildwood Flower" as a featured performer with Hank Thompson and His Brazos Valley Boys. And in 1966 he entered the singles listing for the last time, with the song "John Henry, Jr."

By that time his status as a country elder statesman was well established, and it carried him through the remainder of his career. In 1970 he was voted into the Songwriters Hall of Fame. Five years later—the same year he joined Chet Atkins on the Grammy-winning *Atkins-Travis Traveling Show* album—he was named a Pioneer of Country Music by the Academy of Country Music. By 1979 he was a Country Hall of Famer (its Nashville headquarters displaying a prototype solid-body electric guitar that he'd conceived in the late 1940s).

Prior to his death of heart failure on October 20, 1983, there was a final flurry of activity: He made a series of recordings for the CMH label, one of which, 1981's *Travis Pickin'*, earned a Grammy nomination. In 1982 he appeared in the Clint Eastwood film *Honkytonk Man*.

Travis left behind a reputation not only as a musician but as a kind of country renaissance man, a writer and cartoonist as well as a picker, singer, songster, actor, and raconteur. "Sometimes people will say, 'I like your poem writing,'" Travis once observed, "or sometimes they'll say, 'I like your songwriting.' Then others will come along and go, 'Merle Travis. You're a folk singer, aren't you?' . . . I never have figured out what the heck I am."

RANDY TRAVIS

In the mid 1980s the Country Music Association conducted research that revealed that country fans wanted young performers who sang authentic, traditional country music. Enter Randy Travis, the epitome of what country fans wanted, and he delivered. With his country baritone voice that could span several octaves and his awe-shucks attitude, fresh-faced looks, and sensational songs, he exploded on the chart in '86 with solid, stone-country records like "1982" and "On the Other Hand." He's credited with finishing what Ricky Skaggs and George Strait started in the early 1980s, as he kicked the door open for the line of neotraditionalists that has paraded through since.

Travis (b. Randy Bruce Traywick, May 4, 1959, Marshville, North Carolina) was raised in a small town near Charlotte, the son of a jack-of-all-trades father. "He did everything," Travis remembers, "from construction to farming to raising various animals, cows, horses, and even turkeys." His father also raised a couple of kids with talent: Randy and his older brother Ricky. Travis was 10 when they started performing together as the Traywick Brothers. "We played together in bands up till I was 15," he says. "Ricky didn't like singing that much, so he played guitar and I'd do the singing."

The brothers had wild streaks that led them to run-ins with the law and resulted in Travis' brother

TOP ALBUMS

WALKIN' THE STRINGS (Capitol, '60)
TRAVIS PICKIN' (CMH, '81)
MERLE TRAVIS STORY—24 GREATEST HITS (CMH, '89)

TOP SONGS

CINCINNATI LOU (Capitol, '46, 2)
NO VACANCY (Capitol, '46, 3)
DIVORCE ME C.O.D. (Capitol, '46, 1)
SO ROUND, SO FIRM, SO FULLY PACKED
  (Capitol, '47, 1)
STEEL GUITAR RAG (Capitol, '47, 3)
THREE TIMES SEVEN (Capitol, '47, 4)
FAT GAL (Capitol, '47, 4)

Additional Top 40 Country Songs: 5

Randy Travis

TOP ALBUMS

STORMS OF LIFE (Warner, '86)
ALWAY AND FOREVER (Warner, '86)
OLD 8 X 10 (Warner, '88)
HEROES AND FRIENDS (Warner, '90)
THIS IS ME (Warner, '94)

TOP SONGS

ON THE OTHER HAND (Warner, '86, *1*)
FOREVER AND EVER, AMEN (Warner, '87, *1*)
I TOLD YOU SO (Warner, '88, *1*)
HARD ROCK BOTTOM OF YOUR HEART
   (Warner, '90, *1*)
WHISPER MY NAME (Warner, '94, *1*)

Additional Top 40 Country Songs: 19

song peaked at a disappointing number 67, but even though radio programmers had been reluctant to play such a traditional new artist, they apparently loved the record. They subsequently embraced his second release, "1982," and it hit number six. Then, in a brilliant move, the label rereleased "On the Other Hand." That set up the unique situation of having his first chart song become his third chart entry and his first Number One hit.

Between 1986 and '90 Travis scored 11 hits with such memorable tunes as "Diggin' Up Bones," "Forever and Ever, Amen" (which earned the Country Music Association Single of the Year award), "I Told You So," and "Deeper Than a Holler."

Behind the scenes, Travis' success was altering the industry. At a time when gold albums were tough to achieve, his were selling multiplatinum. That meant that he was reaching beyond the audience of country purists, appealing to the sector of disaffected pop fans who had begun to sample and like country music—the very audience that would drive the explosive growth of country music in the 1990s.

Travis eventually married Lib Hatcher (who continues to guide his career). He also took a year off, in 1993, to rest up from the road and concentrate on making films. His chart action dipped accordingly, but in 1994 he returned with three top 10 hits to reclaim his place in the country foreground. "I would like for people to think that I was one of a small group of people who came along and brought country music back to where it was supposed to be, as far as what kind of songs were being recorded and the way they were produced," says Travis. "Also, that I was part of that group of people that started selling to the pop audience, that younger generation of people."

going to jail. Randy seemed destined to follow him until he met a Charlotte club owner named Lib Hatcher. She hired him to sing in her Country City U.S.A. club—and did it just in time. "I was standing before a judge, who told me that the next time he saw me I'd better bring my toothbrush, because I was going to prison," Travis recalls. "But Lib stood up in front of that judge and assured him that I had a job, that I was changing and had a future, and he let me go."

In 1979, Travis recorded briefly for Paula Records and charted ("She's My Woman," number 91) under the name Randy Traywick.

Hatcher knew her protégé belonged.in Nashville. In 1982 she sold her club and took over as manager of a popular Nashville tourist spot, the restaurant-bar-club near Opryland Amusement Park called the Nashville Palace. Travis was both cook and crooner for the establishment. "I'd be flipping steaks or washing dishes one minute; the next minute they would call me out to emcee or sing a couple of songs," he says. "I worked there three and a half years right up till after my second single came out." During that time they released an independent album he recorded as Randy Ray just to sell to the tourists who came by the club. That record, and Hatcher's tireless assault of people in the record industry, finally landed him a contract with Warner Bros., who suggested the name change to Travis.

In the summer of 1985 they released "On the Other Hand," and a curious thing happened. The

TRAVIS TRITT

He's among the Big Four of the class of 1989—one of several artists, the others being Clint Black, Alan Jackson, and Garth Brooks, who issued their first singles that year and went on to become big stars. Travis Tritt was the hatless one, the R&B and southern rock dabbler who was still country to the core. It was at age 26 that he rose to the surface with "Country Club," a song released in the fall of 1989 that hit the top 10. Tritt would go on to transform country music with soulful ballads

Travis Tritt

like "Anymore," tunes with an attitude like "Here's a Quarter (Call Someone Who Cares)," and a charismatic stage presence that few peers could rival.

Tritt (b. James Travis Tritt, Feb. 9, 1963, Marietta, Georgia) was raised in a family where the father, who was a laborer all his life, didn't want his son to pursue music, while the mother wanted him to become a gospel singing star. That he loved music was not a secret to his family. "I had arguments with my folks because music was my only interest," Tritt recalls. "They got worried about me, because before school and the minute I got home from school I would glue myself to the record player and try to pick out tunes on my guitar." The guitar was a 12-string Epiphone his folks had given him for Christmas when he was 12 years old.

When Tritt turned 18 his father put pressure on him to give up music and settle for a practical life. "I tried hard to be like my family wanted," says Tritt. "I worked construction, house framing, made furniture, and worked at a printing company. I even got married twice and divorced twice by the time I turned 22."

Music remained a part-time job and a full-time dream until Tritt went to work at a heating and air-conditioning company. The vice president of the company was a good guitar player who had once thought about pursuing a music career but never took the chance. He told Tritt how much he regretted not at least giving it his best shot. That's when Tritt decided to quit trying to please his family and concentrate on music.

In 1982 he went to a private studio to record demos of some original material. The studio was in the home of a fellow named Danny Davenport, who worked for Warner Bros. Records' pop division. "I was just cutting a guitar vocal, and Danny walked in," remembers Tritt. "He heard the second song, and his jaw dropped to the floor, and he says, 'Kid, where in the world have you been?'"

Where Tritt had been was working the Atlanta area honky-tonk circuit, including a place called Miss Kitty's (Confederate Railroad played there regularly, and Tritt once sat in with a visiting artist named Billy Ray Cyrus). Tritt had also recorded some gospel music and briefly considered becoming a Christian artist to please his mother. The problem was, he had listened to too much southern rock, Eagles-style country rock, and straight country music—the sounds that would set the direction of his music over the next several years with the guidance

of mentor Davenport. "From '84 to '88 we were recording my first album basically, finding songs and working on them," Tritt says. Warner Bros. Nashville signed him up, and in 1990 his debut album, *Country Club*, hit the record stores.

There were three consecutive top 10 singles: "Country Club" (number nine), "Help Me Hold On" (Number One), and "I'm Gonna Be Somebody" (number two). He then dipped to number 28 with "Put Some Drive in Your Country," a driving southern-rock tune. Although a staple of his live show, it showed Tritt how far he could stretch country boundaries before alienating radio, and it led him to reassert his country credentials. "My true love, even in school, was always country music," he maintains. "I played rock and roll, bluegrass, Christian, but country was always my first love."

Tritt was one of a minority of new 1990s artists who opted not to wear a cowboy hat. Another was Marty Stuart. The two became close friends, mounted a successful tour called the No Hats Tour (1992), and scored a pair of top 10 duets, "The Whiskey Ain't Workin'" (number two, 1991) and "This One's Gonna Hurt You (For a Long, Long Time)" (number seven, 1992).

"On the list of assets and liabilities of Travis Tritt, you put at the top of that list live performance," says Ken Kragen, Tritt's manager (also the manager of Lionel Richie, Kenny Rogers, and Trisha Yearwood). "So when we wanted the industry in Nashville to understand who Travis was and such,

---

TOP ALBUMS

COUNTRY CLUB (Warner '90)
IT'S ALL ABOUT TO CHANGE (Warner, '91)
T-R-O-U-B-L-E (Warner, '92)
TEN FEET TALL AND BULLET PROOF (Warner, '94)

TOP SONGS

HELP ME HOLD ON (Warner, '90, *1*)
I'M GONNA BE SOMEBODY (Warner, '90, *2*)
HERE'S A QUARTER (CALL SOMEONE WHO CARES) (Warner, '91, *2*)
ANYMORE (Warner, '91, *1*)
CAN I TRUST YOU WITH MY HEART (Warner, '92, *1*)
FOOLISH PRIDE (Warner, '94, *1*)

Additional Top 40 Country Songs: 10

we did a live show for them. Every time when we wanted to launch a new album, we satellited a live show around the country."

Tritt's writing ability—demonstrated on the Number One hit "Foolish Pride"—adds the final brush stroke to a portrait of one of the most versatile stars of the 1990s.

ERNEST TUBB
. . . .

The Texas Troubadour, E.T. to his colleagues and fans, Ernest Tubb is a legendary figure in the history of country music. An innovative bandleader and musician, a composer of classic songs, a tireless touring performer, and an emotional vocalist, Tubb was not merely a part of country history, he created much of it. He put honky-tonk on the musical map, was one of the first country artists to use electric instruments and drums, helped make Nashville the recording capitol of the country world, and created a recorded legacy that is one of the most cherished in all of American music.

He was born Ernest Dale Tubb on February 9, 1914, on a cotton farm in Crisp, Texas. He didn't express much interest in music until age 13, when he began listening to the music of Jimmie Rodgers, the Singing Brakeman. Over the next few years, he became an ardent Rodgers fan and performed much of his hero's music at local talent shows and dances. When he was 20 he learned to play the guitar and moved to San Antonio, securing a job on a local radio program singing Rodgers songs.

While he was there he learned that Rodgers' widow, Carrie, lived in San Antonio, and he met her. She loaned Tubb her husband's guitar and subsequently set up an audition with RCA Records for him. He received a contract and recorded several songs, but his singles "The Passing of Jimmie Rodgers" and "Jimmie Rodgers' Last Thoughts" failed, and RCA didn't renew the deal. Undeterred, Tubb moved to Fort Worth in 1938 and became a performer on KGKO sponsored by the Gold Chain Flour company, a subsidiary of General Mills. For a weekly salary of $75, Tubb became the Gold Chain Troubadour.

His appearances in this new role brought him to the attention of Decca Records in Houston. In 1940, Carrie Rodgers set up an audition with the label, a deal was concluded, and Tubb was on his way.

In 1941 he recorded his own song "I'm Walking the Floor over You," which subsequently sold more than a million copies and established him as a major new artist. The record was also an important watershed in the evolution of country music, being one of the first by a country artist to use an electric guitar. Until that time, most of the genre's purists believed that electric instruments were too new for a "rural" form of music.

In that same year he appeared in the film *Fighting Buckaroo*. There would be Tubb appearances in other of the decade's films that had a western or country slant, including *Ridin' West* (1942), *Jamboree* (1943), and *Hollywood Barn Dance* (1947).

In 1943 he moved to Nashville and joined the Grand Ole Opry, one of the bastions of traditional country music. With his band, the Texas Troubadours, Tubb began to loosen up the musical framework of country. Just as he had introduced the electric guitar, Tubb was one of the first bandleaders to include a drummer as part of his sound. His fervent if somewhat raw vocals also brought the gut-busting feel of honky-tonk to the more melodic, folk-inspired bluegrass sound that was at the core of country music.

His move to Nashville also proved to be crucial to the city's evolving role as the capital of country music. Along with such artists as Eddie Arnold, Tubb was one of the first to use the city as the base for most of his recordings. He also put his own stamp on the burgeoning music center when he opened his Ernest Tubb Record Shop (near the

---

TOP SONGS
. . . .

TRY ME ONE MORE TIME (Decca, '44, *2, 15 Pop*)

SOLDIER'S LAST LETTER (Decca, '44, *1, 16 Pop*)

IT'S BEEN SO LONG DARLING (Decca, '45, *1, 23 Pop*)

RAINBOW AT MIDNIGHT (Decca, '46, *1*)

FILIPINO BABY (Decca, '46, *2*)

HAVE YOU EVER BEEN LONELY? (HAVE YOU EVER BEEN BLUE) (Decca, '48, *2*)

I'M BITING MY FINGERNAILS AND THINKING OF YOU (Decca, '49, *2, 30 Pop*)

SLIPPING AROUND (Decca, '49, *1, 17 Pop*)

BLUE CHRISTMAS (Decca, '49, *1, 23 Pop*)

GOODNIGHT IRENE (Decca, '50, *1, 10 Pop*)

Additional Top 40 Country Songs: 72

Ernest Tubb

Opry's Ryman Auditorium) in 1947 and began airing his "Midnight Jamboree" program on WSM. The program, which was broadcast after the Opry shows every Saturday night, became a Nashville tradition.

From the beginning of his career in the 1940s through the '70s, Tubb was one of country music's leading artists. In the '40s and '50s he amassed an astonishing 58 top 40 country hits, most of those making their way into the top 10. The classics included "It's Been So Long Darling," "Soldier's Last Letter," "Slipping Around," and "Goodnight Irene" (recorded with Red Foley).

Tubb was also an ardent touring artist. With the Texas Troubadours he performed onstage constantly, all over the world, touring as many as 300 days a year. As country lore has it, his fabled tour bus, Green Hornet Number One, was retired after it had passed two million miles, giving way to Green Hornet Number Two.

When he began to record his 1979 album, *Legend and Legacy,* a wide range of the biggest names in country music—most of whom he had influenced over the years—agreed to participate. The album yielded a new version of "I'm Walking the Floor over You" (with Merle Haggard, Chet Atkins, and Charlie Daniels) that hit number 31 on the country chart. It was his last entry before his death on September 6, 1984.

Tubb was elected to the Country Music Hall of Fame in 1965, the sixth artist to receive that honor.

TANYA TUCKER

Rolling Stone once referred to her as "the Holy Grail for prepubescent boys." That's because she was a darned cute, major country star by her mid-teens, thanks to such early hits as "Delta Dawn," "What's Your Mama's Name," and "Would You Lay with Me (In a Field of Stone)." A confident performer with a lusty, gritty voice, she was a consummate song person and dedicated pro from the beginning. With guts, a naughty-but-nice reputation, and tons of personality, she has maintained her status as one of the most important and influential country artists for over 20 years, with no signs of slowing down.

Tucker (b. Oct. 10, 1958, Seminole, Texas) was raised in west Texas, Arizona, Utah, and Nevada as

her father followed work. Her first exposure to music was taking saxophone lessons at age six. By age eight she knew she wanted to be a singer, and she even talked her way into a slot on Mel Tillis' road show when he came through their town. "He was sitting in a station wagon, wearing a Nudie suit," recalls Tucker, "and I went up to him and said, 'I just want to know how you get to be a country singer.' And he said, 'Well, are you any good?' I said, 'I don't know.' He said, 'Let me hear you sing.' So I sang something, and he said, 'How many songs do you want to sing on the show?' I sang four or five songs that night."

Encouraged by such events, she was nine years old when she went to her father, Beau, and made a bargain with him: "I told him that I wanted him to help me to become a country star, and that I would do anything it takes if he would help me do that." Tucker's father agreed and dedicated all his efforts to developing his daughter's talent. Her career became the family focus and the main source of income for Tucker, her parents, and two other children. When she was 12 the family drove from St. George, Utah, to Nevada. Says Tucker, "My dad came in the house one night and said, 'Come on, we're going to Las Vegas to record a demo on Tanya.'"

They had exactly $20 to their name when they headed off to Las Vegas. Tanya literally sang for a place to stay. She performed for a lady who rented them a trailer near town based on her belief that Tucker's voice could earn enough money to pay the rent. Tucker's father then took the few dollars they had left and spent two days and two nights playing keno until he had won $1,100, just enough to pay for the recording session. The gamble literally paid off, because it was that demo tape that made its way to Nashville record producer Billy Sherrill. He went all the way to Nevada to meet the little girl that belonged to that mature-sounding voice, "to see if I had the right look and the right attitude," she says.

In Nashville, signed to Columbia Records, Tucker proved to have amazing instincts about songs when she was offered one called "The Happiest Girl in the Whole U.S.A." (the song that launched the career of Donna Fargo). "We were in Sherrill's office," Tucker recalls, "and after the publisher played the song for me, everybody looked at me like, 'How does Mikey like it?' And I said, 'I like the song, but I just don't think it's for me.'" Sherrill agreed but was nonetheless impressed by his protégée's instincts. The very next day he played Tucker a song

Tanya Tucker

he'd seen Bette Midler sing the night before on "The Tonight Show" called "Delta Dawn."

"Delta Dawn" was released in the spring of 1972, and Tucker's producer tried to keep the age of his new singer a secret, "He wanted the song to go over because it was a great record, not because I was an oddity," she says. "Word kind of got out, but there are still people who think I was 41 when I cut it." The single rose to number six on the country chart.

The mature sound of her 13-year-old voice explains, in part, her instant success. It allowed her to perform songs no other teenager might have attempted, including her first three Number One hits, "What's Your Mama's Name," "Blood Red and Goin' Down" (a song about murder), and the suggestive "Would You Lay with Me (In a Field of Stone)." Tucker seemed to grow up quickly, but she remained the darling of country music thanks to chart-topping songs like "Lizzie and the Rainman" and "San Antonio Stroll," both from 1975.

Tucker turned 20 in 1978, and she briefly turned away from Nashville. With her pop-oriented album *TNT* she projected a sex-kitten image that alienated some sectors of her audience. She also earned something of a "bad girl" reputation through the late 1970s and '80s due to bouts with drugs and alcohol and her much-publicized stormy relationship with Glen Campbell.

Tucker's success on the country chart was spotty at best in the early 1980s, and in 1983 she quit recording and performing for the better part of three years. But she renewed her recording career in 1986, and beginning with "One Love at a Time" (number three in that year), she began her most consistent

period of success, placing nearly every release in the top 10.

Tucker entered the 1990s with a renewed desire to achieve as much as she could in country music. "I'm working so hard now because I want to build something for my children Presley Tanita and Beau Grayson," she said at the time. Twenty years after her debut, Tucker was as successful a hitmaker as ever, with nine of her singles charting in the top five (five of them at number two) between 1990 and 1993.

Tucker has given much of the credit for her success to her father, who has remained her personal manager throughout a career that has lasted longer than some of Tucker's current competitors have been alive.

CONWAY TWITTY

A onetime rock and roller with a Number One pop hit, Conway Twitty turned to country music in the mid-1960s. It was the right decision. Ten years after making the switch, he held a show business record of 40 Number One hits—12 of which he wrote or co-wrote—putting him among the most successful country artists of all time.

Five of those hits were created with Loretta Lynn, his partner for 10 years in one of country music's most popular and acclaimed recording duos.

Twitty's accomplishment rested on a seemingly simple formula: make records that aim to reach everyone—with special consideration for women. A Twitty song needed "a Conway Twitty melody, a Conway Twitty-type story, that doesn't put a woman down, that's always got something nice to say about the lady," as he told Tom Roland in *The Billboard Book of Number One Country Hits*. "I try to find a song that says something I know a man would like to say to a woman but doesn't know how. . . . He appreciates the fact that you've said it for him." Many are the Twitty song titles that reflect this approach, including "She Needs Someone to Hold Her (When She Cries)," "I Can't Believe She Gives It All to Me," and "I Want to Know You Before We Make Love."

Such was Twitty's unerring knack for picking hits that when a song brought controversy and a radio station boycott—as happened with 1973's "You've Never Been This Far Before" due to lyrics perceived

---

TOP SONGS

DELTA DAWN (Columbia, '72, 6)

WHAT'S YOUR MAMA'S NAME (Columbia, '73, 1)

BLOOD RED AND GOIN' DOWN (Columbia, '73, 1)

WOULD YOU LAY WITH ME (IN A FIELD OF STONE) (Columbia, '74, 1)

LIZZIE AND THE RAIN MAN (MCA, '75, 1, 37 Pop)

IF IT DON'T COME EASY (Capitol, '88, 1)

STRONG ENOUGH TO BEND (Capitol, '88, 1)

DOWN TO MY LAST TEARDROP (Capitol, '91, 2)

TWO SPARROWS IN A HURRICANE (Liberty, '92, 2)

SOON (Liberty, '93, 2)

Additional Top 40 Country Songs: 43

as sexually suggestive—he still shot to Number One, and even crossed over to the pop chart.

So consistently did Twitty hit the top of the charts that anything less was unusual, an exception to the rule. Of his 97 country chart singles, only 22 scored below the top 10.

Born Harold Lloyd Jenkins on September 1, 1933, in Friars Point, Mississippi, he grew up in Helena, Arkansas, and gained early exposure to guitar, the Grand Ole Opry, the blues, and gospel music. By age 10, Jenkins was a member of a group called the Phillips Country Ramblers and performing with them on radio. Also a baseball enthusiast, Jenkins was skilled enough by high school graduation to attract the offer of a contract with the Philadelphia Phillies.

Instead, he answered the call of the military draft. He went to serve in the Far East, during which time he performed in a group called the Cimarrons. When he returned to the States the Phillies offer was still open, but Jenkins, excited by Elvis Presley and the burgeoning rock and roll movement, opted instead to go into music.

He recorded for the same label that had launched Presley, Sun Records, but the sides weren't released. Then, with a name change to Conway Twitty (a combination of Conway, Arkansas, and Twitty, Texas), he cut some tracks for the Mercury label that were unsuccessful. Finally, on MGM Records, he released a song that he'd co-written called "It's Only Make Believe," and in 1958 it became a Number One pop record, paving the way for Twitty's continuing rock career (and appearances in the soon-to-be-cultish films *Sex Kittens Go to College* and *College Confidential,* both in 1960).

But the pop hits faded, and so did Twitty's interest. He wanted to become a country singer, and in 1963 he saw one of his tunes, "Walk Me to the Door," become a country hit for Ray Price. In 1965, Twitty walked off the stage of a New Jersey club in the middle of a performance to give up rock and move permanently into country. Before the year was out, he'd been heard on tape by veteran producer and Nashville Sound architect Owen Bradley and offered a contract as a country artist with Decca Records.

Four songs reached the country top 40 in 1966–67—enough to build some momentum, lend him country credibility, and bring him stage dates opening for the likes of George Jones, Loretta Lynn, and Buck Owens. Twitty's first top five country hit,

Conway Twitty

"The Image of Me," arrived in 1968. And "Next in Line," his next chart entry, became his first Number One hit, validating his shift to country, solidifying his relationship with Decca (until '73, when he moved to MCA), and providing a springboard for 24 more chart-topping songs created in collaboration with Owen Bradley.

Three more followed in 1968–69. Along the way, Twitty made a non-music business move, founding a fast-food concern he called Twitty Burgers. It didn't catch on, but many other Twitty ventures would, including his Twitty Bird Music publishing company and, years later (starting in 1982), his Twitty City nine-acre theme park in Hendersonville, Tennessee, complete with multimedia retrospective of Twitty career highlights.

In 1970 that career reached a high point with the release of "Hello Darling," a Twitty composition that became his fourth Number One and the first country song to put him back on the pop chart (at number 60).

Prior to that, he had already begun getting to know singer (and Twitty fan) Loretta Lynn. In 1971, having discovered their similar musical tastes, the two began working together. They were immediately successful, their first single, "After the Fire Is Gone," reaching Number One country and 56 pop and garnering a Grammy Award for Best Vocal Performance by a Group. The two continued to work together—scheduling roughly one record release per year to avoid conflict with their solo releases—and over a decade scored 12 hits while earning honors as the Country Music Association's Duo of the Year for four years in a row (1972–75) and the Academy of Country Music's Vocal Group of the Year for three years. They also partnered a successful booking agency, United Talent, starting in 1971. The duo's last chart single, "I Still Believe in Waltzes," peaked at number two in 1981.

But Twitty's chart run was far from over. Having ended his production relationship with Bradley in 1978, Twitty went on to new producers and new sounds, including a grittier, more soulful album, 1979's *Crosswinds*, that yielded three chart-topping songs. Ironically, given his early abandonment of pop, Twitty's later material included such pop-oriented songs as "Slow Hand" (previously a hit for the Pointer Sisters), "The Rose" (once cut by Bette Midler), "Heartache Tonight" (a onetime Eagles hit), and "Three Times a Lady" (a Commodores song). They seemed to complete a cycle for Twitty, neatly tying together the separate threads of his early and later career.

Twitty's recording activity continued into the 1990s, completing a 35-year run of success. After his death at the age of 59 on June 5, 1993, his voice

climbed the chart one last time on the single "I'm the Only Thing (I'll Hold Against You)" in 1993.

PORTER WAGONER

Porter Wagoner was one of the biggest stars on the country music scene of the 1960s and '70s. As a solo performer and as part of a vocal duo with the young Dolly Parton, he hit the charts on a steady basis, and his widely syndicated television program was an important force in popularizing his music—and, for that matter, country music in general—in the vast entertainment marketplace.

Wagoner was born on August 12, 1930, in West Plains, Missouri. He taught himself to play the guitar as a child and began singing along with country songs on the radio. In his late teens he got a job as a grocery clerk and, during lulls in the day, would sing and pick his guitar in the store. His boss heard him and agreed to put him on a local radio program to promote the store.

That program came to the attention of KWTO in Springfield, Missouri, in 1951, and he was offered his own show. A few months later, Red Foley began broadcasting his fabled "Ozark Jubilee" program on KWTO, and Wagoner was offered a part on the nationally televised edition of that show.

Based on the vast exposure provided by his performances on "Ozark Jubilee," Wagoner secured a record contract with RCA in 1954. He was a hit from the start, with his 1954 debut release, "Company's Comin'," hitting the top 10 on the country chart. He topped that list with "A Satisfied Mind" in 1955 and joined the Grand Ole Opry in 1957.

That made him a part of the country establishment, and as such he continued to have hits through the rest of the 1950s with "What Would You Do? (If Jesus Came to Your House)," "I Thought I Heard You Call My Name," and four other singles in the top 30.

But it was with the start of his own television program in 1961 that Wagoner became a major country artist. Performing with his group, the Wagonmasters, and vocal sidekick Norma Jean, Wagoner set the tone and the visual style for much of country music. With his slicked-up hairdo and his sequined and spangled outfits (that came with sparkling depictions of various cowboys symbols such as brands

TOP ALBUMS

NUMBER ONES (MCA, '82)
THE VERY BEST OF CONWAY TWITTY AND LORETTA LYNN (MCA, '79)

TOP SONGS

NEXT IN LINE (Decca, '68, 1)
HELLO DARLIN' (Decca, '70, 1)
AFTER THE FIRE IS GONE (with Loretta Lynn, Decca, '71, 1)
SHE NEEDS SOMEONE TO HOLD HER (WHEN SHE CRIES) (Decca, '72, 1)
YOU'VE NEVER BEEN THIS FAR BEFORE (MCA, '73, 1, 22 Pop)
I SEE THE WANT TO IN YOUR EYES (MCA, '74, 1)
TOUCH THE HAND (MCA, '75, 1)
HAPPY BIRTHDAY DARLIN' (MCA, '79, 1)

Additional Top 40 Country Songs: 77

and cactus), Wagoner became the symbol of the contemporary country performer.

While his music was hardly revolutionary, Wagoner did provide a few innovations. On one of his shows, Buck Tren became the first major picker to use an electric banjo in country music. And when Norma Jean was dismissed from the show and replaced by Dolly Parton, Wagoner also began to use contemporary pop-inflected flourishes in his music.

In fact, Parton's addition was a watershed for both of their careers. It was Parton's first big break, and it increased the fan base of Wagoner and his program. When that program debuted it hit 18 markets, primarily in the South. By the late 1960s it was syndicated in 100 markets in the U.S. and Canada.

Wagoner's new career with Parton was an immediate success on the charts. Their debut hit, "The Last Thing on My Mind," reached number seven in 1967, and they consistently hit the top 10 over the course of the succeeding seven years. In 1968 they were named the Vocal Group of the Year by the Country Music Association and in 1970 and '71 the CMA's Vocal Duo of the Year.

Wagoner continued to have hits of his own. In 1968 he made the country top 10 three times with "Be Proud of Your Man," "Big Wind," and "The Carroll County Incident." And the success of his television program established Wagoner and the Wagonmasters as one of the most popular touring acts in country music.

TOP ALBUMS

Down in the Alley (RCA, '65)
The Carroll County Incident (RCA, '68)

TOP SONGS

A Satisfied Mind (RCA, '55, 1)
Eat, Drink, and Be Merry (Tomorrow You'll Cry) (RCA, '55, 3)
Misery Loves Company (RCA, '62, 1)
Skid Row Joe (RCA, '65, 3)
The Cold Hard Facts of Life (RCA, '67, 2)
The Carroll County Incident (RCA, '68, 2)

Porter Wagoner and Dolly Parton:
Please Don't Stop Loving Me (RCA, '74, 1)
Making Plans (RCA, '80, 2)

Additional Top 40 Country Songs: 56

In 1974 he and Parton hit the top of the charts with "Please Don't Stop Loving Me." But problems began to emerge. That same year, Parton left the program and the duo to pursue a solo career.

From that point, Wagoner's musical career began to fade. He continued to have hits in the 1970s and into the '80s, especially with occasional recordings in duet with Parton. But he became increasingly eclipsed by a new generation of country artists. Now semi-retired from the music scene, Wagoner is a successful businessman in Nashville.

CLAY WALKER

He went to high school with Mark Chesnutt, played on the same basketball team as Tracy Byrd, and eventually followed those two other natives of the Beaumont, Texas, area into country music stardom. Clay Walker made a spectacular entrance in 1993, taking his first single, "What's It to You," all the way to Number One. Within two years he had put five songs at the top of the chart, establishing himself as one of the most important young singer-songwriters to appear in the mid-'90s.

Walker (b. Aug. 19, 1969, Beaumont, Texas) grew up the namesake of a country music–singing father. Walker was nine years old when his father taught him to play guitar. "From that moment on it was only a matter of *when*, not *if*, I would become a country performer," Walker says. He wrote his first song at age 15. Then, inspired by a successful stint performing at the nearby Jones Country theme park, he declared his independence and moved out of his house at age 17.

Predictably, he found the going tough. "I was sitting around my living room in my new apartment, but I had no furniture," he admits. "I used my P.A. system for furniture. I remember I had a big Peavey column-speaker stack for a couch. I used an amplifier for a table, and I slept in a sleeping bag."

When he couldn't get enough club work in Beaumont, Walker took to the road. "I went all over the Texas, Oklahoma, and Louisiana area," he recalls. "Then I went up to Canada. I toured all over the U.S. and Canada and just worked real hard for several years." By the early 1990s he was back in Beaumont, where his seasoning on the road paid off and he was able to find steady work.

His father had predicted that if Walker stayed in one place long enough, the right people would discover him, and he was right. A local businessman who had connections to Nashville brought him to the attention of Giant Records chief James Stroud, who traveled to Beaumont to meet Walker. "I'm not the greatest singer, writer, or performer," Walker says, "but I'm strong enough in all those areas that I think I looked like a pretty good package to Stroud. He signed me up and became my producer."

A "pretty good package" proved to be an accurate assessment of Walker's potential when his first release shot to the top of the country chart. It happened again in early 1994 with his second single, a song he wrote called "Live Until I Die." At the same time, through his manager Irv Woolsey (who discovered and manages George Strait), Walker was able to get his live performance before huge audiences by opening shows for Strait through much of 1994. Smooth, confident, and charismatic in concert, Walker projected a laid-back, wholesome image that is similar to Strait's and that attracted a growing legion of fans.

By 1995, Walker's success as a touring act and hitmaker had pushed both his self-titled debut album and his second release, *If I Could Make a Living*, past platinum status.

Walker's experience exemplifies the volatility of country careers in the 1990s. In two years he grew from a 23-year-old virtual unknown to a national headliner complete with a full road complement of three buses and semi-tractor-trailer trucks hauling full sound and lighting equipment. "There is a lot of responsibility that comes along with success," Walker reports. "Back in my Beaumont honky-tonk days

Clay Walker

the most responsibility I had was to show up on time. Now I have 50 people depending on me for their living. . . . When I look around me, I realize everything I have, the buses, the money, that's all temporary. The people are permanent, and that's the way I measure success, by the way I treat other people and the way they treat me."

STEVE WARINER

One of country music's triple-threat entertainers, a top guitarist, songwriter, and vocalist, Steve Wariner was a protégé of three country stars, Dottie West, Bob Luman, and Chet Atkins, before he began his own recording career in the late 1970s. He broke through in the early '80s with "Your Memory" (his first top 10 hit) and "All Roads Lead to Me" (his first Number One). It was in the latter part of the 1980s, when he amassed eight more chart-topping songs, that he assured his place as one of country music's leading performers.

Steve Noel Wariner was born on Christmas Day, 1954, in Noblesville, Indiana, the son of a part-time professional musician. Roy Wariner was a weekend warrior who played all the local clubs, and if his children showed interest in the country music he was

TOP ALBUMS

CLAY WALKER (Giant, '93)
IF I COULD MAKE A LIVING (Giant, '94)

TOP SONGS

WHAT'S IT TO YOU (Giant, '93, 1)
LIVE UNTIL I DIE (Giant, '93, 1)
DREAMING WITH MY EYES OPEN (Giant, '94, 1)
IF I COULD MAKE A LIVING (Giant, '94, 1)
THIS WOMAN AND THIS MAN (Giant, '95, 1)

Additional Top 40 Country Songs: 2

making, he would put them in the band. "I started singing in public when I was 11 years old," Wariner recalls. "My brother played bass and I played drums in dad's band. He let me sing a couple of songs each night." From that start, Wariner picked up the bass and guitar and became one of the hottest pickers and singers in mid-Indiana.

His big break came at 17, when he attended a local appearance by country star Dottie West. "The opening act was a band I'd worked with, and they got me up to do a song with them. I sang a song called 'Shelly's Winter Love.' Dottie's daughter is named Shelly, and I guess she heard the song, and next thing I know, Dottie is out on stage singing with me." They ended up performing three songs together, and Dottie offered Steve a job as a bass player in her band. After convincing his parents it was a good thing, Wariner joined Dottie West on the road, where he earned his high school diploma by correspondence, taking his final exams in the back of her tour bus as it went down the highway. He worked with West from 1971 through '74.

From there, Wariner went to work as a sideman for Grand Ole Opry star Bob Luman. "Luman was a great live performer," says Wariner. "I learned a lot from him about how to work with an audience."

At a recording session for Luman in 1976, Wariner befriended guitarist Paul Yandell. He was impressed with Wariner's voice and musicianship and brought him to the attention of RCA Records executive Chet Atkins. Legendary picker-producer Atkins not only brought Wariner to the label but

Steve Wariner

also worked with him to improve his guitar playing. "Chet was a good role model," Wariner remembers, "and I picked up a lot about practicing and preparation before performing." Between his signing and the start of his solo concertizing, Wariner toured with Atkins whenever he appeared in concert.

Wariner's recording career got off to a slow start. He posted six sub-40 chart records between 1978 and late '80 before connecting with three top 10s that included his first Number One record. He then charted with "Midnight Fire" (number five, 1984) and "Lonely Women Make Good Lovers" (number four, 1983) before switching to MCA Records (where he remained until signing with Arista Records in 1991).

The MCA years (1984 to '91) were his most fruitful. Beginning with the number three "What I Didn't Do," he enjoyed a run of 18 consecutive top 10 songs that included such Number One hits as "Some Fools Never Learn," "The Weekend," and "You Can Dream of Me." One of the top 10s he scored during this period was a duet ("The Hand That Rocks the Cradle," number six, 1987) with the man he was most often compared to vocally, Glen Campbell.

Although Wariner's writing is often overlooked, he wrote or co-wrote a number of his biggest hits,

TOP ALBUMS

LIFE'S HIGHWAY (MCA, '85)
GREATEST HITS VOL. II (MCA, '91)
I AM READY (Arista, '91)

TOP SONGS

SOME FOOLS NEVER LEARN (MCA, '85, 1)
YOU CAN DREAM ON ME (MCA, '85, 1)
SMALL TOWN GIRL (MCA, '86, 1)
THE WEEKEND (MCA, '87, 1)
LYNDA (MCA, '87, 1)
WHERE DID I GO WRONG (MCA, '89, 1)
I GOT DREAMS (MCA, '89, 1)

Additional Top 40 Country Songs: 30

including "Hold On," "Precious Thing," and "I Should Be with You."

For most of his recording career, Wariner was primarily a singles artist, meaning he scored big chart hits but not huge album sales. While his albums always sold respectably, he didn't collect his first gold record until the 1994 certification of his 1991 Arista album, *I Am Ready*.

GENE WATSON

In 1975 he hit number three with "Love in the Hot Afternoon" and decided he could finally quit his job at a Houston auto body repair shop. During the late 1970s through the late '80s Gene Watson became one of the most consistent chart hitters in the business with songs like "Paper Rosie," "Farewell Party," and "Fourteen Carat Mind." Often overlooked, his pure country voice earned him the respect of his fans and peers alike as one of the finest vocalists to ever sing country music.

Watson (b. Gary Gene Watson, Oct. 11, 1943, Palestine, Texas) was raised in a poor family that traveled from one sawmill town to another to find work in the mills or picking crops. The converted school bus they rode in was also home when they got to where they were going. They finally settled in Paris, Texas, where the family engaged in the auto salvage business. "I would get out of school and ride my bicycle to work, where I'd take cars apart to sell the used parts," Watson remembers.

It was a hard life, but the family escaped the misery through music. "We did most of our singing in the Pentecostal church," says Watson. "My dad also played the blues. A lot of blacks lived around sawmills, and I used to sing a lot of black kind of blues. . . . Singing was a way of life back then. Music came naturally to me. I did it all the time. I couldn't imagine anybody would ever pay me for doing it." He was a teenager the first time he did get paid for his talent. He and his brother performed in Fort Worth in an event called "Cow Town Hoedown." Later, Gene formed a band with his brothers and cousins called Gene Watson and the Other Four.

Watson settled in the Houston area, and for several years he was mostly a weekend performer. He got married at 18, and to support his family he had to hold down a steady job at Southwest Lincoln-Mercury as assistant manager of the body repair and paint shop. He recorded briefly for small labels—Tonka in 1965 and Resco in '74. In late '74, Resco released Watson's version of a much-recorded song called "Love in the Hot Afternoon." "Jim Ed Brown, Willie Nelson, and I think Waylon Jennings had cuts on it, but it was never a hit," Watson says. The song brought him to the attention of Capitol Records, who signed him up and rereleased the record under their label in '75. "When that song hit, I was still working at the body shop, but I put my tools away and haven't used them since."

More top 10 hits followed, including "Where Love Begins" (number five, 1975), "You Could Know As Much About a Stranger" (number 10, 1976), and "Paper Rosie" (three, 1977).

Watson was not the breakout kind of success you find today. He wasn't flashy; just a simple, blue-collar guy who entertained with the sheer power of his voice. He was a "utility" hitter who could be counted on to chart in the top 40 and often the top 10 (totaling 21 top 10 hits from 1975 to 88). He scored three high-impact hits in 1979 alone—"Farewell Party" (number five), "Pick the Wildwood Flower" (five), and "Should I Come Home (Or Should I Go Crazy)" (three)—but spread a bunch more over a long-term career.

In the early 1980s, when he felt Capitol Records was taking him for granted, Watson switched to MCA. "I asked Capitol for some extra promotion effort," he explains, "and they told me, 'Gene, you

---

TOP ALBUMS

THE BEST OF GENE WATSON (Capitol, '78)
GREATEST HITS (MCA, '85)
TEXAS SATURDAY NIGHT (MCA/Curb, '86)

TOP SONGS

LOVE IN THE HOT AFTERNOON (Capitol, '75, 3)
FAREWELL PARTY (Capitol, '79, 5)
PICK THE WILDWOOD FLOWER (Capitol, '79, 5)
SHOULD I COME HOME (OR SHOULD I GO CRAZY)
   (Capitol, '79, 3)
FOURTEEN CARAT MIND (MCA, '81, 1)
YOU'RE OUT DOING WHAT I'M HERE DOING
   WITHOUT (MCA, '83, 2)
MEMORIES TO BURN (Epic, '85, 5)

Additional Top 40 Country Songs: 30

KITTY WELLS

Gene Watson

The Queen of Country Music began as an unlikely honky-tonk singer, entering a rowdy, raunchy, male-dominated world from a life as a devoted wife and mother who'd learned to sing in church. But Kitty Wells, starting with her 1952 Number One hit, "It Wasn't God Who Made Honky Tonk Angels," brought a new perspective—a female perspective—to the popular honky-tonk topics of cheatin', drinkin', and losin'. With her plaintive vocal twang and emotional but restrained delivery, she conveyed her message to a wide audience. By doing it consistently over a long career—and by being the first woman to score a Number One country hit—she paved the way for all successful female country singers to follow.

Musically, Wells' world was one of dim lights, thick smoke, and lovers doing each other wrong in songs like "Cheatin's a Sin," "Lonely Side of Town," "Jealousy," "Your Wild Life's Gonna Get You Down," "Heartbreak U.S.A.," "She's No Angel," "Unloved Unwanted," and "This White Circle on My Finger."

But offstage, Wells appeared a model of decency and old-world values, married to the same man since teenhood and projecting an image of sweetness and quiet dignity.

Born Muriel Ellen Deason in Nashville on August 30, 1919, she picked up guitar from listening to her father and developed her voice in part by singing gospel music. By the mid-1930s—in her teens—she was on WSIX radio in Nashville crooning with her siblings under the name the Deason Sisters.

Musician Johnnie Wright came into her life, and she married him in 1937. It was the beginning of a long professional as well as romantic involvement. In an early stage, she and he performed with his sister Louise as Johnnie Wright and the Harmony Girls. Meanwhile, Johnnie also forged a musical partnership with his brother-in-law, Jack Anglin. Around 1940, calling themselves Johnnie and Jack, they set out to find fortune and fame in the music business.

For a while they caravanned from town to southern town, with Wells (renamed by Johnnie from a traditional tune about "Sweet Kitty Wells") adding vocals to their act. When they did a stint on the Grand Ole Opry in 1946–47, Wells mostly stayed home and took care of the couple's baby boy. But she joined Johnnie and Jack in a lengthy tenure on

sell consistently enough, we don't need to spend any more money on you.' So I left them." Watson was seeking a Number One record when he made that move. He finally got it with his third MCA release, 1981's "Fourteen Carat Mind."

In the late 1980s, Watson became one of many veteran performers who lost priority status at a label due to an influx of younger artists. He was one of the few to have the head of his record label at the time (Epic) tell him personally that's what had happened. "I talked to him long distance on the phone," Watson recalls. "He said, 'We're into new artist development. I might as well be honest with you. We're developing new artists, and it's at your expense.'" In 1988, Watson moved again—this time to Warner Bros.—and in early '89 scored the number five hit, "Don't Waste It on the Blues."

Watson currently records for the big Nashville independent label Step One Records and is still ranked by many as one of the best singers in the business.

Kitty Wells with husband Johnny Wright and son Bobby

WSM-Shreveport's "Louisiana Hayride" program starting in 1948.

Wells cut some tracks for RCA (with the Johnnie and Jack band backing) in 1949, but they were not successful. She was all but ready to pack it in when Paul Cohen at Decca Records—having been approached by Johnnie—came up with a tune he thought would be good for her to record. It was an answer song to Hank Thompson's recent ditty "The Wild Side of Life," which bemoaned the fate of men at the hands of faithless women and contained the line "I didn't know God made honky tonk angels." The 1952 Wells single gave the topic a female spin, casting men as the source of women's problems. "It Wasn't God Who Made Honky Tonk Angels" outsold the Thompson disc, established Wells as a star, and forever laid country music open to the female point of view, which Wells soon expressed again in "Paying for That Back Street Affair," her follow-up chart single and an answer to Webb Pierce's "Back Street Affair."

The remainder of the 1950s proved to be a professional heyday for Wells. She scored 23 top 10 hits during that period, including four in duet with country radio star Red Foley. And although the rankings of her singles would dip in later years, Wells would build an impressive overall track record: 61 top 40 hits in her lifetime, with 35 in the top 10.

Among the women who entered country music through the door that Wells opened was Patsy Cline, whose more urban, pop-styled Nashville Sound would bring contrast to Wells' hard-country honky-tonk. It, too, would be vastly influential, making Cline a competitor for the crown of country queen.

Wells, after scoring her third and last Number One hit with 1961's "Heartbreak U.S.A." (1954's Foley duet, "One by One," had been her second), remained on the country chart through the 1970s. Her last charting single was a 1979 version of "The Wild Side of Life," the song she'd answered with her first hit.

Wells was inducted into the Country Music Hall of Fame in 1974. Thereafter, she continued to tour with Johnnie, appear on the Grand Ole Opry, and run a museum on the outskirts of Nashville. In 1987 she sang with Loretta Lynn, Brenda Lee, and newcomer k.d. lang on a track called "Honky-Tonk Angels Medley," produced by veteran Wells producer Owen Bradley for lang's *Shadowlands* album. And in 1991, Wells was honored with a Grammy Lifetime Achievement Award.

DOTTIE WEST

Dottie West's career was as vast as it was varied. A top solo performer and a successful duo partner with Kenny Rogers and others, West was also a talented arranger and songwriter as well as an award-winning composer of songs for commercials, most notably the "Country Sunshine" campaign for Coca-Cola.

West (b. Dorothy Marie Marsh, Oct. 11, 1932, McMinnville, Tennessee) was the oldest of 10 children. Raised on the family farm, she grew up learning to work the cotton and sugarcane fields. But she was also talented as a musician, and she eventually gained a degree in music from Tennessee Tech in the 1950s.

While she was pursuing her studies, she met and fell in love with fellow student Bill West, a steel guitar player. The two began performing onstage at local college shows. After graduation they got married and moved to Cleveland, where they appeared on local television programs in the mid-'50s.

During a trip to Nashville in 1959 they were signed by Starday Records. When their initial releases failed, West switched to the Atlantic label, but the results were equally disappointing. She finally scored when she moved to RCA in 1963. "Let Me Off at the Corner," her RCA debut, hit the top 30.

TOP ALBUMS

THE GOLDEN YEARS (Rounder, '82)
COUNTRY HIT PARADE (Stetson, '87)

TOP SONGS

IT WASN'T GOD WHO MADE HONKY TONK ANGELS (Decca, '52, 1)
ONE BY ONE (with Red Foley, Decca, '54, 1)
MAKIN' BELIEVE (Decca, '55, 2)
SEARCHING (FOR SOMEONE LIKE YOU) (Decca, '56, 3)
YOU AND ME (with Red Foley, Decca, '56, 3)
I CAN'T STOP LOVING YOU (Decca, '58, 3)
JEALOUSY (Decca, '58, 7)
HEARTBREAK U.S.A. (Decca, '61, 1)

Additional Top 40 Country Songs: 53

Dottie West

Can't Take It Anymore" with Don Gibson, followed by 1971's "Slowly" with Jimmy Dean. During that time she also played a role in establishing the career of Larry Gatlin, who was a vocalist on her hit "Just What I've Been Looking For" in 1974.

She delved into writing music for commercials and found success, her "Country Sunshine" song for Coca-Cola hitting number two on the country chart in its release as a single in 1973.

But it was in the late '70s, when she teamed with Kenny Rogers, that West reached the peak of her success. She had displayed a pop sensibility over the course of her career, and with Rogers—who was enroute to becoming one of the all-time great crossover artists—she used it to commercially rewarding ends. From 1978 to 1984 West and Rogers hit the top 20 of the country chart six times and went all the way to Number One with "Every Time Two Fools Collide," "All I Ever Need Is You," and "What Are We Doin' in Love." Along the way they were named Vocal Duo of the Year in 1978 and 1979 by the Country Music Association.

West remained successful on her own, hitting the charts on a consistent basis with such hits as "A Lesson in Leavin'" and "Are You Happy Baby?" Her daughter Shelly West (by her first husband) also became a country performer, first with vocal partner David Frizzell and then as a solo artist.

In the mid-1980s, after a full two decades of hitmaking, West began to recede from the country music foreground. She died on September 4, 1991, from injuries suffered in an automobile crash.

When her subsequent release, "Love Is No Excuse," hit the top 10 in 1964 her career was established. Its momentum increased—gaining her recognition for both singing and songwriting—with "Here Comes My Baby," a number 10 country hit for West and a pop hit in a version by Perry Como. Her record won a Grammy Award in the category of Best Country and Western Vocal Performance, Female.

Through the remainder of the 1960s, West pursued a wide range of musical and creative activities as her career mushroomed. She hit the charts with songs like "Would You Hold It Against Me" and "Paper Mansions." She was an arranger with the Memphis and Kansas City symphony orchestras. And she appeared in various films, including *Second Fiddle to a Steel Guitar* and *There's a Still on the Hill*.

In the early '70s she began performing vocal duets. The first to reach the country chart was "Til I

TOP SONGS

Would You Hold It Against Me (RCA, '66, 5)
Rings of Gold (RCA, '69, 2)
Country Sunshine (RCA, '73, 2)
A Lesson in Leavin' (United Artists, '80, 1)
Are You Happy Baby? (Liberty, '80, 1)

Kenny Rogers and Dottie West:
Every Time Two Fools Collide (United Artists, '78, 1)
Anyone Who Isn't Me Tonight
   (United Artists, '78, 2)
All I Ever Need Is You (United Artists, '79, 1)
Til I Can Make It on My Own (United Artists, '79, 3)
What Are We Doin' in Love (Liberty, '81, 1, 14 Pop)

Additional Top 40 Country Songs: 35

Keith Whitley

KEITH WHITLEY

His life and career were cut short in 1989, and he recorded only five solo albums, but Keith Whitley's prestige continues to build in the 1990s. The 1994 release of *Keith Whitley: A Tribute Album* by BNA Entertainment (featuring Whitley songs recorded by Alan Jackson, Tracy Lawrence, and others) is only the most obvious indicator of his growing recognition. He died just shy of his thirty-fifth birthday, but in a career that encompassed childhood performing, years of playing bluegrass, and five consecutive Number One country hits, he accomplished far more than most, and in the process influenced many.

He was born Jessie Keith Whitley in Sandy Hook, Kentucky, on July 1, 1954. (His birth date is often incorrectly given as 1955.) It didn't take his family long to realize they had a talented boy on their hands. "I started out singing in tent shows at two, three years old," Whitley said. "That sounds early, but I was really singing before I could walk real good. I don't remember not singing." Whitley credited his early start to his family. "My mother played guitar and piano. My dad played harmonica. My grandfather was a real good, old-time clawhammer banjo player. He was a big influence on my music." By age four, Whitley had put together a little act that won him $25 in a talent contest. "I had a big black cowboy hat and toy Fanner Fifty guns, and I'd walk out onstage and sing Marty Robbins' 'Big Iron.' Then I'd unbuckle the gun belt and let it fall on the floor, take off my cowboy hat, and sing the old George Jones gospel hymn, 'A Wandering Soul' . . . and one of the judges told my dad, 'Get that boy a guitar.'"

At age eight he was playing guitar and singing on the Buddy Starcher radio show out of Charleston, West Virginia. At 13 he put together the first of several bluegrass bands, although he once stated that his heart always belonged to country music: "There just weren't any steel players in my part of Kentucky, so if you wanted to make music you played bluegrass."

One of the bands he formed was called the Lonesome Mountain Boys. It included a great young picker and singer from 20 miles away named Ricky Skaggs. Whitley and Skaggs became friends and ended up forming a duet act that sang mostly Stanley Brothers material. After Carter Stanley died, Ralph Stanley hired Whitley and Skaggs for his Clinch Mountain Boys band. Between 1970 and '72, Whitley recorded seven albums with Stanley, including *Crying from the Cross,* the bluegrass Album of the Year in 1971. From 1973 to '75, Whitley worked with a couple of different bands before returning to the Clinch Mountain Boys, with whom he recorded five more albums before departing the group again in '77. His last job before going solo was with J. D. Crowe and the New South from 1978 to '82. He recorded three albums with that group. "The first two albums were a mix of bluegrass and country," Whitley noted. "But the third on Rounder Records, *Somewhere Between,* was a straight-ahead country album. It was that album that got into people's hands at RCA Records and helped me get my deal in '84."

Whitley got off to a shaky start, initially recording hard-core country for his debut album, *Hard Act to Follow,* and posting only three singles at sub-40 positions on the country chart. But his second album, *L.A. to Miami,* yielded the number 14 hit "Miami, My Amy" in early '86. That broke the ice, and he followed up with three top 10s: "Ten Feet Away" (number nine, 1986), "Homecoming '63" (number nine, 1986), and "Hard Livin'" (number 10, 1987).

In spite of that success, Whitley was unhappy with the uptown-country direction his music was taking. In late 1987 he talked his label into shelving a newly recorded album that contained more of the same. He said at the time, "I just went to Joe Gallante [head of RCA Nashville] and said this music just isn't me. They understood and let me go back in with another producer." Whitley chose Garth Fundis, who had recorded New Grass Revival and Don Williams. The result was the album *Don't Close Your Eyes,* from which came Whitley's first three Number One songs, "Don't Close Your Eyes," "When You Say Nothing at All," and "I'm No Stranger to the Rain"—all released before he died of an alcohol overdose on May 9, 1989.

Just before he died, Whitley had completed *I Wonder Do You Think of Me,* his fourth RCA album, which yielded three posthumous top 10 hits, including the Number One songs "I Wonder Do You Think of Me" and "It Ain't Nothing."

Whitley had married singer Lorrie Morgan in 1986, and her career was just taking off when he died. She was at a loss to explain the drinking problem that ultimately killed him. "He never drank in public, and he couldn't tell me why he drank," she says. "I think there was some deep hidden reason he couldn't reveal, but now we'll never know." What remains are his songs and his musical impact, which reverberates to this day through the music of a new generation of country performers like Tracy Lawrence and Tim McGraw.

TOP ALBUMS

L.A. to Miami (RCA, '87)
Don't Close Your Eyes (RCA, '88)
I Wonder Do You Think of Me (RCA, '89)
Kentucky Bluebird (RCA, '91)

TOP SONGS

Don't Close Your Eyes (RCA, '88, 1)
When You Say Nothing at All (RCA, '88, 1)
I'm No Stranger to the Rain (RCA, '89, 1)
I Wonder Do You Think of Me (RCA, '89, 1)
It Ain't Nothin' (RCA, '89, 1)
I'm Over You (RCA, '90, 1)

Additional Top 40 Country Songs: 9

DON WILLIAMS

With salt-and-pepper beard, modest cowboy hat, and plain garb, Don Williams has a simple and down-home appearance that is anything but slick. His music is the same way. An unfettered, straightforward country-pop sound surrounding his deep and laid-back vocal, it established its own corner of calm in '70s and '80s country music, and it brought Williams an impressive 17 Number One hits on the country chart.

As popular as he was in the United States, Williams was also a major hit in Europe and especially England, where in 1980 he was named Artist of the Decade in *Country Music People* magazine.

Williams (b. May 27, 1939, Floydada, Texas) first came to public attention as the lead singer of a folk trio, the Pozo-Seco Singers, that included fellow Texans Susan Taylor and Lofton Kline. Formed in 1964, the singers made it to the pop charts with six songs on Columbia Records in 1966 and '67. Two of them, "I Can Make It with You" and "Look What You've Done," were in the top 40. The group stayed, together for seven years, disbanding in 1971.

Convinced of neither the commercial viability of his voice nor the desirability of glittering stardom, Williams headed to Nashville with the aim of working as a songwriter. In time he landed a job with Jack Music, Inc. (JMI), a business run by country singer Jack Clement. Although Williams began there as a writer and song plugger, he recorded demos for JMI and in 1972 began issuing singles as a solo artist.

The market performance of his debut, "Don't You Believe," gave little reason to believe that anything approaching major success would follow. But five subsequent singles made the top 20 in the country chart, and one of them—"We Should Be Together"—reached number five.

Meanwhile, Williams' first album, *Don Williams Vol. 1,* introduced the spare sonic approach with which he would come to be identified. "Anything I feel is a distraction from the song, I just try to avoid," he once told writer Kelly Delaney. "And so I try to have songs that I feel are good enough that I don't have to come up with a super-slick instrumentation to make it happen."

Williams departed from the Clement organization and signed with Dot Records in 1974. The initial release for the label proved to be his breakthrough: "I Wouldn't Want to Live If You Didn't Love Me" became Williams' first Number One. It also

Don Williams

launched an amazing run of hits: from mid-1974 through 1991, 44 of Williams' 48 chart singles reached the top 10. By the time his most successful single arrived in 1980, a million seller that reached Number One country and number 24 pop; it was appropriate that the title was "I Believe in You."

There were music industry accolades. In 1978, Williams was voted the Country Music Association's Male Vocalist of the Year, and the single "Tulsa Time" was named the Academy of Country Music's Single of the Year. By that time, Williams had cracked the international market, his popularity abroad reminiscent of Jim Reeves' in the 1960s.

Williams also made forays into film. Along with country stars Jerry Reed and Mel Tillis, he appeared in his friend Burt Reynolds' movies *W.W. and the Dixie Dancekings* in 1975 and *Smokey and the Bandit II* in 1980.

Ironically, given his initial plan to become a songwriter, Williams tended to go to other writers for his hits. Among them were John Prine, Dave Loggins, Bob McDill, Wayland Holyfield, and Danny Flowers (the guitarist in Williams' backup Scratch Band). Of his chart-topping songs, the only one Williams wrote by himself was 1979's "Love Me All Over Again."

By the early 1990s the days of hitmaking seemed to be over, with Williams having long since shown that glamour, flamboyance, and frenzied music are not always the prerequisites for long-term popularity in country music, that sometimes a little less—at least in the hands of a Don Williams—can go a long way.

TOP SONGS

I WOULDN'T WANT TO LIVE IF YOU DIDN'T LOVE ME (Dot, '74, 1)

YOU'RE MY BEST FRIEND (ABC/Dot, '75, 1)

TIL THE RIVERS ALL RUN DRY (ABC/Dot, '76, 1)

I'M JUST A COUNTRY BOY (ABC/Dot, '77, 1)

TULSA TIME (ABC, '78, 1)

LOVE ME OVER AGAIN (MCA, '79, 1)

I BELIEVE IN YOU (MCA, '80, 1, 24 Pop)

LORD, I HOPE THIS DAY IS GOOD (MCA, '81, 1)

IF HOLLYWOOD DON'T NEED YOU (MCA, '82, 1)

HEARTBEAT IN THE DARKNESS (Capitol, '86, 1)

Additional Top 40 Country Songs: 42

HANK WILLIAMS

Canonized after his death, revered as the king of country music by every subsequent generation of country performers, and studied by everyone from backwoods deejays to music scholars, Hank Williams acquired a reputation that dwarfed his humanity. He lived a brief and troubled life, and he recorded for barely six years. Yet his simple, emotionally charged songs connected with country listeners to such a degree that his work now stands as a milestone in the evolution of country music.

Williams (b. Hiram King Williams, Sept. 17, 1923, Mount Olive, Alabama) was raised by his mother when his father was permanently hospitalized due to injuries suffered in World War I. His mother was the organist at their church, and Williams did his first singing with her accompanying him. He got his first guitar at age eight. By his teens he had become a local star in the Georgiana and Greenville, Alabama, areas where he lived. He later won a spot on radio station WSFA in Montgomery, where he became a regional hit and stayed for more than a decade. In 1947 he was signed to MGM Records and scored a big debut top four hit with "Move It On Over."

His musical style was an amalgam of influences. As a child he was taught guitar by a black street singer from Greenville, Alabama, called Tee-tot (Rufe Payne), and black music served as a key ingredient of Williams' sound ("colored music is real natural music," he once said to interviewer Melvin Shestack). He also drew from southern gospel music and such country precursors as the Carter Family, Bill Monroe, and especially Roy Acuff. Mixing blues with country and processing it through his own sensibility and swinging country style, Williams created something fresh and highly accessible.

Country music fans responded to it immediately, and in 1948 he hit the top 10 again with "I'm a Long Gone Daddy." The next year he charted eight more hits, of which "Lovesick Blues" stayed at Number One for 16 weeks. The eight top 10 hits of the following year included the Number One classics "Long Gone Lonesome Blues" and "Why Don't You Love Me."

Williams became known for the cowboy hat and elaborate Nudie western suits he wore. Paradoxically, Alabama-born Williams was not able to relate to "western" music, yet he was sufficiently enamored of the Old West to name his band the Drifting Cowboys (and briefly record some moralistic songs under the pseudonym Luke the Drifter).

Year after year, Williams released such future country standards as "Cold, Cold Heart," "Hey, Good Lookin'," "I Can't Help It (If I'm Still in Love with You)," and "Jambalaya (On the Bayou)."

But hidden behind his success was a persistent drinking problem that would threaten his career and ultimately bring on his demise in 1953.

Ironically, Williams' premature death may have helped ensure, and perhaps even bolster, his place in music history. "Dying the way he did is what made Hank Williams the greatest star in country music," observed Jack Hurst of the *Chicago Tribune*. It lent credibility to his work that Williams was killed by the very problems about which he sang.

Hank Williams drank in part because he had grown up in a setting in which it was condoned and in part to deaden the constant pain from a deformed back. A stormy marriage to performer Audrey Sheppard (from 1944 to '52), which began to fall apart as he reached the top, added to his problems. Dysfunction became entrenched: the cauldron of emotional conflict in which his psyche stewed also served as a creative well into which he dipped for such songs as "Your Cheatin' Heart," "Cold, Cold Heart," and "I'm So Lonesome I Could Cry."

In a kind of country music martyrdom, Williams' death certainly elevated him in stature. Yet his importance ultimately boils down to the legacy he left, rather than the death that gave his life the quality of myth. There was his charisma as a live performer, which Grand Ole Opry star Little Jimmy Dickens once described as "that thing, that 'it' that

---

TOP SONGS

LOVESICK BLUES (MGM, '49, *1, 24 Pop*)

LONG GONE LONESOME BLUES (MGM, '50, *1*)

WHY DON'T YOU LOVE ME (MGM, '50, *1*)

MOANIN' THE BLUES (MGM, '50, *1*)

COLD, COLD HEART (MGM, '51, *1*)

HEY, GOOD LOOKIN' (MGM, '51, *1*)

JAMBALAYA (ON THE BAYOU) (MGM, '52, *1, 20 Pop*)

YOUR CHEATIN' HEART (MGM, '53, *1*)

KAW-LIGA (MGM, '53, *1*)

TAKE THESE CHAINS FROM MY HEART (MGM, '53, *1*)

Additional Top 40 Country Songs: 30

people like Elvis and Garth Brooks have, that cause people just to love them." There was Williams' son, Randall Hank Williams, who became a country superstar in his own right as Hank Williams, Jr. Finally, there were his classic compositions. Every night, somewhere in America, artists play them. To witness a contemporary star like Alan Jackson and his band bring a huge crowd to their feet with a rousing version of "Mind Your Own Business" is to know that the music of Hank Williams endures.

HANK WILLIAMS, JR.

He was just three years old when his legendary father died. He has no independent memory of Hank, Sr., but when he speaks about his father, it seems like he knew him all his life. That's because the senior Williams' fans, friends, and widow, Audrey Williams, sought to keep Hank, Sr.'s memory alive through his son. Randall Hank "Boce-

Hank Williams, Jr.

phus" Williams made his public singing debut at age eight, dressed in a replica of his father's white Nudie suit and singing all of Hank, Sr.'s great hits. He remained the incarnation of his father until his late teens. In 1974, with his album *Hank Williams Jr. and Friends,* he began forging his own identity as a writer and singer. Williams has since produced a total volume of work that far exceeds his father's while leaving his own indelible mark on country music.

Williams (b. May 26, 1949, Shreveport, Louisiana) remembers his first public appearance fondly. "It was in Swainsboro, Georgia, on a show with a bunch of people—Webb Pierce, Grandpa Jones, and Ernest Tubb. I just stood there with my hands in my pocket and started singing 'Lovesick Blues.' Then I sang the rest of his big songs." During his childhood, Williams didn't really mind being the boy clone of Hank, Sr. He enjoyed the attention and was always the hit of the show. "Big stars on these package shows fought not to follow me. They'd say, 'We're not following him!' Then I'd go out there and do my Hank Williams repertoire and tear their butts up." He made his first appearance on the Grand Ole Opry at age 11 singing "Lovesick Blues." Four years later—in '64—Williams began his recording career and, not surprisingly, scored a top five hit with his first release, a Hank, Sr., song, "Long Gone Lonesome Blues."

When he turned 16, the fun of being the living repository for everybody's memory of his father had

---

TOP ALBUMS

HANK WILLIAMS JR. AND FRIENDS (MGM, '76)
FAMILY TRADITION (Elektra, '79)
GREATEST HITS (Elektra/Curb, '82)
MAJOR MOVES (Warner/Curb, '84)

TOP SONGS

ALL FOR THE LOVE OF SUNSHINE (MGM, '70, 1)
ELEVEN ROSES (MGM, '72, 1)
ALL MY ROWDY FRIENDS (HAVE SETTLED DOWN)
    (Elektra/Curb, '81, 1)
HONKY TONKIN' (Elektra/Curb, '82, 1)
AIN'T MISBEHAVIN' (Warner/Curb, '85, 1)
BORN TO BOOGIE (Warner/Curb, '87, 1)

Additional Top 40 Country Songs: 70

---

worn off. He released a song he wrote called "Standing in the Shadows" that symbolized his feelings (it became a number five hit). For a while he performed contemporary rock as Rockin' Randall. Later, after he turned 18, his life began to spiral downward due to drug and alcohol abuse (even as he scored Number One hits with "All for the Love of Sunshine" in 1970 and "Eleven Roses" in 1972), leading to a suicide attempt in 1974. It was in its aftermath that he began to carve a country music personality in his own image.

His first attempt yielded the album *Hank Williams Jr. and Friends,* a fusion of country and southern rock recorded in Muscle Shoals, Alabama, and including such country-rock stalwarts as Toy Caldwell, Marshall Tucker, Chuck Leavell, and Charlie Daniels. Ahead of its time, the album was not accepted by the Nashville establishment.

Plans were made for a follow-up disc. But they were interrupted in 1975, when Williams fell 482 feet down the snow face of a Montana mountain, crushing his face and splitting his skull. He miraculously survived the fall, and over the next few years underwent several reconstructive operations.

During his recovery he planned his next musical moves. One of the results was the 1979 album *Family Tradition* and its number-four–charting title song—both representing a nod to his past and a break from its stranglehold.

The subsequent albums *Whiskey Bent and Hell Bound* and *Habits Old and New* produced more major hits, including "Whiskey Bent and Hell Bound" (number two, 1979), "Texas Women" (Number One, 1981), and "All My Rowdy Friends (Have Settled Down)" (Number One, 1981). Williams practically owned the chart from 1979 to '90, scoring 29 top 10 songs to add to the 13 top 10s he scored in the first half of his career. (In total, he amassed 10 Number One hits.)

The new audience he gained during this period was a young, rowdy crowd, but they were nonetheless aware of the connection to his legendary father. Although he had escaped his father's shadow, he told stories about him, referred to himself as Bocephus (the nickname given to him by his father), and included many songs—and references within songs—that paid tribute to Hank, Sr.

In 1989, Williams was able to "appear" with his father when an acetate demo surfaced of Hank, Sr., singing "There's a Tear in My Beer"; Williams added a vocal track and took the duet to number seven on the chart. Eerily, an accompanying video electronically united father and son in the same scenes.

It was a career-capping moment, adding to such other highlights as winning the Country Music Association's Entertainer of the Year award (twice: in 1987 and 1988) and having his song "All My Rowdy Friends Are Coming Over Tonight" adopted as the theme for ABC's "Sunday Night Football" telecasts. "It was a thrill to become a part of something that is such an important part of Americana," he said of the latter.

BOB WILLS AND HIS TEXAS PLAYBOYS

Combine jazzy 1930s dance music with the sound of a country string band, add hot solos and enthusiastic hollers, and you get western swing, Bob Wills style.

The undisputed Kings of Western Swing were Bob Wills and His Texas Playboys. Of the few who concocted the form in the 1930s and '40s, Wills and gang played it the longest and took it the furthest. By the time they were done, western swing was an important country subgenre with legions of practitioners. Merle Haggard, Buck Owens, Ray Price, and George Strait were among the influenced; Asleep at the Wheel among keepers of the flame.

Although the sound was complex, a mix of country, blues, popular tunes, big band music, and folk, Wills boiled its formula for success down to one simple and fast rule: "I won't play nothin' you can't dance to."

Wills (b. James Robert Wills, March 6, 1905, Limestone County, Texas) grew up in a family of fiddlers: his father was a skilled one, and so were his granddads and uncles. Bob backed up his dad for a spell, playing mandolin and guitar at dances around the town of Memphis, Texas, where he grew up. He pinch-hit on fiddle for his absent dad on one date, and he got hooked.

In 1929, 24-year-old Wills was in Fort Worth, Texas, fiddling and doing comedy routines in a medicine show. He met a guitarist there named Herman Arnspiger, and they worked in a pair as the Wills Fiddle Band. With dance audiences of the time demanding hot jazz sounds, the duo began working "modern" material into their repertoire.

A singer, Milton Brown, joined the two and brought along his brother Durwood on guitar. By 1930, this group was being heard regularly on a WBAP radio show sponsored by the Aladdin Lamp Company, and they were called the Aladdin Laddies. When sponsorship was taken over in 1931 by the Burrus Mill and Elevator Company (makers of Light Crust Flour), the band name changed to the Light Crust Doughboys. Millworkers by day, the Doughboys—when not on radio—would make extra money by playing dances. When Burrus Mill boss (and future Texas governor) Lee O'Daniel demanded exclusivity and prohibited such moonlighting, Milton and Durwood Brown quit, spinning off a new group called the Musical Brownies. They, too, would become highly influential western swing players, until Brown's death in 1936.

Wills, meanwhile, hired smooth-toned vocalist extraordinaire Tommy Duncan to replace Brown, and the Doughboys continued broadcasting and building popularity. But he finally left the show in 1933, taking most of the band with him to Waco, Texas, and forming the Playboys. In 1934 he moved again, this time to Tulsa, Oklahoma, where the name became Bob Wills and the Texas Playboys and the glory years began.

For starters, they landed their own daily broadcast over KVOO radio (which would continue for the next 23 years). During this period, Wills expanded the band, carefully picking top-flight musicians and developing the musical idiosyncrasies that would prove so influential. Wills was the front man, leading with fiddle, entertaining with showmanship, and exhorting his sidemen to play knockout solos, and if they did, hollering approval. The big-beat drums of Smokey Dacus were brought into the band (a Wills innovation that would provide one of the foundations for '50s rockabilly and early rock and roll). Electric instruments were added, notably the steel guitar of Leon McAuliffe, whose playing would help put the steel sound permanently in country. Wills was smart enough to hire fiddlers better than he, Jesse Ashlock in particular, and brought in Al Stricklin on piano. Later, reeds and brass made the sound even fuller.

By 1935, the group was recording for the American Recording Corporation (the McAuliffe showcase "Steel Guitar Rag" a key track from the period) and playing to packed dancehalls across the Southwest. Their sound and popularity spread further when the band's 1938 instrumental recording of "San Antonio

Rose," written by Wills, hit the national pop chart and climbed to number 15.

As the Playboys got better, they also got bigger. Eldon Shamblin, an electric guitarist whose single-note lines were reminiscent of jazzman Charlie Christian, joined in 1938. By the 1940 release of "New San Antonio Rose," a remake with a vocal by Duncan, the band was up to 18 pieces and comparing favorably with the big swing bands of the day.

A succession of songs kept them on the pop charts, and in 1944—when *Billboard* introduced its first country list—the Playboys started a run of top five country hits that would total 18 by the end of the '40s. Meanwhile, Hollywood took notice, leading to Playboys appearances in the 1940 film *Take Me Back to Oklahoma* and several others.

Following World War II, Wills moved to California and kept the Playboys going, but as a smaller unit (using steel guitar and electric guitar to cover the horn parts—another soon-to-be-copied Wills inno-

Bob Wells

vation). Key recordings were created in 1945–47 for Oakland's Tiffany Music: a set of over 200 songs pegged for national sale to radio stations. (These acclaimed recordings are available today as *The Tiffany Transcriptions* on the Kaleidoscope label.) In the face of diminishing interest in western swing, the band traveled widely to make money, moving to Oklahoma City in '49 and to Fort Worth in '50. The Playboys went through numerous personnel changes (fiddlers Johnny Gimble and Tiny Moore and steel player Herb Remington among those passing through) while recording for a succession of labels that included MGM (1947–55) and Decca (1955–59). Duncan, who had left the group in 1948 and been replaced by a number of singers, rejoined Wills in 1959 for some recordings on Liberty ("Heart to Heart Talk" and "Image of Me") that made the country chart—Wills' last visit to that list while alive.

In 1962 he had the first of a series of heart attacks, the second of which, in 1964, forced him to disband the Playboys. But he still cut some recordings, including sessions for the Longhorn and Kapp labels with varying personnel. He also began receiving recognition from his peers. He was inducted into the Country Music Hall of Fame in 1968. Two years later, Wills fan Merle Haggard recorded the album *A Tribute to the Best Damn Fiddle Player in the World*.

In 1973, Wills met with some of the old band members to record a reunion album. He only made

it through one session, suffering a stroke that put him in a coma until his death on May 13, 1975. The album, which included some fiddle playing by Merle Haggard, was entitled *For the Last Time*.

TAMMY WYNETTE

Tammy Wynette is the self-styled First Lady of Country Music, a title that is as much fact as hype. Over the course of a 30-year career, Wynette has reached the peak of country achievement with such signature hits as "Stand by Your Man," one of the top-selling singles by a woman in country history. With her sultry, sexy image, blonde hairdo, and personal history of stormy relationships (particularly with former husband and musical partner George Jones), Wynette has also become the symbol of the country female star.

Wynette's love of music began in her childhood. Born Virginia Wynnete Pugh, May 5, 1942, on her grandfather's farm in Itawamba County, Mississippi, she was the daughter of a local musician who died when she was eight months old. "The only legacy he left me was his love of music," she recalled. "He made my mother promise him over and over again that she would encourage me to take an interest in music if I had any talent at all. She kept her promise—until I wanted to make a career of it; then she, along with everyone else in my family, thought I'd lost my mind."

It would be a while, however, before Wynette pursued that career. In 1943 her mother moved to Birmingham, Alabama, to do war work, and Wynette was then raised by her grandparents. While at their farm she taught herself to play her father's instruments and was given singing lessons.

But her musical career was postponed when she got married at age 17 and subsequently had three children. When the marriage broke up in the 1960s, she was forced to work as a beautician to support her family.

Her career finally started in 1965 when she began performing on a Birmingham television program, "The Country Boy Eddie Show." In 1966 she moved to Nashville and began auditioning at various labels. She eventually came to the attention of producer Billy Sherrill at Epic Records and was signed to a contract.

Her debut record, "Apartment #9," was a mod-

TOP ALBUMS

THE GOLDEN YEARS (Columbia, '73)
BEST OF THE TIFFANYS, VOL. 2 (Kaleidoscope, '83)
ANTHOLOGY (1935–1973) (Rhino, '91)

TOP SONGS

WE MIGHT AS WELL FORGET IT (Okeh, '44, 2, 11 Pop)
SMOKE ON THE WATER (Okeh, '45, 1)
STARS AND STRIPES ON IWO JIMA (Okeh, '45, 1)
SILVER DEW ON THE BLUE GRASS TONIGHT
(Columbia, '45, 1)
WHITE CROSS ON OKINAWA (Columbia, '45, 1)
NEW SPANISH TWO STEP (Columbia, '46, 1, 20 Pop)
SUGAR MOON (Columbia, '47, 1)

Additional Top 40 Country Songs: 18

Tammy Wynette

est hit in 1966, but it offered nary a hint of the success that was to come. The rise to fame began with her subsequent release, "Your Good Girl's Gonna Go Bad," which hit number three on the country chart in 1967.

From that point on, the hits flowed, putting Wynette on track to become one of the most successful female vocalists of the time—and of all time. The Number One records scored over the next nine years would add up to an astounding 17, including such classics as "I Don't Wanna Play House," "D-I-V-O-R-C-E," and Wynette's signature song, "Stand by Your Man."

During that period, Wynette hit the top 10 again and again. And her career hardly diminished even after it peaked in the late 1970s. She remained a major star and a consistent presence on the charts in the 1980s and '90s (although at lower rankings than in her '70s heyday). All told, Wynette has sold more than 18 million records.

Along the way, Wynette gained notoriety for her romantic relationships. She has been married five times, creating the biggest stir with her 1969 marriage to Jones. During their six years as husband and wife they toured together and recorded a succession of hit duets that included "We're Gonna Hold On" and "Golden Ring." While their relationship—which received much attention from the press and public—didn't last, it did add to the stormy imagery that colors their careers as well as a vast number of country songs. And given the media coverage of Wynette's various relationships with others, including Rudy Gatlin of the Gatlin Brothers and actor Burt Reynolds, it sometimes seemed as if Wynette was playing out her music in her life.

TOP SONGS

My Elusive Dreams (Epic, '67, *1*)
I Don't Wanna Play House (Epic, '67, *1*)
Take Me to Your World (Epic, '68, *1*)
D-I-V-O-R-C-E (Epic, '68, *1*)
Stand by Your Man (Epic, '68, *1*)
Singing My Song (Epic, '69, *1, 19 Pop*)
The Ways to Love a Man (Epic, '69, *1*)
He Loves Me All the Way (Epic, '70, *1*)
Run, Woman, Run (Epic, '70, *1*)
Good Lovin' (Makes It Right) (Epic, '71, *1*)

Additional Top 40 Country Songs: 47

That life became the subject of a best-selling autobiography that was subsequently turned into a popular 1982 film, both of which came with the fitting title *Stand by Your Man.*

TRISHA YEARWOOD

Trisha Yearwood provides a contrast to the up-from-poverty, coal miners' offspring of a generation or so back. A banker's daughter, she rose from a little higher on the ladder and paid some of her dues earning a music business degree and singing background vocals on the albums of country superstar Garth Brooks. With a voice most often compared to that of Linda Ronstadt, she became one of the top female acts to emerge in the 1990s.

Yearwood (b. Patricia Lynn Yearwood, Sept. 19, 1964, Monticello, Georgia) has cited as country credentials the fact that her father, while a banker, is a *farmboy* banker, boasting a degree in agriculture along with the 30-acre farm Trisha grew up on. "My parents had a healthy love and respect for country music," she says. "We watched 'Hee Haw' on TV, and my parents watched the Porter Wagoner and Dolly Parton show. . . . My singing just came naturally. I remember deciding I wanted to sing back when I was a little-bitty thing."

For a while, Yearwood's musical outings were limited to talent contests and occasionally sitting in with house bands at a couple of Atlanta area clubs. In college she was the singer in a top 40 band called Straight Lace.

In 1985, Yearwood moved to Nashville to finish her last two years of study toward a degree from Belmont College. An internship in the publicity department of MTM Records provided her first close-up look at the music industry. After graduating from school in 1987, she began working as the label's receptionist. "Seeing how some things worked in the record business makes me wonder why I didn't head back to Georgia," Yearwood says. "But I saw so many young performers doing what I wanted to do that it made me very serious about trying to get in the business."

Just before MTM shut down in 1988, Yearwood began getting demo and session singing work. She fell in with a crowd of young, hit singer-songwriters that included Pat Alger and Garth Brooks, and she was brought in to sing harmony on what would

Trisha Yearwood

become the latter's multi-million–selling debut album. She also frequently backed up Alger when he would sing at local writers' clubs. "One night I was singing with Pat at Douglas Corner," she recalls, "and producer Garth Fundis was in the audience. He became interested in me and helped set up a show-case for me. Tony Brown of MCA Records saw me and offered a deal right on the spot."

In the early summer of 1991, "She's in Love with the Boy" hit the top, putting Yearwood on the fast track. Her album debut, *Trisha Yearwood,* fueled the momentum with the top 10 follow-up singles "Like We Never Had a Broken Heart" and "That's What I Like About You."

Some glitches marred the rapid takeoff. In mid-success came the chaos of divorcing her husband of four years. At the same time, she was booked as an opening act for Garth Brooks before she was ready, and she consequently fired her first manager. Insta-bility reigned until big-time artist manager Ken Kra-gen (Lionel Richie, Kenny Rogers, Travis Tritt) signed on with her, a luxury she could afford thanks to record sales.

With order established, Yearwood began hitting her stride on her second album, *Hearts in Armor,* a million-seller that featured the number two hit "Walkaway Joe" (1992), a duet with Eagles member Don Henley. She repeated the achievement in 1993 with the title song from her third album, *The Song Remembers When.*

In 1994, Yearwood collected her second Number

TOP ALBUMS

TRISHA YEARWOOD (MCA, '91)
HEARTS IN ARMOR (MCA, '92)
THE SONG REMEMBERS WHEN (MCA, '93)

TOP SONGS

SHE'S IN LOVE WITH THE BOY (MCA, '91, *1*)
LIKE WE NEVER HAD A BROKEN HEART (MCA, '91, *4*)
THE WOMAN BEFORE ME (MCA, '92, *4*)
WRONG SIDE OF MEMPHIS (MCA, '92, *5*)
WALKAWAY JOE (with Don Henley, MCA, '92, *2*)
THE SONG REMEMBERS WHEN (MCA, '93, *2*)
XXXS AND OOOS (AN AMERICAN GIRL)
    (MCA, '94, *1*)

Additional Top 40 Country Songs: 3

One hit with "XXXs and OOOs (An American Girl)," the title theme from a TV miniseries set in Nashville.

DWIGHT YOAKAM

Back in 1985, a Nashville pundit looked at two recent signings by Warner Bros. Records, Randy Travis and Dwight Yoakam (Reprise), and said, "One of them is a 20-year act, the other a two-year act." The one he thought lacked staying power was Yoakam, a sort of hip Hollywood honky-tonker with an attitude. A decade later, that "two-year" act was still around, more eccentric and hip than ever and still turning out his distinctive brand of turned-on honky-tonk country sound.

Yoakam (b. Oct. 23, 1956, Pikeville, Kentucky) was born in Kentucky but raised in Columbus, Ohio. He first picked up guitar as a toddler and was strum-ming by age six. Through his mother's record club, he gained exposure to albums by Hank Williams, Buck Owens, Johnny Cash, and Johnny Horton, with the latter proving especially appealing. "I was just infatuated with his sound and style at a very young age," he explains. "It was pure country, but it had an emotional integrity that allowed it to be alive." By high school Yoakam was regurgitating his musical learnings in various rock, rockabilly, and country bands.

After a short stint at Ohio State University, Yoakam made a serious run at Nashville in the late 1970s. He struck out at a time when the "urban cowboy," contemporary-country fad was in full swing, with no room for a newfangled hillbilly-style singer such as he.

Yoakam headed for Los Angeles with lead gui-tarist Pete Anderson, and together they began hitting the local club scene. "Every club we played, we got fired from," Anderson told *US* magazine. "They wanted us to play Alabama stuff, and we were play-ing Hank, Sr., and Merle Haggard."

In the early 1980s the cowpunk scene emerged in Hollywood. Rockers were fusing with country, country pickers were fusing with rock, and the results were idiosyncratic, sometimes very good, and not incompatible with what Yoakam was into. Sud-denly Yoakam found himself playing at as many punk clubs in Hollywood as honky-tonks in the San Fernando Valley, sometimes sharing the stage with such rock extremists as the Dead Kennedys and the Butthole Surfers. Even though he was a willing participant in that scene, and it all seemed to work, Yoakam later bristled when classified as cowpunk. "I will always be in debt to the cowpunkers who embraced our music," he said. "But we are American honky-tonk; we're pure American country music and that's it."

In 1984, Yoakam scraped up $5,000 to record a six-song EP. "The money came from car insurance money I was supposed to use to fix the fender on my El Camino," he recalls. "And there was a music professor at U.C.L.A., Dr. Robert Winter [creator of a number of classical music CD-ROMs], who staged a benefit for me." That independent record began to get him a lot of airplay on local alternative radio stations and helped bring him to the attention of Warner/Reprise Records.

Yoakam's debut album, *Guitars, Cadillacs, Etc.,*

TOP ALBUMS

GUITARS, CADILLACS, ETC., ETC. (Reprise, '86)
HILLBILLY DELUXE (Reprise, '87)
BUENAS NOCHES FROM A LONELY ROOM (Reprise, '88)
IF THERE WAS A WAY (Reprise, '90)
THIS TIME (Reprise, '93)

TOP SONGS

HONKY TONK MAN (Reprise, '86, 3)
STREETS OF BAKERSFIELD (with Buck Owens, Reprise, '88, 1)
I SANG DIXIE (Reprise, '88, 1)
AIN'T THAT LONELY YET (Reprise, '93, 2)
A THOUSAND MILES FROM NOWHERE (Reprise, '93, 2)

Additional Top 40 Country Songs: 17

Dwight Yoakam

Etc., yielded a top three debut single—not surprisingly, a Johnny Horton song called "Honky Tonk Man." He followed it with the album's title song, his tribute to the Bakersfield Sound; it went to number four. Yoakam was on his way, finally connecting with a vision that would continue to reflect country music's past, both in covers like "Little Sister" and "Suspicious Minds" and his own authentic-sounding, new American honky-tonk numbers like "I Sang Dixie" and "A Thousand Miles from Nowhere."

Yoakam's original music earned him so much respect from Buck Owens, pioneer of Bakersfield honky-tonk, that Owens agreed to come out of retirement to record the duet "Streets of Bakersfield," which took them both to Number One in 1988.

Said Pete Anderson, summarizing Yoakam's old-new musical synthesis, "No matter how much we do what we do in keeping with the traditions of country music, there is still a uniqueness to it that came from going in Dwight Yoakam's ear at six, seven, eight years old, bouncing around in his mind for the next 15 or 20 years, then coming out of his mouth in his 20s. The form is there, but it's changed."

FARON YOUNG

Nicknames have long been a country tradition, going back to Jimmy Rodgers (the Singing Brakeman) and Hank Snow (the Singing Ranger). Usually the name reflects an aspect of the performer's real-life background. In the case of Faron Young, known widely as the Singing Sheriff, it came from a role he played in a Hollywood movie. That derivation seems somehow appropriate for a onetime honky-tonker dubbed the Hillbilly Heartthrob who later became one of the biggest of the big-time Nashville stars, a cross-media entertainer as comfortable with show-biz glitter as with hard-core country grit.

Young (b. Feb. 25, 1932) grew up outside of Shreveport, Louisiana, on his father's small dairy farm. A guitar came into his possession on that farm. By his teens, he was a singing musician of budding talent. At 19, he was performing professionally with honky-tonk singer Webb Pierce.

In those parts, and at that time, the best place to showcase singing talent was the KWKH "Louisiana Hayride" radio program. Young was good enough,

and he got his chance to prove it, leading to a stint as a "Hayride" regular. On the side, Young honed his live performing skills in the nightspots and honky-tonks around the area. "I worked places down there," he told Chet Hagan, author of *Grand Ole Opry,* "when you'd come in they'd say, 'You got a gun?' You'd say, 'No.' And they'd say, 'You want one?'"

The road to better things started with a record, "Tattle Tale Tears," that Young waxed for the small Gotham label in 1951. Capitol Records became interested enough to buy out the Young-Gotham contract in 1952, and in the same year the Grand Ole Opry's program manager, who had heard a Young recording, invited him to Nashville for a two-week try-out. Young passed muster and stayed on for the duration. "Back then the Opry could make a star out of you," Young told Hagan. "They took me and literally made me into a big name, and it was just because of the exposure on the Opry itself."

But before fame kicked in, Young served his nation during the Korean War. Assigned to the Army's Special Services, he did his share of entertaining fellow troops. Meanwhile, a song he recorded while on leave, a rocking teen paean called "Goin' Steady," hit the country chart in 1953, while Young was still serving. That meant that when he returned to civilian life and the Grand Ole Opry in 1954, his career was already under way (another song, "I Can't Wait," having hit number five in summer 1953).

Young kept up the momentum, starting with a trio of top five hits: "A Place for Girls Like You" (number eight), "If You Ain't Lovin'" (number two),

---

TOP ALBUMS

ALL-TIME GREATEST HITS (Curb, '90)
THE CLASSIC YEARS 1952–62 (Bear Family)

TOP SONGS

GOIN' STEADY (Capitol, '53, 2)
IF YOU AIN'T LOVIN' (Capitol, '54, 2)
LIVE FAST, LOVE HARD, DIE YOUNG (Capitol, '55, 1)
ALL RIGHT (Capitol, '55, 2)
ALONE WITH YOU (Capitol, '58, 1)
COUNTRY GIRL (Capitol, '59, 1)
HELLO WALLS (Capitol, '61, 1, 12 Pop)
IT'S FOUR IN THE MORNING (Mercury, '71, 1)

Additional Top 40 Country Songs: 66

and his first Number One, the signature "Live Fast, Love Hard, Die Young."

Living fast is what Young did in the 1950s. He scored a number two hit with his own composition, "All Right," in 1955 and then, in the following year, pulled out another soon-to-be-signature rave-up, "I've Got Five Dollars and It's Saturday Night." With blinding speed he branched out to other media, in 1955 appearing in the film *Hidden Guns* and consequently acquiring the Young Sheriff label (he'd later change it to the Singing Sheriff). Ten more films would cast him, and many a television show would host him, making Young an increasingly broad-based entertainment commodity.

Several key songs filled out his list of hits in the 1950s and early '60s. He cut the Don Gibson tune "Sweet Dreams" in 1956, predating the Patsy Cline version by seven years. Two singles—"Alone with You" and "Country Girl"—topped the chart in 1958 and '59, respectively. And in 1961 he hit Number One again with "Hello Walls," a career booster for writer Willie Nelson and a venture into the country-pop Nashville Sound for Young (it reached number 12 in the pop Hot 100).

Proof of Young's durability was yet to come. After he left Capitol Records and moved to Mercury in 1963, his chart activity hit a relative lull (*relative* meaning rankings in the 30s and 40s rather than just the top 10) that lasted through the rest of the decade. Yet in 1969, starting with the number two honky-tonk hit "Wine Me Up," Young returned to his vintage, full-bore, steady-stream-of-hits form and rose to a peak with yet another career classic, the Number One "It's Four in the Morning" (1971), the Country Music Association's chosen Single of the Year. By the end of the 1970s he had essentially completed his run of high-ranking chart singles, and the overall record was impressive: of 76 releases from 1953 to 1978, all but four of them were in the top 40.

Young stayed active in the 1980s, racking up a smattering of country-charting songs. That they were little noticed probably didn't matter: Young had long since amassed a varied array of business interests that included Nashville's *Music City News,* some publishing entities, and a structure bearing his name, the Young Executive Building, smack in the middle of Music City.

INDEX
••••••••••••

PHOTO CREDITS

The authors gratefully acknowledge the following sources, who generously supplied the photos used this volume:

Arista Records: Brooks & Dunn (photo by Mark Seliger), Diamond Rio, Exile, Freddy Fender, Alan Jackson, Pam Tillis, Steve Wariner (photo by Susan Shacter)

Artists Consultants, Inc.: Johnny Cash

Asylum Records: Linda Ronstadt (photo by Martha Swope)

Atlantic Records: Confederate Railroad, Tracy Lawrence, Neal McCoy, John Michael Montgomery (photo by Karen Miller)

BNA Entertainment: Lorrie Morgan (photo by Ruven Afanador), Doug Supernaw

The Brokaw Company: Glenn Miller

Capitol Records: Glen Campbell (photo by Kathy DeVault), Billy Dean (photo by Beth Gwinn), Barbara Mandrell (photo by Ric Boyer), Anne Murray

Columbia Records: Chet Atkins (photo by Deborah Fiengold), Babby Bare (photo by Beverly Parker), Mary Chapin Carpenter (photo by Caroline Greyshock), Roseanne Cash (photo by Melodie Gimple), Rodney Crowell (photo by John Guider), Vern Gosdin (photo by Alan Messer), Dolly Parton (Randee St. Nicholas), Ray Price (illustration by Robert Hunt), Ricky Van Shelton

Curb Records: Bellamy Brothers (photo by Jim McGuire), Hal Ketchum, Lyle Lovett (photo by Peter Nash), Tim McGraw (photo by Peter Nash), Buck Owens (photo by Peter Darley Miller), Sawyer Brown (photo by Peter Nash)

Elektra Records: Roy Acuff, Jerry Lee Lewis (photo by Jim Shea), Mel Tillis (photo by J. Clark Thomas)

EMI/America Records: Barbara Mandrell (photo by Dick Zimmerman)

Epic Records: Charlie Daniels (photo by David Michael Kennedy), George Jones (photo by Jim McGuire), Patty Loveless (photo by Victoria Pearson), Colin Raye (photo by Frank Ockenfels), Johnny Rodriguez (photo by Beverly Parker), Joe Stampley, Doug Stone (photo by Randee St. Nicholas), Tammy Wynette (photo by Harry Langdon)

Frist Generation Records: Ernest Tubb

Giant Records: Clay Walker (photo by Jim McGuire)

The Jim Halsey Co., Inc.: Brenda Lee

Kragen and Company: Dottie West

Liberty Records: Asleep at the Wheel (photo by Jim McGuire), Suzy Burgess (photo by Randee St. Nicholas), Gatlin Brothers (photo by Mark Tucker), Lacy J. Daulton (Ron Keith), Willie Nelson (photo by E.J. Camp), Nitty Gritty Dirt Band (photo by Glann Hall), Tanya Tucker (photo by Randee St. Nicholas)

MCA Records: John Anderson (photo by Peter Nash), Razzy Bailey, Tracy Byrd (photo by Dean Dixon), Patsy Cline, Vince Gill (photo by Victoria Pearson), Waylong Jennings (photo by Wayne Williams), Loretta Lynn (photo by Peter Nash), McBride & the Ride (photo by Susan Teas), Reba McEntire, Bill Monroe, Oak Ridge Boys (photo by Alan Messer), George Strait (photo by Jarrett Gaza), Conway Twitty (photo by Dennis Carney), Trisha Yearwood (photo by Randee St. Nicholas)

Mercury Records: Lynn Anderson, Tom T. Hall, Sammy Kershaw (photo by Glenn Hall), Kris Kristofferson, Kathy Mattea (photo by Peter Nash), Charly McClain (photo by Ron Keith), Johnny Paycheck

Polydor Records: Toby Keith (photo by Dean Dixon)

RCA Records: Alabama, Clint Black (photo by Jim McGuire), Earl Thomas Conley, John Denver, Foster & Lloyd, the Judds, Ronnie Milsap, Juice Newton, K.T. Oslin, Elvis Presley, Charlie Pride, Eddie Rabbitt, Eddie Raven, Restless Heart, Shenandoah, Aaron Tippin (photo by Frank Ockenfels), Keith Whitley, Don Williams

Reprise Records: Emmylou Harris (photo by Peter Nash), Kenny Rogers (photo by Kelly Junkermann), Dwight Yoakam (photo by Kip Lott)

Sire Records: k.d. lang (photo by Albert Sanchez), Charlie Rich (photo by David Gahr)

Universal Records: Carl Perkins (photo by Dennis Carney)

Warner Bros. Records: Crystal Gayle (photo by Empire Studio), Gary Morris (photo by Randee St. Nicholas), Mark O'Connor (photo by Kip Lott), Randy Travis (photo by Aaron Rapoport), Gene Watson (photo by Jeff Katz)

ABOUT THE AUTHORS

Neil Haislop, who wrote approximately half the entries in this book, has been writing about country music since 1978, when he began as an interviewer for the award-winning radio program *American Country Countdown with Bob Kingsley*. For several years he wrote, produced, and appeared on the syndicated video show *America's New Country*. He is currently the writer and co-creator of *Bob Kingsley with America's Music Makers*, a writer and co-producer of country music radio specials for ABC Watermark, and a contributing editor and columnist for *Country Fever* magazine.

Tad Lathrop, editor and originator of the Billboard Hitmakers series, is a former Senior Editor for Billboard Books, staff writer for Cherry Lane Music, and editor with Holt, Rinehart and Winston. He is co-author of the book *Cult Rockers*.

Harry Sumrall is the author of *Pioneers of Rock and Roll,* another volume in the Billboard Hitmakers series. He has also written for *The New Grove Dictionary of American Music,* the *Washington Post, The New Republic,* the *San Jose Mercury News,* and the Knight Ridder News Service. He unwittingly prepared for this book in the 1960s while growing up in Houston, where he spent Sunday afternoons with his dad listening to local country hero Utah Carl and the Gulf Coast Furniture Warehouse Jamboree Boys. He lives in San Francisco with his wife, Leslie, and their son, Sam.